"Tracee McDaniel has offered a gift to the world in her it she tells with great courage her story of growing up a non-conforming person in the Deep South. Tracee begins by weaving into her personal story compelling family and cultural history to help the reader understand the context in which she was raised. She goes on to share details about her and her family's struggle to make sense of the ways in which she didn't fit into the gendered roles and expectations of her based on the body into which she was born. I was moved by her compassion, understanding, love, and respect for her mother, despite her own limitations in accepting Tracee's differences growing up. I was also floored by the tenacity Tracee demonstrated time and again to stand up for herself and others in the face of abuse or mistreatment. Tracee's passion for music and the name she built for herself as a performer was a consistent thread throughout the memoir, as she included memories of the songs she danced to into each chapter; The result is that the music itself tells a story of her and her development. If there is one word to sum up how I felt after reading this memoir it is "resilience." Tracee McDaniel's life story offers hope to other transgender and gender non-conforming people – hope that others not only have survived the challenges of living in a society based on a binary system of gender, but have thrived and gone on to live productive, happy, and fulfilling lives. Tracee McDaniel is an inspiration and role model for all people about triumph, love, commitment, and generosity in the face of adversity."

Erika Pluhar, Ph.D., Professor, Emory University

To Minister Robert
Thank you for your
continuous love and support.
It is such a pleasure
knowing such a genuine person.
Always Tracee 04.28.2013

Tracee McDaniel

TRANSITIONS

Memoirs of a Transsexual Woman

Editor: Phyllis Alesia Perry

Book Cover Photo: Robert Hale Photography

Book Cover Design: Amber Taylor,JaiJoint and Tracee McDaniel

Introduction Written by: Tracee McDaniel

Book Back Cover Photo from: Tracee McDaniel Archives

All Photos Courtesy: Tracee McDaniel Archives

Publisher: Nephrititi Publishing, LLC.

For more information contact: juxtaposedcenter@bellsouth.net

Library of Congress Cataloging-in-Publication Data

McDaniel, Tracee Memoir

Transitions

1. Title. ISBN 13: 978-0615547374 (Nephrititi Publishing)

10: 0615547370

Manufactured in the United States of America

"Transitions" is dedicated to my Creator, ancestors, birth mother B. W. McDaniel, thank you Ma for generously financially sponsoring my book edit. Spiritual mother, K. Smith Mother Chinue, my husband K. Washington, our four-legged babies, Savannah, Bear, Sheba, Solomon, consultant Creative JaiJoint, my transgender, gender non-conforming predecessors and all of my detractors!

Publishers' Note:

This is a non-fictional recollection of the authors' memory in her own words referencing her unconventional personal journals, scrap books, calendars and interviews. Names in this story have intentionally been altered to protect the privacy and identities of those that may choose to remain anonymous.

BOOKS ARE AVAILABLE AT QUANTITY DISCOUNTS WHEN USED TO PROMOTE
PRODUCTS   OR SERVICES. FOR MORE INFORMATION, PLEASE CONTACT
juxtaposedcenter@bellsouth.net JCT MARKETING DIVISION NEPHRITITI PUBLISHING

USA, INCORPORATED

Introduction

Since there were no positive trans images to model during my youth, the hesitancy to willingly disclose personal information about myself and family dynamics is diluted by the need to ensure that more positive transgender and gender non-conforming stories are told in our own words. I believe that it's imperative for the younger generation to see vibrant, responsible and resilient images thriving in modern time that are contrary to the stereotypes often rotated on talk shows for entertainment purposes. Moving forward, I use as my sword and shield the Holy Bible referring to eunuchs, the biblical reference to what we know today as the transgender and gender non-conforming person existing within society since written history! I am brave and strong enough mentally and physically to show up, participate and stand up to be counted and accountable for improving my life and environment. I am visible, guided, protected, maintained and sustained mentally and physically. My intention is to not allow our many positive contributions to society to be diminished and forgotten. I see transgender and gender non-conforming people reclaiming our positions of relevance and honor within society, which was intended by our Creator. I also see human rights protections and equality for all human beings regardless of orientation or race.

So it is, it is done, ashe', amen!

"May The Work I've Done, Speak for Me"

May the work I've done, speak for me, may the service I give, speak for me, sometimes it feels like nothing at all, but when I've done the best I can, I want to hear the Lord say well done ,so may the life I live speak for me."

*Paraphrased lyrics from one of my favorite old time gospel songs that my mother played on Sunday mornings. I loved listening to it growing up!

CONTENTS

Chapter One

My Beginning!

The year was 1967. It was a cold and wet morning in the small town of Sumter, South Carolina. A 16-year-old girl, Bee who was pregnant with her second child, assisted her mother, tirelessly laboring from sun up to sun down, hand-washing the laundry of her 13 sisters and brothers, using only homemade soap, tubs and a wash board to scrub their clothes clean. Due to Bee being close to her due date, her mother cautioned her to limit hanging too many clothes on the clothesline because the constant reaching motion would stretch her umbilical cord. Later that evening after they'd completed the numerous loads of family wash, they went inside the house for a cup of hot coffee to warm themselves from the winter's chill.

According to Bee, immediately after drinking her first cup of coffee, she went into labor. Her mother's limitations weren't limited enough. During the birth, the community midwife reached into Bee's womb to unwrap the umbilical cord from around the infant's neck.

Several hours later after being freed from the umbilical cord once again, I entered the world on January 20, 1967, at 9:05 p.m., a cold, wet night. Born on the cusp of Aquarius and Capricorn during the height of the Civil Rights Movement, I was given the first name Anthony and the middle name Douglas, after abolitionist Fredrick Douglass, whose writings and speeches were influential to ending slavery in the United States. As I grew older I've just exchanged the Y at the end of my nickname Tony to Toni.

According to my mother, considering I was born at home, I was a fairly healthy baby, though I was later diagnosed with a heart murmur. In my early childhood, I suffered with debilitating fevers and extreme bouts of tonsillitis during the winter months.

Although I missed weeks from school early on, I fortunately grew out of both health challenges and excelled in school. Born in 1911, my maternal grandmother, Bertie Lee Wingate was part Black Foot Indian. She married my grandfather Arthur McDaniel when she was 12 in 1923, when girls were considered mature enough to marry at an early age.

The number of children they had together reflected their love and commitment to each other. Unfortunately, I never met my paternal grandfather because he died from pneumonia in 1955, five years after my mother was born. I treasured the moments when Ma reminisced about her life before her father died and, according to her, granddaddy was a hard-working family man who owned and farmed several acres of land off Red Bay Road across from the train tracks in Sumter.

Although granddaddy was directly affected by the systematic racism and discrimination prevalent throughout the South, he persevered over hurdles placed before black farmers whenever they tried accessing United States Department of Agriculture resources.

The farming assistance program was established by the government to aid all farmers during times of drought and other natural disasters affecting their crops, and it's unbelievable to me that the heirs of those American farmers whom were discriminated against are still, in 2013, fighting to bring closure to the Pigford vs. Glickman lawsuit brought by black farmers against the United States government.

Ma recently shared with me that she didn't become aware of Jim Crow until adulthood; however, she confronted that old, rotted cancer firsthand when she and her siblings experienced public, white and black, separate water fountains and restrooms. She recalled black and white schools, which contributed to her and her siblings walking three to four miles both ways to their schools, although the bus ran right in front of their house.

Additionally, she recalled life being difficult and miserable during that time, because white folk did everything within their power to limit black folk from prospering and moving ahead. She shared a vivid story of working all day harvesting peanuts for this particular white farmer, and when it came time to pay her for her labor, he'd make excuses for not having her salary. Since she was hungry and looking forward to buying food after finishing her work, she wasn't afraid when she told him off about not having her money and then was surprised when he later apologized to her for not having her hard-earned wages.

As a result of the frustration, she recalled once when some white kids rode by on their bicycles and called them nigger and other disgusting words. She picked up a soda bottle and threw it at them, producing blood after it shattered on one of their heads. Ma and her siblings thought they were going to be in trouble with the boy's parents and other white folk in the community, but no one retaliated. Those boys never called them names again.

Ma also remembered the time when the stores wouldn't sell Coca-Cola to black folk because they thought the cocaine it contained would cause them to become aggressive. Wow! The inability to purchase a soft drink was the least of black folk's worries.

They were more concerned about the white soldiers that were randomly raping black girls, which is why females were kept inside whenever the armed forces were in the area. Although she doesn't hate anyone, Ma recalled being angry at the injustice and discrimination she experienced, which contributed to her rebelling against not being allowed to look white folk in the eye. Ma didn't feel inferior to anyone.

Also, during those days black people were required to go around to the back door of restaurants to place their food orders, with the exception of McLellan's Department Store. It allowed them to sit in seats at the end of the lunch counter designated for black folk only.

Ma recalled sitting there for undetermined periods of time if she wanted to place food and fountain drink orders. She was served only after all of the white customers were served, even those that arrived after her.

The Jim Crow era empowered segregationists and racists to legally discriminate against black people in South Carolina and surrounding states. I would assume that it's a challenge for those whom haven't experienced blatant oppression to imagine what black people endured. I wonder how the privileged would feel about paying the same amount of money for services and taxes as others, but be required to wait outside of a restaurant at the backdoor to place food orders.

Even though the Confederate flag is offensive to most black people because it represents hate and bigotry, it's unfathomable why it is still displayed on governmental grounds in Columbia, South Carolina.

I wonder how white folk during those oppressive days would feel if they were owned as property, beaten, and denied voting rights and basic education. Would they be forgiving? Just ask those communities that have and still continue in the 21st century to be oppressed and treated inhumanly in their daily lives solely based on their ethnicity, gender identity and orientation.

Thankfully, we were always nurtured and protected by our mother. I was oblivious to the racism and discrimination that she endured while we were with her in public places. All I remember are the fun times during our adolescence, like me sitting on Santa Claus' knee with a lollypop and my brother on the other knee dressed in matching outfits, also with his cherry flavored lollypop posing for our Christmas photo. As a pre-teen, I also distinctly recall visiting the Jasmine Mall and posing with cuddly baby tiger cubs.

Most of all, I'll never forget sitting wide-eyed in amazement, watching Michael Jackson, Diana Ross and Lena Horne on the big screen when Ma took us to the downtown theater for the very first time!

Before that experience, whenever the adults went to the movies, Ma would always bring us buckets of buttery popcorn, so I felt very grown up and special sitting there eating popcorn with her on our special night, watching "The Wiz."

Unfortunately, after Granddad's untimely death, none of the fruits of his labor were passed down to his heirs, due to my grandmother's grade-school education and her inability to read or write her name. Her lack of education contributed to her being swindled out of all of the land during tax time by her boyfriend. Also, according to Ma, it was very difficult for them after Granddad's passing. In an attempt to provide for her family she had to quit school, get a job, and become the primary breadwinner at 8 years old.

Ma cooked and cleaned for white people, some rich and most not. She often hid food that she was given to eat, and sometimes stolen table scraps outside of the house, to feed her mother and siblings. When she wasn't cooking and cleaning for others, she also labored back-breaking hours in the scorching Southern heat, picking cotton, tobacco, cucumbers and other produce to earn a living. I wish that I could take away the pain that I hear in her voice to this day whenever she talks about growing up in the South.

Although Grandma was illiterate, she possessed commonsense in teaching her children to not pick at other people, but insisted that if they were threatened by anyone, they were to stand up and defend themselves. She'd threatened them that if they ran home without defending themselves; she'd beat their butts and send them back to face their opponents.

Of course, Ma and her siblings were often involved in fights and altercations with some of their schoolmates and neighbors, because they were tired of constantly being harassed and teased about their color, clothes and the condition of their house. "I hated that our house was the worst conditioned house in the neighborhood, in such disrepair after Daddy died."

Ma painfully recalled in detail," From inside of the house I was able to see the chickens underneath the house pecking and scratching around for food. There were also many times as a child that I was frightened at the thought of a snake crawling through the holes in the floors."

Not only was it rough dealing with Jim Crow racists, she also constantly dealt with the negative treatment from the upper-class black folk who thought themselves superior to them. I now know from whence I received my courage and strength after Ma told me the story she'd overheard from the so-called bad girls from the country in the school stalls.

The girls were talking about her raggedy clothes and shoes as compared to their shiny patent leather shoes and freshly pressed outfits. According to Ma, she waited outside the bathroom door until they exited, and she let them know that she'd heard them talking about her behind her back, and invited them to say to her face after school what they'd said in the bathroom.

Remember, those were the self-described, roughest girls around, so after school I'm sure that they were caught off guard when she beat the ring leader while her crew watched. Later that evening, the girl and her family members came to retaliate. Unbelievably, it turned out to be the only time that Ma recalled Grandma ever standing up for her.

She recalled Grandma standing on the front porch with a shotgun. She threatened serious consequences if anyone else jumped into the fight between the two girls. Of course, no one jumped into the fight, and the instigator ended up with the tip of her finger severed, and Ma never had any problems with those girls again.

Ironically, those girls turned out to be crack-heads and trouble-plagued people in their adulthood, and whenever the sister of the one Ma had beaten saw her, she'd immediately turn in another direction.

Ma recalled being enraged by the constant teasing and taunting she'd experienced due to her circumstances, and she thanked God she didn't hurt or kill anyone during her rages.

I never had a relationship with my dad. I vividly recall the first time we held a conversation with each other the night after my junior prom. I was in my mid-teens. My best friends, Alonzo, aka Asia, Marvin, aka Miss Patti, along with our other cohorts Earnest, aka Monica, and lesbian couple Charlene and Carol all decided to go to the neighborhood hole-in-the-wall juke joint, Romey's, after the prom to hang out and act crazy.

I'd worn a black penguin-tailed tuxedo with a Prince-inspired white ruffled shirt, black shiny Stacy Adams and my freshly touched-up jerry curl to the prom. I was looking fabulous, ready for some fun and show off time with my friends. I danced the night away at school with the girls that I remained friendly with from my former crew, and we all seemed to have had a good time!

As far as I was concerned, it wasn't about hooking up with girls or boys. I just wanted to have fun. And I was sure that the after-hour party at Romey's was most likely going to be a blast to continue dancing and showing off.

My friends and I always felt safe at Romey's place and were able to freely express ourselves, because in addition to Mr. Romey liking that the gender non-conforming and trans girls livened up his Club for the better, his older son who wore women's wigs, clothes and make-up was also gender non-conforming.

That night Asia, Marvin and I had gotten a ride from school to the club after the prom with one of Asia's many boyfriends. Arriving at Romey's before the other girls, we scurried to the back to blot and cool off at the screened door.

We knew that the rest of our crew always tipped into the club from the back door. As we stood huddled there patting and blotting our faces with wads of bar napkins, Asia spotted one of her other boyfriends, and that girl almost broke her neck dashing out the door in a three-piece suit, tipping through the uncut weeds and up the dark alley to get around to the front of the club, trying to catch that man before he drove away.

Marvin was twirling on the dance floor with the middle-aged lady that you could always count on to become extremely drunk before the end of the evening and turn the club out. I stood at the back door keeping an eye out for the other girls and watching Marvin instigate the drunk lady to act even more outrageous.

Since the others were fashionably late as usual, I figured that I would join him on the dance floor. But, when I turned around, I was intercepted by this fairly handsome stranger who intentionally blocked my path. I'd previously observed him hanging out in the corner of the club earlier that evening, observing us from a distance. At first, I thought that he was possibly coming on to me, when he approached me in that manner. I really didn't have any idea how to respond once he engaged me in conversation.

However, looking back now, although I couldn't put my finger on what it was during that time, I felt that there was something quite familiar about his energy. Anyway, after a few moments the conversation became extremely uncomfortable for me when he started talking about my family and asking personal questions about my mother, uncles and aunts.

In my mind, I was thinking who could this stranger possibly be whom was asking about my family members and what were his motives for doing so? By then, I no longer suspected that he was coming onto me, nor was I comfortable with the direction he was going trying to discuss my family, so I wanted to get away from him as soon as possible. Discussing my family with a stranger was never going to happen because Ma always taught us to keep our family business in the family.

He was certainly a stranger to me, so I was relieved when the rest of our crew sashayed through the back door where we were standing causing a commotion. I awaited an opportunity to politely excuse myself from the awkward conversation. My mind was on joining my friends in our reserved booth, where they were touching-up their eyeliner, mascara and face powder before getting the party started.

After prom night at Romey's, I thought no further about the encounter with the stranger, that is, until weeks later, I was hanging out at Asia's house getting dressed to go out on a Friday night when she unexpectedly asked, "Toni, do you remember the guy that was talking to you at the back door of Romey's two weeks ago at the club?"

Her voice was serious so I hesitantly replied, "Girl, he was kind of strange and I didn't like it when he started asking me personal questions about my family." Her question wasn't offensive or a surprise to me because Asia knew almost everybody from Romey's.

I'd anticipated her saying the guy was interested in me, when she stopped applying her foundation and looked across the room at me, replying, "Well, he and I were talking last weekend at Romey's and he told me that he was your father. Is that true, Toni?"

I was shocked and slightly agitated as I continued lightly applying liquid Posner honey-glow foundation and powder although not yet dressing in full drag, pretending to not be irritated by her question. I didn't respond as she continued revealing that he'd also shared with her some really personal information about my family members. As I listened, I knew deep within that there was a good possibility that he was who he'd claimed to have been.

But, I faced her responding to the jarring information she'd just delivered and denied that he was telling the truth, adding, "He's not my father because a real man takes care of his child. They as the fathers should have a strong presence in their children's lives, which is what my father did before he was killed in a car accident when I was an infant."

I ended the conversation about him by turning and facing the mirror to continue moisturizing and styling my hair with gel and a little spray activator so that we could leave her house sooner than later for our night out.

I was unconcerned if Asia was convinced or not about whom this man was because I felt that his approach was cowardly. In my opinion, if he was a real father, he would have revealed to me who he was before approaching me in a club. Maybe it's a good thing that he didn't reveal himself at Romey's?

I label him a coward, because he'd approached me in a club and not on a more personal manner in an appropriate environment so that I'd be able to properly understand his motives for engaging me in conversation.

Since he'd always known where we'd lived, according to Ma, if he was really concerned about my well-being and family I feel he should have made a better effort at making his presence known before that night.

What was his point for approaching me in that manner in a club environment, clearly aware that I'd had no idea of what his relationship was to me? I might have preferred that he at least let me know who he was at some prior point, instead of placing me in such an uncomfortably awkward position with my best friend telling me that a man I'd just recently met, in of all places, Romey's club, was my daddy. Not father; huge difference.

During that conversation with Asia, I'd realized the rumors were true about the boy in my neighborhood that I would often get into fights with at the bus stop after school. He lived up the street from us with his mother, whose younger son rode the same school bus with me. As I recall, he also shared a similar facial bone structure, and it didn't surprise me when he turned out to be my half-brother.

I used to wonder how many other half brothers and sisters I might have that the stranger from Romey's helped to conceive and then abandoned. I recall there was this one time when Asia asked me if I knew this girl from their neighborhood that looked so much like me. According to Asia, the girl could have been my twin sister.

As I'm writing this memory, I realize that sometimes I wish that I'd pursued being introduced to this person Asia thought looked so much like me. Asia had already set the record for knowing more about my sperm donor dad before I'd really known him. It's quite possible that the girl could have been a relative. Who knows at this point?

Although I'm grateful that the stranger from Romey's contributed to my conception, I feel that he should have done everything within his power to have been a part of my life in some capacity. But instead, he'd chosen to be a deadbeat who went to our home many years later, out of the blue way after I was an adult, exclaiming that he'd all of a sudden become concerned about me.

Imagine his audacity. Although he wasn't an issue for me growing up, I was somewhat unpleasantly affected by his actions in Romey's. However, I'm not defeated by his continued absence. I expressed this sentiment to Ma after she informed me he showed up unannounced at the house, wanting to talk to her about me. Since he wasn't around during my childhood, I do not need or desire to know anymore about him.

However, I am aware that blaming and resenting him for not being in my life does me no good. I'm also grateful that, according to Ma, when he was present during my infancy, she never allowed any unsupervised visits with him because she didn't want to have to kill him for being irresponsible with her baby.

I also know that in order for me to continue successfully healing and moving forward with my purpose, I must forgive his shortcomings for my own sake. I remain open to an acknowledgement and gesture from him that may help move the healing process forward to further assist me with understanding my paternal heritage. However, I'm not holding my breath.

Quite recently, I questioned Ma for research to gather some additional information about him to write this memoir, and she shared with me that he was once the love of her life and that I looked like his mother, with the same eye color as hers.

Unfortunately for me, I have never had the privilege or opportunity to meet my paternal grandparents. I can only wonder about the kind of influence that they may have had on my development if they had been in my life growing up?   Well, at least I now know why I'm the only one in my immediate family who was born with hazel eyes, or cat-eyes as Grandma called them.

My heart is full recalling our conversation on a cool afternoon as my mother and I burned trash in the backyard. "E.D. disappointed and deeply hurt me after I found out he'd cheated with someone close to me."

I really didn't know how to respond to her informing me who it was that had sex in a pathway with E.D., so I just continued staring into the fire, hoping that the conversation about him would soon conclude before going back into the house.

I have never felt comfortable enough to tell my mother about the encounter between the stranger and me at Romey's until now. She knows that the man that I consider to be my father was named Manley and, according to Ma, he was a hard-working man who married us when my brother and I were infants.

In life and in death, according to Ma, Manley stepped up to the plate and took responsibility for ensuring his family's needs were met, as if we were his biological children. Most of all, she said he loved, respected and cherished her. I've tried to remember more details about him, but unfortunately due to being almost 3 years old, all I recall is Ma taking my brother and me to the funeral home on Manning Avenue to view his head after he was killed in a mysterious car accident.

Also, I recall Ma being dressed in black the day of his funeral and crying while her family members comforted her during the burial. I wanted to comfort her as we walked in the funeral procession towards his grave site, but I was restrained from going to her by one of our other chaperones.

Additionally, according to Ma during another of our recent trips back down memory lane together, I eventually ended up in her arms, sitting quietly and content with finally being close to her during his burial.

After the internment, my brother was passed over the grave, which is our family's Southern custom after a death of someone who is in or close to the family. They "passed" infants and toddlers over the deceased person's grave hoping to prevent the spirit from coming to the children during the night.

Ma said as an infant I'd usually slept peacefully throughout the entire night, but after Manley's funeral that night, I was in an unusually restless and fussy state. Grandma eventually asked Ma, "Did you pass that baby over the grave?"

Ma said she regrettably replied, "No ma'me Ma, since Tony was sitting contently on my lap during the burial, I didn't feel the need to cross him over the grave."

Grandma replied, insisting, "You need to go and take Tony back to the graveyard and 'pass' him over Manley's grave."

The end result was that night my Uncle Gene drove Ma and me back to the cemetery, in a storm, to cross me over the grave. Afterwards, I immediately fell asleep quietly throughout the rest of the night, undisturbed by Dad's spirit. During my Aunt Rebecca's funeral I recently observed my cousins continuing the tradition of "passing" their babies over her grave.

When we were several years older, Grandma told us that my father was found decapitated on the side of the road and that Ku Klux Klan members were suspected in his death. The story goes that my brother and I were with him visiting Grandma the night before his death, and when he was ready to leave, Grandma suggested to him that since it was so late in the morning and that we were already asleep, he should let my brother and I spend the night.

The next day my father was found on the side of the road with some of his body parts conspicuously placed on the roadside. I've never wanted to cause Ma any additional pain by asking her to recall the alleged circumstances that contributed to his death, so I've chosen not to question her about those details which tragically altered our lives.

Although Ma recently provided me with a copy of his death certificate, I've steeled my nerves to read it entirely. So, I can't honestly say yea or nay if his death was the result of a car accident or a life senselessly cut short by hate and bigotry.

Chapter Two

My Mother Bear

I've recently questioned my mother about her hopes, dreams and the aspirations that she'd given up after becoming a young and single mother of two. It came as no surprise that as a child she wanted out of the poor living conditions, which contributed to her being hungry all of the time.

During our conversation I was pleasantly surprised when she'd unequivocally stated that she hadn't given up any of her significant dreams other than wanting six children in total, three boys and three girls! I'd always wished for more brothers and sisters growing up and I often wondered what our family dynamics would have been like with additional siblings.

Another dream of hers that became a reality was marrying Manley, whom also adored her children as his own. Her career dream was to become a nurse or work within the medical field in another capacity, which she accomplished by working for the State Board of Disabilities and Special Needs and then later retiring as a certified nurse assistant!

I've always idolized and received great inspiration from my mother's strength and ability to work all day long in the kitchen and hours on the farms of others in order to provide for her babies. Later, during our adolescence and teen years, I recall her laboring grueling hours in sewing and manufacturing factories to give my brother and me a solid foundation.

I am so proud that all the while she later attended adult education evening classes after working all day at her job to graduate and receive her diploma from my high school for what was supposed to have been my junior and senior year at Sumter High School!

Considering that she didn't have very many positive role models to emulate during her development and she was still a teenager herself when she'd given birth to my brother and I, God has innately blessed her with intuition, wisdom, intelligence, commonsense and strength.

Lastly, but not at all least, Ma later told me that she'd vowed to herself that me and my brother would be provided with a better life and environment that was totally opposite her childhood experiences.

She'd also unselfishly sacrificed things that she needed for herself in order to ensure our needs were met. She was focused on making sure that our lives were different from the life of poverty, insecurity and hopelessness that she'd felt after the untimely death of her father.

The mother bear protecting her cubs is an accurate description of the loving, protective spirit that God ordained to be my mother! Everyone that really knew her also were aware that she was dedicated to her children. Ma wears her heart on her sleeve whenever she continues to give someone in need clothes off her back and even brand new clothes that she'd purchased for herself with labels still attached.

However, when it comes to her children, she did not play at all. I also recall her often emphatically stating, "I'll walk through Hell backwards in gasoline drawers before I let somebody hurt my children!"

My mother's maternal instincts were tested very early on when I was an infant born with extreme bowlegs, which prompted concern from the doctors about how I'd develop. They suggested to her that I would not be able to walk properly if she did not allow them to intervene and actually break my little legs in order to reset them in hopes that they'd straighten out.

Of course and instinctively she refused to give them authorization to experiment on her baby by inflicting unnecessary pain upon me! She wisely went on faith that my legs would eventually work themselves out to become what they were supposed to be on their own which they have, thankfully!

It's ironic that before Ma told me this story about my bowed legs, I found bowlegged people very attractive, and during adolescence I used to fix my legs and pretended that I was Bow-legged to walk like them!

Earlier on I wasn't aware and extremely unappreciative of the sacrifices that Ma made for me and my brother. Looking back, we were divinely blessed to have a mother who really dedicated herself to our wellbeing after our birth, making it clear to any potential suitors that the three of us were a package deal. You can't have one without the others.

I currently possess more cognizance of how hard it was for our mother to have financially maintained a household without a father figure in the home to lean on whenever times were challenging and she needed a soft place to land.

Although we'd basically grown up together, considering she was practically a child herself when my brother and I were born, she was smart with her insistence that we developed a strong sense of character, morals and values! Another golden nugget that I recall is that she'd always told us, "Be leaders, not followers."

She instilled in us that we should respect our elders and ourselves at all times. To this date, Ma beams with great pleasure about the number of compliments that she's often received on how well mannered and respectful we were as children into adulthood!

Although everybody in the neighborhood knew that she didn't play when it came to her children, we were also taught, as she was previously by her mother, to never go out bullying others just because we could.

Whenever those rare times occurred when we first moved into the neighborhood that an ill-thought parent of some of the other kids inappropriately approached us about a childhood quarrel that we may have had with their children, Ma made it clear to them that in no uncertain terms any adults should address her first and foremost before they'd approached us about any accusations from their children or any others. She'd always stressed to us, "Your word is your bond, so if you always tell me the truth, I will stand up for you tooth and nail to the end." So, whenever anyone unfairly tried accusing us of something that we hadn't done, I told her the truth so that she would not look like a fool defending me whenever I was in the wrong.

Reflecting back to my earlier childhood many years before moving to our new house on East Calhoun, there came a period for the very first time in my life that I recall my sense of being traumatically shifting into the unknown and uncertainty.

Around the age of 5 years old my foundation abruptly shifted after Ma informed Perry and I that she was leaving us with Grandma while she moved to Coco Beach, Florida, with her boyfriend, Singleton, in search of jobs and better opportunities.

Ma said, her intentions were only to leave us until she was able to get a job and find a stable place to live and then she'd return for us. After my mother left, it was extremely hard on me trying to adjust to being separated from her, to my recollection, for the first extended period of time in our lives together.

My little brain wasn't able to process why we couldn't have gone with her. While she was gone, I suffered through the worst case of untreated chicken pox that covered my entire lower frame with the most unbearable lesions and puss-filled wounds on my fragile stick-sized legs.

The itchy sores were more inflamed by the early morning dew while waiting at the school bus stop. I was in such despair and all I wanted was my mother to make the pain go away as she'd previously done.

During the time that we were left to live with Grandma, we were regularly exposed to her alcoholic boyfriend Mr. C, who went on expected cursing tantrums for hours after he arrived home from work drunk. Although he worked every day of the week at Roy Timmons Used Car Lot, he never bought home a pay check.

I recall once when he'd carried on so badly for hours and Grandma must have gotten tired of him nagging her, so before anyone knew it we were startled by a gun shot. After Mr. C continued to not heed Grandma's warning to leave their bedroom with all the cursing, grandma retrieved her pistol from underneath her mattress and shot Mr. C in the foot.

When we all entered the room, there was Mr. C bleeding from the bullet hole and yelling, "Burt, you shot me."

I am unable to recall exactly how Grandma got away with shooting Mr. C in his foot. I do, however, remember the extended periods of time when we lived without electricity and running water because the bills were not being paid by grandma or any of the other adults living within the household.

I also recall with certainty another time when the lights were cut off the almost day and a half later once the frozen fish completely thawed out in the freezer from the hot summer heat. The smell of rotted fish became intolerably ingrained in my senses for several years following. Why an adult didn't dispose of the fish before it decomposed to that extent baffles me.

Also during that time, my Aunt Duck had to dig a hole in the ground in the back yard that she covered with the oven-rack from the stove to cook breakfast and dinner. Cooking outside with my aunt was like a camping adventure to me and the food sure tasted good!

Perry and I were not aware of the fact that Ma was regularly sending grandma money to ensure that we were being fed and properly cared for. The money Ma was sending home went elsewhere, because it certainly wasn't used on food and paying the utilities.

During those days I often flipped through magazine pages and imagined being magically able to sink my teeth into the creamy chocolate cake advertised on the pages and whenever the pancake commercials came on television, showing the light stacks of fluffy and buttery pancakes floating on air and then being smothered in Mrs. Butterworth's syrup.

After being reunited when Ma finally returned for us, I was relieved and exuberantly overjoyed once again! I knew that from then on, things would be much different than our environment and living situation with Grandma!

Ma has confided in me that when she returned for us after getting settled in Florida, she was beyond horrified to the point of breaking down and almost weeping when she saw the gaunt and emaciated condition that I was in. Also, she's shared with me, to my surprise and amazement, that it was only a three-month period of time when we were left to live with Grandma until she was able to get established in Florida.

It seemed more like three years to me and an eternity that she was gone. Although I recall the challenging times that we'd experienced living with Grandma during those days, I also fondly remember some of the great times we'd had during the years following!

In addition to Ma having a great influence on me, I was also influenced by my Aunt Mae and Aunt Dinah Lee, also affectionately called Aunt Duck. I looked forward to helping Aunt Mae prepare the holiday family dinners!

Although I was the first of the children to hold my cousin, Mary Ann, when she was brought home from the hospital, I don't ever recall Aunt Mae being pregnant with her and since the baby was such a mystery to me, I was happy with the honor to hold and closely inspect her as I'd passed her to Grandma!

I remember Aunt Duck and I regularly practicing singing and creating routines to the latest pop groups like Chi Chi & Pepe, Evelyn Champagne King, Peaches and Herb, so forth and so on!

Since Aunt Duck was the baby sister of the family and somewhat closer to our age, I was very intrigued by her pregnancy. She was the very first pregnant woman who was related to me that I could observe!

It was amazing to me that there was a baby actually growing inside her stomach! It saddens me that my Aunt Dinah Lee McDaniel recently died from cervical cancer. I choose to remember how vibrant she was when we used to dance to Marvin Gaye's hit song "Got to Give It Up"! Rest in Peace Aunt Duck. I love you.

As time passed, Ma has also recently acknowledged her mistake and regrets for leaving us with Grandma for any period of time, taking into consideration her childhood experiences after her father died. According to Ma, she'd mistakenly thought that since she was sending money home on a regular basis, we would be provided for until her return.

After that horrifying experience, she'd vowed she would never leave us to be cared for by anyone other than herself ever again. She also committed to us that if she would ever have to leave town for an extended period of time ever again, Perry and I would go with her no matter what!

Ma has also shared with me that when we were younger, she often prayed to God that she would live long enough to see the day that we were old enough and able to take care of ourselves if, God forbid, something was to ever happen to her. She was often concerned that if something were to happen to her, no one else would protect us in the manner she's done.

I was still 5 years old and life for me was great after Ma rescued us and took us to Florida to be with her! I recall the lush orange orchards in our backyard where my brother and I spent as much time as we were allowed playing tag and helping ourselves to the juiciest, huge sun-sweet navel oranges that I've ever tasted!

At first, I was content during our adjustment period of getting to know Singleton because I was safely back with my mother and as long as I was with her I felt reassured that no matter what, everything from that point forward would be okay!

We were enrolled in Pine Needle Elementary School upon our arrival, which is where I had my very first major crush on this really cute, light-skinned sort of bad boy named Tyrone! He was in my homeroom class with the most perfectly styled afro and he was very nice, sweet and unaggressive toward me as compared to the other boys in our class thatTyrone used to beat up during recess!

Tyrone and I often manipulated our teacher into permitting us to use the restroom together so that we were able kiss and smooch! Yes, and I'll agree just this once if you're inclined to label me a little hot ass at such an early age.

I may have been continuing, as Iyanla Vanzant refers to, "Patterns" from my childhood pathology -- living without my mother in a home with male adolescent relatives also responding to their hormones.

I looked forward to going to school every day to see Tyrone! However, life at home was a totally different situation starting after a period of time when Singleton's attitude and actions were very clear that he really didn't care for me and my little girlie ways.

Singleton started being more comfortable with calling me names when Ma was gone. He was always careful to not overtly be too cruel towards me in front of her and whenever he slipped up in doing so, although she didn't do it in front of us, I knew that she'd chastised him for being overly aggressive and strict.

Nevertheless, I recall hating being forced to wash his dirty, four-door Cutlass Supreme car, enduring him being especially short and condescending to me whenever I made any mistakes.

I also clearly remember hating him during the many times when I was unjustifiably beaten and abused by him for things that I hadn't done. I now know that hate is a strong word. However, that hate I'd felt was coming from a child's perspective.

As time passed on the day after Singleton arrived home from work with me and Perry there alone with him until Ma was to arrive home later that evening. Well, he was in rare form when he'd started calling me sissy, Little D meaning Little Dummy and other cruel names that I'm so grateful are currently closed wounds from the past that have no power over me.

Singleton was full of himself that afternoon. I remember him trying to force me into doing after-school chores that Perry was responsible for completing. Although Singleton might have been feeling invincible, I recall being fed up with his cruelty towards me. It just didn't sit right with me when he'd insisted that it did not matter whose chores they were, he wanted me to do them.

Singleton was a giant compared to my tiny little self during that time, but I didn't back down and continued rebelling against his authority. I guess up to a breaking point he felt that he didn't have to debate with a child, so he then lost control, trying to physically attack me for disobeying him.

No matter how much bigger I'd perceived him to be, I was strong enough to have pushed him away after he'd grabbed my arm. I then bolted out the kitchen door with him in hot pursuit behind me and I was fortunately too fast for him to catch as I sprinted around the house like Flash Gordon!

After dashing back through the kitchen door, I ended up locking myself in me and my brother's bedroom refusing to unlock the door until Ma arrived home from work!

Although I was really scared when he'd started banging on the door threatening to unhinge it if I didn't come out, I thought to myself shivering in the corner on the floor next to the dresser that he'd have to break the door down to get me out because I was not going out on my own.

Finally later that early evening after Ma arrived home several hours later from her nurses' aide job at Cape Canaveral Hospital, I felt it safe enough to come out of the bedroom. Singleton had already told her his side of the story on the phone after the incident occurred earlier that day for sure.

After I finished informing her that Singleton was trying to force me to do Perry's chores, I recall that evening being one of many times to come that my mother would stand up for me.

Once informed of the truth, she didn't feel it necessary to place me on any further punishment, because I'd completed all of my assigned chores! Of course the cause and effect was that the abuse started to progressively escalate during the time one afternoon that Perry and I were home alone doing our regular after school chores.

I busied myself dusting and vacuuming the living room carpet while watching "The Mickey Mouse Club" on television when my brother suddenly yelled for me to come into the kitchen!

When I came to where Perry was in the kitchen and saw the light shade shattered on the floor he proceeded to claim that he'd accidentally hit the shade with the broom trying to kill a huge black widow spider that was supposedly crawling on the kitchen ceiling.

I never saw a spider. I just stood there in disbelief, warning him that he was going to be in deep trouble when Ma notices the light shade gone.

He then suggested that nobody would notice the missing shade, and he'd even managed to convince me to not tell what he'd done. Later that evening when Ma and Singleton arrived home from work, I thought that Perry was going to do the honorable thing and tell them that he'd broken the light cover trying to kill a spider. If you think the coward told the truth for once, you'd be wrong.

Instead of protecting his baby sibling, he didn't say a word when we were questioned about the missing light fixture. I'm not sure why I'd resisted being a tattle-tale rat when I didn't bring the light shade to their attention earlier on and for a brief moment, we both thought that they weren't going to have noticed the missing shade.

But, the deception by omission didn't last long when Singleton remained at the dining room table after dinner cleaning his eye glasses.

Since our homework was expected to have been completed before Ma arrived home from work so she could check it, I was enjoying a rare reward watching a special featured Disney movie airing on a week night! From where I sat on the living room couch watching television, I was able to overhear Ma and Singleton converse during commercials.

My heart raced faster than normal after hearing Singleton remark to Ma that the kitchen seemed unusually bright for some reason? I saw them both look up at the ceiling and after seeing that the shade was missing, they called us into the kitchen asking what happened to the light shade?

I recall this time period being when I'd noticed and became more aware that Perry started lying because he could get away with it. It seemed that he'd received some sort of pleasure out of us both being punished for something that he'd done.

I'd foolishly proceeded thinking that Perry was going to "fess up" to what he'd done, but he didn't take responsibility. He lied instead, saying that he knew nothing about the light shade. When they turned and asked me what happened, I had no choice but to tell the truth because I didn't want to lie to Ma.

The true story was that Perry told me when I'd entered after school was that he'd broken the light shade trying to kill a spider. I was deeply hurt when my mother didn't believe that I was telling her the truth about not breaking the glass shade because I wasn't even in the kitchen when it was broken.

I guess that due to them having no way of knowing who was telling the truth, I recall us both being brutally beaten by Singleton for lying and placed on punishment. Since it was just a light shade, I still don't know why we were beaten so brutally for something that could have been easily replaced.

I resented being beaten in that manner and punished for things that Perry had done just because it was his word against mine. In addition, that torturous incident was a sadistic form of child abuse that drew blood and caused me intense discomfort sitting during school for several days.

I never told any of my teachers because we were taught to keep family business in the house. I was frustrated that Ma would not believe that I was telling her the truth. Nor did I comprehend why she'd found it necessary to punish both of us for things that Perry usually did?

Those experiences in CoCoa Beach, Florida, were the first time that I really started to feel I was somewhat on my own, because my big brother whom was supposed to look out for me could not be trusted.

Perry was rather good at lying and manipulating our mother for reasons unknown to me during those days. So, now I had to deal with both my untrustworthy brother that would throw me under the bus without any remorse to look out for only himself and Singleton's consistent disdain for me just because I was a little too effeminate for his taste, which caused us to continuously clash with each other.

Singleton didn't like me and I mutually did not care for him one bit. Resulting from being taught by Ma to not be disrespectful, I reluctantly followed some of his commands and by some means we'd managed to tolerate each other for my mother's sake.

Thankfully, Ma usually kept him in check whenever he'd crossed too far over the line with us progressing forward. As for me, other than the challenges of the unjustified punishments that in my opinion didn't cross the abuse line as the shattered light shade incident had, our environment was much better than the circumstances that we'd previously faced living back in South, Carolina with grandma.

At least we didn't go to bed or school hungry, wearing raggedy clothes, we always had electricity, running water and, most importantly, I was finally back where I needed to be, with my mother!

Living in Florida that period of time wasn't always bad. I felt very special after being given permission by Ma to go on a class fieldtrip to have witnessed the 1972 Cape Canaveral rocket launch to outer space!

However, there were the times that I was so frightened by the extreme weather during hurricane season. Once I thought the world was coming to an end during one particular horrible lightening, thunder and extreme downpour from a hurricane knocking out all of the power throughout our neighborhood.

I remained awake all night cowering underneath my covers throughout the entire storm scared to move in the pitch black dark! All I could do was cover my head with the sheets and pray to God to please save our lives.

The following morning, we awoke to the television news alerts on every channel about massive flooding and drainage systems being overwhelmed and backed-up with debris. You'd think that the schools were damaged during the storm, but they weren't and we were still required to go to school due to no school closures announcements on the news.

My brother was in a different school than me, so he left for his bus a little earlier than I and when I walked outside to leave the house and out our gate, I was startled by these really huge dead stiff black eels that were washed up during the storm!

I literally had to step over those scary monstrosities covering the streets throughout our entire neighborhood on the walk to the bus-stop. I recall catching eels during our fishing trips back in South Carolina, and I don't remember ever seeing an eel the size of those pre-historic reptiles washed up on the streets in Florida!

During that time, I developed into a very precocious child and, unfortunately, I also picked up some of the bad habits from my grandmother's boyfriend Mr. C when we lived with them back in South Carolina.

I recall going through this phase whenever I was away from Ma that I would curse like a little sailor at the bus-stop and around the neighborhood. On one unfortunate Saturday afternoon for me, Perry and I were riding our bikes in the front yard up the driveway and out the gate to the stop sign on the corner within view of Ma while she and Singleton were detailing their cars. I was having a good old time trying to keep up with my brother on our bikes!

My bright sunny playful afternoon all of a sudden came to a screeching halt when some local older teenage girls from the neighborhood and school came strolling by our house carrying on a casual conversation amongst themselves.

Unbeknownst to me at the time, Ma must have overheard with her bionic ears when one of the girls pointed me out to her friends and stated, "That's the little boy with the green eyes that's always going around cursing people out!"

Oh my! I heard Ma call those girls into our yard and reconfirmed with the one girl what she'd just overheard her say about me. After the girl confirmed to her that I was going around the neighborhood cursing, Ma turned facing me and asked, "Is what she saying about you the truth, Tony?"

It was as if she was able to see right through me as she continued, "Are you going around cursing?"I knew that if she'd found out that I was intentionally lying to her face I'd be in deeper trouble.

Her direct gaze transfixed on my eyes let me know without any additional words that she wasn't playing and I would be better off telling her the truth from the start. So, I didn't even attempted to lie and deny that I wasn't running around the neighborhood cursing like I was grown.

Ma thanked those girls for bringing my behavior to her attention and, after they left, let us just say that the butt whipping and punishment that I received taught me a valuable lesson about not cursing and being disrespectful.

By the way, this is the reason why I respectfully don't use profanity in front of Ma as an adult. I'm baffled by those adults that feel comfortable enough to let curse words roll off their tongues in front of their parents. Don't get me wrong, there are those times when a curse word or two might be appropriate in certain situations. I just personally feel it disrespectful to curse in from of my mother in any circumstance.

As time progressed on over the years, I'd eventually started to notice the changes in Ma and Singleton after she'd found out that he was cheating on her. I remember the afternoon that we were in the car when she was driving like a detective in pursuit of a suspect through traffic after she'd caught him in his car with another woman.

I was ecstatic after she packed up our things and we went directly to Boston, Massachusetts, to live with Aunt Rebecca and her five children. Most recently, she informed me several years ago during a conversation with Singleton that he'd suggested the next time I visited home from living abroad he wanted my brother to bring me to his house for a visit with him.

I've expressed to Ma the level of disdain I still harbor for Singleton resulting from the abuse that I'd experienced at his hands and I will never forget the way that he'd treated me. I didn't comprehend what hating someone meant at that time and now I understand for the first time in my life that I really hated him for mistreating me.

Although moving forward I've forgiven him in my own way in order to heal myself, there is absolutely no reason I would ever willingly choose to go visit with him for anything pretending that his actions didn't cause damage to my psyche when I was a child. Not in this lifetime.

Progressing onward after Ma left Singleton, I recall the distinct smell of the Greyhound buses during the trip to Boston. After our arrival at Aunt Rebecca's, it was not without its challenges adjusting from living in tropical Florida to bone-chilling Boston, Massachusetts. I was frightened by and steered clear of the hot steam sizzling out of wall oversized radiators in all of the rooms in the apartment.

Those hot smoking large steamers unexpectedly turned out to be a source of comfort and warmth during those cold winter snowstorms blanketing the neighborhood! In addition to the cold weather, we'd often get into physical altercations and fights with the neighborhood Puerto Rican gang members, escalating to the point that we were forbidden from going anywhere alone without an escort, even to school. I loved seeing my mother standing outside of the classroom peering through the window observing and waiting to take me home after the bell rang!

Once, on one cold and wet winter night when Aunt Rebecca sent my older cousin Chris and I out to the store for milk, butter, oatmeal and sugar for breakfast before school the next morning, everything went smoothly on our walk to the market around the corner.

After paying for the groceries and immediately upon walking outside of the store before turning the corner heading home, we were accosted by this Puerto Rican guy that followed us out of the market who robbed us with a knife!

Even though Chris had given him all of the left over change from our purchase, which obviously wasn't enough because the thug insisted that he had more money to give and he then tried sticking his fingers into my cousins' eyes.

No one did anything to stop the attack right in front of the grocery store. I was afraid that he was hurting my cousin, so I grabbed the thug's jacket and screamed at him, "Leave my cousin alone!"

I didn't know what was going to happen when the thug turned his attention to me stating before running away, "I'm not going to hurt you green eyes."His exact words! Since the attack happened so quickly, I don't know where the courage and strength came from that allowed me have stood up in defense of my cousin to a perpetrator who was almost five times my size.

I was just gratefully relieved that my cousin wasn't permanently injured during the robbery at knifepoint and I was also thankful I wasn't hurt during the unsettling ordeal! Other than the constant fights with the gangs, my memories of Boston are mostly okay.

I'll never forget those crab cakes that were so delicious, nor have I tasted anything that even comes near going to the corner store for giant, hot fresh cakes by the dozens!

Also, I remember there being a lot of students per class and very long lunch lines. I'd anticipated being able to hang out after school with my older cousin, Debbie, whenever Ma wasn't able to pick me up from school, because she'd take me to see drama class productions accompanied by her boyfriend, Hannah!

He was a nice guy who was obviously liked and trusted enough by Ma to have allowed him to take me to the movies by myself to see Pam Grier in her 1973 movie "Coffy"! My favorite scene remains when she was locked in the sauna and she used a rock to sharpen a hair pin that she later used to escape from her captors and proceeded on a rampage enacting her revenge!

There was also this very nice Asian couple living in the apartment below us that received permission from Ma and Aunt Rebecca to take each of us on individual day outings, concluding with bags of candy and other tasty treats when they arrived back home!

At that time, I was always competing for attention living with my brother and all of my cousins, so I was really disappointed when I was selected to be the last to have gone on my outing. I'd anticipated my turn to go candy shopping and each week I watched everybody else return home with bags of goodies.

I was really disappointed and wondered why I was the only one not allowed to go shopping for my brown bag of candy? I guess Ma didn't trust the couple as much as she'd trusted Hannah?

We lived in Boston for a few years or so. It was after my mother was forced to defend herself against a physical altercation with my aunt's boyfriend after he'd gotten drunk during a card game that we left Boston on another Greyhound bus back to South Carolina!

Although I recall the bus smell and cold winter, I don't remember much about how long it took for us to arrive back in Sumter. I do remember when it was just the three of us back in our home town, I often felt that Ma was more impatient and harder on me than she was with my brother.

Those feelings were reconfirmed the time after I'd returned from running a corner store errand for some neighbors who were more like extended family members to us. When I jumped off my bike after returning from the store, they'd obviously didn't hear me outside of the house listening to them discussing their observations about the difference in the treatment that my brother and I were receiving.

I've always been very protective of my mother no matter what and even though their observations validated my feelings, I wasn't about to allow anyone to talk negatively about her. So, I quietly tiptoed away from the screened door and jumped back on my bike pedaling as fast as I could to get home and tell my mother about what I'd overheard!

After informing her of the details, we were not allowed to run anymore errands for them and our interactions became slightly estranged.

During the time when it was just the three of us, I was often conflicted when it came to the protective spirit that I possess for my mother because on one the hand, I didn't want anyone to hurt her, and on the other, I was in constant pain due to the ways she'd mistakenly dealt with my gender identity nonconformity as I grew older.

Overtime, the built-up resentments that I'd been containing about the unfair treatment that I'd received compared to Perry started simmering on medium heat. Every day I questioned God. Why was I being treated so severely and why was I born into the wrong family?

This was also around the time when I'd had a very frightening, unexplainable weird experience when I was around 7 years old that I'll never forget. I recall that I was lying in bed one morning half awake and somewhat slightly still asleep. Although it's difficult to fully explain the experience, I remember being aware of my surroundings as I tried to wake up completely, but I was not able to move.

There was this really strange constant ringing sound that frightened me even more as I was being pulled back to who knows where. I was really frightened and aware that something wasn't right about the way I was feeling, slipping deeper and deeper back to sleep, so I tried screaming, but no sound came out!

As the ringing increased and I continued feeling as if my life-force was being sucked right out of me, I continued fighting harder to just make myself move. I was so scared and I knew that if I was able to just move one limb, I'd be okay. I continued struggling and fighting to move until finally, I broke free and released myself from whatever it was that had a hold on me! This was a very strange incident that I haven't shared with anyone until now and I still wonder what that morning battle alone in my lower bunk-bed was all about. Oh well, whatever it was, I'm still here!

It was shortly after the unexplainable, outer-body, nightmarish experience that I met my Uncle Gene's wife, Diane, and her family. As time passed, I was seemingly more able to be myself around them and observed how open the communication between them seemed as compared to my almost invisibility in my family.

I wished that my family was as open and communicative as theirs was. I felt that I didn't have a voice in my family and it appeared as if the only time I received attention was when I was being punished. I didn't want that type of attention and I'm so glad that I didn't adopt the idea of it in order to get attention I'd have to be punished!

Observing Aunt Diane's family led me to think that since they were so open and communicative with each other, they were the right family that I was supposed to have been born into. Foolish me thought that the only way to be with them was to run away from home for the very first time to escape my perceived torment!

I planned the run-away all out in my little head, knowing that the best time to make my escape was after school while Ma was still at work! Due to Perry and I being in different schools once again, I usually got home before him, but I knew it wasn't too much longer before he was expected.

So I had to hurry home after school that afternoon! After jumping off the bus, I ran all the way home as fast as my legs would carry me from the bus-stop and once I entered our bedroom, I started stuffing clothes and personal items into three grocery store plastic bags that I'd previously set aside the night before for easy access!

I then quickly ran outside and jumped onto my little black and yellow striped bicycle that I'd previously gotten for Christmas! My perception was that if I pedaled as fast as I could toward Manning Road, I'd soon be united with my rightful family!

The cold wind ferociously slammed against my face and impeded my progress by blowing clothes out of the bags back towards home as if warning me that I should not be doing what I was doing.

But, I was determined to make my getaway so I jumped off the bike and dashed up Manning Road to catch up with my clothes then immediately continued toward my perceived freedom pedaling against the consistent Jack Frosted wind gusts!

Finally, after arriving to turn off Guignyard Road onto the street that Aunt Diane's family lived on, I felt nervous and a little apprehension about what I was doing because they didn't have any idea about my intentions. However, the apprehension didn't last too long.

I had no idea of what to expect as I walked up to ring their door bell, and when Aunt Diane answered the door, she was surprised that I was there so far away from home alone on my bicycle. She'd questioned, "Tony, does your mother know where you are?"

It was clear that she was astonished when I told her, "Aunt Diane, I've run away from home to live with you!" Immediately after my revelation, she called Uncle Gene to inform Ma that I was at their house. Considering that they'd become unwilling participants in my plot for acceptance, they handled the situation in a respectfully supportive manner.

After getting off from work later that evening when Ma arrived at their house to pick me up. I knew upon sight of her that I was in deep trouble for running away from home.

I also knew that she wasn't happy at all about what I had done or having to come to get me after a long, hard day at work.

During the visit to retrieve me from Aunt Dianes' house, Ma was her usually poised and composed self as they conversed about the situation.

I was somewhat baffled that even after we'd left Aunt Diane's house during the drive home, Ma still remained unexpectedly calm and silent until the torturous ride concluded underneath our carport.

Once in the house back on Dent Street, in addition to not knowing what was going to happen to me, I was also numbed with fear wondering how extreme my punishment was going to be once again.

I was ready to except whatever punishment that was to come due to the infraction being mine and not my brother's for once. I'd braced myself for an extensive punishment and was surprised that all I received compared to what I'd expected was a good chastising for running away from home and placed on punishment for a very long time. Whew! I was prepared for another sore butt for another week. Thank you, Jesus!

Unfortunately, I don't recall ever being asked why I'd run away in the first place. I'm not even sure if I would have been able to give an intelligent answer that would've made a difference in the way I'd felt about feeling misplaced within my own immediate family.

Over the next several years, I should have been more grateful that Ma continued working hard to build our first home that I recall from the ground up! She continued struggling, performing back-breaking long hours in the sewing factories providing for us.

I am now more appreciative of her sacrifices for us even through the tough Reagan years that I recall, when the American manufacturing industry started to be outsourced to foreign countries at an alarming rate.

Although Ma recalls another house that we'd previously lived in when I was much younger which was built from the ground up, I will never forget being old enough to witness our house off Calhoun Road being built to her specifications!

We temporarily lived up the street from the almost three-acre lot where our new three-bedroom, large full kitchen, one-and a half bathroom home was being constructed.

Our temporary rental residence was at the very end of a small two-lane road called The Strip. The suburban road was often used by the older neighborhood guys and their friends as a race track due to its direct and extended length!

We usually excitedly stood at a safe distance watching them burn rubber just before emerging from smoke plumes from their stinky burnt tires!

During our mid teens a group of us often got together, after receiving permission from Ma, of course, to jog up to the end of The Strip that seemed endless at the time without a car. As a reward for detailing her car, Ma usually allowed us to drive up the Strip to practice parallel parking at the DMV testing location!

I usually cruised through Friendship Apartments at the end of The Strip to show off to my friends that I was driving alone before going back home!

It wasn't out of the ordinary during the time leading up to before our final move into our new home going with Ma to meet with building inspectors and contractors while inspecting the building progression. Ma especially loved selecting her favorite carpet colors, cabinets and wall paneling designs for our new brick house!

We were all excited after the construction concluded, which allowed Ma to sign all of our names in the freshly poured carport cement a week before we were to start moving in! Since we'd already helped Ma start packing and boxing up our possessions in the rental many weeks in advance of our move, we were ready to go after receiving final word of completion!

Perry and I were very excited about choosing our own bedrooms and immediately after we completed moving into our new house, I started plastering my bedroom walls with posters of Michael Jackson, The Jacksons, Prince, Boy George, Madonna, Andre Cymone, Jody Watley, Jesse Johnson's Revue , Cyndi Lauper and any pictures of my other favorite hot recording artists I could get my hands on from the teen magazines!

Other than the typical childish quarrels, we'd adjusted quite well to the other kids and their families in the neighborhood and on any given summer weekend our front yard was filled with some of the kids jumping on the trampoline whenever Ma allowed us to pull it from the backyard to the front!

As for those that were observing our family dynamics from the outside looking in, they mistakenly thought us to be rich just because a couple years after getting settled Ma gave me and Perry matching tangerine mopeds!

Perry and I progressively filled our yard with wisteria vines, green shrubs, red blooming rosebushes, fruit bearing trees, juicy bullet vines in the back and plum bushes in the front yard bearing the larges and sweetest crimson plums! My best friend's grandfather used to regularly comment to Ma during his visits, "If I had your hand, I'd turn mine in!"

Once one Sunday afternoon when my brother and I were exiting the church bus in front of our house, I overheard some of the ladies who saw our house for the first time question in disbelief to each other, "Do they really live there in that big house with a garage and huge fenced in yard?"

They had no idea that we were far from being monetarily rich, but we did have a mother who made wiser decisions about our finances as compared to others, who always set everybody up with rounds of drinks and whatever else they required on the weekends, nonstop partying the way that I've often observed other people doing with their hard earned money.

Admittedly and although Ma liked going out often on the weekends during her younger days, she always made sure that everything was in place at home before she went anywhere and she never allowed people to run in and out of our home.

Ma was still young, so it's understandable that she enjoyed going out and having fun with her sisters and brothers! However, after she'd realized that Perry and I both needed more of her attention when Perry started acting out in school and then it was suggested that he consume a mind-altering Attention Deficit Disorder drug those doctors tried convincing Ma to administer to him.

She wisely, emphatically, declined their suggestion to take the easy way out and drug my brother just to deal with his behavior issues. She then decreased going out as much on the weekends and pivoted to exposing us to activities and environments which stimulated our minds, because she wanted us to be prepared to meet the many challenges that we'd be faced within society as thriving adults!

It was around this time that she'd purchased the entire collection of Charlie Brown reading and vocabulary books so that she was able to measure our progress at home. I also remember at the beginning of every school term we'd go on our annual excursion downtown to Berger's to shop for new outfits and other school supplies!

Ma lived up to her commitment of ensuring that we weren't teased like she and her siblings were growing up. I'm happy that our Mother Bear compensated for her unhappy and poverty-stricken childhood by making a conscious effort to expose us to culture and surrounding communities!

My cherished memories include receiving chocolate and vanilla cones from Dairy Queen during our regular Sunday adventures after being loaded into the car and then driving to visit surrounding cities, state parks and peach orchards where we'd handpicked the sweetest fruits that were comparable to the juicy navel oranges in Florida!

Other memories and gifts that my mother has given to us that I will always keep close to my heart are the regular fishing trips to Santee Lake where we'd once found an injured pigeon underneath a bridge!

After tugging on her heart strings, we persuaded Ma to allow us to take the bird home with us in hopes of helping it to heal from its injuries! When we got the bird home, we placed it in the bird cage that previously housed a pet bird that accidentally died after it opened its cage door and had gotten into some rat poison.

After a few weeks, we took the pigeon outside and opened the cage door to see if it was able to fly and miraculously, it flew away! We thought that would be the last time we would see the bird, but a few days later after we'd arrived home from visiting our grandmother's house and to our surprise, the pigeon was perched outside underneath the carport! The pigeon frequently returned to visit us for quite some time after its release!

A few summers after we were settled into our new home, I was around 11 years old on the day that we'd just returned from summer football camp excited about Ma driving us to visit Grandma's house to play with our cousins!

I don't recall the events leading up to us being in the most horrific car accident I've ever experienced that knocked me unconscious immediately upon impact.

According to Ma, we were sitting at the stop light on that sunny afternoon waiting for the green light to change, when all of a sudden, this lady who wasn't paying attention when she ran the red light plowed directly into our car. Immediately after the collision, I was out and didn't wake up until several hours later in Toumey Hospital.

In addition to my concussion, Ma sustained extensive knee injuries when the shattered jagged-edged materials from the dash board splintered into both of her knees. God had enfolded us in his arms because even though the dashboard fragments were in her knees, the Lycra mixed material black pant that she was wearing were not torn, quite possibly minimizing the damage that could have permanently disabled my mother! It was simply a miracle that she wasn't permanently wheelchair bound after such a tragedy.

Most recently, Ma shared with me that she still has those pants in a drawer reminding her to be grateful that God was watching over us during that horrific accident!

Perry's ankle was broken and I'd received a horrible head injury to the left front side of my brain causing me to be the only one admitted into the hospital for two days due to the head trauma.

I remember later that evening after the accident at the hospital begging the nurse to let me please go to sleep, but because I had a concussion, she had to keep me awake for an extended period of time for observation.

During her visits, Ma brought me new pajamas and underwear for my stay in the hospital and after I was finally released for what seemed to me like two weeks, I was restricted from returning back to school for a period of time until after fully recovering.

Psychologically, you never really forget receiving a head injury such as the concussion that I'd received on that unfortunate day. Recently while looking through family albums, I've seen the photo that Ma still has of the car in a photo album taken after the accident and upon seeing the level of damage on the side of the car where I was sitting from an adults perspective, I know for sure that if it were not for the grace and mercy of God, we could have all possibly died in that accident.

Chapter Three

Who am I, and why am I different?

The love for flowers is something that I am for sure Ma and I had in common during that time. However, no matter how many plants I'd transplanted in the yard to make her happy, there remained the conflict between mother and child just because I identify as female.

Although I wasn't really aware then, I now have no doubt that there were times that Ma feared for my safety and physical well-being. I'm sure that she was also sometimes embarrassed that I was acting as they'd perceived to be gay, which contributed to the inevitable time during puberty when her cub began rebelling.

Her fear was that I'd be stigmatized and someone would cause me physical harm due to my two-spiritedness contributed to her ill-conceived attempts at shielding and preventing me from exiting the hibernation chamber in exploration of my surrounding environment.

I refused to accept that there was something wrong with me just because I didn't fit into the molds ascribed by her and society. I also often dreamed of receiving independence from Mother Bear in order to develop my own identity.

During those days you were either called a sissy, gay or homosexual and other unmentionable horrible names if you acted contrary of your birth sex, but I'd emphatically denied being gay or homosexual when questioned by Ma.

Although I wasn't familiar with the term transsexual, transgender or gender non-conforming at that time, I was most certain that those inaccurate gay and homosexual socially constructed labels didn't fit who I perceived myself to be then, nor now.

I didn't buy into those gay labels, no matter how many times I was forced by Ma to read the homosexual condemnation to Hell verses referenced in the Holy Bible, in hopes that they'd scare me straight. By the way, they caused me to resist even more at every turn against her attempts at forced conformation into what she wanted me to be.

I've often wondered how much better my life would have been if I had read from the book of Isaiah, chapter 56, verses 1 to 5, that I gladly paraphrase, "Thus said the Lord, neither let the son of the stranger that hath joined himself to the Lord speak, saying, the Lord hath utterly separated me from his people. Neither let the Eunuch say, Behold, I am a dry tree. For thus said the Lord unto the Eunuchs that keep my Sabbaths, and choose the things that please me while taking up my covenant: Even unto them will I give in mine house and within my walls a place and a name better than of sons and daughters. I will give them an everlasting name that shall not be cut off."

I imagine that *my* adolescent years would have been quite different if I would have also been forced to read the book of Matthew, chapter 19, verses 1 to 19, that I also joyfully paraphrase, "And it came to pass, that when Jesus had finished these sayings, he departed from Galilee and came into the coasts of Judaea beyond Jordan. But he said unto them, All men cannot receive this saying, save they to whom it is given, for there are some Eunuchs which were so born from their mothers' womb and there are some which were made Eunuchs of men, and there are those that have made themselves Eunuchs for the kingdom of Heaven sake. He that is able to receive this let him receive it." I am empowered with this knowledge!

I recall that just before the first dividing wedge was driven between me and Ma, I'd always loved being surrounded by nature because I never felt judged and unconditionally accepted amongst the animals, flowers and trees! I spent a lot of time with myself on summer breaks from school exploring the forest across the train tracks from our house!

I'd especially reveled during the rare times I snuck off to the Milk Dairy for a quick visit with the dairy cows! On my way back home, I'd always picked the sweetest seasonal fragranced yellow and white honeysuckle vines and the most vibrant golden daffodils that were growing wildly around the security light post in front of our house!

I knew that the flowers made Ma happy after a long day at the sewing factory when she'd arrived home to freshly picked flowers in vases I'd strategically placed all over the house. I don't recall a time that I didn't always want to make my mother proud of me, so I also transplanted in our yard sweetly fragranced pink tea rose bushes that were also growing wildly near the ditches across the train track.

Rewinding just a few frames back to right before when I was in my early teens when we were old enough to stay home by ourselves during the day on our breaks from school, Ma used to drop us off at Grandma's house to stay until she'd gotten off from work.

I liked spending the day at Grandma's because the limited supervision allowed me to get involved with this really cute guy Rick Fox looking older teenager named Roy Lee who visited during the day to play with us.

Although I don't exactly recall how the attraction between Roy Lee and I crossed over from playful to physical contact or who initiated the first move, I do recall one of our favorite games being hide and seek.

Roy Lee and I covertly hid together in obscure places in order to make out with each other. Once, when we'd become distracted and carried away out in the open under the kitchen window on the back side of the house, we were startled by my Aunt Duck.

We were carelessly passionately kissing each other unaware that Aunt Duck had come to the window to check on us. I heard her voice above us asking, "What y'all doing?"

We both immediately popped to our feet and I began throwing rocks behind him as he ran away through the pathway leading to his house. I don't know who I thought I was trying to fool when I'd started throwing those rocks after we were caught red-handed, but I had to do something.

Afterwards, I begged and pleaded with Aunt Duck not to tell my mother about catching me kissing Roy Lee and I believe that her being one of my favorite aunts contributed to her not telling.

Flashing forward to after we'd started staying home by ourselves during our summer breaks from school while Ma was at work, we were given strict rules and regulations, and adherence was expected at all times.

We weren't allowed to leave the house, nor have any unsupervised company over, and we had daily chores that were expected to be completed before Ma arrived home from work. Ma taught us both to cook so that she wouldn't have to come home from back-breaking work all day in the manufacturing plant and prepare dinner, and I did most of the cooking. I really didn't mind doing my share of the domestic chores!

My brother, on the other hand, rarely contributed to getting what we were expected to do during the day done, and if it wasn't completed to her satisfaction, we'd get into trouble. So at one point in time, in an effort to avoid being unnecessarily grounded or punished, I did the majority of the house work.

That summer the rendezvous between Roy Lee and I continued because he was old enough to drive his mother's car all the way up The Strip to see me during the days that Perry was out doing his thing!

Although we were both forbidden to leave the house, I'd often sneak across the train tracks in front of our house to meet with Roy Lee while Ma was at work and we'd then park on a pathway off the dirt road where we wouldn't be seen.

Both our ages most likely have contributed to Roy Lee never suggesting that we'd engage in intercourse, which was okay with me. It felt good just making out and passionately kissing him in his back seat.

The only problem with Roy Lee was whenever I'd told him that I had to leave and go home, he would begin the slapping, accusations and threats. These started during our times together at Grandma's house, when he talk about what he'd do to me if he found out I was leaving him to see another boy from the neighborhood, which wasn't the case at all.

My dilemma that afternoon wasn't that I wanted to leave Roy Lee to go be with someone else, because there was no one else. I was more concerned about Ma doing one of her surprise early returns home to catch us off guard, and I wanted to double-check that all of my chores were done before she arrived home from work.

I never liked being hit by Roy Lee, and I knew at that early age it wasn't right for him to be abusive just to prove his perceived feelings for me. I'd warned him many times that he'd never see me again if he continued to be abusive for no reason.

Of course, he always apologized and promised he would not do it again, but it didn't take too long for him to forget his promises. He continued accusing me of being involved with other boys from my neighborhood and also threatening that if he saw me with one of them, I'd be sorry.

I wisely took his threats to heart, knowing that I needed to start distancing myself from him by limiting the contact between us, so whenever he called to arrange for us to get together I lied about not being able to meet with him.

As time passed, Roy Lee continued calling often, pleading for me to meet with him. I might say that he put forth his best efforts for several weeks at trying to persuade me to just meet with him, but I refused.

As far as I was concerned I meant it the last time when I warned him that I was not going to continue tolerating the constant abuse and untrue accusations from him. I hoped that he'd gotten the message that I was serious about not seeing him again after continuously refusing to meet with him, but he was persistent and continued calling until that surreal morning when our relationship was revealed.

I had no idea earlier that morning that Ma had called off sick on what was expected to be an ordinary summer break home, completing chores and making up choreography. It was far from the usual routine because I had no idea of what was unfolding when I was awakened from a deep sleep by her voice during the time that she was supposed to have already left for work.

I was startled by her voice coming from her bedroom, commanding that I pick up the phone! After rubbing sleep from my eyes as I walked up the hall to the kitchen to pick up the receiver, my heart started racing and I knew that we were busted upon hearing his voice on the extension after drowsily saying, "Hello."

Roy Lee proceeded to insist upon coming and seeing me later that afternoon while continuously professing his love and affections for me. I didn't know what to say because I knew that Ma was listening to our conversation from the extension in her room.

All I could think to do was to pretend not to know what he was talking about and questioned why was he calling me? Instead of the fool taking the hint, he continued begging me to meet with him continually expressing his undying love and need to be with me.

With nothing else left to do I tried hanging up the receiver, but Ma was on the other end and she'd by then stretched the long phone cord wire from her room up the hall into the kitchen where I was and silently motioned a command to continue talking with him.

I began wishing that I could just wake up from that horrific nightmare, but I was already awake and there was nothing that I could do except for continue listening to him tell me over and over how much he loved and needed to see me.

All the while Ma continued listening until she'd finally heard enough and made her presence known to him by asking, "Roy Lee, why are you calling Tony?"

He'd remained silent as she informed him that she was listening to the whole conversation and then reminded him that I was still a minor. She proceeded to warn without interruption from him that if he came anywhere near me, he would be sorry.

It seemed as if it had taken forever for the idiot to have finally gotten the clue that I was trying to give him all along to end the conversation and hang up the phone because my mother was eavesdropping on our conversation.

After he'd hung up his receiver, I knew that I was in deep, deep trouble when Ma commanded me to get dressed. After I was dressed and sitting in the living room nervously waiting for her to emerge from her bedroom, there were no doubts in my mind about where we were going after we'd gotten into the car to leave.

I sat quietly during the ride over to where Roy Lee lived frightened to death about what was going to happen once we arrived at our destination. I was relieved when Ma passed Roy Lee's house and turned onto the street that lead toward Grandma's house.

But when we turned the corner, Roy Lee was in the middle of the field weeding his uncle's garden that was right across the street, a few yards up from Grandma's house.

My heart skipped a couple of clicks when I saw Roy Lee standing there with his back turned to us hoeing the rows of cabbage, tomatoes, corn and melons. It seemed as if we were moving in slow motion as Ma pulled the car onto the side of the dirt road carefully avoiding the ditch next to the garden where Roy Lee was bent over shaking dirt from the weeds, oblivious to our presence.

Several seconds passed before he almost jumped out of his skin when he'd finally looked up and saw that we were parked right up on him!

After turning off the ignition, when Ma opened her door to exit the car it wasn't necessary for me to have been told to stay my little butt in the car. After closing the door she then leaned up against the car front end once again asking, "Roy Lee, why are you calling my son?"

He stood there ankle deep in dirt like a deer in headlights holding the hoe looking obviously shaken and scared! It was as if he had no idea of what he was going to say in response to her question. Finally, he decided that he'd deny ever calling me. "Miss Bee I don't know what you're talking about, but I didn't call your house."

When Ma then reached into the car to obtain her cigarette purse from the console, he must have thought that she was reaching for a gun or something. He dropped the hoe and then struck out, running away as fast as he could, kicking up dirt and dust!

Ma yelled after him, "I'm not going to do nothing to you Roy Lee, you don't have to run!" He knew that she knew without a doubt it was him talking to me on the phone earlier that morning, so she yelled out after him. "If you're not guilty Roy Lee, why are you running?"

After lighting her cigarette and leaning back against the car, he stopped in his tracks creating a dust storm after realizing that she was just reaching for a cigarette, obviously relieved he didn't get shot as the dust storm slowly settled.

From my viewpoint on the passenger side looking out the car window, he shivered slightly while listening intently to Ma once again warning that I was still a minor, and that he'd be arrested if he contacted me ever again.

After taking one last draw of her cigarette before flicking and distinguishing the butt into the sand Ma also informed him as she started getting back into the car to leave, "Don't think that you've gotten away with anything Roy Lee, I'm going to wait for your mother to come from work so I can tell her that you're calling my house and having explicit, perverted conversations with my son."

I was so relieved after she'd gotten back into the car and driven a few yards over to Grandma's house! Although I wished that I could stop my descent deeper into the rabbit hole, I exhaled a slight sigh of relief as I exited that car for some fresh air.

Still moving in slow motion, I followed Ma inside the house, going directly to a place then sitting quietly as a mouse on the couch that was as far out of her reach as possible. I was really embarrassed when she told the sordid details of the early morning situation to Grandma, my aunts and cousins. I quote:

"I followed my mind when something told me to call off from work this morning, even though I wasn't sick, and right after I turned over to go back to sleep, the phone rang. When I answered it the first time, I questioned to myself why Roy Lee was calling to speak to Tony?"

In between the looks and stares at me that could have killed, she proceeded with the story. "The first time that he called, I told him Tony was still asleep and I hung up the phone."

I couldn't do anything but just sit there and try to stay clear of her glares at me as she continued. "Less than five minutes later, he called right back, which caused me to become even more suspicious, so I woke Tony up and made him get out of bed to talk to Roy Lee."

It wasn't enough that I had to listen as she'd precisely recalled the incidents leading up to that point in time, I was also forced to sit there glued to one spot for hours from early that morning until late that evening enduring what seemed like an eternity waiting for his mother to arrive to their house from work.

I was relieved Aunt Duck didn't tell Ma that she'd previously caught Roy Lee and I kissing each other underneath the back kitchen window.

Finally, when Ma was informed by one of my cousins that Roy Lee's mothers' car was parked in their yard, my heartbeat increased a few notches. She threw another dagger at me with her eyes and then sternly ordered, "Let's go!"

I don't remember getting back into the car or the drive around the corner to Roy Lee's house. I do recall that when we arrived at their house, I continued the almost numbing outer-body experience on the slow walk from the car to their front door.

Roy Lee's mother had no idea that her world was just about to be rocked after a long day at her job in response to being told that her son was having an illicit relationship with me during the day while both of our mothers were at work.

After Ma rang their doorbell, his mother answered the door and greeted us. Ma greeted her in return and then proceeded to inform her about the details of what had occurred earlier that morning.

His mother listened without interruption as Ma calmly informed her that she'd overheard Roy Lee on the phone expressing his inappropriate feelings for me and asking if he could come over to our house to see me while she was at work.

After Ma finished, his mother called him to where we were standing at their front entrance and asked, "Roy Lee, is what she saying about you calling Tony true, did you call her house this morning, Roy Lee?"

Of course Roy Lee lied and denied that he was calling me. After his mother chose to believe her son, it was obvious that she was in denial about him being intimately involved with me.

In response to his denial, Ma advised his mother, "If your son ever call or come near my child again, I will have him arrested and prosecuted for sexual contact with a minor." Before we left their house, I believe that deep down inside his mother knew we were having an improper relationship, which is why she guaranteed Ma that Roy Lee would never ever contact me again as we walked away.

After that humiliating incident involving my mother and his mother, Roy Lee never attempted to contact me again. In response to the Roy Lee incident, I was once again placed on punishment for an extended period of time.

Since Roy Lee began being more abusive towards me as we grew older, I didn't try to challenge Ma after she'd forbade me to ever see him again.

As a result, Ma tightened the reigns and continued forcing me to read those old familiar Bible verses on a more regular basis condemning homosexuality to hell. When that didn't work, she thought she could beat the demons out of me.

It's my opinion migrating forward that I'd received an overly excessive level of unjustified corporal punishment during those days just because I wasn't a "normal" boy. There's nothing like waiting for your vengeful brother to go cut the switch that was going to be used for your whipping.

Sadly, when the switches were no longer effective, Ma also started improvising with extension cords and other home-made devices attempting to exorcise whatever she thought possessed me.

The physical abuse affected my behavior at school and I started cutting class to hang out with my friends that Ma forbade any association with.

As I grew older, I became even more aware and resentful about the discrepancies in the treatment and consequences that I paid for misbehaving verses my brother's punishments. He was allowed to do random things that teenagers did, but I was not because Ma thought my friends were a bad influence on me.

She'd especially disliked my best friend during that time, Kelvin, of whom she'd uncompromisingly forbade me to hang out with because he was openly gay and she thought that he was influencing me to be like him.

I continued enduring being forced to read over and over about Sodom and Gomorrah, knowing very well that Ma wanted me to be the masculine boy she'd given birth to. In an effort to relieve the torture and not be condemned to hell, there were brief times earlier on when I even pretended to be masculine.

It was ironic that at school I'd only hung out with the same group of about five girls up to ninth grade. I also briefly pretended to date a couple of them to satisfy Ma because she was happy whenever they came home with me after church on Sundays for a visit.

They say that most boys would not turn down an invitation to be sexually intimate with a female, but I was the least interested in being intimate with another female when opportunities were presented for me to do so.

It seems to me if it was in my nature to be sexually attracted to females I would have been intimate with one ever since middle and high school, when I'd had my fair share of those girls that tried tempting me by showing their breasts in math and science class.

I recall this one girl, who shall remain nameless, thinking that her newly formed breast cores were turning me on when she pulled back her training bra revealing them to me. Not! I was more turned on just by admiring the basketball team captain, who shall also remain nameless.

I fondly remember the older women who were overly aggressive in their attempts to have sex with me, resulting in literally having to physically protect myself from being raped by those that were insistent upon taking my virginity.

Additionally, I can't forget about the others that were left in a state of shock and disbelief after I'd bluntly informed them I wasn't interested in sex with a female in response to their desire to do so with me!

To date, I don't wonder nor desire to experience intimacy with another female, lesbian transsexual or gay person, although I am aware of the saying "Never say never." However, in my case I am pretty certain that willingly having sex with another biological female at this point will most likely not happen. I guess I'll see you "Next Lifetime," as poetess and lyricist Erykah Badu so eloquently stated!

We can be sisters, go shopping along with all of the other girlie things that sisters do, but for me to consciously engage in intercourse with anyone other than a masculine man will not be happening. I don't bump purses!

I don't ever recall a time I wasn't more attracted to the cute guys no matter how wrong I was constantly told my feelings were, which contributed to the continued challenges that Ma had with my gender identity as I grew older.

I'm reminded of the time in the late '70s when my rebellious nature really started escalating into overdrive when my brother Perry and his friends started bodybuilding at our house.

They'd also regularly competed in local bodybuilding contests and talent shows that I was allowed to attend. The escalated rebellion happened on a warm bright Saturday morning that Ma allowed me to go with them to the mall for a bodybuilding demonstration.

I'm sure that when she'd dropped us off that afternoon, the thought of me meeting a much older guy at the event would likely not have happened. I'm equally sure she'd thought that I wouldn't get into any trouble being with my brother and his friends.

But, fast little old contrarian me met a guy as I was admiring the other muscular professional bodybuilders demonstrate their posing and weight lifting techniques to the audience!

After a period of time observing the bodybuilders, this guy whom I'd noticed was also watching the show from the other side of the crowd eventually made his way over to where I was sitting and asked, "Are you enjoying the show?"

I responded. "Yes I am, are you?"

He then replied, "I am, are you here with someone?"

I pointed out my brother and his friends posing in the amateur portion of the demonstrations as I replied, "I'm here with my brother and his friends over there."

After a brief moment of small talk about weightlifting, which I had no interest in other than the baby-oiled glistening muscular men in their tight speedos, he told me his name. "My name is Gerome, what's yours?"

"My name is Tony" I replied.

"Hello, Tony. I don't mean to be presumptuous, but if I gave you my number before you leave and I never see you again will you call me later so we can talk?"

It was obvious that he was flirting with me so I replied, "Okay, you can give me your number so we can talk later!"

Gerome, whom by all means could have been described by others as a predator, passed me his phone number that he'd obviously written on a piece of paper upon planning his initial approach. I quickly glanced over at my brother and his friends to make sure that they didn't see what was transpiring between us before taking the paper and quickly placing it in my pocket. I felt special that this older, attractive man was showing interest in talking to me!

Remembering back to that time in my life, I wonder if my attraction for much older and more mature guys were in some way an attempt to compensate for not having a father figure in my life on a consistent basis?

Anyway, moving on after the bodybuilding demonstrations were over, I couldn't wait to get home then run across the field to tell my best friend Kelvin about the man that I'd just met at the mall!

Since Ma was gone, Kelvin accompanied me back to the house so that we could call Gerome, and I was really nervous dialing the numbers, almost hanging up the phone after hearing his voice on the other end answering, "Hello?"

I replied, "May I speak to Gerome, please?"

He responded in a very sweet voice, "Hello, Tony this is he!"

"Hello, Gerome. How did you know that it was me?"

"I'll never forget your voice!" He replied, with a smile on his voice.

We talked for about 30 minutes or so while Kelvin sat listening in on the conversation in disbelief that Gerome invited me to the drive-in theater with him to finally see sexy John Travolta's movie "Saturday Night Fever"!

I was very nervous about going out with him alone, so I suggested that my friend Kelvin join us on our first date with each other?

He replied without hesitating. "Sure, do you think that he'd be interested in meeting a friend of mine after the movie?"

Gerome never questioned me about my age, nor did I question him about his exact age. I just assumed that he was probably in his mid-30s or so.

When we arrived at the drive-in, Gerome and I ended up transitioning from the front to the back kissing and making-out while Kelvin sat alone watching John Travolta strut his sexy self on the big screen.

I managed to have watched segments of the movie in between the necking and afterwards, Gerome took us to introduce Kelvin to his friend Jordon. From the first moment Jordon and I were introduced, he nicknamed me Green-Eyes.

Jordon and Kelvin seemed to hit it off with each other and whenever we visited Jordon's house they'd often ended up in Jordon's bedroom doing whatever they did with each other.

Gerome and I were usually in another bedroom or sometimes on the living room couch fully clothed making-out! Up to that point, although I'd previously experienced making out with boys, I had not yet crossed the threshold of engaging in intercourse with any of them, much less a much older man. To his credit, Gerome never once initiated anything other than kissing and such.

Although I had a nice time at Jordan's with Gerome, I never stayed out too late into the evening whenever I'd sneak out after Ma left the house for a weekend night out. I made sure that I was always home, just in case Ma returned early from going out with my aunts!

After arriving back to our neighborhood, I insisted on Gerome letting me and Kelvin out of the car way up the street way out of sight from my house, because I knew there stood a slight possibility of Ma coming home earlier than expected to catch us off guard.

Since I thought only about becoming the person I innately identified as, Gerome was an opportunity to run away from home again for good this time in order to do so. I was a stupid little child, feeling that I'd be successful since I was much older than compared to the first few times when I'd ran away. Ma always found out where I'd gone and then forcefully retrieved me to return home.

I felt that this time would be different, because I was running away to stay with someone she didn't know! I was really confident due to her not having any idea as to where I was going that time! Perfect plan, so I thought.

A few weeks after meeting Gerome, I'm sure that I was the one who broached the idea about running away to Kelvin since he was having the same issues with his grandfather. We misguidedly thought that we'd devised a fool-proof plan to finally make our getaway!

As a result of being young, dumb and somewhat desperate to be ourselves, we half-wittedly felt that we'd found our knights in black armor, who would take us away from all of our problems at home to live a phantasmal fairytale happy-ending life!

Can we talk about stupidity and naïveté? After several dates with Gerome and Jordan sometimes just hanging out together watching their band practice, we quickly moved to floating into an extra sensory perception-concocted zone in our minds where we'd be able to live at Jordon's house with them and no one would know where to find us!

We were on summer break from school and the ill-conceived plan was to run away the upcoming week while Ma and his grandfather were both at work. I guess that time was passing a little too slowly for Kelvin because, due to his anxiety, he felt the need for reassurance that I was still following through with our plans.

I still don't know to this date why he was concerned about me not sticking to our conspiracy. It was, after all, my idea initially and only a day had passed since we'd discussed the schematics of the vanishing.

So, evidently too much time had passed in his judgment since we'd last spoken, which caused him to compose a note inquiring if we were still going to run away. He then stupidly gave the letter to my brother, Perry, as the delivery source.

Of course, Perry read it before giving it to me. After receiving the letter from Perry, I knew that he'd most likely have read it, but I was still determined to follow through with our running away from home undertaking.

We'd previously arranged to meet up with each other that following Friday afternoon and then rendezvous with Gerome across the train tracks whenever the coast was clear! Gerome didn't have any idea that we were going to arrive at his car carrying almost everything we owned, so he was visibly surprised upon seeing us, although he went along with the flow!

However, one could only imagine the response after we arrived at Jordon's house and informed him that we'd run away to live with them. He immediately hit the roof in disbelief, replying, "Oh my, Gerome, these kids are still minors and they trying to get me locked up, Lord Jesus!"

Jordon was very dramatically expressive when excited! He, rightfully so, flew off the handle, because he knew very well that there would be trouble and consequences to pay if he allowed us to stay at his house.

So, he continued hysterically, "Oh, my baby love Gerome, these children got to go back home, because I don't want any problems with their parents or Miss Alice coming to my house!"

Gerome managed to calm Jordon down enough to convince him to let me stay, but Kelvin was taken back home the following morning.

Two days later, on a warm clear Sunday morning, we were awakened by Jordon in another panicked state telling us to look out the window! When I peered out and saw my mother, Kelvin and his grandfather standing outside of the gate, my heart seemed to have instantaneously dropped from its chest cavity through the floor.

All I wanted to do was magically vanish and join my heart underneath the house with Jordon's cats, because I knew that I was in deep trouble and the situation wasn't going to be pretty.

Jordon became even more frantic as time went on in response to Ma starting to call for me to come out of the house and continuously yelled, "I know that you're in there Tony, you better come out before I call the police."

She then also added to the mix, "God made Adam and Eve, not Adam and Steve!" What did she say that for? Jordon continued freaking out at maximum decibels, because he was still in the closet and didn't want his neighbors to know that he was gay!

He sat on the couch rocking back and forth chanting as if he was in church, "Lord Jesus, my neighbors don't know that I'm gay and this child mother is out there spilling all of my tea, oh, my baby love, what am I going to do?"

My immature thought was never mind Jordon still being in the closet, I was scared stiff about what I was going to do. Finally after 15 minutes or so, I got up the nerve to walk out the door to face the wrath of my mother due to me knowing that she was not leaving without me.

I also knew that if I did not come out of that house, ultimately the police would be called, creating an unnecessary spectacle. As a dead man walking out of the gate toward where they were standing in front of the car, I could see that my mother was enraged the closer I got.

She was so furious that when I was within reaching distance from her, she grabbed and began continuously slapping me in my face. There was nothing that I could do but endure the pain and embarrassment.

Later that afternoon, after dropping Kelvin and his grandfather off at their house, I was left alone with Ma and her fury. Before we went into the house after getting out of the car, she continued slapping me and expressing her disgust.

As the pain became more and more unbearable, I don't know what finally came over me when for the first time I had found the strength to stand up to my mother. I was somewhat surprised when a voice that I'd never heard before came from deep within my soul started angrily and forcefully reciting, "Ma, I am sick and tired of you slapping on me, you need to make this your very last time that you put your hands in my face."

My life would never be the same after confronting my mother that day. We were both surprised and stunned that I was the least concerned about the repercussions resulting from the very first time that I recall taking a definitive stance against being abused in that manner again.

I just knew that I had finally reached my limit for tolerating physical abuse being used to change me into something I would never become. I was also tired of the beatings and done with being forced to read those Bible verses having nothing to do with who I am.

Most of all, I was tired of being forced to deny who I was born to be. I was amazed that I'd miraculously managed to come out unscathed after the confrontation with Ma that afternoon underneath our carport, which ultimately ceased the physical abuse after that encounter!

However, although I'd stood up to Ma and ended the abuse, she let it be known that she was still in control and running the show. I was placed on restriction whenever I'd blatantly acted out in ways that I knew were prohibited.

I always knew that my mother was in charge for as long as I was a minor, which is why I anticipated my 18th birthday! In the meantime, something from deep within me knew that it was wrong to continue enduring being punished for my gender identity, which was totally out of my control.

I would have never had the courage or nerves to stand up to my mother like that if it were not for divine intervention being at work taking over my actions. Looking back to that moment, the Lord was truly embracing and protecting me during that evolutionary time in my life!

After that inevitable clash of the Aries ram and the Aquarian water bearer, I continued sneaking around to be with Gerome whenever I was able to get away with it! As divine intervention continued its influence, after a period of time with Gerome, during one of our rendezvous I became suspicious and questioned him after snooping and finding a bottle of pills in his glove compartment that I wasn't familiar with.

It was another sunny afternoon when I confronted him about why his eyes became so bloodshot red. He didn't know that I had previously found the pills after plundering through his things when he'd left me alone in the car to go inside the filling station to pay for gas.

His excuse for the constant red eyes was he had severe allergies that he was taking medicine to help manage. Intuitively, I didn't believe him and I thought that he was probably a hardcore drug addict or something so we'd eventually mutually agreed to just be friends with each other.

As a symbol to celebrate our newly found friendship, he took me to the Candy Shop club in Columbia, South Carolina, and we danced the night away to our favorite songs "Caribbean Queen" or anything else by Billie Ocean, "Cutie Pie," "Juicy" by Mtume, "Head" by Prince and our favorite song, "Let's Get Closer" by Midnight Star.

By the end of our celebration into the following morning I was extremely exhausted from dancing all night long on the drive back to Sumter. So, I slept with my head on his lap, unaware that our night together would be the last time seeing each other. Many years later, Ma informed me during one of my visits home that she'd read his obituary in the Sumter Daily Item, stating that Gerome had died from AIDS.

She's my Mother Bear, and her job, which in my opinion she has done very well, was to protect me as much as possible from falling into the pitfalls that were on my pathway. She was rightfully concerned about my health.

I am extremely grateful that although I don't foresee being in a position to not care for myself, she made me promise that if I was to ever be in a situation where I was not able to physically care for myself, I would go home so that she would be able to care for me.

Many years later in the early '90s during a visit home, Ma asked me point blank, "Did you contract the AIDS virus from Gerome?"

It was only by God's' love, grace and mercy that I was able to emphatically tell her that I had not been infected by Gerome because not only was I not engaging in intercourse with any guys back then, Gerome and I have never even seen each other completely naked.

I shudder to imagine what my young life would have been like back then living in Sumter, South Carolina, infected with HIV/AIDS. I thank God that my mother instilled in me a sense of respect for myself and the desire to live by a set of values that have saved my life!

As I reflect back on those experiences, I also thank God that Gerome never tried having intercourse, sentencing me to an inevitable death. I am also thankful that he was always respectful to never have tried to convince me to do anything beyond just kissing and making out with him. I pray that he rests in peace…

Although I'd desperately wanted to make my mother happy by stopping my attractions to guys, having sex with a female was not a compromise that I was willing to make. It has never been my desire to hurt any biological woman by using her to marry me so that I would be able to fool my mother, others and even myself into thinking that I was something that I am not.

Maturity has taught me moving forward that Ma and my family members have lived their lives, so I feel entitled to also live mine to my satisfaction as long as I'm not hurting myself or others.

Unfortunately, the only other choices that I had back then, other than not living a big fat lie, was to either eventually numb myself with drugs and alcohol or commit suicide like others that I've personally known. Suicide has never been an option for me.

Platonically, I love females and believe that they are the mothers of the Earth divinely created by our Creator. Although I identify as a female, I don't want to be a biological woman, because I am more than content with being the transsexual woman that I was created to be!

Furthermore, I believe that it was divinely intended for me to not have any of the extremely negative body image issues that most trans-people have about their bodies. I currently don't possess the strong urge or need that others may have about gender reassignment surgery to make themselves complete.

Most importantly, I strongly feel that I was born completely and exactly the way that I was intended to be by my Creator, Mother, Father, God and Universe!

My only challenges from a very early age were with being told that I was supposed to act like a boy. Although I was okay with my gender identity at an early age, I overtime became emotionally stressed out due to, on one hand, identifying as female and, on the other, my mother and society continually insisting that I was not.

Before I go any further, I don't want to mislead anyone into thinking that I was miserable at all times growing up. I give Ma credit that even though I'd faced more restriction as compared to Perry, she did support and encourage me with her permissions to join the school concert choirs and performing in talent shows.

Instead of girls or boys, I focused on the only outlet that allowed me to fully express myself during those days. I felt safest communing with nature or performing on stage during school events.

In the beginning, I started out creating the safe and acceptable male characters that wouldn't cause Ma any concerns about what I was doing. I distinctly and fondly recall my very first talent show win at Croswell Elementary School when I performed "I Want to get Next To You" by Rose Royce from the original "Car Wash" movie.

The picture remains clear as my then pretend girlfriend Joyce Ray sat in the front row cheering me on from the audience during my expressive performance and after the principal announced that I was the first place winner! I was so excited and proud of myself because I'd spent countless hours in the living room choreographing each move to the lyrics.

I feel that I need to reemphasize that my attention wasn't always on boys during my adolescence. I'm just saying! Instead, after completing my chores I passed free time during summer breaks from school occupying myself with spending a lot of time alone in the house making up random performance routines to Madonna, Michael Jackson, Prince and other favorite artists during that time.

Before I started raiding my mother's fabric remnants bag, I used towels and sheets to create costumes to wear while practicing my performances.

During those days we weren't allowed to leave the house while Ma was at work and, thankfully, I was gifted with a first pair of roller skates for my birthday that year, which prepared me for future roller-skating rink outings throughout my teen and adult years. I'd almost lose myself remembering routines that I'd made up on our driveway!

I had no problems with finding creative things to do after completing my chores, attempting to stay out of trouble when Ma was away from home! If Perry hadn't already blown out the speakers or damaged the needle on the stereo practicing their bodybuilding poses, I also placed the stereo speakers in the window, turned the volume up as loudly as possible, then make up choreography skating up and down our driveway for hours!

I had a specific choreographed routine for "I'm Coming Out,", "Upside Down" by Diana Ross, "Loves Coming At Cha", "The Other Side of The Rainbow" by Melba Moore,

Shannons' "Let The Music Play" album, any and everything Prince, Michael Jackson, Roy Ayers and all of my other old-school favorites thrown in for extra measure!

Another memorable time was performing "Ben" by Michael Jackson in another Black Heritage Club show! Everybody was there, even a really cool lesbian named Sally, a mutual friend of me and my best friend Kelvin. She also drove our school bus and rarely attended after school functions. She became so moved by my performance that she wept like a baby during the entire song!

As I performed, I remember reflecting back to when I first saw the "Wiz" and became inspired to emotionally move others the way that Michael Jackson, Miss Ross and Lena Horne affected me! Another unforgettable performance that I really connected with from deep within happened the year I joined the Drama Club. I played a character in a stage-show production of "Flowers for Algernon" who fit me perfectly due to feeling for a very long time voiceless and sometimes almost invisible in my family unit.

Near the end of junior high school I'd gone, in one big swoop from performing those safe and conservative characters to wearing full make-up for the very first time during a Black Heritage Club variety show at Haynesworth Street High School auditorium!.

When requesting permission from Ma to be in the evening time show, I didn't discuss details with her about what I was planning to perform because I'm sure that she would have had major issues with me impersonating such an androgynous person if I had told her that I was attempting to look like Boy George.

Project Boy George was on the right track after successfully rescuing the most important element of my whole vision from Grandma's bedroom trash can. I was gifted with being there greasing and brushing her hair when she'd thrown away one of her old wigs!

After volunteering to empty Grandma's trash can out back onto the trash pile, I snatched the hair out the garbage and hid it with my bag of personal items that were going home with me.

Nothing was going to stop me from accomplishing my goal to capture the essence of the hottest artist at the time, so I studied his choreography and the pictures on my wall that I'd carefully removed from Tiger Beat magazines. I studied Boy George's make-up and costume designs for inspiration.

Since there were no digital video recorders back then, I was glued to the television watching the music videos whenever they'd air, which allowed me to complete the choreography and illusion.

Designing my costume went off without incident, due to Ma regularly bringing remnants of materials home from the sewing factory. I was ecstatic to have found the perfect materials to complete my costume after removing and raiding her remnants bag from the broom closet when she wasn't at home!

It didn't take too much time cutting up the red, gold and green pieces of material into ribbons that I'd then braided into the wig to finish my hair.

There were also great large pieces of black and white leopard-print material that I used to make my top and oversized bottoms, topping the ensemble off with a flowing black choir robe that I don't recall from where I'd pilfered.

As I prepared for my performance, it never occurred to me that my talent choice may have caused issues with the school or my schoolmates. Happily it didn't!

Although briefly during my living room rehearsals I was slightly nervous about performing such an extremely feminized character, I quickly reverted back to the idea that the audience would really love my production due to Boy George being such a popular, top-charting artist during that time.

Additionally, I moved full speed ahead checking off the list of items needed by using my allowance savings to purchase from the drugstore downtown other supplies, including foundation, powder, black laced gloves that I cut the fingers to really set it off.

It was the most exciting evening of the most amazing moment since I'd first started performing in front of my classmates and friends! If I recall correctly, Ma most likely dropped me off at the school campus a couple hours before the showcase.

The night finally arrived when all of the hard work that I'd invested into creating something memorable and entertaining was about to be presented to my peers, teachers and everybody else that were anticipating another Black Heritage Club spectacular.

I was unexpectedly a little nervous backstage because I wasn't sure how the crowd was going to react to me performing in androgynous make-up, hair and costume. Up to that point, they'd only seen me singing in the choir, modeling and performing male artists in the school talent shows.

That night during the Black Heritage Club event I stepped completely out of the box by impersonating someone considered by most to have been an over-the-top entertainer. Going in, I knew I'd have to make a grander entrance that was more exciting than just walking onto the stage from behind the curtains like the other performers did.

So, I nervously waited for my turn to perform outside of the auditorium front entrance after the audience was completely seated and the auditorium door entrances were closed. After I was introduced and my music finally started playing, I burst through the auditorium doors on cue, dancing and sashaying my way up the aisle. And when the crowd turned around and saw me entering from behind with the music precisely tuned and blasting through the sound system, they erupted in loud screams and cheers!

I was overwhelmed with energy when they started jumping out of their seats, loudly applauding and spilling out into the aisles dancing as I passed to ascend onto the stage! They were so out of control that the fire Marshall eventually threatened to shut the event down because the beyond capacity venue had people spilling into the aisles dancing and creating a fire hazard!

That was certainly one night I won't soon forget! As a result, I didn't expect that the very next day at school, this guy whom I've never previously conversed with before approached me on the yard during our lunch break and informed me, "Tony, I told my sister, Annette about your performance last night and she wanted me to ask you if you'd be interested in auditioning for her fashion troupe?"

After talking for the first time with the boy that I'd previously seen around school and expressing a real interest in being a part of a fashion troupe, I knew that I would have to be on my best behavior if I was going to be successful at convincing Ma to let me audition for a group that would be traveling out of town to adult clubs on the weekends.

I also knew that all wasn't lost and she may be more inclined to allow me to audition if I told her that I was also going to be paid a salary. Still, I knew that persuading her to let me audition wouldn't be easy and, to date, I still don't know how I did it, but I managed to persuade her into letting me go to Sky Diver club to audition!

The one contingency was that she would only consider giving permission after meeting face to face with the show director, Annette. She required certain rules to be set and assurances from Annette that she'd take personal responsibility for my safety. Only then did Ma consent to the audition.

Considering that I was still a minor, there must have been a rare astrological alignment occurring at those very moments for Ma to have even entertained my request to perform in adult night clubs.

It was the summer before 9th grade when I started rehearsing with a very diverse troupe consisting of another soon-to-be-best friend named Victor Richardson, Annette, Stanley, Darrielle, Lorraine, and another older flamboyant transsexual who was attending Benedict College in Sumter named Miss Kris.

Although I was restricted to the dressing room during the engagements because I was the youngest and newest edition to the group, I felt so mature during my summer breaks from school traveling around in a passenger van and sometimes carpooling from city to city on the weekends, appearing at the most obscure and sometimes one-room country clubs with wood-burning potbelly heaters in the corner.

Some of the favorite skits that we received rave reviews were to Run DMC's "What People Do For Money,""When Doves Cry," by Prince, and one of my all time favorites that I'd eventually persuaded Annette into letting me do with Kris wearing women's clothes, make-up and hair, "Another Man Is Loving Mine," which was a song about a woman who finds out that her man is cheating on her with another man.

If Ma had known about me performing in that skit dressed like that, she would have pitched a fit and made me immediately quit the production team on the spot. Whenever I left home to go anywhere, she always cautioned before allowing me to leave the house, "Be Yourself."

I knew that she was telling me to straighten up, un-bend my wrist and stop being so effeminate. I would have agreed to almost anything just to have been allowed to leave the house, knowing all along, deep down inside, there was no doubt in my mind that I was incapable of being anything other than my true self.

So, unbeknownst to Ma, I chose to take her cautions literally and acted naturally away from home being the androgynous little two-spirited person that I was born to be, because it would have been extremely challenging to do otherwise.

After I was first allowed to join the modeling production company, my friend,

Victor, used to line my eyes for me because I didn't know how to apply it myself. I really wanted to learn how to put on my own eyeliner, so I figured that I'd use my mother's make-up to practice while she was out one night.

Big mistake sneaking into her bedroom in search of her make-up bag and, while I was at it, I also retrieved a Pam Grier-styled afro wig from the top of her closet. I had my eyes on that hair ever since she'd previously looked so beautiful wearing the night she and Aunt Diane had worn matching pantsuit outfits!

I remember Ma sitting at the sewing machine cutting and creating the two-piece outfits that she and Aunt Diane wore along with Uncle Gene to one of their favorite party spots, Pop and Son's in the country!

Anyway, I stupidly took her charcoal black eyeliner and started practicing lining my eyes so that I didn't have to continue hearing Victor complain and fuss every time I asked for his help with my make-up.

After I finished practicing and performing in the living room, I was able to take off all traces of the lipstick and blush in the shower, but removing the charcoal black eyeliner pencil without any eye make-up remover presented a unique challenge for me.

I scrubbed as much of it off as possible, but I was not able to remove all of it. So, I did my best to steer clear of Ma when she returned home later that night, hoping that she wouldn't notice the eyeliner residue on my eyes.

I did everything possible to avoid immediate eye contact with her, but after taking one look at me, she immediately knew what I'd done and went off! Needless to say, Ma wasn't one bit happy about me wearing make-up.

You best believe that I was placed on punishment for some time after eyeliner-gate, which also meant no more touring with Nephrititi Productions, and my extracurricular activities were limited to school activities only.

As time ticked forward, I tried walking the "straight line," pretending to be what Ma wanted me to be following the eyeliner blow up.

Eventually, I was able to convince Ma to allow my Aunt Mae to put a Care Free Curl in my hair! It didn't take very long for me to have tested my mother's patience again after going to my hairdresser and friend Victor Richardson for a touch-up. God rest his soul.

Vic lived in Lee Wood Projects, which was a neighborhood not too far from where Grandma lived on Coffy Street. When we met for the first time at the annual Christmas parade, he was the very popular and charismatic Lee Wood High School drum major. His school band showed out with their performance that year!

When I first laid eyes on Vic, I thought that he was very handsome and we later made an attempt to date before I'd joined the fashion troupe several years later. However, on the day I snuck away from Grandma's house to meet with him one-on-one for the very first time, I found him to be a little too effeminate for me, so we didn't pursue the dating idea any further, instead becoming very good friends and dancing partners at the gay clubs.

Anyway, on the day of the visit to the salon for my Curl touch-up, he sewed in a curly hair extension that I couldn't resist after he offered to add fullness and length to the shag! I was so happy with my bouncing and behaving hair, but when I got home later that afternoon the exuberance was immediately deflated when Ma saw how long my hair was in the back and once again, she hit the roof!

I was so embarrassed when she made me go right back to Vic the very next day for him to remove the extension after not charging me anything to sew it in. Needless to say, he wasn't happy that I'd returned after all the work that he'd done on my hair just the day before and I was devastated over losing my long hair.

Ma previously compromised on allowing me to get the curl in the first place and she insisted that I look like a boy at all times, so adding unnecessary length to my hair was not a compromise she was willing to make, thus continuing our battle for control.

Anyway, at the beginning of high school during another drama club assignment that year I received an A-plus performing "Automatic" by Prince with just my natural shag!

I'd always listened to the WWDM radio station in the mornings while preparing for school and I called in for a contest that was announced as I was brushing my teeth after breakfast. I was so shocked when DJ Romeo told me that I was the right caller to win the latest albums by Vanity Six, The Time and Prince, being given away to promote their concert at the Sumter Exhibition Center.

Knowing that, due to my age, Ma would never allow me to attend the concert, I didn't dare ask. However, winning those albums that morning before school was the next best thing!

I also had to meet with a school therapist that same year to find out what was wrong with me. Ma wanted to know why I was still attracted to boys and, most importantly, how to fix the problem since nothing else worked.

She probably hoped that the therapist would be able to prescribe a magical pill or something that would turn me straight! But after several sessions, the therapist explained to her that there was nothing mentally wrong with me.

He then suggested that I just needed to be allowed the opportunity to participate in some of the appropriate activities for teenagers my age. He also suggested I needed to be reassured that I was loved, supported and accepted by her.

I'm not exactly sure how she'd felt about that conversation with the therapist. I can only assume she was determined to not accept that there was nothing wrong with me and she wasn't going to be supportive of my female gender identification.

During that time, I was inspired by this guy named Chris Gist, who was the first and as far as I know, the only Sumter High School male cheerleader. I don't know what I was thinking when I decided to push my luck, building up my nerves before asking permission to try out for the high school cheerleading squad, but Ma wasn't having it. Allowing me to become a cheerleader was a non-negotiable discussion, end of conversation. Period.

However, the therapist did manage to convince her to loosen up the reigns just a bit, so that she signed the track team permission slip as a compromise. Now, I was the least interested in running track, however, this was an opportunity to hang out with my friends after school who joined the track team along with me.

My friends and I often spent most of track practice fooling around and acting crazy! During a break from the gang to get a drink of water, minding my business alone sipping the cold and refreshing hydration from the water fountain, I was approached by this white guy proceeding to question if I was black or white.

Since this was the very first and last time that someone had ever blatantly attempted to challenge or question my race, I was taken aback that he'd found it necessary to do so. I responded by telling him assuredly that both of my parents are black so that also made me a person of color.

Throughout the brief encounter with the racist, he kept insisting that because my skin tone is light and I have light green hazel-eyes that made me White. I told him he didn't know what he was talking about, concluding with calling him an idiot that didn't have the sense God gave a billy-goat.

Then I turned walking away and leaving him standing there looking stupid! Now, I don't deny the possibilities of being mixed with another race. I'm an African-American born and raised in South Carolina with an Irish last name, which somewhat increases those odds. However, I definitely didn't need to argue or justify my race to him.

Although I grew up in the segregated Jim Crow South, I've never chosen to discriminate against or think less of anyone based on their race or cultural background. I love all people and I am aware that we were all uniquely created in the image of our Creator for a specific purpose.

Furthermore, I personally believe that we come in all colors, shapes and sizes with love as the formula and foundation for us to harmoniously co-exist together on this magnificent planet provided to us with everything necessary to be all that we've been created to become.

The following year, after becoming a sophomore, I promise you that I was unconsciously back to the boys while continuing to struggle with denying who I was for the sake of keeping peace within the family. I promise!

I'd done okay up to almost the end of the term. I hadn't gotten into any major trouble due to my boy craziness! That is until the time I'd briefly further explored my sexuality with a Caucasian guy who was a senior upperclassman two years ahead of me.

I was a library assistant when the unexpected white chocolate consumption spark ignited right before the end of the school year! I remember sitting alone, minding my own business, studying for a final exam in the school library that day after my library volunteer shift concluded. Just as I was comfortably studying and memorizing the U.S. Constitution Preamble, I noticed how handsome this guy was walking into the library.

I was taken off guard when the attractive guy sat at the table directly across from where I was and faced me. I wasn't one to continue staring at him and the thought of anything beyond just admiring his looks never occurred to me until I also noticed that every now and then when I looked up from studying, I'd catch him staring directly at me! He'd then quickly looked away, pretending to be staring at something located within my vicinity.

I definitely wasn't going to say anything to him and as time passed he eventually got up from his seat and sat in the chair right next to me proceeding to ask, "Your name is Tony, right?"

Not only was I shocked that he knew my name, I was also surprised by his boldness to sit right next to me and then engage in a direct conversation without concern for what others may have been thinking! I nervously replied, "Yes, my name is Tony. Who are you and how do you know me?"

He responded. "My name is Bryant Touchberry and I remember seeing you when our class was invited to your Drama Club performance!" He then smiled as he leaned in closer peering over at my books as he continued. "What are you studying?"

I replied, astonished that he seemed so nice, "Oh, I'm just studying for a civics exam tomorrow."

I noticed his minty fresh breath as he leaned closer to me replying, "I passed civics with an A plus. Do you need some help studying?"

Feeling slightly uncertain as to where the conversation was headed, I replied. "No, I think that I've got it covered. Thank you for asking, though!"

He looked directly into my eyes with his piercing ocean deep blue eyes and seductively whispered almost without taking a breath, "Tony, I have to admit that I've thought about you ever since I saw you performing Prince and I've been watching you file away books and studying in here alone ever since! It has taken me since the beginning of the year to even approach you like this, would it be possible for me talk with you on the phone after school sometime?'

Astonished, yet slightly blushing I replied. "What is it that you want to talk with me about after school, Bryant?"

He appeared confident that I wasn't going to tell him to get lost because he then removed a piece of paper from his biology book on which he'd already written his name and phone number. After passing his contact information to me, he replied, "I find you very attractive and I'd like to know more about you."

Wow, this fine-ass white guy really admitted that he found me attractive! Of course I took his number.

Throughout the remainder of the day, I anticipated being able to talk with him again on the phone after school to see what was really going on.

After repeatedly checking throughout the rest of my classes to make sure that his phone number was still safely secured in my clear, vinyl pencil case, I noticed that he'd had the most perfect handwriting while recalling how dreamy he was!

Bryant was the first guy in high school whom had ever directly approached me in that manner, so after school when I arrived home later that afternoon, I called him and we talked for several hours about school and general stuff at first!

By the end of the conversation, we'd made plans to meet after school the following Friday hence, starting regularly shared intimate moments just making-out together in secret places close enough for me to get back home before Ma arrived from work!

Bryant Touchberry was a very sweet guy whom I shared some precious moments with, dispelling the myth about only black guys having "Big-Egos." He also taught me some very interesting things about myself that up to that point, I've never experienced or considered before!

Although Bryant Touchberry was charming and magnetic, I refused to give him my phone number after he'd requested it several times. I didn't give him my number because I didn't want another Roy Lee phone situation between him and my mother. No, no, no!

Mind you, this was way before cell phones, so after his sister found out that I was a person of color, she started intercepting his phone calls and made it very difficult for us to communicate with each other.

For a little while whenever I called Bryant's house, I attempted disguising my voice trying to sound white giving her a fake name when she answered their phone. I'm not certain if she knew who I really was or not.

Eventually, I stopped calling Bryant because in addition to my gender identity, I also suspected that the black and white scab relative to mixing the races in South Carolina would have made it even more challenging for us to have pursued anything other than the precious teenage crush times we'd spent together!

Until now, I've never told anyone about how exciting and stimulating it was to be with him; not even my best friends knew that Bryant and I were secret lovers! I feel comfortable with telling the Bryant Touchberry story now because I cannot be placed on punishment by my mother for something that's occurred so many years ago. Thankfully, Ma never knew about me and Bryant. Or did she?

I'm also comfortable with telling the Bryant Touchberry story to show that although there were a lot of racist people in my school who were taught by their parents to hate black folk, such as the one who approached me during track practice, I'm encouraged that Bryant Touchberry didn't appear to be one of them, and that there are also others whom don't hate another person simply based on race!

As for my mother, I'm sure that if she had known about Bryant, she wouldn't have given me permission to join a local band that one of Perry's friends and his cousins formed called "The Cash Money Millionaires" that briefly played at local parties and social events at the Masonic temple and the mall during summer break.

Furthermore, I found the Bryant Touchberry summer to be ironic due to the summer before when we'd gone on a weekend road trip to visit our aunt and cousins Gail and Judy in Greensboro, North Carolina. We were not allowed to go outside to play the whole weekend because the Ku Klux Klan were rallying and causing a disturbance nearby where our aunt lived.

The next summer and most summers thereafter, Gail and Judy stayed with us during their summer vacations. One day during the summer break, Ma, Gail and I were in the car getting ready to go to grandma's house where Judy and Perry were already there waiting for us to return.

I will never forget that day, which was when it was absolutely re-enforced that my mother was still not at all happy that I continued behaving so effeminately.

I'll never forget when I was in the back seat with my legs crossed, acting like I was one of the girls excited about going to play with my cousins!

Ma was focused on securing her seat belt. Gail, however, was more attuned to me when she turned to Ma and commented after she'd observed the feminine way that I was sitting with my legs all crossed, "That boy is going to grow up to be a little faggot sitting with his legs crossed like that Aunt Bee."

Ma immediately became almost uncontrollably enraged when she saw how feminine I was acting, angrily responding, "Uncross your legs and sit up straight in that seat, Tony." She removed her seat belt and then continued lashing out at me. "There is only one woman living in this house and that woman is me, so you better straighten up and act like you are supposed to!"

I was embarrassed and hurt that she was still expecting me to reach an unobtainable goal and, although I remained conflicted, I knew that there was no way that I could continue pretending being something I wasn't, because my previous attempts were futile.

I've never wanted to disappoint and hurt my mother and it's understandable that she remained challenged with my two-spiritedness due to her and my aunts briefly hanging out with a transgender friend of theirs named Gillie.

I recall the times when they'd all occasionally hang out at our house playing cards and music underneath the carport! Once after that card game, I overheard Ma and my Aunts talking about the crazy and self-destructive things that Gillie was doing terrorizing the town with her antics.

It was no surprise to me that I never saw Gillie again after that conversation, because I'm most certain Ma didn't want me to be any further influenced by her.

Maturity has contributed to me understanding that my mother was concerned that I'd be disdainfully mistreated by society the same way she'd observed Gillie being treated by those within the community.

Also, I am more aware of the sense of loss that Ma feels about not having the little baby boy that she'd given birth to, while also reconciling that she'd most likely not have any grandchildren from me. I wish that I was able to give her grandkids!

Although I understood her concerns and desires for me during that time, it was extremely difficult for me being an androgynously effeminate teenager being forcefully locked in the closet and pretending to be macho.

It was also challenging being forced to become robotic in reaction to having all of my interactions with others dissected and analyzed by Ma. However, overtime, I grew really tired of being treated differently and constantly getting into trouble just because Ma felt I shouldn't act the way that I was behaving.

I was also sick and tired of unjustifiably being punished or put on restrictions as a result of my brother continuing his manipulating lies to cover up things that he'd done to break the rules.

Although I understood why I was being punished for my attractions to boys, I didn't feel it fair that I was also being punished for things that I had not done. So, I'd started directly questioning Ma about why Perry was allowed to get away with almost everything short of murder.

I'm sure that it was because I was different, which wasn't fair at all. As if the unfair mistreatments, lies and manipulations weren't enough, I was beyond furious that Perry constantly called me names and gotten away with it. I was also tired of the jerk regularly eavesdropping in on private conversations between my friend Kelvin and I so that he'd have something he could use to blackmail me later.

Once when me and Kelvin were sitting outside of our house on the front steps reminiscing about our first adventurous Saturday night with our friends Sally and her girlfriend at "The Candy Shop" in Columbia, twirling the night away to Nona Hendrix, Prince, Chaka Khan, and Samantha Fox. And anytime the DJ played "Swept Away" by Diana Ross, everybody simultaneously cleared the dance floor because we all knew that Miss Ammoca would enter flying through the front entrance, performing as if she was in a pageant!

We had so much fun throughout the years at "The Candy Shop"! After Kelvin left to go home later that afternoon, Perry wanted me to do his chores and when I refused, he threatened to run and rat on me to Ma that I was still gay and I had gone to a gay club with Kelvin.

It's funny to me now when I think about it that Perry was very hypocritical when he often ratted on me for the things that I'd done. However, I refused becoming a rat and expose his kinky little secrets. I'm not going to go into those details because he knows exactly what I'm talking about.

Throughout the years we'd often fought with each other like cats and dogs, ever since adolescence. Ma would make us kiss to make up after a fight when we were younger.

I'd immensely hated when we were punished by being forced to kiss and apologize after fighting each other, which, by the way, was extremely disgusting having to kiss my brother. Yuck!

So, to the best of my ability I avoided confrontations with him in order not to kiss him and, of course, he used my disdain to his advantage. There were those lingering times that I felt outnumbered and the inevitable time to fight back was just around the corner when I decided to defend myself against being punished for things I should not have been disciplined for!

Setting the scene, we usually switched off chores from week to week so at that point in our living-room on an ill-fated warm sunny afternoon, you might say that although I was somewhat unhappy about it being my week to do the heavier-duty cleaning, I was still getting it done in a timely manner.

Perry was assigned to cleaning and mopping the kitchen and his bedroom. I was responsible for the living room in addition to cleaning our bathroom and not excluding Ma's bed and bathroom.

My frustrations boiled over after he'd done his usual routine, hanging out with his friends lifting weights all day long and then leaving their house returning home right before Ma was scheduled to arrive from work, very much aware that he'd ran out of time to complete his responsibilities.

His awareness that he'd ran out of time to complete his chores attributed to him audaciously declaring that I was wrong about the individual chores we were each to complete for the week!

It's unfortunate during that time, I unimpeachably felt it might not have mattered to Ma that my chores were completed, because I was going to be in trouble anyway. However, I was done standing passively by while Perry continued lying and getting me into trouble resulting from his devious, deceptive manipulations.

I was not going to take it anymore that afternoon! He kept insisting that it was his turn to clean the living room then threatening to tell Ma when she returned home he'd cleaned it. I was fuming inside at his arrogant certainty that she was going to believe him.

But wait a minute. I didn't care nor was I going to argue with him about who was in charge of cleaning what chore. He knew very well that it was his week to clean and mop the kitchen.

He remained overtly cockily full of himself, trying to snatch the feather duster from my hands once again threatening, "I'm going to tell Ma that you and Kelvin went to a gay club if you don't do my chores."

I responded angrily, "I have no idea of what you're talking about. I'm almost finished cleaning in here and you know that it's your turn to clean the kitchen!" I turned away continuing to finish dusting the coffee table and he once again antagonistically tried snatching the duster from my hands.

I was sick of his arrogance and cockiness, so I took all of my pent up frustration out on him. We fought what would be the most brutal knock down fight that we've ever had even though he was much bigger and stronger than I was.

Due to all of his muscles from bodybuilding, I had to fight back against him with all of my might and held my own, kicking like David versus Goliath.

I bit and kicked, all the while remembering that I was previously warned by Ma not to scratch his face with my fingernails again. Nevertheless, we fought so hard that we turned over all of the house plants, totally wrecking the living room! The fight didn't stop until we ended up breaking the edge off the coffee table.

We immediately stopped fighting and knew that we'd be in deeper trouble, so I joined forces with him to try and glue the corner of the table back into place before Ma arrived home. Since it was both our faults that the table had gotten broken, we both rushed to straighten up the living room, vacuuming potting soil from the carpet that we weren't able to place back into their pots and prayed the glue we'd used would dry before Ma got home.

We then hit the kitchen with a swift cleaning and mopping! I don't know what we were thinking, but we actually tried covering the broken edge of the table with decorations that were usually in the center. Then we also thought that we were going to actually get away with it if we didn't say anything about our fight when Ma arrived home later that afternoon.

Usually on the days that she was bone-tired, when Ma arrived home from working all day she'd take dinner that I'd most likely prepared from the oven and retire to her bedroom to watch television for the rest of the evening to unwind.

So, we stupidly thought we'd dodged a torpedo after she'd taken a shower before bedtime, but the truth always comes out in the end and it did that following weekend when Ma was entertaining some guests in the living room.

The assumption is that after she noticed the broken table she waited until the following morning to confront us and needless to say that she was very upset when she called us into the living room, asking, "What the hell happened to the coffee table?"

Of course, Perry did his usual placing all of the blame on me and, unfortunately, Ma believed him and then, also as usual, we were both placed on restriction. Other than our regular tiffs and Perry's ever-present lying nature as time continued ticking, I don't recall any other major physical blowouts after the coffee table brawl.

Since I felt that I would get in trouble regardless of the situation other than when it was my fault for acting out with boys, I also continued rebelling at every turn. I completely stopped hanging out with the group of girls that I'd previously hung out with ever since elementary and then in junior high school.

At the point when I started exclusively hanging out with my gay friends, I honestly didn't care anymore about what anyone thought about my abrupt peer group association shift. I believe this was also around the time that other schoolmates whom were in the closet also shifted their associations after knocking their closet doors off the hinges!

It was no surprise to me that a couple of those people coming out had been in denial that they were gay and lesbian. I knew it all along hanging out with them that they were family members. However, I respected their wishes to remain in denial up to that point as I had.

Although they didn't say anything, I'm sure that the group of girls I'd previously hung with in middle school found my actions surprising! They really shouldn't have been surprised. I mean, really!

Chapter Four

God's Grace, Love and Mercy!

Considering my age during my junior year in high school, it's a miracle that I didn't get into any major, life-threatening trouble! I continued taking advantage of every opportunity presented to get away with sneaking out of my bedroom window late at night after being sure that Ma had fallen asleep.

I was usually on a mission to go hang out with my friends during our road trips to Columbia, South Carolina, to dance the night away at "The Candy Shop" or stay in town whooping it up at Romey's!

During our nights out on the town we never had any major problems with the girls at the "Candy Shop" in Columbia and the only issue that we'd ever had at Romey's was with these other much older queens who were well in their 30s and late 40s, who must have felt threatened by our youth.

On the scenes at cookouts or the club they always had something sarcastic and condescending to say about certain members of our crew. They were evidently aware that the rule for us was that we didn't bother anybody. They were however, unaware that if someone messed with one of us, we'd engage our code words: "Let's bash!" Once enacted it meant that you are going to have a problem with all of us!

After previously learning how messy and two-faced some of those older queens were, I purposely avoided them whenever we were by happenstance in the same environment.

Anyway, one Saturday night we all got fed up with them after they'd tried humiliating Miss Monica in front of everybody in the one-room club.

Since we didn't want to disrespect Mr. Romey's place, we bided our time after activating codeword – "Let's bash!"– to stand up to the bullies! We'd patiently endured the taunts until the time was right to strike. They were foolish enough to bite the hook by following us outside.

It was on! We had no intention of sneak attacking them because it just wasn't our style. We wanted them to know with certainty that we didn't appreciate their actions in the club.

At first, they didn't say a word to us until after they'd gotten safely inside their car. Then immediately they started rolling the windows up and down, taunting and teasing us. We stood there un-amused by their cowardice and immaturity.

They thought that they were being funny until one of our lesbian friends named Charlene snuck around to the back of the car and eased her way to the other side, waiting until one of them rolled down the window.

When the opportunity presented itself, Charlene stuck her hands inside, unlocking the door and holding it open until one of us was able to grab the driver's necktie then banging his head up against the door panel several times!

I'm not promoting violence, but some people get what they deserve. Someone else from our crew opened the back doors and went in on the queens in the back seat while someone else grabbed the folder containing all of the sheet music that the lead harasser was flaunting and showing off in the club earlier in the evening, informing the entire bar he was playing at a wedding the following morning.

But, before it was all said and done, thousands of pieces of ripped up sheet music decorated the ground like snowflakes in front of the club by the end of that morning!

Our friend, Josephine, revealed to me many years later that those queens were at his house earlier that evening before going to the club. Due to Joseph's mother being aware of their track record for bullying others, she'd cautioned them to not go out picking at other people.

I bet after we'd finished with them on the streets in front of Romey's that night they probably wished that they had heeded Joseph's mothers' warning.

Thankfully, during that time we were out of school for summer break when the confrontation occurred, and I'm also thankful it was two days later on Monday morning after Ma had already left for work, leaving me alone at home, when the doorbell rang!

Upon opening the front door, there was an intimidating deputy sheriff standing there asking in a deep voice, "Are you Tony McDaniel?"

It never occurred to me to lie so I replied, "Yes, sir."

He proceeded, "I have a summons for you to appear in court to respond to an assault and battery incident that you were involved in at Romey's club this past Saturday morning."

Since I knew exactly what incident he was referring to, without replying I unlocked and opened the glass storm door, taking the white folded papers from him.

After he left, my heart skipped a beat or two when I read that those queens had pressed charges against us for battery and destruction of personal property.

Of course, I didn't inform Ma of me being summoned to court. Come to think of it, I'm not sure why a judge presided over a legal hearing without the presence of our parents.

However, I feel that since we were still minors and in addition to the judge finding that those adult queens provoked the fight, we were only ordered to complete community service hours washing police cars on the weekends.

Although our punishment was to wash police cars and be jeered by the police officers, bringing their cruisers to the service station to be detailed because there were sometimes leftover traces of eyeliner and foundation on our faces from the night before due to us staying out really late.

In the end however, it was well worth it. We never had any more problems with those Queens ever again upon inadvertently being in the space at the same time!

As time pressed on, I managed to get away with sneaking out of my window for a while until Ma discovered what I was doing. Then she took my house key away. You would think that taking my keys away would have had an effect on me, wouldn't you?

Well, it didn't stop me from sneaking out of the house. Due to Ma sometimes snoring hard like Grandma when she slept, when I was sure that she was out for the night, I climbed out of my bedroom window to go to a party with Kelvin at his cousins' house who were living in Friendship Apartments at the end of The Strip!

I had a great time dancing and hanging out with people from school that night, but upon returning home later the following morning and attempting to climb back through my window, I found that it was locked and bolted shut from the inside with nails.

I ended up sleeping in the laundry room that night and the next day, once I was allowed entry into the house, there was no way that I was going to bed attempting to sleep in late recovering from being out all night.

Although I had to do chores all day as punishment, that wasn't the last time I'd sneak out of the house because I thought that I was grown.

In my defense, I was doing what I had to do in order to rebel against purposeful confinement. Recalling those memories in adulthood, I now understand and am in many ways thankful that Ma was stricter on me as compared to my brother, because I was a little hot you know-it-all.

During those full-forced pubescent latter high school years, I disliked the way that I looked with extreme acne that my mother used to love popping with her fingernails after forcing me to lie on her lap for easy access.

I was still testing the boundaries to see how much I could get away with, and I really wasn't ready when the time soon arrived and it felt like a ton of reality came crashing into me like a Mack Truck.

On that ominous day there was no mistaking that I had disappointed my mother beyond repair when we'd reached a level within our tug-of-war, causing the police to become involved. They were called by her to retrieve me from a rendezvous with another older boyfriend named Peter.

Peter was a tall, Sydney Poitier-colored, handsome guy who overtime became the very first guy that I went all the way with. The courtship, as I refer to those times, started on a balmy, full-moon Saturday night when Asia, Monica, Miss Patty, The Duchess, Miss Josephine and myself gathered for a night of fun and adventures at Romey's.

It all happened after we did our usual twirl through the back screen door of the club. I immediately noticed this mysterious, dark and handsome guy, who I later learned was 25years old. He was leaning like James Dean in the corner near the back entrance, sipping on a beer, and it seemed from the moment our eyes met we were drawn to each other like a magnet to metal!

Since I wasn't going to approach him first, no matter how attractive he was, it took him almost the entire evening before he finally stopped just staring and approached, offering to buy me a drink.

After paying and tipping the bartender for my Coca-Cola, we retreated to the back of the club and stood near the screened door for the rest of the evening, just talking. After that night concluded, I felt so mature when Peter used to pick me up from school and we'd make all of the other children on the bus jealous when they saw my friends and I being picked up by Peter driving away in his sports car!

Once we finished dropping everybody else off at their designated stops, our favorite pas time was driving to Hayward Pond across the tracks to hang out before it was time for Ma to arrive home from work.

On one occasion when he was exhausted from working at Shaw Lumber Company all day and I must have been tired from hanging out the weekend before and school, we both fell asleep in the back seat of his black and yellow Trans Am.

When we fell asleep, we were fully clothed the entire time that we were together, because we had not yet reached the point of doing anything beyond just kissing and making out with each other. We were unaware of how much time that had passed until being startled and awakened to flash lights banging on the car window!

When I woke up, I was immediately concerned when I saw that it was dark outside and after Peter rolled down the car window we were greeted by one of two cops we called "Miss Alice" asking in a very stern voice, "Are you Tony McDaniel?"

I replied, "Yes Sir I am."

"Get out of the car, "he commanded and continued, "Your mother is looking for you."I tried explaining to him that we weren't doing anything and that we'd just fallen asleep, but he was not interested in what I was trying to tell him.

As I exited the car, I overheard the other officer on the opposite side of the car asking Peter his name and age. After Peter informed him that he was 25 years old, the officer issued the following warning, "Are you aware that you could be arrested and go to jail for being with a minor?"

Peter did not respond until the other police officer commanded me to go home and then he offered to drop me off at my house. "I'll give you a ride home."

"No, you won't, he will walk!" The officer commanded. Nothing else was said between me and Peter after the officer responded to him dropping me off at home. I just turned and walked away with the awareness of being in serious trouble on the short walk from Hayward Pond to my house.

Although Peter and I were not having intercourse with each other at that time, and when we later became more acquainted with each other in that manner, we were never intimate in a car.

On his days off, Peter usually reserved a hotel room for us to be together on

Thursday evenings at the Sumter Downtown Motel.

On that evening when we fell asleep at the pond in his car after school and awakened by "Miss Alice", we were just hanging out enjoying spending time with each other!

When I arrived home, there was no convincing Ma that we were not having sex in the car, and during our conversation I knew that she was not happy about me once again disappointing her so greatly when she commented, "My brothers are not like that. Why are you like that?"

Translation, why are you gay? I didn't know how to respond to her, I just stood there enduring the wrath of a hurt and angry mother, when she went on to say, "Sometimes, I wish that you were never born."

I was deeply hurt and wounded after hearing those devastating words coming from her. It felt like she'd thrust a poisonous stake through my heart and then taking her hand ripping out my heart.

I was crushed immeasurably, hearing that my mother wished I was never born. I was never the same after hearing those hurtful words coming from the person whose approval meant everything to me.

If I had possessed the power to change from who I was so I could become the person my mother expected me to be so that I never heard those words from her, I probably would have changed. That incident was the dramatic turning point in our relationship which changed things between the Mother Bear and her cub for years to follow.

Regrettably, the relationship between Ma and I became even more estranged from that moment forward since I knew I would never be the person she wanted me to be. Every night after that devastating incident, I prayed to God to speed up the time when I would be old enough to leave my family and live on my own so I'd be able to truly be my authentic self.

It hurt me to my core after hearing those wounding words that summer, spoken to me by the person that I loved the most with all of my heart and soul.

The look in my mother's eyes haunted me for days and years, because I never wanted to disappoint her like that again. What was I going to do? Deny who I am and make my mother happy, which meant a psychological death for me, or be myself and live fully as the gender and orientation that I identify with regardless. All I wanted to do was get as far away from the pain as possible.

I wish that I was more focused on preparing to graduate from high school instead of sneaking around with Peter, continuing my rebellious nature. I wasn't thinking about school during that time because my attention was on being grown and doing what I wanted to do.

Peter and I continued seeing each other until the end of the school year! He inevitably lost his job and relied on living with his family for support, which meant that there was absolutely no way that my knight in THE shiny yellow Trans Am would take me away to live happily ever after in our very own trailer park.

Many years later after Peter, every now and then during my visits home whenever I visit with Jordon the person whose house my friend Kelvin and I previously ran away to with Gerome, he'd informed me that although Peter's currently married to a biological woman with kids, he continues asking Jordon about me whenever they run into each other! Nice to know, but I'm never going back because forward progression remains my middle name!

However taboo to others the previously mentioned intimate encounters were with those guys, they were my experiences.

I currently do understand that most of those early sexual experiences with those guys were too fast and too soon in my youth. However, I view the others as a natural progression of almost any average teenager who is attracted to someone that their parent may find objectionable or inappropriate.

It's just that my experiences were contrary to what was and remains by the majority of society to be normal attractions to the opposite sex. However wrong or right those experiences were for me, I strongly believe that they were my preparation for the future.

I'm conclusively sure that I might have felt differently if I were a mother doing everything within her power to protect her headstrong child from himself and the uncontrollable outside harm and dangers associated with being transgender and gender non-conforming.

Chapter Five

Schenck CCC Job Corps 1985!

I was one year away from graduating high school the very first time I left South Carolina for an extended period of time on my own. As previously stated, I wished that I was more focused on graduating from high school instead of focusing on being as rebellious as possible and running the streets with grown men.

Not graduating with my class is my one regret up to this point, because everything I required to have graduated was achievable if I'd only put forth the effort; Ma provided me with every tool academically to have done so.

Since I didn't tell any of my friends where I'd suddenly disappeared to upon my departure, it's understandable that there were various untrue speculations about where I had gone and why had I later not returned home with them.

According to my closest friend, Asia, several years later, after I'd finally returned to South Carolina for a visit, one specific most jarring untruth was that I'd passed away after being infected with AIDS by Gerome.

I currently understand those lies about me were due to my practice of never really telling everybody all of my personal business, because my mama taught me so. I felt that they didn't have to know every aspect of the exact details about my Kool-Aid.

I also knew that no matter what, they were going to assume and exaggerate whatever outlandish ideas that happen to pop into their imaginations, regardless of the facts. I'd purposefully kept details about any guy that I may have been intimate with from them because it wasn't their right to know. Messy queens always mess up the festivities, if you know what I mean!

Some of them relished in gossiping and speculating about what's really going on, so you had to really keep both eyes on them at all times! Drama queens simply put. Not that I feel the need to explain to anyone outside my family why I made the choices I did during that period. However, the undisputed truth was that I left home for no other reason than I needed to be able to become the person I was created to be.

Something deeply within knew that without a shadow of a doubt that I would never bloom into the beautiful butterfly my creator kissed breath into for specific unknown reasons living in such a restrictive and confining environment.

I also felt that South Carolina wouldn't have been able to nurture or provide me with the necessary resources and opportunities that I would require to evolve mentally and physically.

Additionally and, most importantly, I made my exodus from home because I never wanted to see that disappointed look in my mother's eyes ever again, just because I was uncontrollably attracted to guys and not females.

After that through-the-chest, heart-piercing incident between Ma and I, the need to run away was even more reinforced within me. So, where could I run this time?

Everywhere that I'd previously gone after running away, Ma always found and forced me to return home, continuing our duel. I knew that if I was going to be successful moving forward with my escape plan, this time I needed to convince her to willingly give permission for me to leave home without intervention.

My brother's graduation from high school the year before was a perfect opportunity. I could use the example of the things he was allowed to do in comparison to the limits and restrictions that were placed upon me growing up.

Since Perry seemed to have been doing very well after enlisting into the Job Corps, I thought that this would possibly be a brilliant proposal to present Ma in hopes that she'd let me go also.

Due to me still being a minor, Ma had to sign the papers giving her authorization and I'm most certain that I would not have been allowed to go if not for Perry going in first. Be it as it was, I was beyond excited after finally wearing her down to agree and drive me to the unemployment office to sign the admission paperwork!

I'm almost sure that by that time she must've most likely saw my going away into the Job Corps as an opportunity to take a much needed break after reaching the point where she was just ready to rid herself of the constant challenges that I'd created within the family unit.

I absolutely did not care about the reasons for her allowing me to go, I was just exuberantly overjoyed after completing the admission forms! During the process I had no idea of what I was really getting myself into, all I knew was that in addition to finally being given permission to move away from home, I was also signing up to take a culinary arts trade and continue my education.

I was thrilled about finally getting away from Sumter, South Carolina, and filled with almost uncontainable anticipation about leaving during the weeks leading up to my departure date.

It seemed that time couldn't pass quickly enough, counting down the days, and I was beyond ecstatic on the morning that I was scheduled to take a mysterious journey to a Job Corps Center in North Carolina. Ma took me shopping for underwear, toiletries a trunk and duffle bag at the country store that she'd taken us to ever since we were toddlers.

I'd pre-packed so that all of the personal things that I was planning to take with me were ready to go, and I awoke before sunrise that anticipatory morning to be dropped off after breakfast at the Greyhound bus station by Ma on her way to work.

When we arrived at the station, she told me to call once I arrived at my destination and that she loved me, in addition to offering her usual precaution, "Be Yourself." After hugging and kissing Ma on the cheek, I went inside the Greyhound station with my wardrobe trunk and duffle bag in tow waiting for my bus to arrive at the depot in a window seat!

Once it was announced that my bus had arrived, I found another window seat at the very back to begin the ride from South Carolina to Brevard, North Carolina, wondering what was ahead of me once we reached my final destination.

After starting the trip earlier that morning, intermittently stopping along the way to pick up other passengers, we didn't arrive at Schenck CCC Job Corps Center until later that evening, way after sunset.

Since it was extremely dark when the bus finally arrived at our destination in Transylvania County, I had no idea of where we were and it never occurred to me that I was assigned to an all- male facility until after we arrived at the center.

Once there, we were taken to a building with large windows called the duty office, where we were processed and individually assigned to one of the four dorms across the courtyard from the duty office. This was not turning out to be at all what I was expecting, because it was almost like being in the military.

As I sat there with the three others that had arrived with me, I was really nervous and concerned about fitting into a militarized environment. As time passed that night during processing, I started to feel like a character in a carnival or a county fair sideshow when large group of guys started gathering on the porch outside of the duty office and just stood there peering through the large windows at us.

Once we were all finally processed, I was assigned to Pisgah Hall named, after the National Forest that the Job Corps Center resided, and when I stepped inside of the dorm for the first time, there were guys sprawled out lounging around on the couches and chairs, some shirtless and in their thermal underwear, watching televisions that were mounted on both sides of the common area.

I felt somewhat uneasy about my adjusting abilities to the barracks-style living quarters that seemed to have 10 to 12 individual bays extending from one end of the hall to the other. My dorm manager wisely assigned me to a bay with one other person that was close to his office.

Since it was so late into the evening and since I was also feeling uncomfortable with the environment, after placing my belongings into an assigned locker and making my bed for the night I slept fully clothed over my sheets.

The following morning, I awoke at the crack of dawn to prepare for the weekly scheduled 6 a.m. muster roll calls in an extremely unfamiliar space. I'd been at summer camp before so I'd planned to shower and brush my teeth as early as possible before the mad rush of the others into the bathroom.

When I stepped outside of the dorm, inhaling the crisp cold air and then realizing that the center was surrounded by majestic snowcapped mountains and giant hundred-year-old federally protected trees, I felt a little more at ease, although we were isolated in what seemed to be our own little world!

As I walked over the bridge dressed in my military-issued uniform, a tan button-down shirt, matching khaki pants, and steel-toed combat boots – all topped off with a heavy military green utility overcoat. We'd all been given four of those shirts and matching pants, in addition to four dark blue khaki pants accompanied with four white shirts for the kitchen.

Before reaching the designated assembly point where we'd answer roll-call, I was comforted by the flowing creeks filled with the most vibrantly colored koi fish that I have ever seen before up to that point. I was also placed at ease feeling that things would probably be okay living in such a serene and beautiful environment surrounded by nothing but nature!

After making it through muster roll-call without a hitch, I later learned that contrary to the names answered to during Muster, most of the corps members were addressed by their last names or other nicknames associated with their home towns or states.

Our orientation lasted a few days, consisting of touring the facilities, including the laundry facility where we obtained laundry bags that we'd use later to drop off our laundry to be laundered on designated days. We then toured the school and various trade facilities, including the mess hall where I'd be learning my technical cooking trade!

Finally, after the orientation business was done, we were then treated to a bus tour of the majestic Pisgah Forest! I was mesmerized by the snow-covered mountains as we drove to levels above the canyon that enabled me to see Schenck positioned in the valley below!

Our tour guide was very entertaining and humorous as he'd driven us on an extremely small one-lane road that seemed to have extended up to heaven and at one point pretending to lose control of the bus, which would have resulted in our immediate death upon impact.

Thankfully, we were never in any danger of being hurt during his little prank. My most cherished memory of the entire bus tour was seeing the Vanderbilt Castle nestled high within the white clouds on a mountain top near the center. At that time Gloria Vanderbilt perfume was my favorite fragrance of choice before going into Job Corps!

Until such time arrived that I was fully comfortable with my environment, I'd usually occupy myself after class and work with borrowing a boom box from one of my dorm members who was nice and accommodating to me, and I'd go and lounge for hours upon hours alone by the koi-filled creek!

I passed many hours alone inhaling nature and listening to anything by Freddy Jackson and Ready for The World, in addition to playing Whitney Houston's very first album ragged on cassette tape so much that I ended up having to replace it with a newer one!

(It pains me to say those words as the tears wells up in my eyes, Rest in peace,

Whitney Houston. You have and continue to influence me on a daily basis, my dear sister.)

At first, I thought it would be wise to go into the closet as a means of self-preservation, so I remained reserved and to myself. I continued working hard at adjusting to living around so many guys at one time who were either court-ordered criminals or juvenile delinquents ordered there by the court system as an alternative to jail and prison terms. However, there were also those that were there to learn a skill and trade like me.

Before signing up for Job Corps, since I'd previously dropped out of school near the end of my Junior year to run away from home a third time to escape from the constant emotional challenges I'd face living at home, I decided that I would take advantage of the opportunities that Job Corps had to offer me.

I was a smart kid back then, and if only I'd just applied myself in high school I would have graduated on time. So, I also decided to not squander the second opportunity to finish what I'd started. I focused on school, not boys, and excelled, receiving my diploma in record time, according to my teacher, Ms. Vitale!

Shortly after that accomplishment, I received my driver's license and was regularly complimented by our driving instructor, Mr. Waverly, who said that I was one of the few students with whom he felt at ease enough to remove his foot from the breaking pedal on his side of the floorboard and relax during our long-distance driving excursions.

I'm sure that my practice driving and parallel parking on The Strip back home after detailing our family car, in addition to passing the high school driving course I'd previously taken really helped.

Since I've always been a nature person, I appreciated and thrived in the natural environment, even though I wasn't allowed to leave the campus to explore the surrounding woods like I did growing up in my neighborhood.

However, it was a treat after cashing our weekly stipends to board the bus for a trip to town where we spent our money on personal supplies at Kmart and other department stores.

In addition to really enjoying those trips off campus, I was content with sitting for hours underneath the tree at the rolling koi-filled streams.

Strangely enough, I even found the lingering smell of the skunk spray that filled the cold and crisp morning air somewhat invigorating on my short walks before dawn from the dorm to the mess hall to begin prepping and cooking for the early breakfast shifts!

I'm happy to report that my life on campus progressed forward fairly well, and on the weekends, I regularly called Ma to give her updates on how I was doing!

She was extremely happy when I informed her that I had received and mailed my diploma to her, and that I was chosen as valedictorian to speak during our class graduation!

I could tell that she was so pleased with my accomplishments and she also encouraged me to continue to do well. Whew, it really felt great that I was finally making my mother proud of me once again!

I really liked the arts and crafts instructor, Mrs. Ann Lowery, because she was also very encouraging and a genuinely sweet and kind person to me. She encouraged me to express myself through various creative avenues, including learning how to mix and pour clay into variously themed molds to create beautiful ceramic figurine statues and pottery that I later hand-painted.

Mrs. Ann also rewarded a group of us from the arts and crafts class with an evening at the movie theater to see the latest releases, which is where I first fell in love with Glenn Close in her blockbuster movie "Jagged Edge"!

It didn't take too much longer to completely immerse myself in being creative when the adjoining town Davidson River, North Carolina scheduled their annual Halloween parade and Mrs. Ann asked if I was interested in participating in the festivities in some manner.

After agreeing to participate in the parade, I didn't have any idea of what we were going to do until one cold and brisk night inside the warm dorm while watching music videos in the common area I instantaneously became inspired to choreograph and re-create a routine to Michael Jackson's music video "Thriller."

"Thriller" was the hottest song and music video going at that time, so we were very excited about starting rehearsals! Of course, yours truly organized things, recruiting participants and casting myself as the Michael Jackson lead character. Included in our production was with Kiwi, Miss Tico, Miss Anthony, Miss Olive Oil, Miss Michael, her boyfriend and even my arch nemesis, Miss Ray, whom had a crush on the guy that would later become my boyfriend.

We had a great cast of other really cool corps members that were secure enough with themselves to participate in our skit joining in on the fun. We had less than three weeks or so before the parade to get our routine together, so no time was wasted before starting regular rehearsals after school and work and on the weekends!

We joyfully rehearsed on the courtyard outside of the gymnasium, aware that the macho guys were pretending not to be interested in what we were doing as we re-created the choreography from the video.

However, during our rehearsals I felt that there was an important element missing in order for us to make a memorable impact. I knew that we would have to do something more than just dance and march up Main Street looking like a bunch of fake zombies.

My solution for adding pizzazz to our production was persuading Mrs. Ann to ask the guys in the wood works shop to build a portable coffin with wheels that could be pulled up the parade route in addition to being sturdy enough to safely hold and fit me inside.

During the final rehearsals with the coffin, some of those same macho guys continued unsuccessfully pretending not to be amused by what we were doing. Their attitudes abruptly shifted when they started gathering around on the sideline watching our production using the coffin. After getting applauds from those guys, we knew that we were ready to entertain the crowd on the parade route that following morning.

The giant boom box that blasted "Thriller" was disguised to look like a Tombstone carried by a dancing zombie, and when we were stopped in front of the judges and various points in the parade route, I slinked out of the coffin and the crowd erupted into continuous applauds and cheers!

We'd copied to the best of our ability the exact dance moves from the "Thriller" music video. Afterwards, we were so proud of being awarded with the first place trophy for "Most Creative" in the parade!

Unfortunately, the trophy was later stolen from my bay by an ex-bay-member who'd perpetrated a fraud in front of his boys about being disgusted with people like me. He later flirted and revealed his true feelings towards me just before he was expelled from the program for physically attacking another corps member with his steel-toed boot in the Culinary Arts break room. His physically assaultive actions contributed to the break room later being turned into a dry goods storage space.

Several months later for homecoming, I wasn't expecting that girls from an all-female Job Corps Center were scheduled to arrive for the weekend, staying in a designated dorm to participate in the homecoming activities.

It turned out that our dorm, Pisgah Hall, was the designated dorm they were assigned to for the weekend. My dorm members and I were randomly assigned to the other dorms for the remainder of the time that the girls were on campus.

I was assigned to Brevard Hall where this guy resided who had previously expressed interest in me.

He was a nice guy, but he was not my type because he was kind of rougher around the edges than the guys that I was usually attracted to, and the fact that he smoked and probably did other things that were a turn off to me.

There was just something about him that I couldn't specifically put my finger on that didn't win him any points, although he'd put up a persistent secretive effort into seducing me into liking him.

I also didn't pay him any attention due to it being too soon to come out of my self-imposed closet. So, we never went there with each other because during that time, Mrs. Lowery once again encouraged me to enter the homecoming talent show, which consisted of a modeling and talent portion that I was preparing for.

Thinking about a guy was the last thing on my mind leading up to homecoming revelries after confirming with Mrs. Lowery that I was going to participate in the talent show. I knew exactly what I was going to model because I already had the modeling requirements down pact from my previous modeling experiences in school talent shows and with Nephrititi Productions!

My conflict was that I had no idea of what I was going to do for talent. Once again, while watching music videos in the dorm I'd received a light bulb moment after resolving that I wouldn't have been allowed to perform "Dress You Up" by Madonna, so in order to not rock the boat and out myself, I decided on the safest and next best alternative, which was to perform "Do Me Baby" by Prince.

In my opinion, Prince was the hottest and sexiest performer who was uninhibited about expressing his sensuality during that time!

Once I'd chosen the song selection for the talent portion, I called with a list of items that I'd needed from home and asked Ma to Federal Express to me, including the penguin-tailed black tuxedo that she'd previously purchased for my junior prom and some of my other boy clothes and shoes that I had intentionally left behind.

For my talent, I wore a Prince-inspired, crisp, white ruffled shirt and a pair of black fitted jeans that were similar to a pair Prince had worn in one of his music videos. For a dramatic effect, I placed a portable bed from the dorm on stage that was incorporated to perform an erotic routine.

I unconsciously stepped one foot out of the closet during the Friday night before homecoming, because I'd hung out with Kiwi, Miss Tico and Miss Anthony at the dance in the gymnasium, dancing to all the latest hip-hop songs by Slick Rick, "The Show," Doug E. Fresh, "Dana Dane" and other hot pop artists during the time.

The following Saturday night before the show, I remained low-key backstage out of sight, because I didn't want anyone to see my costumes before entering the stage! After the fashion portion that left the audience all excited, it was finally time for the talent segment.

I don't recall where I was in the line-up, because all I remember is that when my music started, the audience went crazy as I stood posing at the microphone in shadow before the spotlight came up on cue.

I knew going forward with my plan to win the homecoming title, that I had chosen the perfect song for my talent after I left the stage and ascended into the bleachers and passed out long-stemmed plastic red roses that I'd previously purchased on one of our regular trips to town for personal supplies.

I tell you that I was grabbed and kissed by the girls like I was actually Prince whenever I handed them a rose, and during the climatic point of the song near the end, I climbed into the bed covering myself with the white sheets and started emulating sexual motions to the moans and groans during the erotic conclusion of the song, which sent the girls into a hysterical frenzy!

Later that evening, I was crowned homecoming king after sweeping all of the categories! Although I was crowned king, I felt more like the queen riding solo, draped with my royal white and red robe seated in the back of a shiny rented convertible sports car during the parade after the girls had returned to their center.

I also felt like a real celebrity whenever the girls came to my dorm to meet me and attempted to use their feminine wiles to seduce me for the remainder of their stay on campus that entire weekend. They weren't allowed to go inside of the dorms, so they'd send other guys in to ask me to come out and talk to them.

I was not interested in those girls, so I refused go out whenever they gathered outside the dorm and for the majority of the time that they were there I purposefully did everything to avoid them as much as possible.

Fortunately, I was allowed by our culinary arts instructor, Mr. Nick, to have breakfast, lunch and dinner before the rest of the corps members and girls were scheduled to eat, because they would not leave me alone.

Mr. Nick was really cool and down-to-earth when he sometimes affectionately teased me about not being interested in the females. Some of the guys tried encouraging me to hang out with them so that they could get a girl and I was also often teased by some of them, because I showed no interest in dating any of those females that they thought were so pretty.

Finally, when the time arrived for the girls to leave, I was relieved after watching them load onto the bus to return back to their center!

Who was I kidding, pretending to be straight when I first arrived on campus? I was this petite, Jerry-curl-wearing, hazel-eyed effeminate person that was fooling no one but me into thinking that I was successfully convincing others that I was something that I was not.

I only fooled myself when I first consciously decided that I'd initially, purposefully avoid the other gender non-conforming and gay corps members, which inevitably didn't last very long after homecoming weekend.

During another special celebration six months or so later, when the girls returned for another weekend on the Center, I busted the closet door completely off its hinges when I decided to perform "Out On A Limb" by Teena Marie.

My song selection was due to me developing a serious secretive crush on a fellow corps member, and after that performance, there was no mistaking that I was not interested in girls Period.

I still had a few admirers, some obvious and some not so obvious. Two of my favorite fellow dorm members were obviously attracted to me by the look in their eyes whenever we were conversing with each other while hanging out in my bay or in the common area.

The leader of the Cheech and Chong motley crew duo, Bates, became a surrogate adopted brother to me, and he and his best friend, John, didn't perpetrate like the other corps members.

I was aware that Bates was extremely attracted to me and since I wasn't attracted to him in the same way I was happy that we overtime became more like brother and sister! No one would mess with me because Bates was very protective and always looked out for me, in addition to making sure that I had everything that I needed.

When he and John returned back from one of their weekend off-campus passes drunk as skunks, they usually stopped by my bay to hang out with me if I was lying in bed reading and listening to music. They weren't worried about what others would say when they'd both lounge on my bed with me.

There was never anything sexual between any of us, and I found them to be really cool guys! Bates was aware that there were other guys who were attracted to me, and he often teased me about his observations of their body language during our interactions.

I knew that Bates liked me more than in a sisterly manner and since I didn't want to hurt his feelings by showing interest in other guys, I often pretended to not know what he was talking about.

They often both teased me about always being the last to go to bed, unaware of what was really happening after everyone else were in bed. The time arrived when I finally told Bates about a senior dorm monitor that was in charge of signing off on our nightly chores before we went to bed.

He often refused to sign off on my assignments so that I was forced to be the last one up with him in the bathroom stalls doing illicit things I felt forced to engage in.

I was afraid to report him to the duty officer because he was this very muscular, popular guy named Capone. I felt no one would ever believe that this highly decorated corps member was forcing me to go down on him.

Bates tried convincing me to report him after my revelation, but I refused so Bates and John agreed to take turns staying up with me until I went to bed in order to block his attempts at forcing me to engage in the unsolicited sexual activities with him in the bathroom stalls.

Thanks to my adopted big brothers, Bates and John, that nightmare finally ended, but there would immediately be another bad dream that soon followed named Miss Charles.

Before Miss Charles arrived back on the campus, I'd already heard the urban myths referencing this other transgender corps member that was on an extended leave during my arrival at the center who was a force to be reckoned with! The word was that she was on a job interview in preparation to graduate from the program.

Several weeks after my arrival, Miss Charles blew back onto the campus like Hurricane Katrina's big sister, making her presence known to all. Observing her from a distance, she was extremely flamboyant and aggressively forward and l thanked God that she wasn't in my dorm!

She was a big fat bully and I intentionally chose to avoid her like the plague. However, it was inevitable that our paths would eventually intertwine, which they did one Saturday afternoon after sitting with Miss Anthony in the gym bleachers watching this boy named Carlton Keizer who always showed off and acted silly to get my attention.

After growing bored with watching the boys play basketball, Miss Anthony and I left to go outside to the commissary for soft drinks and snacks. Shortly thereafter we were sitting on the courtyard wall outside of the gymnasium and had been enjoying our snacks for about 15 minutes when the earth seemed to tremble like an earthquake, interrupting the peaceful moment.

When I looked up and saw Miss Charles and Kiwi appear between Brevard and Pisgah halls, walking rapidly and with a purpose in our direction, Miss Anthony commented, "Look out Tony, here come trouble with a capitol T!"

This would be my first direct encounter with Charles, and at first she verbally started confronting Miss Anthony about something that had happened in their dorm. Then she abruptly flipped the switch and turned her venom on me when she'd started uncontrollably pointing her fingers, stating untrue accusations, "As for you, you stuck-up little bitch, I will kick your ass if I catch your little skinny ass messing around with my man!"

I had no idea of who or what she was talking about, because before Charles arrived at the center, I'd just ended a brief, not-too-serious, somewhat undercover courtship with a guy named Ilya, who became overly jealous and possessive with me very fast to the point of threatening physical violence if he felt threatened by other guys, although I wasn't even thinking about another guy at the time.

Ilya and I never made out with each other or anything other than just sneaking to hold hands in the dark on the bus during skating rink and supply shopping outings.

As for Miss Charles, I was thinking, as she continued threatening bodily harm if I went near her boyfriend, what the Hell was I going to do if this big-ass bitch got those huge Dusty Rhodes arms around my neck?

I quickly processed my options as she continued flapping off at the mouth. I could either let this big bull crush me, break me in half and then proceed to kick my ass all over the campus for something that I didn't do, or I could stand up to her and defend myself.

I knew that if I showed any signs of fear, it would be all over and I'd never be able to live in peace on the center as long as she felt threatened by me. I chose the latter.

So, I decided to stand my ground after slapping her talons away from my personal space, responding, "I don't have a clue about who you are accusing me of messing around with, but you need to back the hell out of my mug, Miss Charles!"

Fortunately, Kiwi, who was a mutual friend of ours, stepped between me and Charles to separate us. When Miss Charles saw that I was not backing down, nor was I intimidated by her size and that I was ready to go down mano a mano with her if it was necessary, she backed off.

I exhaled, thanking God that the giant left when Kiwi pulled her away to leave. However, no matter how concerned I was due to her weight, I was prepared to deal with the consequences of what might have happened.

Miss Charles had to know that regardless of her size and threats, I was not going to be bullied by her or anyone else on that campus. Fortunately for me, that was the first and only incident that I had with her. She eventually got a job in a restaurant and left the center a few weeks later, never to return. Thank you Jesus,   that I didn't have to contend with her any longer!

I later discovered that the guy Miss Charles was accusing me of messing around with, Glenn, was in Pisgah Hall with me, and he turned out to be one of my admirers. Glenn had previously revealed his feelings toward me when we were alone in the shower one evening after dinner.

Glenn was a very handsome and nice guy who treated me with respect and, although we flirted with each other from time to time, I knew he was a player and a little too certain I would become a willing participate in sneaking around to be with him whenever no one else was present.

I had no interest or delusions of being romantically involved with someone that was playing Miss Charles and one of the girls from the female center that previously visited during homecoming named Elizabeth.

I'd previously spoken with Elizabeth on the phone whenever she called the dorm for Glenn. She seemed like a sweet girl during our brief conversations.

Now that I think about it, after I continued spurring his Casanova advances, I realized Glenn was the kind of narcissistic person who would have purposefully placed some sort of misleading bug in Miss Charles' ear referencing me just to stir up the scene and then sit back watching the fireworks go off!

Although Glenn wasn't a top boyfriend prospect, there was this other tall, dark and handsome guy from Chattanooga, Tennessee named Durk who later caught my attention in culinary arts class.

His swagger was so intriguing that I found it interesting the way he always playfully teased me whenever we encountered each other on campus or the cooks' lounge. Up to a certain point, we'd only interacted one-on-one in our trade course whenever he wasn't hanging out with his homophobic friend, Chung.

On another casual evening in the gym with Miss Anthony, while we were watching the basketball team practice for an upcoming away tournament, I noticed right off when he started making it obvious to me that he was intentionally making an effort to have extended moments of eye contact with me.

Even Miss Anthony pointed out how hard he stared whenever he came to retrieve the basketball after it bounced out of bounds in our direction on the bleachers.

Durk was a senior cook in the culinary arts program and he was also the captain of both the football and basketball teams. Overtime, the teasing eventually turned into overt flirting on his part.

Although I was extremely attracted to him, I never considered that he'd be interested in anything other than just teasing me to pass time.

However, to my surprise, it was after we'd finished a long early morning preparing and serving breakfast for the entire campus that the flirting went to another level. I wasn't prepared for when Durk shifted into full idle with the direct flirting after we entered the break room!

The break room was a lounge where the cooks rested between breakfast and lunch shifts before it was later converted to a dry storage unit.

It was usually pitch black in there, with the exception of the television and the light from the entrance whenever someone entered or exited. I was stunned that he didn't first come at me with an expected joke and seemed serious when he started revealing that he liked me!

I was taken completely off guard that his teasing had advanced to such an unexpected level!

As the conversation between Durk and I continued in the cooks' lounge that afternoon, he also informed me that he'd admired the way that I carried myself from the first time I'd arrived on campus.

He also revealed that he was one of those groups of guys standing outside staring into the duty office the night of my initial arrival, trying to figure out why there was a girl on the all-male campus.

Durk proceeded, jokingly asking, "Who do you think you were fooling pretending, to be all macho?" As I reminisce back to those private moments that we shared, I'm still not certain why there wasn't anyone else from the shift in the lounge for as long as was required for him to continue wooing me.

He continued, "I could see that you were a little girl with your little tight, white jeans on and Jerry Curl when I first laid eyes on you, sitting there in the duty office looking scared as hell. I also knew that you'd be mine!"

After he concluded, I replied in astonishment, "I don't know what I was thinking back then, pretending to be something that I was not. I do know that I was scared stiff sitting there in that duty office while you all were standing outside peering in like I was an alien from out of space or something."

I continued only after allowing for time to have digested that he'd really just blatantly expressed his intentions and attraction to me. "What made you so certain that I would be interested in you?"

He smiled and arrogantly responded, "There's something you should know and never forget is that I run this campus, and I always get what I want."

I'd never really dated any guy from high school or who was close to my age as boyfriend and girlfriend for a long term so I was engulfed by Durk's directness.

I continued listening in amazement and disbelief as he shared with me that during times when a group of us were hanging out together after breakfast service, he'd often fantasized about me sitting on his lap as his girlfriend!

I didn't put up any resistance at that moment when he'd become my unstated secret lover and protector! As required in almost every fairytale, there exists another corps member, named Cowboy, who was also arrogantly thinking that he was running things and also thought he'd get what he wanted in his attempt to win my affections.

Cowboy had previously expressed his interest in me, confidently thinking his mere interest and pretty-boy looks was all that was required to get my attention.

Although Cowboy was cute, he was a little too pretty for me with his Jerry Curl and metro-sexual dress style, as compared to Durk's masculinity and ruggedness, which was more my type.

However unstated to others the relationship between Durk and I was, even Stevie Wonder could have observed by our energy with each other that we were a couple, which didn't deter Cowboy from making a foolish mistake in flexing his muscles one bright summer afternoon under the large tree by the Koi creek.

Cowboy decided that it was time to compete with and directly challenge Durk by mistakenly choosing the wrong time and place to reveal his feelings towards me in front of the entire group, which was casually hanging out on the bench having fun teasing each other!

There was almost a collective gasp as Cowboy jokingly and conceitedly commented out of the blue, "If I wanted you, Tony, you'd be mine!"

Immediately after he completed releasing that unexpected statement from his lips, everybody had this look of shock and disbelief on their faces that he'd even made such a bold unedited statement in the presence of others!

I couldn't believe what he'd just stated in front of so many people, nor did I really know how to respond. My only thought was why would he say something like that in front of Durk, joking or not, with the awareness that he was much taller and stronger than Cowboy! Wait, there's more!

The day that I refer to as the Matrix 3D action series further took everyone by surprise when Durk grabbed Cowboy by his collar and threatened, "Look here, boy, if you ever disrespect me like that again, I will throw your ass in that water, and if you ever approach Tony like that again, I will kick your little ass all over this campus, Now what?"

After Durk made his feelings known to me in the break room, except for a couple of others who found out later, it was supposed to have remained an unspoken secret. But I was delusional.

The cat was yanked out of the bag and, of course, the news of the incident quickly spread throughout the campus like a raging wild fire in Pisgah Forest, confirming that Durk and I was an item!

After it was confirmed to everyone on campus that there was no doubt Durk and I were a couple, no one, I mean not a single soul, ever approached me in that manner again as long as Durk was present.

After officially becoming Durk's girl, it seemed as if I was also even off limits from being harassed by the duty officers and dorm managers.

I also quickly learned moving forward that you really couldn't keep very many secrets on the campus for a long time before someone eventually found out what was really going on, because it seemed as if the dorm walls had ears and were filled with guys that gossiped more than the girls.

Our relationship caused few conflicts with the other corps members, because they all respected Durk and also knew not to bother me, especially after hearing that he'd physically threatened Cowboy in front of so many people.

I'm quite sure that center staff members were aware of our relationship and as long as we weren't openly breaking the rules, they didn't feel the need to question their star athlete about the rumors or the extent of our togetherness.

As the seasons changed, I remained smitten with Durk, often ignoring the unsolicited attention from the new arrivals on campus, because I only had eyes for my man from Chattanooga, Tennessee!

However, once I made what I considered an honest big mistake when the football team was on an away game. Myself and some other corps members decided to release some pent-up up energy in celebration of the weekend, horse-playing around with each other after the last dinner service was finally completed!

It later occurred to me that one of Durk's boys most likely observed our innocent activities and could not wait to inform Durk that I was wrestling around with other guys while he was away.

The following day, my happiness that he'd be returning to campus later that afternoon came to an abrupt halt. I was filled with anticipation that once he'd finished getting settled into his dorm, he would come to mine and hang out with me!

When he finally arrived at Pisgah Hall, I was informed by another corps member from my dorm that he was waiting for me outside for me. Mind you, it was a big deal for Durk to have come to my dorm and ask for me, because corps members were not allowed to go inside any other dorm that they were not assigned to.

It made me feel very special that Durk didn't care what others were saying whenever he sat on the bench waiting for me on our porch!

I was very excited as I rushed outside to greet him! I could immediately tell as I sat next to him by the cold way in which he'd responded to me that he was upset about something, so I questioned him about what was wrong."Are you okay, Durk?"

After not responding to me for several minutes, he eventually replied, "I really don't appreciate hearing about you rolling around on the ground with other people while I was away, Tony."

I was totally wrong in thinking that he was upset because they must have lost their game or he'd been injured in some manner. It was a whole lot more serious than just a basketball game. He pulled the letter that I'd previously written to him from his jacket pocket.

Then he coldly continued, "If you really meant what you wrote in this letter, professing how much you care for me Tony, you would not be letting another guy put their hands on you while I'm away."

After making his statement Durk stood and then dropped the love letter on my lap before turning to walk away without giving me an opportunity to respond. I was not going to let him just walk away without hearing my side of the story, so I tried convincing him that it was only innocent horseplay. "Durk, I was not rolling around on the ground with nobody; we were bored and just acting crazy to pass time that is all."

Durk was not buying it, and I'd never seen him that angry at me before, so I desperately called after him as he continued ignoring me and walking away. "Durk, I made a mistake, and I am sorry. I promise it will never happen again!"

He continued ignoring me and kept walking back to his dorm directly in front of mine across the courtyard and all I could do was watch his back as he entered, letting the heavy door slam behind him.

Writing about Durk causes me to realize that he was the very first guy that I've really hurt and yearned for to that extent after ending our relationship. I thought my world was coming to an end watching him walk away, leaving me alone on the dorm porch in disbelief that he was so upset.

Although in all honesty I never once rolled around on the ground with another corps member, I concluded that I would never horseplay around again, innocently or not. I also resolved that I was going to do whatever I could to show Durk that I was remorseful about getting carried away with other guys.

Later that evening, alone in my bay, I committed to doing whatever that was required to get him to forgive me, because I couldn't handle the thought of him continuing to be angry with me for too much longer.

The following day, during our brief times alone in the cook's lounge before anyone else came in after the breakfast shift ended, it was excruciating that he avoided talking to me throughout the entire breakfast service and break.

I tried apologizing to him once again for what I'd done and promised I would never cross the line like that again with another guy, and as I poured my heart out to him, I slightly suspected he believed I was sincere. Instead of forgiving me right away, he drew out my torture a little bit longer.

As day two slowly turned into three, he didn't know that I was aware that he was observing me from the other side of the kitchen to see how I interacted with the corps member he'd accused me of being interested in. Although still refusing to forgive me and deciding to prolong my agony by refusing to talk to me, I'd also observed that he'd always made sure none of my other admirers were allowed any opening to lounge close to me in the break room.

Durk still would not talk to me, however, but the fact he wouldn't let anyone within an inch of me provided hope that he'd eventually come around and forgive me for my transgression!

Even though I found out later that another corps member, Fred, was rumored to have transferred from welding to culinary arts because he was attracted to me and wanted to be close enough to make his move. But I only had eyes for Durk.

Whenever Fred approached me during or after service, I made it clear to him in no uncertain terms that Durk was still my man no matter what was going on between us.

Since I'd soon know for sure that Fred liked me, I only engaged in conversations and interactions with him which only pertained to our required interaction in school or the mess hall.

It took three long days before Durk decided to stop being so stubborn, once he was satisfied that he had proven his point about me not getting physically close to another guy again. I was surprised after he finally stopped torturing me when he grabbed my hand in the cook's lounge and kissed me on the cheek in the dark!

I was overjoyed that he'd finally forgiven me for my indiscretion, innocent or not, and I agreed to meet him after work later that evening to sneak off campus for one of our intimate secret rendezvous! Don't judge that I'm right back to the boys.

Life was good after getting back on track with Durk from that point forward, until a month or so later when I'd received the devastating news from him about his graduation in a couple of weeks. In addition, he would be traveling to Georgia for a job interview the following week.

Although I was happy that he'd gotten the job in Atlanta when he returned back on campus after his interview, I dreaded each day leading up to his final departure. We spent every moment possible with each other leading up to the morning that Durk left the center for the final time and, believe you me, it was challenging remaining composed on the final breakfast, lunch and dinner service line.

I struggled to fight back the tears to keep from weeping all over the eggs, bacon and sausages that I was serving, because I knew that I'd most likely never see Durk again. However, I couldn't help but hope that there might be a slight possibility that he would stay in touch with me after getting settled in Atlanta!

I also foolishly hoped that we might be together at some point in the future. Wishful thinking!

The afternoon that Durk left, "Silly" by Deniece Williams became my theme song, although most of the boys from his crew futilely jockeyed to see who would be the first to make me their girl.

One of these was his right-handman, Michael, who informed me one evening on his dorm side steps that it was his duty and responsibility to protect and take over where Durk had left off.

Whoa, Nelly! Wait a minute! I wasn't able to get over Durk that easily so, although I welcomed his protection with open arms, our relationship remained platonic until the day he left the campus.

Another one of Durk's boys who lived in my dorm, Go-Rock, had previously made it clear to me that he was against Durk and my relationship from the beginning, but there was nothing he could do about it as long as Durk was a willing participant.

Three days after Durk left, Go-Rock stole Durk's identification card, which he'd given to me the night before his departure and that I proudly displayed in my locker. Go-Rock was fuming that his home-boy was so unconcerned about what others thought of our relationship and that he even gave me his ID in the first place.

So, he made threats to take it from me if I didn't remove it from display whenever he walked through my bay. Since I felt that it was more than just Durk's picture hanging as a reminder so visibly in my locker that caused him to be so angered, I refused to do as he'd commanded.

I really believed that there were instances when Go-Rock was coming onto me and he, overtime, became more frustrated that I continued not responding to his advances. I just was not attracted to him in that manner.

After he continued refusing to return Durk's identification card, I rubbed it in that he would never take Durk's place, and when he finally realized that he stood no chance with me he eventually backed off.

Several weeks after Durk's departure, there was an incident in the mess hall with a fellow corps member who tried to intimidate me in front of his boys after intruding in on a private conversation that I was engaged in with Miss Anthony.

He thought that it was funny when he left his table to walk across the room over to me and started making homophobic and derogatory remarks, which ultimately resulted in him threatening to kick my ass after I read and shamed him in front of his crew.

He was physically much bigger than I was and I felt threatened when he lunged at me, stating, "Yeah faggot ass faggot, your boyfriend not here to protect your ass now!"

So, without thinking and in self-defense, I picked up a hot sauce bottle from the center of our table and smashed it over his head. He grabbed the side that was saturated with the hot sauce dripping down on his uniform, stumbled backwards in shock as his boys laughed at him looking stupid.

I'm so thankful that he was just stunned and not injured from the glass shattering upon impact. As a result, we were both written up and I was the only one called to appear before the review board because I had used a "weapon."

I was represented during the appearance before the disciplinary review board by one of my instructors, Mr. Williams, whom everyone used to tease that he could have been my father due to our similar eye color and skin complexion.

During the review process, since they were informed by my culinary arts instructor Mr. Nick that I was much more advanced than others in our class. I possessed the ability to make a mean pineapple upside-down cake that made you want to slap somebody. In addition, he was impressed at how quickly I'd mastered the grill, achieving the ability to scramble dozens of eggs while simultaneously turning hot and fluffy pancakes in record time to feed the entire campus.

During the two weeks of uncertainty waiting for the review board to complete their deliberation, I wasn't satisfied that I'd became hardened, defensive and guarded as a means of protecting myself physically due to past experiences contributing to my current predicament facing the disciplinary board.

I was also disappointed in myself due to blowing an opportunity to have transferred to a different Job Corps Center that was offering college courses. I'd visited this center one weekend just a couple months before my termination.

Since I wanted to be responsible for my actions, I prepared myself to accept the consequences before being informed that my choice to use the weapon during the incident contributed to their expulsion conclusion.

I was also informed that although the other corps member's actions were inappropriate, they'd terminated me because, in their opinion, I'd successfully accomplished all that Job Corps was designed to offer, more than the average person at the center during the length of my stay.

Although I'm not proud of the actions which contributed to my termination from the program, I was proud to have walked away with receiving a culinary arts certification, driver's license and, most importantly, my General Education Diploma, allowing me to possibly attend college in the future!

I was also glad that my focus wasn't just on the boys and that I'd acquired quite a bit of useful tools and skills as I packed my belongings from the locker preparing to leave. I couldn't help but be both scared and uncertain about leaving the place that had quickly become a source of security, growth, and order for me.

There was really no one left that I had to see; the majority of the people that I'd associated with had already left the campus for one reason or another. During the wait in the duty office for my departure transportation, I remained okay, accepting the punishment and moving forward with dignity and with pride about my accomplishments.

I probably would have not accomplished any of those achievements if not for me being there at that specific time because, before my enrollment, I was rebelliously fast, thinking that I was grown, sneaking out my bedroom window to attend clubs and date older guys, although I was still under-aged. My, my, my, what was I thinking back then?

How did I pull off being admitted into adult venues during those times when it was so obvious to almost everyone that I wasn't of legal age, I wonder?

I exited the duty office for the last time to board the Greyhound bus, I resolved that the training I'd received there in Brevard, North Carolina, will always benefit me no matter where I go or what I do in the future. That chapter in my life came to an end as I once again settled into a ticket-out-of-town window seat at the back of the bus. I also became intrigued with the sense of awareness that I'd received relative to the unrealized abilities I had possessed in contributing to causing a very popular ladies' man jock to throw caution to the wind and risk his reputation to become intimately involved with me.

It was as if it didn't matter that he was well-respected by others and previously involved with a biological girl from the female Job Corps Center before my arrival. Another intriguing aspect of the situation was that he'd been treated respectfully during our entire time together and no one confronted him, questioning his manhood! That's the kind of man that I like, yes!

Additionally, as the sun began to set swiftly reflecting through the pine trees as we drove to the main highway leaving Pisgah Forest, I'd started to embrace the gift of being born unordinary for a specific purpose that I am yet to fully comprehend!

I wonder if one of the other reasons I'd been so boy hungry and rebellious early on was to prove my mother and society wrong. To prove that was I supposed to have been gender non-conforming from the beginning.

Back in South Carolina, it was at first somewhat of a challenge re-adjusting to civilian life due to missing the routine of being on the Job Corps campus. I'd had a taste of independence and there was absolutely no doubt that I was way beyond the point of permanently living in Sumter under my mother's roof again.

Due to my certifications and achievements at the center, Ma and I never discussed the details as to what contributed to my return home. I was embarrassed to tell her the whole truth.

I was determined that the return home was only going to be brief enough to fully regroup and figure out what I was going to do with my life next in order to maximize and capitalize on the newly discovered abilities.

My newly recognized potentials were vibrating within me and I was illuminated to such a degree that I knew I would not be content with the way things were before leaving home!

I was sure that there was absolutely no way that my mother and hometown would ever allow me to openly express and fully become the person I am, even now, constantly evolving into.

I recall wanting something more than Sumter, South Carolina had to offer and I am thankful that I took the leap of faith and left my hometown when I did to explore other horizons!

Currently, and unfortunately, all of the close friends that I grew up with of whom chose to remain in Sumter are dead, with probably the exception of the one who is alleged to be strung out on heroin in New York City.

For a brief while upon my return back home, I was excited about the possibilities of getting a job and permanently moving out of my mother's house into my own place after traveling to Columbia, South Carolina with my neighbor Darlene E., to apply for employment at a hotel where her brother's girlfriend worked.

However, it was quite possibly due to my inexperience that the employment search didn't go as planned in my hometown or in Columbia. But a great opportunity was presented when Ma told me she'd read in the Sumter Daily Item newspaper that the city had created a program to supply a transit bus free of charge to the unemployed to seek employment.

Monday through Friday were the designated days that those from Sumter and surrounding cities could travel the two-hour drive to seek employment opportunities that were not available in our towns.

It was evident that some people just used the free bus ride to spend a day of sun and fun at the beach! The exception being me and my friends, we took advantage of the trips to look for jobs.

Ma showed her support by taking me to the designated pick-up and drop-off site downtown on her way to work. It didn't take too long for me to find work after presenting my culinary arts certifications to the manager who interviewed and hired me on the spot to work as cashier and front customer service representative at Burger King.

I was very happy about receiving a job offer on my very first interview at Burger King, since our most recent vacation was on Kings Highway in Myrtle Beach, South Carolina and Burger King remains there!

It made it even better that most of my friends were also hired for other positions within the restaurant. To get to that job, we rode over four hours back and forth, not accounting the delays during stops to drop off the people living in Conway, South Carolina and cities in between the beach and Sumter.

I'd be remiss if I forget about the precious hours that we'd spent on the broken-down bus waiting for repair trucks after a long, hard, tiresome day at work. We seriously began considering the possibilities of living on the beach to alleviate the frustrations and inconveniences!

As far as I was concerned, it wasn't a question or debate to team up in groups of two and rent adjoining rooms at one of the extended stay hotels on Atlantic Beach, South Carolina, which is also referenced by some as the Black Beach.

Although we were young, crazy, adventurous and partying after work on the weekends, we were responsible with being to work on time and doing our jobs well. At least I was. It's ironic that my trade was for culinary arts and I've never worked a grill or fry station since those days of scrambling dozens of eggs at once in the kitchen at Job Corps.

The exception being those occasional times (being a team player and in an effort to keep the team running efficiently) when I placed some burgers and buns on the burner during those mad lunch rushes!

During those crazy lunch and dinner rushes, we ran that restaurant like a well-tuned engine working together! However, we also had fun during those slow-down, in-between periods that we'd all usually be in stitches when Miss Patti used to act out, abusing the meat before placing it on the burner!

We'd also be rolling around on the floor laughing at his crazy self while waiting in the dining room for the bus after our shift ended, watching him tip-toe up behind the fragile elderly lady named Miss Betty that worked the salad bar and almost giving her a heart attack when he'd shouted her name, "Miss Betty!" Miss Betty reacted startled and disgusted, replying, "What?"

Due to my history, you'd think that since I was no longer under my mother's watchful eyes and the restrictions that were associated with my time in Job Corps, I would have gone absolutely boy crazy, wouldn't you?

It was quite the contrary. Although I admit that there were a couple of guys that I crushed on, I only made out with one of them the whole time I remained on the beach. His name was Donnie and you'll hear more about him a little bit later!

Anyway, during our off days we explored Atlantic Beach, discovering this restaurant/club where we'd felt safe hanging out on the weekends called The Cotton Club.

It had a connected gift shop owned and operated by these two entrepreneurially gifted sisters named Linda and Coby.

The older sister, Linda, nicknamed me Pearl because she admired how white my teeth were and everybody else called me Dominique after my favorite television diva-vixen, Miss Diahann Carroll from the television show Dynasty.

Eventually, in addition to working at Burger King during the day, I started working part-time for the sisters taking photos in their souvenir photo booth directly across the street from the club! I spent many hours after my day job during Biker Week, Memorial Day, Labor Day and other busy holiday weekends snapping away.

My friends, on the other hand, were using their antics to lure customers into the restaurant and gift shop next door whenever "Stir It Up" by Patti Labelle and "Neutron Dance," or anything else by the Pointer Sisters played on the loudspeakers that were strategically placed out front by Coby.

The rest of my crew loved being the center of attention, performing for the thousands of tourists that filled the sidewalks walking up and down the beach.

Call me prissy if you want, I don't care. I was always the more reserved, serious, and about-business one, which wouldn't allow me to put myself on public display and make a clown of myself in that manner.

So, while they were living it up, performing and entertaining the tourists on the streets in front of The Cotton Club, I was hard at work across the street managing and taking souvenir photos of the drunken tourists.

I saved all of my partying and cutting loose for after work during After Hours at Pumps' Patio just up the street on the ocean. It has since been demolished by a hurricane.

Some of my favorite letting-loose, cut-up songs at that time to relax and unwind after a long day and night at work were, "I Can't Wait," and "Pass The Point Of No Return" by Nu'Shooz, "Pleasure Principle,""When I Think Of You," and "Wait A While" by Janet Jackson, "Word Up" and "Single Life" by Cameo, in addition to anything by pop groups like Club Nouveau or the Timex Social Club.

As time passed, I eventually evolved into producing, directing and performing "Kiss" by Prince in a well-attended fashion show that I was never compensated for. Anyway, some many years later, I figured that the best revenge would be to boldly let them meet my husband and our babies to see show them that their expectations were wrong about me. Yes, I did say husband, you'll find out more about that mystery man much later! Be patient!

I wanted to show them that out of all of my friends who also worked or were previously associated with the sisters, I am still here! Mentally and physically contrarily living opposite of what they'd expected!

It was my intention to rub my success in their face during a recent Christmas vacation when the memories of my time previously living on the beach came flooding back as if it were yesterday. My husband and I took our babies for the first time together on the two-hour day trip from my mother's house to Myrtle and Atlantic Beach!

It was a little after lunch that afternoon when we stopped by the Cotton Club to grab a bite to eat and pay a visit, but they were already closed when we arrived.

Since they were already closed, I went to the back where the living quarters were, where I'd previously resided those many years ago, to knock on Coby's door, but there was no answer.

As I turned to leave, I was intercepted by a former Cotton Club co-worker named Kris, who was not still employed there the last several years ago since Josephine and I last visited before his recent death. More about Joseph's untimely death is forthcoming.

When Kris rode up on her bicycle the day that Tevin and I were there, she didn't recognize me when I'd spoken her name and inquired if Linda and Coby were gone for the day.

Even after speaking her name, I still had to tell her that I was Dominique and then it was like a lightbulb flashed on as the memories all came rushing back to her! I found it funny that the thing that she recalled about me the most was when I'd previously performed Prince during the uncompensated special event fashion show that I produced at The Cotton Club!

It was also funny that, although I had on bottoms, she seemed to think that I had stripped just because I'd removed my oversized jacket during the performance revealing my bare chest to work it out like Prince did in his "Kiss" video. It was interesting to me that she considered that stripping; oh, well.

After moving to the beach in the late '80s, things had gone well sharing a room with my roommate and best friend Asia for several months until she'd started being irresponsible with staying out partying all night long until dawn.

To make things worse, Asia didn't want to get her butt out of bed and go to work when it was time to do so. Over a period of two weeks when she consistently missed work, I became frustrated and tired of paying all of our rent and buying the food for the both of us on my own while she took her money and bought new outfits to wear out every weekend.

After we inevitably got into a rare argument about her being inconsiderate and self-absorbed, she decided that she was homesick and ultimately returned to Sumter when some of our other friends returned back home after the summer season ended.

I was not ready to move back home, so I remained on my own after they all left. My new theme song was "On My Own" by Patti Labelle and Michael McDonald, reminding me about the fun that we shared together when we'd initially moved to Atlantic Beach.

After the summer season ended and the tourists left the beach, I got an additional part-time cashier job paying more money at Harris Teeter Super market! I also continued working part-time at The Cotton Club before eventually enrolling in Chris Logan Beauty College the day after resigning from Burger King.

Almost a year later was when I'd meet and started hanging out with this tall and cute guy named Donnie after he walked into the restaurant looking cool like Shaft in his black trench coat and matching leather brim. I later walked in and found the younger sister, Coby, briefly courting him.

Since the closeness and trust I had in Linda and Coby became greatly diminished after talking to a guy that they'd recruited to drive me to the country and attempt to scare me straight, I started hanging out more at Donnie's apartment after work.

The sister's plan was for this guy to pretend interest in taking me out on a date and then he was supposed to have abandoned me in a dark, unfamiliar place around a group of his male friends that were supposed to frighten me to the point of turning masculine.

Since I was not their family member, I wonder why were they so threatened or concerned about my gender identity?

I thank God that the guy that they recruited to set me up must have had a change of heart after our introduction when he later that evening in his car during the drive revealed what they wanted him to do.

He was a nice person choosing not to take part in their vicious scheme. They had no idea that I knew what they'd planned and the writing was on the wall that I should start preparing to make a move in employment and living arrangements.

I didn't question them about what I was told by the guy, because I believed him and I also wanted time to make other plans.

Since the stranger had no reason to lie to me, I no longer trusted Linda and Coby. When that first plan of humiliation didn't work out to their advantage, they then resorted to promoting a fellow co-worker to management in order to begin harassment and intimidation tactics when they influenced her to try and embarrass me one night that I was hanging out with Donnie at his apartment.

I knew what they were up to, so when she arrived knocking on the door to front on me, I had already started to make other living arrangements and when the pawn became belligerently disrespectful towards me in front of Donnie and his roommates, I let her have it!

Just because I was more reserved than most, she should have known better than to push a queen into a corner trying to embarrass her in front of others, especially a guy that she likes.

I was ultimately officially fired from working for the sisters on the following evening. I returned from school and Donnie's apartment to find my personal belongings all piled outside the room I'd occupied.

Although I had previously started making other living arrangements, they were not yet complete due to finances, so when I walked up on that bone-chilling, cold windy evening and saw all of my things piled outside of the room in the back of the club, I didn't know what I was going to do.

After a few moments of strategizing and analyzing the situation, I decided to ask this elderly gentleman in the neighborhood on the next street over who was always very kind to me if he would use his truck to transport my things until I figured out what I was going to do next.

Years later, I was informed by Miss Josephine that the same pawn that was used to plot against me at The Cotton Club eventually ended up stealing money from the cash registers before disappearing!

I've since learned everything happens for a reason and being fired from the club in that manner presented an opportunity for me to be introduced to another living guardian angel who not only stored my belongings in his storage unit, he invited me to stay on his couch until I'd finished saving up enough money to get my own apartment.

Although I suspected that the former club owner may have had a hidden agenda for being so generous to me, he never approached me in a sexual manner. His generosity and understanding allowed for me to continue going to school and spending time with Donnie without feeling pressured about giving him something in return for his kindness.

I didn't ask Donnie for help initially because we had just recently started courting and I didn't want him to think that I wanted to move in with him. Donnie had a mid-aged man named James as his roommate and co-worker who was also nice to me.

In the beginning, his live-in girlfriend and I grew close so I felt safe hanging out at their apartment with them in the evenings. One memorable evening in Donnie's bedroom, hanging out after I'd finished my homework, he asked me out of the blue, "Dominique, will you spend the night with me and let me make love to you tonight?"

Up to that point, Donnie and I have never gone beyond just kissing and making out fully clothed, so I was taken aback by his question.

Quite honestly, I really wasn't ready to advance to that level, because I was quite content with just being with him and making out.

Back then, I was not giving up my goodies to every Tom, Dick and Donnie. However, I might have later seriously considered his proposal, considering the way that he treated me. It just wasn't the right time due to me not feeling comfortable with the idea of being intimate for the very first time with his roommate and girlfriend in the paper-thinned walled room right next to his.

Also, I questioned his motives for asking me to have sex with him while his roommates were in the apartment. After declining his invitation to spend the night and have sex with him, he didn't pressure me after I explained to him that I wasn't ready to have sex with him yet. However, we did make out that night!

Several days later when his roommate James and I were alone in the apartment together, before his girlfriend and Donnie arrived, he questioned, "Dominique, what did you do to my boy Donnie the other night?"

"What do you mean, James?" I replied looking up from my homework.

"Girl, that boy was upset all day at work for the last couple of days about you rejecting his invitation to spend the night with him."

"James, to tell you the truth, I am really not ready to take that step with Donnie yet, because I'm not sure of what he's expecting from having sex with me."

He replied, jokingly, "Well, I don't know what you've done to Donnie, but he said that whenever you do decide to give it to him, he will not use any lubrication in order to teach you a lesson about rejecting him."

Although I was young during that time, the conversation between James and I didn't seem quite appropriate to me. It confirmed that they were having intimate discussions about me amongst themselves. Before then, I never considered the fact that macho men like that were having one-on-one talks about their sex lives.

Donnie and I continued hanging out with each other, but after a period of time, I kind of felt that I was just a mystery to him which he'd intended to solve by having sex with me. Since I did not want to be used by him as an experiment, we eventually grew apart and less than a month later Donnie moved in with a biological woman who lived in the same neighborhood. I was happy that I didn't allow him to use me sexually just to satisfy his curiosity!

Meanwhile, back at my guardian angel's apartment one evening during the week, I was alone in the living room doing homework when some of his friends, whom I'd previously briefly met in passing, arrived at the apartment.

The one of the two of them whom was affectionately called L.F. reminded me of Bill Duke. He was a gentle giant, well into his sixties, and he started to openly show his affections for me. My guardian angel didn't seem to mind that his friend started showing interest in me or that he also began buying me coats and winter clothes.

I didn't want to lead L.F. on, so I tried dissuading him from buying other gifts and giving me beautiful pendants that I usually wore with closed shirt collars. He insisted that it made him happy to be able to give me things.

Their other friend, Booker, was a jealous creep that pretended to be drunk so he could come onto me whenever we were alone. I did not care for Booker at all because he was an instigator and alcoholic that was also jealous because L.F. didn't care that I was transgender, nor did he care about what others were saying about his obvious infatuation with me.

I had never before had a gentleman so aggressively and openly pursue and take such strong interest in my well-being as L.F. did and, even though he was old enough to be my grandfather, he was determined to make me see him as more than just a grandfatherly figure.

Although I was not attracted to L.F. in a romantic manner, I felt empathy for him after he shared with me his fresh grief over the recent loss of his beloved wife. Also, during one of our conversations he expressed his loneliness and need for companionship.

I felt compassion for L.F. and thankful that he had been so generous to me, so I accepted his invitation when he invited me to move into his house to stay with him and his daughter.

Tessie was in her early twenties and understandably unpleased about her father inviting a stranger to move into their home.

Before I moved into his house, L.F. shared with me that Tessie usually spent the weekends away from home. But, immediately after we were introduced, she started staying at home more regularly. I had no problems with her actions because they were all totally understandable.

One evening almost three nights after I'd officially moved to what was considered the country, when L.F. and I were sitting in front of the fireplace after returning from a day of fishing and oyster harvesting, Tessie didn't go directly into her bedroom as usual.

She chose instead to come into the living room where we were and immediately started confronting her father, who was comfortably reclined in his Lazy Boy, puffing on his cherry tobacco-filled pipe. Tessie nonchalantly walked over, sat down next to me on the couch right across from L.F.'s chair and proceeded interrogating him. "So Daddy, what's going on here between you and Dominique?"

L.F. puffed his pipe and slowly exhaled the smoke creating three well-rounded circles before responding in a deep baritone voice. "Tessie, whatever is going on between Dominique and I is none of your business."

Replying as if I was invisible, she asked while crossings her arms, "But, Daddy, are you and Dominique playing house now?"

Again he replied, in a much deeper bass tone, "Tessie, you are grown now and so am I." He declined his chair and placed the pipe in the ashtray on the end table next to his chair, continuing, "I pay all of the bills around here, Tessie, so I do not have to answer to you about who I choose to playhouse with, as you call it."

Clearly agitated, he continued."Dominique will be here as long as she needs to be, so you better get used to it!" He then rose from the leather recliner and concluded the conversation by stating, "This is the last time that you and I are going to have this conversation, Tessie." He then smiled and winked his eye at me as he walked towards his bedroom concluding, "You ladies have a good night. I am going to bed."

After L.F. exited the living room to retire for the evening in his bedroom, Tessie and I stayed up talking with each other about my intentions regarding her father. She continued somewhat looking down her nose at me, saying, "Dominique, I hope that you're not taking this personally, it's just that after my mother died from cancer, I've been concerned about Daddy."

I replied, completely understanding where she was coming from, "Tessie, I am so sorry about your mother. I can never understand how you feel about her passing and then shortly afterwards coming home to find that a strange person like me has moved into your home."

Since she didn't immediately respond, I continued, " L.F. is a loving and kind man who is generous enough to give me a place to stay until I can get myself together, which is the only thing going on between us."

I guess after that revelation she must have been somewhat reassured that there wasn't any hanky-panky going on between me and her daddy. She twisted her neck before bending it to look over her spectacles, responding, "So how did you meet Daddy, Dominique?"

I continued, hoping to reassure and place Tessie at ease about the situation as the evening progressed during our first real one-on-one conversation with each other."Ever since I met your father at Mr. Washington's apartment almost two months ago he's become like a father figure to me. I'd just lost one of my jobs and not yet able to get my own place and after L.F. found out that I was moving into a weekly rate motel, he then asked me to move in your spare room so that I could continue saving my money to get my own place."

Although she'd remained obviously skeptical, I concluded. "I hope that you and I can get along with each other until I find my own place, which I expect to be much sooner rather than later."

Eventually, Tessie and I formed somewhat of a sisterhood that night after our heart-to-heart conversation and immediately started regularly hanging out with each other!

We both loved listening to "Have You Ever Loved Somebody" by Freddie Jackson whenever it played either on the car stereo or when we were hanging out at the restaurant on the beach up the street from the "Cotton Club" where her secret married boyfriend worked.

I didn't think that it was necessary to reveal to Tessie that her father initially insisted on me sleeping in the bedroom with him when I first moved into their home. I emphatically declined due to not being attracted to him in that manner and, even if I were, there'd be no way that I would have been comfortable even considering sleeping in the same bedroom and bed that his wife slept in with him.

If I had done something that foul, I would've been disrespecting his late wife, daughter, and myself. I certainly didn't need that kind of karma. Although L.F. wasn't happy one bit with my continuous refusal to not sleep in his bedroom and be intimate with him, he continued to express his determination to make me fall in love with him no matter how long it took.

Although it was consistently challenging dodging his insistence on me moving into his bedroom, I managed to keep him at bay as time went on by convincing him that I needed some time to get used to having him as an intimate partner.

A small part of me hoped that I'd grow to see him as something other than just a father figure because he was so kind to me, but no matter how much I tried tricking myself into thinking that maybe my feelings towards him would change, the time never came that I saw him as a prospective longtime sexual partner.

I also knew, delicately stepping forward, that I couldn't continue being dependent upon L.F., especially after resolving that I was not going to be intimate with him in the manner that he wanted.

I was additionally certain that his patience would eventually run out, so I knew that I would have to start making other living arrangements as soon as possible regardless of how much money I'd saved.

As predicted, just short of a month he reached the point beyond resentment because I'd kept refusing to move into his bedroom and be intimate with him.

Thankfully, I had previously formed a friendship and camaraderie with some of my gay classmates, Steve, Toby, and Robert.

Steve was the experienced, crazy, somewhat rough-around-the-edges person who lived with his boyfriend not too far from the where I was. Either he'd given me rides to school and work or another classmate of ours living close to me named Catherine gave me a ride to and from school.

Robert was the really skinny, Nelly one, whose rich parents had recently bought him a new Trans Am after he'd enrolled into beauty school.

Toby was the heavier-set, aspiring performer from North Carolina who always argued with Steve whenever he called her a drag queen.

The four of us usually hung out after school and partied at Offshore Drilling Company, even though at that time I still wasn't old enough to legally get into the clubs. However, when some jealous queens found out about my age, they ratted me out to management because their own underage friends were being restricted from entering the club.

I then resorted to sneaking into the club whenever the manager wasn't on duty. On her nights off, she often phoned the club to question the on shift bartender if I was there. I'm sure that she was concerned about under-age drinking, but I never drank alcohol, beer or used illicit drugs during those times.

I just loved to dance and hang out with my friends! Thankfully, we had one bartender friend who was dating Steve on the side and who would let me stay whenever the club manager was gone.

Not only did the bartender want to be with Steve, he also wanted to join us after the club in Robert's shiny new five-speed sports car to cruise the popular pick-up spot Hurl Rock and main strand.

We passed time sitting in the car by the ocean observing the other gay guys cruising the park near the beach for sex, with Toby and Robert usually cat-calling the cute muscular guys who most likely were male prostitutes on their beats for dates!

Robert often invited the three of us to spend the night at his parents'
bed-and-breakfast on the weekends after we'd hung out late cruising and acting crazy!

Back in the country, once when L.F. was drunk he tried physically restraining me
from leaving the house to go out. He then threatened to physically harm me if he found out
I was seeing another guy, causing me more concern about his drinking and aggression.
After sharing with my friends Steve, Robert and Toby about his threats, Steve insisted that
I spend the night with he and his boyfriend, Lynn, until I found a place of my own.

Although I'd had my heart set on getting at least an efficiency apartment, I didn't
have the total deposit that I'd needed to get one, so I settled on a room at an extended-stay
hotel, which is what I probably should have done before moving into L.F.'s house.

Hindsight is 20-20. The next morning before school, Steve took me to rent an
affordable weekly rate room on Myrtle Beach, and after work that evening, they helped me
move out of L.F'.s house while he was away.

Many years later, when I first returned back to Atlantic Beach with my friend Miss
Josephine before his death to visit the sisters that we'd previously worked for at "The
Cotton Club," I was saddened when Linda informed me that L.F. had died.

I've never shared with my friends the experiences that I had on Atlantic Beach after
their departures because I'd moved forward from those past negative energies, choosing to
believe that the sisters expressed their concerns for me the only way they knew how due to
it being obvious to them that some of the guys on the beach were attracted to me.

It was probably that misinformation that caused them to assume I was having sex
with random guys, which was never the case. Although I did occasionally flirt with one or
two guys, I was very selective about whom I'd chosen to make out with.

I don't regret any of the experiences that I had working for the sisters because I've
also chosen to see the good in the negative. In addition to my mother, I learned many
lessons from the older sister about work ethic and the ability to get things done that I
currently incorporate in my personal life.

I admired that Linda used to put on her little, tight designer jeans, cotton top or
bodysuit underneath and sneakers, then swing a hammer doing repairs around the club
better than most men, while remaining a sophisticated lady.

I also admired her flair for business in addition to the elegant and classy way that she'd used her God-given assets to get what she wanted.

Shortly after I finished relocating from Atlantic to Myrtle Beach, I interviewed at Shrimp and Company seafood restaurant on the main strip. I was hired that same day by the restaurant owner for the last available job bussing tables. I then resigned from my grocery store cashier's job on Atlantic Beach!

I had no choice but to resign from Harris Teeter due to the unreliable commute back and forth to work. Since Shrimp and Company was a seasonal job, I also applied and was hired part-time as a server at Morrison's Cafeteria, along with my friends Toby and Robert.

In less than two weeks, I was promoted to head bus person at Shrimp and Company, managing two other bus-boys, which meant that I did not have to bus anymore tables.

Equally as importantly, the new promotion presented me with a divine opportunity to dress in my own clothes. My dramatic evolution began one Friday afternoon after work and cashing my check then deciding to take a short cut and stroll through the mall.

I figured I'd treat myself to a new outfit for that weekend hanging out with the my Chris Logan crew of friends. When I walked into JC Penney to look for some bargains, I was instantly drawn to the women's department, instead of going into the men's section. I purchased a black and white zebra-print dress just in case we went to Offshore to dance!

I also bought this really cute peach cotton halter top and a pair of white cotton chinos that I wore to work the following day. It turned out to not be a big deal at all when I thereafter started dressing as a girl at work!

My boss and co-workers were all nonjudgmental and very supportive at work. In addition, we shared good times hanging out after work, celebrating our birthdays and other special occasions.

My transition from dressing in male clothes to dressing everyday as a female was unexpectedly seamless enough for me to eventually start wearing light foundation, eyeliner and mascara during the day.

I also started using hair bonding glue to add length to my hair in the front, creating a cute asymmetrical Klymaxx-style curly bang which feminized my features!

After shopping at JC Penney that life-altering sunny afternoon and purchasing only female clothes, when I went home to visit, I decided to not remove the Fire and Ice red lipstick or my female clothes.

By the way, who but a rookie wears Fire and Ice flame red lipstick during the day? I did because I didn't know any better back then. As far as make-up and doing better when you know better, I currently wouldn't recommend wearing Fire and Ice during the day when you're first starting to transition.

I felt that since I was working and taking care of myself, if my mother had an issue with how I was presenting and rejected me, I could have always gone back to the life that I had built away from home.

Thankfully, my gender identity was no longer a constant bone of contention between my mother and I like it previously had been!

Back on the beach, I will never forget my boss, Rocky, at Shrimp and Company because although he was this beer-drinking, macho Italian man's man, he also possessed a heart of gold to have been so supportive towards me!

He interviewed me as a boy and he wasn't offended or blinked an eye when I started, less than three weeks later, wearing female clothes and complimentary make-up in order to express my true self at work! Great boss, I must say!

I distinctly recall that my first official "drag" performance was during Rocky's surprise birthday party that my co-workers and I organized for him at his favorite Mexican restaurant and lounge!

I surprised everyone with a performance of "I Wanna Dance with Somebody," which was my favorite latest hot song by diva Whitney Houston during that time! I wore a long, black curly wig that I had previously purchased for practice and a sexy off-the-shoulder, black lace, knee-high cocktail dress that I'd purchased from JC Penney formalwear!

I must admit that I was looking pretty good for my first performance, because I'd drawn inspiration from veteran performers that I admired like Erica Summers and Miss Gina Latate whom I'd seen whenever I'd successfully snuck into Offshore Drilling Company to see the show!

Rocky and my co-workers were entertained, especially after jokingly pulling out my fake boob and handing the B cup to Rocky at the end of the song!(By the way, snatching and revealing your boob fake or not isn't something that I would recommend to rookies.

During those days it was common for me to purchase costumes and hair to practice performing as my favorite singers, with the intention to one day after becoming of legal age to perform on the stage at the club!

My goal to perform at Offshore Drilling Company never occurred due to the town going into sort of a hibernation mode when the summer tourists left town.

Once Shrimp and Company closed for the off-season, I continued waitressing at Morrison's Cafeteria, which sustained me during the winter months when the other restaurant was closed.

As for Morrison's, there were also never any issues with my feminine appearance as long as my uniform was up to par! However, after the second summer season concluded, Myrtle Beach felt to me like a cold, ghost town. I was slightly depressed at the prospect of spending another harsh winter there, seemingly alone.

The harsh, cold winter rolling in did nothing to cool the heated incident that would soon occur with the beauty college administration about my student loan refund. The surreal scene between Chris Logan and I occurred after she was called to school by management resulting in my walking out because they'd wrongfully tried taking the money that was rightfully mine to use for living expenses after my tuition was paid.

During the conversation in their office where I felt ganged up on, I questioned them about the money that I was due to receive and then the owner, Chris Logan, kept making excuses that didn't make sense to me.

She then became very condescending and belligerent with me after her attempts at persuasion failed. I wasn't giving in to her because I was aware that they'd previously tried running that same game on another one of our classmates.

I will never forget that day when Chris Logan was actually called in to personally try and force me to sign over my refund check to them. I concluded the interrogation by refusing to sign the check and left the school with no intentions of returning.

A few years later I was not surprised that all of the Chris Logan Beauty College international chains lost their accreditation due to alleged embezzlement and fraud charges!

Upon my abrupt departure from Chris Logan Beauty College there wasn't anyone stopping me from seriously considering leaving the beach. Even the attentions of an older Italian gentleman I'd met could not persuade me to stay, though he invited me to spend time at his house and I also loved holding on tightly around his waist while cruising on his Harley-Davidson through Myrtle Beach and the boardwalk.

We were never intimate or even made out with each other, because we just enjoyed each other's company! However, spending time with him did not fill the void enough to make me stay and once I'd made the final decision to leave Myrtle Beach, South Carolina, to strike out on another adventure, I knew without a doubt that I was not moving back to my hometown Sumter!

After contemplating my options, I decided upon going to Atlanta, Georgia! It was bittersweet on the day I went to pick up what would be my last checks from the restaurants because my boss and co-workers at both jobs always made me feel like I was a part of the family.

Rocky was disappointed after I'd informed him that I would not be returning the following season to work for him because I was leaving the beach for good. My manager at Morrison's also expressed disappointment after I tendered my two-week notice to her.

After cashing my checks at the bank, I went to the bus station and purchased a one-way ticket to Atlanta, Georgia. Although I was not in contact with anyone in Georgia, nor did I have any idea of what would be waiting there for me once I arrived, I wasn't afraid to go.

All I knew during the process of concluding my time on the beach is that I was being guided toward a new beginning, and I would be guarded, protected in addition to being blessed with the ability to care for myself, no matter what.

Chapter Six

Atlanta, Georgia, 1988 to 1990

Looking back, it never really occurred to me that I should have been fearful after committing to not moving back home. It was totally opposite, because I was filled with anticipation and excitement on the bus ride to Atlanta from Myrtle Beach!

The bus ride provided an opportune time for me to assess my options moving forward upon arrival in Georgia. I decided to completely change my name to Tracee in response to my new attitude and figured that since my resources were so limited, I needed to conserve the coins that I did have until I had gotten a job.

The idea to temporarily stay in a shelter became the best thing for me to do until I at least obtained a cashiering or waitressing job somewhere – anywhere as long as it wasn't illegal or degrading.

Although I don't recall any of the events or stops that occurred during the bus trip, I do remember being excited stepping foot off the Greyhound bus onto the historical soil of Atlanta!

As I stood there absorbing the energy flow and waiting to retrieve the rest of my luggage, it was unexpected that another guardian angel would walk over to me and asked in a southern accent, "Do you need a taxi, young lady?"

"Sure!" I replied and continued, "Are you familiar with a local shelter that I would be safe at for a period of time until I find a job?"

"Yes ma'am, I am aware of a safe place that you can stay!" He replied as he started assisting with the bags from under the bus and then motioning me to his car to place all seven of them, including my Chris Logan Stylist Kit, into the trunk.

When we arrived at Milton Avenue after crossing the train tracks and then pulled into the driveway of a large building, he proceeded to explain that there were two separate shelters for the homeless operating in the converted schoolhouse.

The front was occupied by a private operator and the back gymnasium was managed by the city. He suggested that I would be safer if I checked into the privately operated facility before offering me his business card.

He then unexpectedly told me to call him after getting settled so that he could come by and pick me up to give me a proper tour of the city if I wanted! I took his card and stuffed it into my canvas shoulder bag and walked up the steps to enter a shelter for the first time in my life.

When I checked into the front facility, I presented myself as a female and I was relieved that my gender wasn't challenged by the staff that processed me into the building that night after viewing my Driver's License.

Out of concern for my safety, I felt that the possibility of being attacked by one of the male shelter patrons was decreased after being assigned to one of the women -only rooms on the second floor.

I awoke early every morning before the other women in order to have the bathroom to myself so that I could comfortably shave my face and use spray adhesive to secure my falsies into place that I'd previously started wearing in Myrtle Beach to keep the illusion of having breasts going.

When I first started using the spray adhesive to secure my falsies onto my chest it was only when we went out dancing on the beach, so after I'd started using it every day in Georgia my skin became very irritated to the constant usage.

I immediately stopped using the spray adhesive and started stuffing my bra with tissue. Thank goodness for the later discovery of padded bras and future electrolysis sessions!

Usually after I finished applying my make-up every morning, I began the business of understanding and familiarizing myself with my new environment to seek out prospective businesses in the area to apply for employment.

A week or so later after my arrival at the shelter, I was called into the office to speak with the operator, Peggy, who then questioned me about my gender. I didn't lie to her when she asked if I was a biological female.

I told her that I was anatomically male and that I did not initially stress that fact to them due to me being concerned for my safety. She seemed to have been understanding and compassionate after my revelation to her. However, I was moved out of the women-only room and placed in a dorm that was occupied by only one of the shelter staff members.

Once my sleeping accommodations were changed to a room immediately across the hall I was relieved that there were no further concerns about my safety as I slept through the night or my personal items because we were the only two assigned to that room.

I was also grateful that the staff didn't treat me any differently by insisting that I use the male restroom and showers after the gender conversation meeting in Peggy's office!

I continued my morning routine of getting up early to prepare myself for a new day in GA, as we affectionately called Atlanta, which I recall was the most desirable destination of most corps members after leaving Job Corps.

After becoming acclimated to the shelter routine, I began to venture outside of the shelter, that weekend taking my guardian angel up on his offer to take me on a tour of Atlanta. After using a pay phone to call and make arrangements with him, the following evening I got all dolled up in my dark Gloria Vanderbilt jeans, a black lace body blouse topped off with a black leather jacket for what would be my introduction to Midtown.

After dropping me off at the Krystal's Restaurant that used to be on Seventh Street and Peachtree, and because he was working the late shift that night he told me to call him later whenever I was ready to return back to the shelter.

I was pleasantly surprised by my guardian angel's generosity. I started out walking up Peachtree, absorbing and checking out the night life until I eventually ended up at Backstreet club for the first time.

When I walked into the showroom, there was Tommie Ross on the stage looking like a million dollars performing "Muscles" by Diana Ross with several gorgeous body builders that were on stage with her posing with weights while she performed.

She was gorgeous and her performance was inspiring to me. The spark was ignited to really start performing occurred in Myrtle Beach and the flames heated up after seeing Tommie Ross!

I was inspired and excited about the possibilities after seeing her perform, and I was also encouraged about the limitless opportunities that Atlanta, Georgia, would have to offer me!

As I sat watching the other performers, I reflected back on the Atlanta earth guardian angel driving a taxi cab appearing out of nowhere and allowing me to experience

Atlanta nightlife in a way that I have never considered possible!

Believe it or not, there were no strings attached to the kindness he displayed to me, going above and beyond the call of duty to voluntarily give me the opportunity to see the city without feeling pressured to be intimate with him.

Neither did he ever request a single penny for driving me around Atlanta! I strongly believe that he knew that I was transgender and it did not seem to have mattered to him because he was a kind guy that was only concerned with my safety and well-being.

Later that evening I called and he immediately returned to Krystal's to pick me up for the drive back to the shelter. I never saw him again after that night. Although I don't recall his name, I will always remember what a gentleman he was and I cherish with fondness the special way that he made me feel upon my arrival to Atlanta!

When I arrived back at the shelter, I was informed by night staff security that I had missed curfew. However, since it was my first infraction against the rules, I was given a warning after promising that I would never break the curfew rules again.

Since I never liked the experience of relinquishing to someone else the power to dictate my comings and goings, I was determined to get a job so that I could afford to get my own place as soon as possible!

It never occurred to me until much later that the majority of the people residing in the shelter were either dealing with domestic violence or drug addictions, which contributed to them being homeless.

Living in a shelter was a completely different experience for me and knowing that it was only going to be temporary made it somewhat tolerable.

As time moved forward and as a result of my surrounding environment not presenting any job opportunities, I knew that I'd have to expand my search the following week. I started learning how to use the public transit system to get where I needed to go and start seriously submitting applications to businesses on the transit line.

One particular sunny, beautiful Sunday afternoon as I was sitting underneath a huge oak tree on the only bench in front of the shelter, circling Help Wanted Ads that I was planning to inquire about employment the following day.

After I finished selecting several prospective employment opportunities, I turned my attention back to the steamy paperback copy of "Dream Girl: My Life As a Supreme" by Mary Wilson that I had started reading on the bus ride to Georgia from Myrtle Beach.

Shortly after reading a chapter or two, my reading was eventually interrupted by this tall and sexy, dark chocolate guy, who had the Tyrese Gibson smoldering and intense look, sat down uninvited on the bench next to me.

Then immediately, smoothly, he began complimenting me in a Southern drawl that seemed to draw me in. "Well, hello there, beautiful!"

I looked up from my book and he continued smiling from ear to ear, continuing, "I haven't seen you around here before. Where did you come from?"

I sarcastically replied, "I've never seen you either. Where did you come from?"

He leaned in with those piercing eyes and melodically replied, "I'm from Georgia and my name is Hilton. What's your name?"

I smiled back and replied. "Hello, Hilton, my name is Tracee, and I just moved here from South Carolina."

He further inquired, "Are you staying in the front shelter?"

"Yes I am," I replied emphatically. He inched closer to me and then jokingly continued as if we had known each other forever, "Has Peggy converted you into her cult yet?"

Smiling as he leaned even closer looking into my eyes and continuing, "The cult members have this zombie-like far off stare. Let me see your eyes."

During the conversation, he alleged that Peggy was suspected of being a cult leader that forced the people living at her shelter to go to her church every Sunday plus three times during the week in order to indoctrinate them into her cult.

After generally conversing for an hour or so, Hilton and I eventually ended up walking to Church's chicken for dinner and then having an impromptu picnic in the park where we continued our conversation into the early evening.

I should have gotten a clue when he shared with me his regret that he was temporarily living at the shelter due to some domestic issues between he and his wife who had previously left town with his little boy and girl.

I also should have delved in deeper to get more information about her reasons for having to abruptly take their children running away to another state, but I chose to give him the benefit of the doubt since we'd just met.

Upon wrapping up our evening in the park, I still wasn't sure if Hilton knew that I was transgender or not. All I knew was that after that night, we started spending as much time together as possible, whenever we were able to, until I felt the need to confirm my gender identity to him.

I didn't expect to be informed that he knew exactly what he was getting into after he'd approached me on the bench the first time! In his eyes, according to him, I was a beautiful and special kind of girl that he wanted to get to know!

During our time together, I eventually shared with Hilton the frustrations that I was feeling about not having any success in getting a job. After I told him that I was job hunting in the city limits, he suggested that I try Sandy Springs, Georgia.

He also gave me the bus and train schedules that I needed to get there. The following morning, after I had gotten appropriately dressed to go out on interviews, Hilton walked me to the bus stop.

My intentions were to submit as many applications that were required until I'd gotten a job somewhere and, fortunately, my first interview was at Burger King. Of course, due to my previous experience working on the beach, I was confident going in that I was also qualified for the job as I walked through the front entrance.

I was overjoyed and happy that I'd taken one step closer to accomplishing my second short-term goal of getting my own place and moving out of the shelter when I was hired on the spot for a cashier and front service position!

When I returned to the shelter later that afternoon after my interview, I shared the great news with Hilton about my new job. He was proud that he'd contributed to my employment success! However excited we both were, I wasn't able to hang out with him late into the evening that night because I was scheduled to start work early the following morning. So, we agreed to meet later that evening after I arrived back at the shelter from my first day at work.

I must have been really tired after training all day on my new job because I overslept during my nap after work later that afternoon. The following morning on the walk to the bus stop, Hilton told me that he had thrown watermelon seeds through the window to try to wake me up to come outside to hang out with him, but he was unsuccessful in waking me from the deep sleep the entire night.

He made me promise not to oversleep again, because he had something very important that he wanted to discuss with me. I wondered why he was being so formal all of a sudden, so the following afternoon after work, I made sure that I didn't oversleep.

After my nap later that afternoon, I rushed outside to meet him on the bench to be presented with an unexpected proposal, suggesting that we become exclusive with each other. Looking back, I was in my early 20s and really naive to fall for only the second guy to have approached me. It was what it was and I can't change the past.

Except for work, we became almost inseparable, just hanging out getting to know each other listening to Soft Rock groups that included Journey, Steve Perry, Whitesnake and 38 Special.

Hilton introduced me to timeless love songs like "A Heart Needs a Second Chance," "Foolish Heart," and "Who's Crying Now?", which are all currently on my IPOD.

Pressing on at the shelter, since I was intimate with the circumstances that contributed to me being in there, I never judged Hilton when he told me about the events that lead to him being there, and the fact that he'd also impressed me when he took me to meet his Jehovah's Witness family, introducing me to his mother, stepfather and four brothers, sealing the deal. I'd never before been taken and introduced to the family of a guy I was sexually attracted to!

According to a conversation between Hilton and I many years later, his family did not know that I was transsexual, other than his oldest brother, Charles, who we used to often hang out with after he returned back to Georgia from the Navy.

Charles even went as far as to have commented to Hilton in my presence that he liked me, because he'd observed how much I cared for him, so it did not matter to Charles that I was not a biological female.

His mother also liked me and thought that I had a positive influence on Hilton and his attitude after suggesting to us that we get married. She also went as far as framing and prominently displaying an 8-by-10 photo of me in her living room that was given to her by Hilton!

Hilton also informed me those many years later that she had no idea I was transsexual until way after we had broken up for the final time. According to Hilton, she was really surprised that I was not a biological woman and that she also accepted his attractions to transsexual women that he dated after me because she had never before observed him as happy and stable as he was when we were together.

As time passed, Hilton also shared with me that it seemed that whenever he was with biological women, he would always end up in trouble and doing destructive activities and drugs.

Although Hilton was handsome and irresistible, in the beginning, after officially becoming a couple, we only engaged in kissing and whispering sweet nothings during our make-out opportunities.

I felt safe and protected being with him, because he always made sure that I had everything that I needed and none of the other guys ever messed with me because they respected Hilton!

In the meantime, back at the shelter a couple of weeks after I began my new job, Peggy and her crew became more aggressive with their relentless attempts to intimidate me into attending her church. She issued me an ultimatum one afternoon during another private meeting in her office with one of her cronies, stating bluntly, "Tracee, if you do not attend worship service this upcoming Sunday, you are going to have to immediately leave my shelter."

As I sat there listening to her threats, I was reminded that my initial intentions were to only be there temporarily anyway. Also due to me not feeling comfortable with being forced to attend her church, I knew that I had to quickly come up with another plan so that I would not have to load onto their church bus to be escorted on Sunday morning to her upcoming indoctrination ritual.

I also knew, sitting there processing my next step, that I would have to appease her in order to buy enough time to come up with a Plan B. So, I smiled as I promised, "Peggy, I am finally adjusted to my new work schedule so I will be ready bright and early come Sunday morning for church!"

After the meeting with Peggy, Hilton was waiting for me outside on our bench and when I told him she'd just threatened that if I do not attend her church on Sunday, I'll have to leave the shelter.

He laughed and teased me in his own charming way. "I warned you about Peggy and I must admit that I'm surprised you held out this long not going to her church sooner!"He then suggested that I should move into the back shelter where he was staying.

Of course and without thinking, I agreed and he helped me to immediately move my things from Peggy's homeless facility to the Task Force for the Homeless City Shelter in the back.

Up to that point, I had not seen the sleeping arrangements inside the back shelter. I never knew until that first night they'd used mats that were pulled out from underneath the stage to sleep on.

However, the five staff members had beds on the stage behind the big curtain and the shelter director slept in a small office off to the side that was converted into a bedroom, which is where he allegedly was with his girlfriend during the times that he disappeared for weeks at a time on crack binges.

That was a totally whole new experience for me, sleeping on the gymnasium floor. At least Peggy's shelter had individual rooms, beds and showers. In the city shelter, the girls bathed in the women's bathroom sinks and the men bathed in the other restroom.

I realized during that humbling experience that growing up, I really took for granted and didn't appreciate all of the hard work that my mother did to ensure that my brother and I were always in a safe and clean environment. That moment of awareness caused me to be more appreciative of my mother's sacrifices to provide for us.

If bathing in a small sink wasn't enough, I also came in closer contact with drug addicts and criminals. I'm extremely grateful for that experience, because it introduced me to a lifestyle that I did not want to become my permanent future.

After the first night in the city shelter and being faced with the reality of what life could be for me if I didn't make the right choices, I became even more determined, persistently working harder to get up out of there, ASAP!

I would not have been able to endure those circumstances if it were not for Hilton being there as my protector, so I decided that I would make the best of the situation and stash away my money so that I could move out of that gymnasium for good!

My goal was to use the first pay check to rent a room at a boarding house until I could afford an apartment.

There was another transgender person on the city shelter staff named Tee, who was the shelter drag mother, so to speak. She had a crush on Gary, Hilton's running partner, and she took care of our personal items that were stored underneath the stage during the day when we were out and the shelter was closed.

I welcomed Tee designating herself my big sister because she was a nice person. I was amazed to witness her taking clothes that were donated to the shelter, deconstructing, and then hand-sewing the materials, creating one-of-a-kind designer garments, one of which she unexpectedly gifted me.

The dress was an original, sexy form-fitting, Roaring Twenties-inspired charcoal grey chiffon number that was perfect for a song and routine(still undetermined)that I would do when I entered the weekly contest at the "Marquette" that she'd previously told me about!

I was anxious about getting a private space of our own and, as fate would have it, things did not go as planned.

Peggy lost the lease to the front shelter and the city secured the lease to the entire building and another location in the West End called West Hunter Shelter, where Tee and most of the other staff members were transferred to. As the events transpired, I was approached by the Task Force for The Homeless program manager, who often visited the shelter for inspections and meetings with the director and staff. I will just call him G.E.

At first, I thought that he might have observed some leadership potential in me after offering me an unsolicited part-time paid staff position to help coordinate the move from the gymnasium to the front building of those desiring to stay at that location.

As previously admitted, I was young and naïve back then. It was well known to others that Hilton and I were planning to leave the shelter, and I did not find out until much later that G.E. had been interested in dating Hilton for quite some time before my arrival on the scene.

After Hilton informed G.E. of our pending departure, G.E. figured that he would use me to get to Hilton. Unaware of his ulterior motives for offering me the job, I accepted the position to become assistant director to the shelter director.

The job offer was a win-win situation for me, because in addition to getting a weekly check to add to my bi-weekly salary from Burger King, we were also given a private room that was padlocked and secured whenever we were not in it.

After accepting the new position, I worked long, hard hours establishing and organizing the new facility, with limited assistance from the director because it was suggested by others that he was on one of his many drug binges.

On the evenings during the adjustment period to my new job, it felt almost like the Twilight Zone as I walked the halls, observing and directing the patrons that were obviously strung-out on drugs, alcohol and dealing with mental health issues.

I don't know why I wasn't more afraid to interact with them, nor ever threatened by any of them because they seemed to be aware that I was there to help. However, I once had to briefly confront this strung-out, enraged woman in the shower room who was terrorizing the other patrons.

Thankfully, she was coherent enough to understand me when I threatened to call law enforcement if she didn't compose herself and act accordingly.

Since I've always had a knack for organization, it didn't take too long to organize the clientele. I worked closely with another recently hired, cool and down-to-earth patron named Danny, who managed the volunteer kitchen staff, that immediately started preparing hot homemade meals!

I also worked in the administration offices with another part-time staff member named Gino from Jamaica. Other than the judgment and moralistic pedestal he often took, he was okay to work with. As I busied myself establishing a routine in the new facility and getting the patrons adjusted to the new environment, unbeknownst to me until much later, Hilton was out stealing and robbing others, in addition to being a dog in heat when he was supposed to be out looking for a job.

At that time, I didn't have any reasons not to trust him when he was gone all day. It never occurred to me then that he was seeing other people until his infidelity was confirmed some weeks later when Gino and I were working in the office during the day while the shelter was closed.

The drama all unfolded after this woman pulled up in a shiny convertible sports car outside of the office window and laid on her horn. I thought that she was looking for one of the other patrons as I stuck my head out of the office window to inquire if I could assist her.

I thought it was strange when she asked for Hilton and abruptly left after I asked who she was to leave a message after informing her that Hilton wasn't there. Although I trusted Hilton up to that point, I questioned why would he have her coming to where we were living to pick him up if in fact they were acquainted?

In less than five minutes, she returned and continuously started blowing her horn again and then became loud and rude after she was informed for the second time that Hilton had not returned yet.

I remained professional until after she'd started name-calling and cursing. I threatened to call the police if she did not immediately leave the premises. After she uttered a few more choice profane words, she sped off.

An hour or so later when I was emptying my desk garbage can in the waste management receptacle outside, she sped into the driveway and got out of her car to confront me. I was beyond annoyed at that point because I had no idea who that enraged person was. Obviously, she knew something about me and Hilton, otherwise she would not have been reacting in such a threatening manner.

I grabbed a long metal pipe from the ground by the garbage can to defend myself ,if need be, while informing her, "Girl, I don't know who you are, but if you don't back the hell away from me, you will certainly come to know that you have chosen the wrong one to fuck with today."

She jumped back into her car and angrily replied as she backed onto the street and then sped away! "I know exactly who you are, bitch, and I will see you again."

What the hell? Since I didn't recall there ever being any previous interaction between me and that person before, my frame of mind walking up the stairs back into the building was simply anger that I'd put my trust in a guy that I really did not know very well.

I was most of all angered that he'd blatantly disrespected and placed me in an unpleasant compromising position to be confronted by some strange woman on my job.

Wait, hold up … there's more! During the incident with the woman, it never occurred to me that she was a transsexual and not a biological female as I'd assumed.

Of course Hilton's boy, Gino, brought it to my attention immediately after I returned to the office and informed him of what had just occurred on my trip to empty the trash.

I fumed throughout the rest of the day after the confrontation with that lunatic, obviously fatal attraction transsexual. I planned to let Hilton have it upon his return. Later that evening after confronting Hilton and unconsciously creating another destructive pattern, I foolishly believed him when he told me that she had previously just given him a ride from Thomasville, Georgia, after he'd missed the last bus. I bought the story hook line and sinker then went on about my business.

After several months, Tee left West Hunter and moved back into the Milton Avenue shelter. She'd been told by G.E. that she would not be able to continue remaining on staff because her obviously transgender identity caused a negative response and reaction from G.E.'s boss.

G.E. claimed that some of the patrons at West Hunter supposedly complained about Tee's appearance – dressing in women's clothing. I didn't believe a bit of that crap, because from my observations the patrons liked Tee very much.

Tee was understandably unhappy that an openly gay man had given her a lame excuse for being demoted and, most of all she could not continue being who she was because so-called other homeless people were offended by her presence.

Back on Milton Avenue, my co-workers were all anticipating conflict between Tee and I upon her return, but we were sisters and I did not feel that I had to compete with her for anything because we had different tastes in men, goals and aspirations.

I'd observed that Tee was at times wild and more uninhibited about the things she'd engaged in and so were the people she'd chosen to do them with. I was a bit more reserved and paired off with Hilton, so we got along very well.

Due to our mutual respect, Tee and I proved the naysayers wrong by joining forces and running that place like a Motor City auto assembly line!

I recall receiving great pleasure helping and doing for others since a very early age. I also remember back when I started cooking dinner for our house, I'd fixed more than enough to take and feed another household that was less blessed with food as we were.

Working at the shelter gave me an opportunity to continue my passion for giving positive energy to others! I really enjoyed my jobs working the early shift at Burger King and then managing the shelter during the evenings. Multitasking, honey!

There were times that I would not see Hilton until way late in the night. It so happened that once, when I'd gotten off from Burger King earlier than expected one afternoon, I walked into the room that we shared, and there was Hilton and a biological female who had recently arrived at the shelter sitting intimately close to each other on our bed.

Hilton and the girl were obviously startled when I entered the room, and I truly believe that if I had not walked in on them, they would have gone to the next level with each other. I calmly told the girl to leave and never set foot in my room ever again. As she scurried pass me out the room without saying a word, the infatuation cloak immediately dissolved making it clear to me that I was in over my head.

The conversation which followed revealed that I was trapped in a situation that I had not experienced before. Admittedly, I was angered beyond measure, going off and warning Hilton, "If you want to entertain other females, do it in the streets and not where I reside and if you ever disrespect me or threaten my job like this again by bringing a client from the shelter into our bedroom, we are done."

Hilton nonchalantly replied, "What are you getting so upset about, Meat, we weren't doing anything but just talking."

I replied, emphatically, "What the hell do you think you're doing in here with that girl in our bedroom, Hilton talking or not. Do you think that I'm stupid *and* blind?"

He responded in an agitated manner, calling me the nickname that he'd previously given me as he stood up and walked towards my direction, "Look, Meat, I told you that nothing happened, so I'm not going to continue this conversation with you no longer."

"No, you look Hilton, if there is something or someone else that you want, please don't let me interfere with your getting them, because you can 'Just Talk', as you claim, with anybody that you want to talk to. Just do me a favor and wait until after I have moved out."

He stopped in front of me, blocking my way as his expression changed from agitated to anger as he replied."Where do you think you're going, Meat?"He backed me up against the wall and threatened, "You not going no damn where without me, Tracee." Then he casually exited the room, closing the door behind him.

Since Hilton was a Bruce Lee and karate fanatic, I was afraid to leave the relationship upon previously witnessing him roundhouse-kicking a guy unconscious. Hilton thought the stranger was showing a little too much interest in me while we were waiting at the bus stop one afternoon after visiting his parents' house.

I was also concerned about the violent and vindictive reaction that most likely would have occurred if he continued feeling that I was seriously contemplating leaving the shelter without him.

I also knew that I would not have lived a moment of peace if I left without him before making other living arrangements as far as possible away from Milton Avenue.

I may have still been slightly naïve during those days, but I wasn't stupid. Hilton was the only person that I really knew in Georgia other than my co-workers at Burger King, and I assumed they were aware that I was transsexual, so I really didn't feel comfortable talking to them about my personal business.

Hilton was the first guy that I had ever really lived with on such an unrestrictive level. His threats that afternoon revealed him to be the kind of person who thought that once he'd gotten his hooks into you, you're not going anywhere without some drama.

I didn't have any experiences to draw insight from on how to deal with the problems that are most likely to occur in one form or another when you live with a guy that you're romantically involved with.

However, after that incident with the girl in our room, I became more aware of my surroundings and also more observant of Hilton's comings and goings. Condoms remained our best friend!

I was no longer living the innocent and carefree life that I'd previously lived on the beach, hanging out with my childhood friends. The time had arrived for me to start growing up and becoming more responsible for myself and my choices. So I also started paying more attention to the events and activities that were occurring between G.E. and Hilton.

Overtime, I observed that Hilton started hanging out more regularly at G.E.'s house with his friends, or so he claimed. When I questioned him about G.E. and the interest he had in him, he reassured me that he was just using G.E. for money and to buy him weed.

I'd never suspected anything more between them because he continuously reassured me that he liked and was attracted to soft and pretty girls like me, not masculine, beard-wearing men like G.E.

So, I didn't think twice that time Hilton called me and claimed that there was a stabbing incident at West Hunter, where he had been hanging out with G.E., and he had to go to the emergency room to seek medical attention for the stabbing victim.

The following morning, he claimed that he had spent the whole night in the busy emergency room with G.E. and the stabbing victim. Yeah, right! I will never know what really occurred between Hilton and G.E., nor will I know if he was really with G.E. that night. All I knew is that his story was very suspicious to me.

Although the shelter director and other staff members were encouraged to live at the homeless facility, I knew that I could not continue living and also working there after resolving that I didn't believe the emergency room story.

It was time to go! I started completing my plan to make other living arrangements after revisiting a boarding house on Capitol Avenue that I saw advertised on the bus line after getting off one day from Burger King.

I didn't know until later that the boarding house was operated by Pop and Son's, who also owned and operated a club that was welcoming to trans people. Hilton had taken me there once.

The room was affordable and it had a separate entrance from the main house, which made it like a small studio apartment with a private bathroom. It was also conveniently located on the bus line right up the street from a Muslim restaurant that served the most delicious homemade tartar sauce and hot fish sandwiches that I had had since leaving my hometown in South Carolina.

Although I was still apprehensive about moving with Hilton, the feelings that I felt back at the shelter later that night when we were packing our belongings to leave were those of joy and excitement!

Several weeks after we finished moving, G.E. came up with some lame excuse about budget cuts that discontinued my salary. I knew that he was actually disappointed about not being able to get what he expected from Hilton sexually.

I really didn't mind discontinuing my employment at the shelter because I was ready to cut ties and totally move on anyway. Since I'd expected the inevitable, I also had already gotten another part-time job styling hair in an all-female stylists salon called "The Hairem" in East Point.

I also eventually evolved from the day shift to a newly created overnight shift, running the drive-through at Burger King, which was perfect for me! Although we'd severed ties with the shelter I remained friendly with Tee whom had no connection to the hair salon. After we had gotten settled into our new place, we invited Tee and Hilton's brother, Charles, over for dinner and then hanging out while the guys drank their 40-ounce Mickey Malt Liquors, climbing trees, acting crazy!

We spent the evening talking about the past, present and future. As time passed, I learned that the much older salon owner, Barry, was interested in more than me just styling hair at his salon.

Barry unexpectedly made his move on a slow Tuesday, when he decided to close for the day and tricked me into going to his house for a quick pit-stop on our way to drop me off at the train station after work.

Since we were not independent service providers and working totally on commission, I didn't mind him choosing to close down shop so early in the afternoon. On our drive to what I expected to be MARTA, he sprung the invitation on me, insisting that it would only take a minute to locate what he was looking for.

What was I going to do? My employer was kind enough to have given me a lift after work and I didn't want to be rude.

Once we arrived at his impressive home, he then suggested during the tour that I could be living in a beautiful, five-bedroom, multilevel luxurious house with him if I wanted to.

He seemed to be respectful and backed off after I told him that I was involved in a relationship, but I eventually had to resign because he became resentful that he wasn't able to persuade me to come his way.

I'm not sure if Barry was aware that I was transsexual or not back then and it really did not matter, because in addition to him being old enough to have possibly been my grandfather, I was not attracted to him in a sexual manner.

Although this could have been a good opportunity for me to completely sever ties with Hilton, I didn't want to use Barry to do so. Neither was I in the mood to go through the process of explaining to Barry that I was transsexual, resulting in quite possibly losing my job, which would have opened up another can of worms that I really did not need to deal with at that time.

I didn't feel the need to explain my gender identity to Barry, because it wasn't his right to know. I also knew that if my gender didn't matter to him, I was going to have to put up or shut up if I moved into his home.

I just knew by his personality that he didn't play any games, so I wasn't going there with him. No way! Once again, and although they may have had their own motives, I seemed to have attracted another much older guy somewhere in his late 50s or early 60s during a major transitional phase in my life for some reason or another. I'm not complaining, I'm just explaining.

Now, as I reflect on my history, I understand why and am grateful that more mature and responsible men are attracted to me.

Overtime, I began to see clearly that Hilton was the type of guy that used his handsome, suave looks and streetwise charm to be kept by the girls and women that he had been previously involved with.

According to Hilton, most of his previous involvements insisted on working and taking care of him while he did whatever he wanted while they were on the job bringing in the regular income.

Hilton wasn't the first guy who informed me that he liked being taken care of by women. If he'd shared that information upon our introduction like the others he would have been toast as far as I'm concerned.

Although I was inexperienced back then, I've never been the type to take care of a grown-ass man and use my hard earned money to buy his affections just to say I have one.

I insisted that Hilton get a steady job other than the hit-or-miss schemes and burglaries that he and his friend, Gary, were doing for money.

Since I wanted him to start contributing financially, I encouraged him to apply for an open position at the Burger King where I was working.

To my surprise during the application process it was revealed to me that Hilton was illiterate.

The explanation Hilton gave for his low education level was that since he'd rebelled against his parents' rules while in high school, he was thrown out of the house. I was astonished that he wasn't able to read.

After he brought the employment application back to our room that afternoon I had to basically fill it out for him. His illiteracy wasn't too much of an issue with me at first and it never occurred to me what effects that it would eventually have on our relationship; he would become even more controlling, obsessive and possessive.

Our main priority at that point was him getting a job. So, I became his personal reference then Hilton interviewed and was hired for the job at Burger King. During the application process we both decided that it would be better if our co-workers did not know that we were in a relationship together.

It was really strange working closely with Hilton and not being able to express our true feelings towards each other. However, we seemed to have managed to keep our relationship a secret. I knew that we were being successful at concealing that we were a couple because, I'd occasionally observed some of our female co-workers overtly flirting with him during the shifts.

Everything was going as we'd planned until the day after Hilton lost his keys and took mine to make copies for himself during his break. Fortunately, as I walked to the bus stop to go home, I discovered that I did not have my keys after checking my bag to make sure that I had everything before getting on the bus.

Oh crap! I had no choice but to go back to the job to retrieve my keys from Hilton. As I turned to walk back up to the restaurant from the end of the driveway, I wondered how I was going to pull it off, approaching him in the middle of the shift change without getting crossed looks from our nosy co-workers.

When I opened the side door to walk back in, it came to me that I would pretend that I had forgotten to clock out. I knew that I would look suspicious if I didn't immediately leave after pretending to check my timecard, which became the inevitable time presented for the cat to come out of the bag revealing our living arrangements.

There being nothing left for me to do but just approach the situation head-on because I had to get my keys. Although I tried to be as discrete as possible when I approached him at the deep fryer to request the keys, you could have heard a pin drop as the other conversations ceased and the jowls of our co-workers literally dropped to the floor as they stood at their cash registers and at the broiler when he reached into his pocket to give me the keys.

I don't know what was said after I left to go home after work that afternoon. However, I am most certain that there were very interesting conversations held whenever we were not at work. Oh, well! Thankfully, we didn't have any issues with management or our co-workers after it was revealed that we were together.

Once, on a very rare occasion that we were scheduled to work the same shift, after a long day at work when we returned to our room and found that we had been burglarized. We were even more infuriated after our transgender neighbors identified Gary as the person they'd witnessed kicking in the door and carrying out the only television that we had, along with our mad money bank, which was obviously not stashed away good enough.

Hilton seemed surprised and angered that his crack-head friend would steal from us. I don't know why he was so disappointed, considering that they had previously perpetrated the very same crimes against so many other unsuspecting, innocent people.

Hilton did not reveal to me until after that incident that they were also breaking and entering into people's homes while they were usually at work. Once, according to Hilton, when they'd broken into an apartment, the person was still at home and confronted them with a baseball bat. They immediately left the scene of the crime without any further incident.

I felt violated when Gary broke into our room, so I understood what those other people felt whose homes they'd burglarize. Hilton went off looking for Gary and swore to physically harm him upon sight, which he never did.

I was angry that Hilton knew that Gary was strung out on drugs and still allowed him to visit us and learn our schedule. Although I was angry with Hilton, I realized that being mad at him for what his so-called friend had done wasn't fair, so we bought another television and he promised that he would never again bring anyone into our home that he knew was on drugs.

Things were going well between Hilton and I until he started taking me for granted and began irresponsibly hanging out late at night, lying about where he had been and with whom he was with.

After a period of time, he also didn't want to go to work. Hilton was the first guy up to that point that I have ever lived with as boyfriend and girlfriend, so I was unaware of what the rules of engagement were when you cohabitate with a lover.

However, although our relationship was an unfamiliar situation for me, I soon saw Hilton for what he was, which was someone that did not have any goals or future plans of advancement because he was content with being illiterate and using his handsome looks to be taken care of by desperate women.

Hilton's actions were unforgivably unacceptable and I made it clear to him that I was not at all happy about his irresponsible actions. His response was to become more aggressive and threatening as time progressed.

His aggression eventually didn't matter to me, because eventually he committed the ultimate deal breaker when he'd stayed out all night and did not return home until the following morning.

I give him credit for having his lie down pat when I questioned him about where he was all night. First, the story was that he had spent the night at his brother Charles' apartment after they'd gotten drunk.

I was quite insulted that he thought I believed that lie for a nanosecond. I finally convinced him that he did not have to worry about me staying mad if he just told the truth.

He admitted that he was with his brother at a club where they met this mother-and-daughter blonde duo.

They'd danced together at the club and were later invited by them back to their apartment where he spent the night with the mother. I immediately went off and started pummeling into him with fists of fury with no fear of his retaliation.

Let us just say that the incident concluded with him getting hit in the lower-back with a large portable radio as he ran out of the apartment because I was beyond furious that he'd disrespected me and thought that there would be no consequences.

When he returned later that night, suspecting that I'd cooled down by that time, I informed him in no uncertain terms, "Hilton, you have been doing your thing from the moment that we met and I've chosen to be in denial about a lot of what you were doing."

I proceeded to inform him that I was not going to deny what he'd admitted to doing, so I needed him to take his things and go back to where he'd slept the night before. His demeanor immediately changed from apologetic to threatening. "Meat, if you think that I'm going to leave so you can bring another nigger up in here, I will set this motherfucker on fire with both of you up in it first."

I defiantly replied, "Hilton, there is no other guy but you. I am just not going to continue risking my life being intimate with someone that I know who is out there indiscriminately slinging your dick into whatever Hole you can find."

At that point, he became extremely hostile when he replied, "Meat, you not listening to me if you think that I will just let you walk away so easily." He bolted the door lock and removed the keys as he continued, "If we not going to be together, I can guarantee you will not be with another nigger, Meat."

Since I'd seen Hilton's vengeance before, I shivered with fear at the thought of his response to seek revenge against me. But at that moment I was willing to take the chance and endure his vengeful actions.

There was absolutely no way that I would tolerate being mistreated like that by him no matter how cute he was.

When I tried to walk past him to leave the room, he grabbed me, throwing me on the bed. His sole intentions were to permanently blind me by taking his fingers and trying to literally gouge out my eyes.

As he continued trying to get access to my eyes, he was telling me, "No other nigger will ever look into these eyes like I did."

I couldn't get away from his strong grip. All I could do was lie on my stomach and try to protect my eyes with my arms, covering them to block his fingers. When he turned me over to face him, I started wildly kicking and swinging to escape his grasp!

As I fought to free myself, I prayed to God to help me. My prayers were answered when Hilton finally gave up and backed away. Before he left the room, he grabbed my purse and took my driver's license and the money from my wallet. He then threatened as he ran out of the room, "If I ever see you with another nigger, you will be sorry, Meat."

Fortunately, I managed to protect my eyes and, thankfully, all I had were red and lavender bruises on my arms that cocoa butter eventually erased.

I was relieved that he'd left and I'd remained in one solid piece without any permanent injuries! I sat there on the bed for several minutes, in disbelief that he was actually trying to blind me just because I'd refused to become one of those girls that would endure mental and physical mistreatment just to be able to say that they have a man.

Although this was the first time that I had ever lived with a guy before, being abused by one was all too familiar. I did not like it then and I do not tolerate it now. After the eye-gouging incident, I figured that I'd go to the Driver's License Bureau to get a replacement temporary identification card the following day and renew my license later because I assumed that I'd have to take a driving test.

I am so happy that I had not cashed my check yet that day. It was hidden it in a secret compartment in my purse that Hilton missed when he searched my wallet, so I wasn't worried about eating and paying my rent.

I remained in the room the rest of the day, afraid and concerned about staying alone that night because I had no idea of what Hilton was planning next. I braced myself for whatever act of violence might be coming, having no choice but to spend the night being afraid yet vigilant, fully dressed and alert, waiting for the black crows to arrive signaling turmoil and tumultuous times.

The next morning, after applying make-up, finding the right long-sleeved blouse to conceal my battle scars and topping it off with an over-sized hat in addition to imitation Jackie Onassis dark glasses, I went downtown to replace my Identification Card.

I didn't allow myself to be too caught up in being happy that I'd made it through the night okay and, as expected, when I opened the room door to leave, there was Hilton standing outside armed with large stones, bricks and whatever else he could find to attack me with.

I thank God that I responded fast enough to close the door. He was seriously focused on physically messing me up as much as possible.

He pelted the room with rocks, stones, bricks and whatever else he could find from the construction site in the next yard. I could hear him saying, in between the loud objects crashing up against the room, "Yeah, I told you that I wasn't going nowhere Meat, did I not?"

I refused to respond to him the entire five minutes or so he continued throwing the stones and rocks. When he finally stopped and left, I was even more fearful of what was to come later. I knew that I'd have to move to a neighborhood that was unknown to Hilton as soon as possible.

I lived in constant fear for several days, with him popping up out of the blue at random times, I assume to see if there was another guy there with me.

I also assume that his concerns were a result of him mistakenly thinking that I was a liar and cheater like he'd been. As for another guy, please! My mind was on making more money and getting an apartment.

I was grateful when Hilton finally stopped terrorizing me after almost a week living under siege. I tried to go on with my life and prayed every day that he would not return. Although I could not afford to immediately move to a new place because I'd already paid an advance on the current room, I refused to allow fear of him stop me from moving forward with my life.

So, I took my valuables to work with me and left all the others with the transgender neighbors that had witnessed Gary breaking into our room. I also decided that I would go ahead and enter the talent show at The Marquette and use the prize money to help reach my goals of relocating a lot sooner!

Yes, I did say use the prize money. I was confident that I was going to win because I needed that money to complete my plans to relocate as soon as possible!

I already had the perfect, one-of-a-kind designer costume that Tee had given me to wear in the contest, and since "Mercedes Boy" by Pebbles was sultry and sophisticated, I was set to go win some cash!

The night that I went to the "Marquette" for the first time by myself to perform in the contest would be the night that someone from my past would unexpectedly re-emerge from the dark shadows.

I never in my wildest dreams imagined that the night of my first performance in Georgia would also be the night that the first guy I have ever cried for after our relationship ended would reappear out of nowhere.

Looking back, I think that I might have seen someone that resembled him on the train several months prior, on the night that Hilton and Tee took me to the "Marquette" for the first time to dance and see the show.

But, I wasn't sure that *was* him on the train and since I did not want to turn around to stare at another guy, I just brushed it off as my imagination playing tricks on me.

Any who, I was excited about performing in my new haute couture costume when I walked into the club on the night of the contest as "Private Joy" by Prince was ironically playing, taking me back to the days at The Candy Shop with my friends!

As I made my way around the bar after being greeted by the assistant manager, Miles, at the front entrance and directed by him to go to the dressing room upstairs, I was surprised to see my former boyfriend from Job Corps, Durk, sitting upstairs on the banquette when I reached the top of the stairs, as if he was there waiting for me!

Although the upstairs room was somewhat dark, this time I was certain that it was him sitting alone. Old, unresolved feelings came rushing over me. I did everything that I could to maintain my composure when he called my name and asked in his nonchalant, cool manner, "What's up Tony, how you doing?"

At first, I could not believe that he was really in a gay club, and as I stood there, stunned, my legs started to feel like they were about to give out, so I sat on the edge of the banquette next to him to keep from falling, as I responded, "What are you doing here, Durk?"

He smiled broadly and responded, "I previously saw you on the train with some other people dressed up in a way that I've never seen you dressed before, and I knew that you would most likely end up here, so I followed you to be sure."

I replied, unsurprised. "I thought that I saw you on the train one night!"

He chuckled. "You looked right at me, Tony, and since I wasn't sure if you were with that dude who got on the train behind you and your friend that you sat with, I decided not to approach you because I knew that I would see you again."

"The guy that you saw shadowing us like a ninja was my former boyfriend who fashioned himself to be a karate expert usually sitting separately on the train because he wanted to present the element of a surprise attack if anyone started to act stupid towards us and I've also changed my name to Tracee."

He replied as he gazed into my eyes, "After I saw you on the train that night, Tracee, I went to the club several times since hoping that you would be here alone."

It took me a while to wrap my head around actually having a conversation with Durk after so much time had passed. Although I was flattered that he'd gone through such lengths to make contact with me after briefly spotting me on the subway, I also wanted him to know how affected I was about him not even attempting to contact me after he'd left Job Corps.

"You should know, Durk, I cried for many days after you left the center and even though those unresolved feelings for you have returned, I am still disappointed that you never tried to contact me after you left for Georgia."

He pulled me closer to him, requesting that I sit on his lap like he'd always imagined us doing when we were in Job Corps. He then proceeded to apologize for not staying in touch with me and, of course, I could not stay upset with him too much longer.

Later that evening, Durk watched from a dark corner in the club as I went on to win the talent show! By the end of the night, I needed closure from the past in order to resolve those feelings that I still harbored for him, so I agreed to meet him at Piedmont Park the following afternoon.

We spent hours on the bench reminiscing about our times together on the center and when he did not invite me back to his place, I figured that he was most likely in a relationship with someone. I didn't press the issue because I surely was not about to invite him back to mine.

Who knows if Hilton would have inevitably reappeared? As the afternoon progressed into evening, I never asked Durk about his current relationship status after he questioned me about mine, because I just assumed that he was probably living with a biological female.

I must be honest and admit that we did kiss and make out to the extent that I was comfortable with in a public park until it had gotten really late in the evening. Although I dreaded having to leave him, I was not yet familiar with the MARTA schedule and I really needed to go home and prepare for work the following morning, so we embraced and passionately kissed for another extended period of time. During that embrace, I knew that evening in Piedmont Park would most likely be the last time that I would ever see Durk Hardy again, which it was.

After getting off the bus back on my side of town, I knew that I still had to take extra precautions whenever I went out into the public until I'd made other living arrangements, because I never knew when Hilton would reappear out of nowhere.

Shortly thereafter, I was thrilled to have moved into another boarding house that Hilton had no idea existed! I also thought it was best to change jobs, so I applied and was hired at Pizza Hut on Roswell Road to wait tables, which was great because I always had cash on hand from my daily tips, and I also had the option of picking up other shifts whenever they needed to be filled.

In addition to Pizza Hut becoming a great source of consistent income for me, I also became acquainted with someone who contributed to me meeting the healthcare provider who changed my life.

I met Tijuana after being hired and we became closer when she started training me. It never occurred to me that she was transsexual, because I just assumed that she was this really nice lesbian with a deep voice.

Her mother, Hazel, also worked there and after they invited me to go to the theater with them after work one afternoon to see a summer blockbuster that we were all excited about, we started regularly hanging out at their apartment.

I remember Tijuana always talking about her husband and kept telling me that she wanted me to meet him, so when we finally met at their apartment after work on the day that we were scheduled to go to the movies again, he turned out to be this guy whom had previously propositioned me outside of Pizza Hut on the day that I was going in for my initial interview.

I'd given him a bogus number when he first approached me because I was not attracted or interested in him. I chose not to say anything to Tijuana during that introduction because I did not think that it was necessary to tell her that her husband previously asked for my phone number.

He definitely didn't say anything to her and to his credit, he never approached me in that manner again.

One afternoon when Tijuana and I were restocking the napkins and condiments on our stations after the end of lunch shift, I picked up on and questioned why she constantly talked about going to the doctor to get some "Mones"?

She did her trademark smacking of the lips and making her usual popping sound before stating, "Girl, I need to go see Dr, Lee for my "Mones!"

Since I had never heard that term before, I asked bluntly for clarification, "Girl, what are Mones?"

She smiled and coyly replied, smacking again, "Honey, we are sisters!"

I immediately knew what she was saying to me as I replied, "I had no idea that you are also transsexual and whatever those "Mones" are that you're taking, I want some!"

Tijuana replied. "Sister, you can go with me on Friday after work to see my doctor in Midtown who is sympathetic to the girls, administering hormone and B12 shots for twenty dollars a pop!"

Although her constant pops and smacks every time she spoke should have given me a clue, it never occurred to me until then that she was also a female-to-male transsexual.

Since I was sold on the possibility of growing my own breasts, we took our tips to see Dr. Lee that following Friday afternoon. His office was located up the street from the Backstreet Atlanta club.

Dr. Lee's nurse collected blood to monitor my therapy and he then injected me with my first estrogen and vitamin B12 shots, one in each hip! I was around 21 years old and I anticipated growing breasts after taking a huge step that I'd suspected would positively change my life forever!

I visited Dr. Lee regularly for several weekly visits on Fridays after working the lunch shift with tips in hand, and I was amazed when my core started tingling as breasts started developing!

At first, they were very sensitive to my clothes and I was no longer able to continue sleeping on my stomach due to the sensitivity of my nipples. Time passed as I literally watched the process in the mirror as my body started slowly acquiring what I'd always felt should have been there at birth!

My relationship with Tijuana later ended on a bad note after she betrayed me. There was an incident when her husband, Shamrock told my future boyfriend at the time that another guy had asked me out on a date one night when we were all hanging out in the pool at our future apartment.

My future boyfriend, you'll become introduced to a little whom later physically abused me on a night after he'd been informed that another guy was interested in me.

While I was in the bedroom dealing with my boyfriend, Tijuana and Shamrock stole money from my purse to purchase crack cocaine, according to Tijuana's mother, Hazel, before she'd moved out of their apartment to move back to their hometown.

I never suspected that Tijuana was smoking something other than "Trees" after she'd commented to me in passing that she was high as a kite at work one afternoon, causing her to abruptly request to take the shift off.

I'm just grateful and appreciative that instead of turning me on to black market hormone pushers, she'd introduced me to a professional medical provider that safely administered my treatment and provided me with a life-changing gift!

I concluded that saga feeling that Shamrock must have still harbored some misguided feelings for me. I also firmly believe that although he knew that I wasn't interested in the guy that approached me at the pool that night, his telling my boyfriend what occurred would distract me so that they'd be able to steal money from my purse to buy crack.

As for the hormones and my development, I began to feel empowered by the physical changes that I was experiencing as my body continued transforming, which inspired me to enter the Tuesday night contest at Loretta's club. In my opinion, Loretta's was several steps up from the Marquette due to the contest prize being larger.

I was both excited and a little nervous about entering their competition because I thought that there'd be stiff competition. I'd visited the week before to scope out the club layout and obtain information on entering the contest.

As I started preparing for the contest, I felt that my life was positively evolving into what I had hoped to have achieved since my arrival in Georgia, until the fearful afternoon that I ran into Hilton on the same bus on my way to see Dr. Lee.

To my surprise, he seemed normal when he approached me after we both exited the bus at the same stop, asking, as I hurriedly walked away in the opposite direction from him, "Can I talk to you, Meat?"

I was very nervous and cautious when I turned to reply to him, "What do you want, Hilton?"

"I just want to apologize to you for the way I treated you. You a good person, Meat, and I am sorry."

I hadn't expected that response so I proceeded cautiously with my reply.

"Hilton, you are right; you were wrong and I accept your apology." Nervously continuing, "But, after all those inconsiderate things you did to me, I can't go back to the lies and cheating again if that is why you are apologizing…"

He interjected before I concluded my statement, "I just wanted you to know that if you ever need anything, Meat, just go to my mother's or Charles' house and tell him to show you where I am."

After that encounter with Hilton, I was relieved that he didn't physically attack me again and that he'd discontinued threatening harm.

I was happy that he seemed to have moved on from being violent and vengeful towards me and after that conversation with him, I felt somewhat safe that he would not just appear to threaten me anymore.

After our conversation, I proceeded on my merry little way, preparing and practicing for my upcoming performance at Loretta's! I decided to once again perform "Mercedes Boy" by Pebbles for the show the following week.

Although I was very disappointed that I did not win that night, I was determined to go back the following week to try again, because I'd observed that Loretta's clientele at the time were a more mature audience.

All I could think about while serving up personal pans and large cheese pizzas at work the following day was what song I was going to perform next.. Later that afternoon I knew that I'd have to find the perfect song to perform for the "Loretta's" more mature crowd, so immediately after arriving home from work I sat on the bed and went through each and every one of my cassette tapes listening to a variety of them on my tape player.

Then I came across a song that I've always loved ever since Ma used to play it when I was still a child. I immediately knew that "Neither One of Us" by Gladys Knight and the Pips was going to be my next performance in the contest since it brought back so many beautiful memories and feelings as I listened to it.

Choosing the perfect song was the major hurdle in my relay race, so now I went shopping at one of the department stores near underground Atlanta and purchased this really cute, strapless cocktail cotton dress that was conservatively ruffled at the knees.

She was topped off with an earth-tone light green shrug that accented my eyes. That following week I won the contest, walking away with $100 and guaranteed future bookings on future Monday Night Madness shows!

During the time of my contest entry, I wasn't aware that the show director named Candy Johnson, God rest her soul, loved Gladys Knight.

As a contest winner I was eligible for future club bookings! When I started performing regularly at Loretta's, I was quickly introduced to what deceitful, bitter and jealous queens really were all about.

Although I knew that envious people existed in the world, I never imagined how far they'd go to sabotage people that they may have felt threatened by. They were so transparent and two-faced in their failed attempts to conceal their dislike for you, just because of the way you looked and presented yourself.

It didn't help that some of them were over the top pageant queens, who saw anyone new on the scene as their competition. There were also those that would steal the heart out of a hot biscuit in the blink of an eye.

They usually prepared for a competition by going into a high-end boutique and hiding out in the store underneath the clothing racks, until closing in order to steal thousands of dollars beaded gowns and accessories to wear in a pageant and other contests.

There was this well-known story of this one queen who had worn a one-of-a-kind designer gown for her evening wear that she'd stolen in that manner. When she walked off the stage after modeling the gown in the eveningwear segment, the boutique manager and a cop arrested her on the spot.

Also included in the host of very eclectic characters was this full-figured queen, who shall remain nameless, whom I personally observed going into a fabric store and walking out with bolts of fabric concealed on her person. It still amazes me to this day that she was able to walk out of the store unnoticed with all that material!

Additionally, I quickly learned my lesson about leaving personal items and valuables unattended in the dressing room at Loretta's after my jewelry, wigs and costumes were stolen from my show bag one night. I was so mad that someone went into my costume bag and took my newly purchased hair that could be worn in two different styles just by reversing how it was worn.

Even though I knew that some of the other performers were talking about me behind my back, I decided that I would continue being myself no matter what they were saying, because Ma always taught me to treat people the way I wanted to be treated. That is what I chose to do until they'd proven that they were not worth me investing precious energy on them.

I also knew that some of the girls associated with Loretta's were thinking that they could take my kindness for a weakness just because I was the new girl on the scene, so I was very selective about those I associated with, purposefully feeding the messier ones with a long- handled spoon!

On the other hand, there were those rare girls, like Miss Cee Cee, who was known for her precise fancy footwork during performances, and Miss Jarvis JonVille, who was also cool and down to earth! I loved when Miss JonVille used to perform "Read It In Your Eyes" by Jennifer Holiday in her one-of-a-kind gowns that were designed and tailored by her then-boyfriend, who I later commissioned to design a couple of costumes for me.

I continued waitressing at Pizza Hut in addition to booking both clubs and creating productions to "Back Down Memory Lane" by Minnie Riperton dressed in a powder blue, silk over-the-top, "Dynasty"-inspired night gown and slippers, performing a routine in a wheelchair with a framed photo of a lost love to add drama!

I also donated my talent to raise money performing in rent fund-raisers for another performer and acquaintance, Christy Lombasia.

During her benefit show at the Marquette, on a night that the club was jumping with the DJ bumping "Funky Cole Medina" by Tone Loc, I danced with this lesbian named Jackie who later revealed to me that she was in love with me and wanted to make love to me with a plastic Caucasian strap-on fake penis that she'd brought to the apartment.

I knew I hurt Jackie's feelings by laughing in her face after she brought out the strap-on dildo from her bag, but I didn't care because I'd never lead her to believe that I was interested in being more than platonic friends with her.

As I walked upstairs to the dressing room to prepare for my turn on the stage after dancing with Jackie that night, my intention was to do something memorable! Up to that point I'd created and practiced every element of a dramatic production to "The Greatest Love of All" by Whitney Houston, and now was the time to show off my talent.

After being allowed a few seconds to set the stage before being introduced, I began my number, elegantly dressed and performing as if I was in a live concert. Then close to the end of the song, I sat at a make-up station on stage and in certain parts of the song, I individually deliberately removed jewelry, lashes, hair and make-up.

I concluded with removing costume, revealing my bare chest and ending up dressed in only a G-string and panty hose!

This dramatic performance was way before my breasts were fully developed from the hormone treatments, and I've realized that, unconsciously, I used that performance to symbolically shed the old body in order to successfully transition into my more feminine, softer self.

That night my performance drew rave reviews from the audience and they showed their appreciation by generously forming a long line at the stage to individually tip me!

I even received a sponsorship offer from a make-up artist for an upcoming pageant. (That turned out to be a disaster; I should have insisted upon him applying my make-up in a practice run first. Never again has that happened.)

After my performance in the fund-raiser, I went to the dressing room and changed into my jeans and blouse before going to the bar downstairs in the showroom for a drink to cool off.

As I stood there waiting to order a ginger ale, I noticed this elegantly dressed girl looking like she had just gotten off from her corporate job and was having a cocktail at the bar before going home.

As we both stood there waiting for the bartender, she and I struck up a conversation. Tara Holiday was her name, whom I affectionately later called Ebony out of Drag! When we first met at the bar, she seemed to be a genuinely nice and down-to earth-person, which probably had something to do with her being from North Carolina and me from South Carolina!

During our conversation that evening, she asked."So, what part of town do you live in, honey?"

"I've just recently relocated to Georgia from South Carolina and I'm currently renting a room at a boarding house," I replied.

She replied, "Well, Tracee, you seem really nice and since my brother. Scott, my boyfriend Greg and I are looking for a new roommate to replace the previous messy queen that lived with us, if you're interested I'd love for you to consider becoming our roommate."

I was aware that I was right where I needed to be at just the right time! I strongly believe that our introduction was preordained. It was unfolding in divine order. I now know for sure that mother, father, god, universe were continuing to provide the people, places and events required to assist with fulfilling my destiny!

A couple days after Tara and I discussed in detail the living arrangements and rent payment business after being introduced to her brother and boyfriend!

In addition to getting a fresh start, I was more than happy with the idea of getting as far away from Hilton as possible, so I jumped at her offer to become their roommate!

Living in a three-bedroom town home in Sutton Place on Buford Highway was a great incentive to change my environment. The day I was scheduled to move in after obtaining my set of keys Tara was at work at the Journal Constitution.

She'd arranged for her boyfriend, Greg, to help me move my things from the boarding house into a vacant third bedroom upstairs that afternoon, thus beginning many adventures, including the creation of Sugar & Spice!

Since Tara and I had immediately connected with each other, it was no surprise to me that we became instant sister-friends! It was my idea for us to perform together because I envisioned us performing the perfect song that reminded me of my high school friends from back in the days when we used to tear it up at the Candy Shop in Columbia, South Carolina.

I fondly remember that anytime the DJ played "Coming out of Hiding" by Pamala Stanley and we were all on the dance floor having a good old fashioned time whooping it up. Those were the days!

As for Tara and I as Sugar & Spice, I designed our sexy costumes --a black and white all-in-one negligees' purchased from Sandy Springs K-mart with knee-high, five-inch boots! Very Madonna!

I've always been a stickler for rehearsing new numbers and during rehearsals in the family room at the apartment for our first partnered production, I also got the brilliant idea to incorporate whips into our routine for some drama and effect!

I figured that the whips would also bring an element of Vanity 6 to our performance. However, I did not take into consideration that Tara liked to have more than a few cocktails before she performed.

We were both excited about doing our first number together at Loretta's, so we arrived there early to claim our spots in the show and dressing room.

I won't forget walking into the club with "Good Life" by Inner City thumping throughout the rooms and the energy was elevated. In the dressing room, we pulled the third spot in the show line-up and we were happy that we were not first, because it's usually always more nerve-wracking to open the show.

We even had enough time for Tara to have a couple more drinks before the show while I used the restroom for what I'd hoped to be the last time before changing into my costume! When we returned to the dressing room, I immediately noticed the energy shift amongst the usual deceitful queens who were in charge of the show line-up. Due to previous experiences seeing how deceitfully they ran the show, I knew that they were up to no good.

So, I suggested to Tara that we should go ahead and start getting into our costumes. Thank goodness that we were ready to perform because they played our music first and then pretended it was an accident.

Since Tara and I were ready to go, we didn't let their deceitfulness spoil our night! The club as well as the stage was beautifully decorated with pastel blue and white balloons and wall to wall streamers, and the showroom was packed with an audience that was clearly ready to be entertained!

After our music started, Tara and I high-fived each other before entering the stage to loud applauds. As the number progressed, we performed and popped those whips to the beat just as we'd practiced, but before the song ended I observed that Tara had gone rogue and off track when she started demolishing the stage with her whip.

I'd suspected that she was really feeling those cocktails around that time so I stayed out of her way on the other end of the stage, performing and keeping a clear view of her.

Even though she almost took a few of the audience members heads off with her whip and utterly destroyed the stage decorations, they still overwhelmingly enjoyed our performance!

Fortunately for me, I managed to finish the routine without getting whipped across the mug! We currently laugh whenever we reminisce about those nights at Lorretta's, both concluding that if they had not been so shady and jealous, those queens' professionally decorated stage would not have been devastatingly assassinated by Sugar &Spice. Oh well, karma is a bitch!

As for our other hang-out spot, some people have questioned why we liked the Marquette. I'm talking about the original, three-level Marquette that used to be on Martin Luther King Jr. Drive.

The "Quette" was slightly edgier and on the wild side, considered by many to be a hole-in-the-wall hood club.

But I liked the Marquette, because, in addition to the money and tips being really good whenever I performed, we could always count the music to be pumping and the down-to-earth people there to be having a great time!

I now smile as I reflect back on those days, because it was just an adventurous time when we lived for the weekend to get all gussied up to hit the scene for a night of dancing and fun!

One funny story that occurred at the "Quette" was when we had just gotten to the club, ready to get down, when a guy that I'd previously danced with pulled me onto floor with him to dance to "I Wanna Dance with Somebody" by Whitney Houston.

Just as I'd started to get my groove on, Tara pulled me to the side and out of the blue and said, "Girl, I got to go!"

"I replied in disbelief, "Honey, we just got here. What's going on?"

She leaned in and whispered, "Girl, look, my face is cracking."

I immediately excused myself from my dance partner and followed Tara, scurrying directly into the ladies room. Upon looking in the mirror, she exclaimed, "Just look at my face! That cheap-ass make-up! Damn, damn, damn!"

I thought that she was exaggerating, but my cynical tune changed after I turned her face to the light and saw the patches and cracks all over her face. It looked like a dried mint julep facial mask. All I could say was, "Girl, what kind of make-up did you use?"

"Tracee, since I wanted to hold onto my money to get this new dress and have a few dollars leftover to buy a couple cocktails, I decided to try this cheap-ass foundation."She tried to stop the cracking by using powder from the compact that she removed from her purse before finally announcing, "Girl, this is not working; I got to go."

Needless to say, that was the end of that night out before it really ever started. There was absolutely no way that I was going to stay at the club without her. We left and, to my knowledge, she has not used cheap foundation or powder ever again. What an adventure!

Throughout all of the adventures and fun-filled times, my inevitable very first fight in Georgia occurred when this other queen, who also performed at Loretta's, started acting crazy one night in the dressing room at the "Quette."

Tara and I, along with Miss Darrel, wanted to have some fun and make some money, so we decided to do the show!

I'd met Miss Darrell several years previously during a visit that her school made to the Chris Logan Beauty College in Myrtle Beach, and we started hanging out after we'd recently ran into each other at Loretta's one night. She was currently styling hair at a salon on the West End.

Although I recalled the vow that I'd previously made to seek alternative solutions to dealing with someone that physically threatened me, there are those times when you just have to back a crazed and out-of-control, sketched-out queen off you. In the dressing room that night, one of those messy queens that I'd fed with a long handle spoon named Michelle asked, "Miss Tracee, can I use your blush?"

"Sure honey, but you got to use your own blush brush," I replied.

Offended, she responded, "Oh, Miss Tracee, you think you all that."

"No, Michelle, it's not that I think I am all that; it's just that certain personal make-up and brushes that I use on my face are not items that I share with others."

After I explained this fact to her, I left the dressing room to go to the bathroom while Tara grabbed a cocktail. When I returned back to the dressing room, I saw that Michelle was using a blush brush that was very similar to mine, so I looked in my make-up bag to be sure that she was not using my brush before saying anything to her.

When I discovered that the brush I had just put in my make-up kit was gone, I secured my make-up returning everything back into my costume bag and then stood up to face her asking, "Michelle, is that my brush you're using?"

She responded by slamming the brush on the table, then intruded on my personal space, waving her finger near my face and speaking loudly."Miss Tracee, you think that you are better than everybody else!"

I took a step back, replying, "Miss Michelle, I know that you are high on crack or whatever your drug of choice is right now, but you need to take a couple steps back off me, girl."

Unfortunately for her, she chose to not heed the warning as she moved forward and continued erratically swinging her finger. Before she knew it, she ended up being thrown on top of the dressing room table, pinned up against the mirror screaming, "Miss Tracee, Miss Darrell let me use your brush!"

I knew that Michelle was really messed up and high, so I backed off and turned to face Miss Darrell and asked, "Miss Darrell, did you go into my bag and give Michelle my brush?"

Miss Darrell shivered cowering in the corner as she replied, "Ah, Miss Tracee, she just wanted to use your blush."

I faced her, using direct eye contact to let her know that I was serious. "Honey, obviously you don't know me that well, so let me make myself clear to you and Michelle. I will fuck you both up if you ever again touch anything of mine that I have not given you permission to use."

As I concluded my statement, Michelle's boyfriend, La'Mont, after learning what happened, interjected, pointing at her with a cigarette between his fingers and a drink in the other hand. "You see, that's exactly what you get Michelle, I told you that touching other people shit without their permission will get your ass kicked one day!"

Tara and I could not believe that Miss Darrell had the nerve to go into my bag and then give Michelle my brush after I had unequivocally told Michelle in front of Miss Darrell that she could not use it.

I bet you one thing: Miss Darrell never went into anything of mine without permission ever again and I assume that the word had gotten out about that only physical altercation that I was ever involved in with another queen the entire time of performing and living in Atlanta.

Ebony and I still laugh about those days and he has even suggested that the reason nobody ever messed with him was probably because they were scared of me. I wonder?

During that time I was performing regularly at Loretta's hot current songs like "Talk About the Lover" by Sheena Easton and "Super Woman" by Karen White. That's when I observed that the claws began to really sharpen after I finished creating a production with a cute guy and props.

Since I didn't wanted to just do the usual walk on stage and then start lip-syncing to songs, I hired a male dancer to re-enact a breakfast dining room scene on stage that I'd choreographed for my Karen White character!

The climax to the performance was when I removed from the bosom of my gown a toy cap pistol to shoot the mentally and physically abusive boyfriend. I don't recall where that idea came from back then.

In addition to accumulating a loyal group of fans, I also gained a larger number of threatened and undeclared enemies from within the show by that time. In my mind, I was not there to compete with them because I was only performing in the shows in order to eat and pay my bills, not to win some title.

Please don't get me wrong: it's not that I am knocking pageant girls or guys, it's just that because of my previous personal horrific experience that one time in the late '80s, I've never acquired the temperament, taste or patience required for properly navigating the behind--the-scenes politics and sabotaging that many engaged in. Personally, I don't think that a title is required to be a well-rounded entertainer.

During my evenings, I performed in the clubs and served up pizzas at Pizza Hut during the day, until one of my favorite managers resigned after she went on maternity leave. She was replaced with the evil witch that none of the employees really liked very much.

I knew that she had it in for me after an incident that I had gotten into with one of her favorite, fake, booty-kissing employees.

Since I wasn't about to take any chances on risking not having a day job, I decided that it would be better for me to apply for different employment.

After working the lunch shift that sunny spring day, I walked up the street to the Kmart that used to be on Roswell Road. I was hired on the spot to by the African-American apparel department manager!

After becoming her assistant, I submitted my two-week notice to Pizza Hut the following day and found myself excited about styling and creating fashion displays at Kmart, where I could wear my own clothes and no longer smelled like tomato sauce all day long.

During my first week at Kmart, I sat next to this beautiful woman named Sanoya on the train ride to work one morning and during our conversation we discovered that we were both Kmart employees.

She was a cashier and during that first conversation, I felt that there was something very familiar about her, but I did not think anything further because I figured that she was just a really nice and down-to-earth person.

After we got know each other, I was blown away to find out that she was also a transsexual woman when, during one of our lunch breaks together, she asked, "Girl, do you know somewhere a sister can find some 'Mones'?"

I was completely flabbergasted because she was so feminine. I replied in shock, "Sanoya, you have got to be kidding me; I had no idea that you are also transsexual!"

"Yes, honey, I used to date this doctor back home and he surgically removed my testicles without completely removing anything else so I am still functional, but I just cannot produce sperm anymore!"

I was intrigued so I inquired, "So why do you still need hormones if you have removed your testicles?"

She smiled and caressed her breast as she replied, "I love what 'Mones' do for my fishiness!"

Although I found her surgery interesting, I did not have any desire to explore that path any further and I gave her Dr. Lee's phone number and address.

During another lunch hour together a few days later she informed me that her roommate was coming in the following day to shop and that she wanted me to meet her.

After the first unexpected revelatory conversation, I just assumed that Sanoya's roommate was also transsexual, so when I later ran into her on the apparel aisle before we were formally introduced, I immediately knew by her appearance that she was Sanoya's roommate.

Upon sight of her I could not believe that she had a Jessica Rabbit body and an almost full beard. I was shocked at her appearance looking tore up from the floor up out in public like that!

After me and Sanoya's roommate briefly acknowledged each other as we passed in the aisle, in addition to her appearance I felt it strange that she was also pushing an overflowing shopping cart and pulling another half-filled one with various merchandise behind her.

Since I was busy, I really did not get a chance to talk with her. But two minutes later I was paged to customer service, expecting to assist another customer.

As I walked up to the counter at the front of the store, I saw Sanoya and her roommate both standing in front of her register handcuffed with four police officers surrounding them.

After my manager informed me about what they had done that caused them to be arrested, I thought how stupid and obvious can you be to risk your job by having your roommate come to your place of employment looking like a freak of the week.

On top of that idiocy, I couldn't understand for the life of me why she then had nerve to try and steal two carts full of merchandise. She should have known that she would draw suspicion and unwarranted attention to herself coming up in a public place looking like that without shaving.

After Sanoya was fired and arrested for shoplifting along with her roommate, I never saw her again. Their arrests are so memorable to me because later that evening, as I was leaving work to go home and when I exited the front door to walk across Roswell Road to wait for the next bus, I was approached by this tall, very handsome man wearing a stylish jacket.

If I recall correctly, his opening statement was something like, "Hello, beautiful lady, my name is Shawn Work. Do you have a moment to talk?"

Since I wasn't really in a rush to get anywhere other than home, I didn't see any harm in hearing what he had to say, so I replied to him as if I was still on the clock in the apparel department helping a customer. "Hi, Shawn, my name is Tracee. How may I help you?"

I was caught off guard when he replied that he'd seen me there before when he was previously shopping and then asked me out to dinner.

I wasn't comfortable with giving him my phone number because I wondered if he was able to tell that I was transsexual. So I replied, "I've just recently moved and my phone hasn't been turned on yet. If you give me your number, I will call you."

I took his phone number with no intention of ever calling him because I was not in the mood to explain to a guy that frequented my place of employment what it meant to be a transsexual woman.

I didn't think about the handsome man wearing the fashion-forward jacket again until that following weekend when Tara and I were waiting in line to get into the Marquette.

As we stood there waiting to get into the club, excited about getting our groove on, I noticed a familiar face crossing the street and then getting into line behind us. After I realized that he was the handsome guy that had approached me at work, we acknowledged each other as he said, "Well, hello again, beautiful lady … we meet again!"

"Hello, Shawn. Fancy seeing you here!" I replied, slightly shocked, and then introduced him to Tara. After the introductions, Shawn and I ended up having a great time dancing the entire night, with only each other. Of course, Tara enjoyed herself as well!

As I look back to that time when I first met Shawn at Kmart, although I thought that he was a very attractive man I never expected to see him at, of all places, the "Quette"!

After that second encounter, we immediately started seeing each other on a regular basis. We had so much in common including our Aquarian birth signs, working in the entertainment industry, loving thrift store shopping, and dancing the night away!

We were together at Loretta's one night several months later, sharing another magical evening before one of my booked engagements in the show performing "Dreamin" by Vanessa Williams!

Right before my number, I was standing in the background on the side of the stage watching one of my favorite of all-time performers and inspirations from Miami named Tiffany Arieagus, who was a guest performer in town, tearing down "Where Is My Man?" by Eartha Kitt. I was captured watching Miss Arieagus elegantly slink across the stage wearing an amazing costume with a removable replica of a sparkling gold and black flared cobra's head.

Shawn was in the restroom as I stood out of view in the back of the show room waiting for him to return and watching Tiffany work it out when this other queen came and stood right next to me. I'd met her before and had chosen to avoid her because she hung out with the other messy girls.

After we acknowledged each other, I continued watching Miss Arieagus seductively crawl across the tables. Mind you, this other queen was much taller than I was. So, when she intentionally dropped her keys into my hair, trying to pretend that it was an accident, I didn't care how tall she was as she attempted to mess up my hair by pretending to retrieve her keys.

I pushed her back away and threw her keys at her warning, "Miss Girl, you are lucky that I have not performed my number yet, but I promise you that as soon as I am done, I will come find you so that we can continue this conversation!"

I didn't immediately tell Shawn about what happened between me and Miss Girl when he returned from the facilities and stood behind me, wrapping his arms around my waist. I just gave him a usual kiss on the lips and excused myself to go to the dressing room and assess the damage.

I mentally composed myself after assessing that there were no major issues with my strategically pinned-up hair. It was nice that there wasn't anyone else in the dressing room as I prepared myself before going on stage.

I intended to not let a jealous queen ruin our night. I was more excited about performing a song to express to Shawn how I was feeling about the time that we were sharing with other.

When it was all said and done, the crowd loved my performance and they were unaware that my only thought throughout the song was quickly changing back into my street clothes so I could finish what Miss Girl had started!

But, of course, she was nowhere to be seen. Since she was such a shady, dirty type of person who'd blatantly attempt to sabotage a girl before her performance, if I would have found her it would have been on like Donkey Kong between us wherever our paths met that night.

When I joined Shawn after scouting the club out for Miss Girl, I chose not to mention the incident to him because I just assumed that Miss Girl could have possibly been someone from his past.

I chalked it up to her being one of those bitter and jealous girls attempting to be catty who misjudged her perceived rival just because she was almost taller than Andre the Giant.

All she was going to get that night was an ass kicking. Not over a man, mind you. It was the principle of the matter, as far as I was concerned, due to her choosing to be a disrespectful bully bitch!

If she was really all that she'd viewed herself to have been, she would have at least attempted to have a civilized discussion with me, woman-to-woman, about her issues instead of the way she handled things.

I really believe that after the incident at Loretta's, if Miss Girl saw me first, she must have gone in the opposite direction, because I never saw her again for the remainder of my time in Georgia.

Later that evening at Shawn's apartment, he introduced me to his roommate, Rick, and, after a bit of small talk, Rick excused himself to go on a date, leaving Shawn and I alone sitting on the couch in their living room.

During our conversation after Rick left, he must have sensed that there was something bothering me when we were at the club so he inquired, "I can tell that something is bothering you, babe, tell me what it is?"

I replied to Shawn, unsurprised that he'd been so connected with my feelings and emotions. "Well, Shawn, I wasn't going to tell you that I'd had a strange encounter with Miss Girl while you were in the restroom when she came out of the blue and tried to sabotage me, attempting to mess up my hair with her keys before my number."

He replied in disbelief, "I'm so sorry about that, babe, I went out with Miss Girl once and after I found out that she was a prostitute, I tried to distance myself from her. Then she started showing up at the apartment unannounced. I will make sure that she never approaches you again, babe."

I wasn't naïve and I didn't foolishly think that I was the only transsexual that Shawn may have ever been involved with, nor was I expecting him to become my husband overnight.

Even though we had only been seeing each other for a short period of time, he reassured me that the relationship between the two of them was over and that I didn't have to worry about her approaching me again.

Although I was very understanding and cool with his reassurances, I just had to let him know, "Shawn, something you need to be aware of is that I don't fight over no man. However, I am not going to let anyone just disrespect me the way that she tried, so you should also know that I did go looking for her after my number, but she was gone."

Reassuringly, he replied. "I know that you can take care of yourself, Tracee, but you don't have to worry about fighting nobody, babe."

I replied, hoping to change the subject, "I am determined to not let her spoil our evening together, so I would rather that we talk about something more pleasant."

Smiling his gorgeous smile in agreement, he replied, "Would you like to hear a song that you inspired me to compose?"

"Of course, Shawn, you know how much I love your music!" I was so moved as I sat listening to him playing his keyboards and singing an original, slow melodic song, sensuously entitled "Take Your Clothes Off" that he had written and dedicated to me!

I was also blown away as Shawn started shedding tears singing a beautiful song that he had written for his mother. I loved hanging out with Shawn "Climbing Trees" in his bedroom or in the living room listening to him play the most amazing original compositions!

We spent countless hours into the wee hours of the morning flipping through his vinyl album collection, playing songs that took me back down memory lane and grooving to old-school classics that I had not heard in such a long time!

It was always an adventure for us to spontaneously go to a park for an impromptu photo shoot and I still have and cherish a collection of his music and compilations that I've collected that he'd gifted to me over the years.

I shall not soon forget the various evenings of multiple orgasmic moments that we shared together in his shower and bedroom!

Shawn's history was that he and his roommate Rick were music writers and producers at that time, producing music for one of the Atlanta Hawks team members. Shawn surprised me once when he invited me to go with him to my first professional basketball game to see the Hawks play a home game.

The night of the game, I knew that I wanted to look great, so I wore my always appropriate Vanessa Williams curly fall and a body-hugging, off-the shoulder, mid-armed, little black hip- hugging dress with mid-length black leather boots. I must admit that I was looking hot!

This was my very first NBA game, so I had no idea of what to expect as we walked into the arena, and at first I felt a little self-conscious and taken aback at the amount of people seeming like all of their eyes were on us as we walked hand-in hand down to our seats.

Shawn must have sensed my nervousness, so he pulled me closer to him with a big smile on his face and whispered in my ear, "They are all staring because you are the sexiest girl in this entire auditorium!" After those comforting words from him, I relaxed and became more at ease after he pulled my hand to his mouth and gently kissed the back of it with his sweet lips. I don't recall anything about that game, all I remember is that I had a great time at my first Hawks game with Shawn.

It was very challenging for me to not fall in love with Shawn after several months of dating because he was very charming. However, I knew that his employment and living circumstances would not allow for us to be more than what we were.

I purposely didn't let my guard completely down enough to even entertain the thought of us being more than what's currently considered by some a no-strings attached situation between two consenting adults just having a great time with each other, which was okay with me!

Even though I'd previously spent nights at Shawn's apartment after a night out on the town, I wasn't expecting for him to, out of the blue, ask me to spend an entire weekend with him at his apartment.

I never saw that coming and since I wasn't working my day job that weekend, I packed an overnight bag and went along for the adventure! Shawn prepared delicious meals for us the whole time whenever we were not eating at restaurants or doing our favorite past time, thrift shopping and taking pictures in the park!

I was impressed at the effort that he was making, never suspecting that the following week he would just disappear without any warning.

Although I viewed our relationship as somewhat no strings attached, it was unsettling when I tried calling Shawn to thank him for the great weekend and wasn't able to speak with him.

I grew more perplexed each time his roommate answered the phone, continuously informing me that he did not know where Shawn was and promising to forward my messages whenever he spoke with him.

I didn't know what to think after leaving several messages with his roommate for him to call me. I was really confused about the situation because Shawn usually would have responded to my calls in a timely manner, so after a few days of not hearing from him since his disappearing act, I finally stopped calling.

I was disappointed that he had just disappeared without a word right after the most romantic weekend that we'd just shared with each other. I couldn't help but to wonder if he had done what most guys do whenever they become conflicted with their strong feelings for transsexuals, causing them to cease all communication.

As the days passed, I began feeling that maybe he'd became scared after getting emotionally involved with me too soon. I was confounded about not being able to talk with him to obtain answers, so I decided that in order to protect my heart, I needed to move on with my life.

I moved forward, filing the time that Shawn and I shared together in my cherished memories safe. During that time Tara aka, Ebony and I were asked by my new drag mother Lady Fabian Sanchez to re-enact a scene from the Broadway play "DreamGirl" in her talent when she performed "I'm Not Going" by Jennifer Holiday for a pageant that she'd entered at Loretta's!

Also at this point, Tara and I shared an apartment together on Argonne and Ponce De Leon affectionately known as All Girls Village! What had happened was Tara and Greg had recently separated due to an incident that occurred between me and Greg on a day that I was off from work the morning after we all had gone to Loretta's the night before.

I'd fallen asleep on the couch watching television downstairs after everyone else retired upstairs. The next morning, I was awakened by someone caressing my exposed legs and when I realized that I was not dreaming about Laurence Fishburne and found Greg's grimy hands on my thighs, I quickly covered my exposed body with the sheet and angrily asked, "What the hell are you doing, Greg?"

He responded, "Scott and Ebony are at work, I have wanted to spend some time alone with you ever since I helped you to move in with us, Tracee."

Shocked and disgusted, I replied, "Ebony is my sister and I would never consider betraying her trust by having sex with you Greg, you need to back off and go back upstairs before I call Ebony at work and tell him what you are trying to do."

Greg persistently tried replacing his hands under my sheet as he commented, "Ebony don't have to know about us. This could be our little secret, Tracee."

He was completely nasty to the core! As Greg continued talking, I pushed his hand away, even more disgusted with his persistence and advances. I knew that he was not concerned about the feelings of the person that I considered to be my friend.

The absolute truth about that whole pointless scene was that Greg was a true idiot to think that I would have ever jeopardized my friendship with Ebony in order to have sex with his disgusting ass.

So, in an attempt to let him know that I was serious about not going there with him at no point, I resorted to intentionally hurting his feelings with my response. "Even if Ebony wasn't my sister Greg, I would not have sex with you because you are just not my type."

Greg immediately became enraged and insulted that I'd turned him down. He finally popped up off the couch and angrily huffed and puffed back up the stairs looking like the stupid fool that he was.

After I heard their bedroom door slam shut, I jumped up from the couch, ran upstairs and locked myself in my bedroom until Scott and Ebony arrived home from work later that evening.

I didn't tell Ebony right away about the incident because I didn't want to start any drama and I hoped that Greg had gotten the message that I wouldn't be interested in him if he was the last man on earth.

I also hoped that his advances would cease, but as time passed, Greg became more and more hostile towards me. I knew that Ebony was smart enough to have observed and questioned to himself the extreme change in Greg's attitude toward me.

One evening when it was just the two of us home Ebony entered my room with a cocktail in hand, sprawled across the bed with me, in her usual Lucille Ball happy go-lucky comedic personality, stating, "Honeychile, I have observed Greg's sudden attitude change towards you from the constant compliments to complaints and anguish."

Ebony took a sip of his cocktail and continued, "I need to know if something has happened between the two of you that brought on this negative situation between the two of you?"

I wasn't surprised that he had noticed the negative vibrations between me and Greg, neither was I going to not tell him the truth so I hesitantly replied, "Ebony, I did not want to hurt you or jeopardize our friendship by telling you that I woke up to Greg caressing my legs on the couch downstairs and suggesting that just because you and Scott were at work, he and I were free to have sex."

Ebony swirled the ice and alcohol around in his cocktail glass and then took a sip as I continued. "Nothing happened between us and Greg then became angry after I informed him in no uncertain terms that we would ever have sex even if you were not my friend."

Ebony replied, unsurprised, "I know that he is a dirty ass dog and I figured it was something like this that would explain why he all of a sudden stopped liking you."He continued reassuringly, "You do not have to worry, honey, I will take care of his ass, and I appreciate you for being a real sister and not sleeping with my man even if he is a dirty ass dog."

As we embraced each other I replied, "I feel so much better that you came to me like a sister giving me the chance to tell you the truth about what occurred. I will never betray your trust by sleeping with Greg or anyone else that you may have been with because that is just not who I am."Shaking the ice around in her cocktail glass and replying before exiting my room, "I will take of Greg."

Later that night after Greg arrived home from work, all hell broke loose between those two in their room! There was a huge, violent fight involving an electric iron being used as a weapon during the fight on the upstairs catwalk and the police being called.

The final result was that Ebony and I shortly thereafter became roommates in All Girls Village, which brings us back to the "DreamGirl" rehearsal on the evening that we were at Lady Fabian's apartment, choreographing and staging her most memorable First Place Talent Winner in the competition!

I had no idea that my life was about to evolve into something that was totally unexpected on that peculiar summer evening. This really cute, tall Will Smith-looking guy who was there named LeRon Goodard came into the room and sat down on the floor in bare feet and started observing our rehearsal.

I noticed that he had really kissable, sexy lips when he started being overtly flirtatious and interjecting unsolicited comments. Since I was not sure if he was dating someone at Lady Fabian's or not, I kept my distance from him until I was certain that he was not involved with anyone.

As the rehearsal proceeded, he continued making sarcastic comments and blatantly flirting with me. I thought about Shawn, but I was not sure if I would see him again, nor was I sure if we were still in a relationship due to not being able to communicate with him.

LeRon intrigued me and I felt that boyish charms would be a great distraction to mask my feelings about Shawn's disappearance. After rehearsal that night, LeRon offered to escort Ebony and I to our apartment, which was a block up from Lady Fabian's.

After our arrival, Ebony went inside, leaving LeRon and I alone outside under a bright moon to talk privately. We must have conversed for hours about everything just so that we would be able to prolong our time together! During the conversation, he seemed mature to me, yet due to his boyish charm I curiously asked, "How old are you LeRon and why are you staying with Lady Fabian?"

He replied, "I just turned 21 this past June and as for why I'm staying with Lady Fabian, my dad and I got into a fight after I defended my mother against him beating on her. I needed to get away, so a mutual friend of ours told me that it would be okay for me to stay at Fabian's until I get it together."

Since I've never believed in getting involved with another girl's man or recent former boyfriend if I can help it, I continued interrogating him. "Have you had any type of current or previous involvement with anyone that was close to or lived with Lady Fabian?"

He confidently replied, "No, Tracee. I'm straight and I never have been involved with anyone there. However, I am really attracted to you and I would like to get to know more about you!"

"Well, LeRon, I think that one of the important things you should know about me is that I'm not sure if I am currently still in a relationship or not, because I haven't spoken to the guy that I was dating for a while now, so to be quite honest I really don't know if we are still together."

I was around 22, going on 23 at the time and up to that point, I had never before seriously dated anyone that was younger or around the same age as me because I've always been more attracted to older mature guys.

LeRon's attentiveness and strong embraces throughout that cool evening as we continued conversing way after midnight caused me to make an exception and throw caution to the wind to become more adventurous!

If I had any idea of what our future would become, instead of getting involved with LeRon, I would have run for the hills that night.

However, I wanted to see if he would be comfortable at Loretta's, so I invited him to go to the club with us to see the pageant.

The night of the show Lady Fabian won first place in talent and LeRon seemed to be comfortable in that type of environment.

We all had a great time at the club and after the pageant, LeRon and I spent the night together that evening alone in my room, getting to know each other further as the discussion eventually evolved to safer-sex, using one condom versus two.

All the while we were both desperately trying to control the sexual tension that had built up between us! Also, that evening he revealed to me that I was the first transsexual person that he was interested in being intimate with beyond just oral sex and I must be honest and admit that I was flattered by his attraction to me.

Yet, my brain kept warning me that he was too inexperienced and that he would be trouble if I didn't proceed with caution, especially after the domestic violence that he'd previously witnessed between his parents in their home.

I was proud that I held out and restrained from engaging in intercourse with LeRon until several weeks later, when my brain inevitably became overruled by lust and decided to go with the flow and enjoy the moment!

I'm currently mature enough now to understand that I really didn't take the time that was required to properly deal with my feelings around Shawn's abrupt missing in action before eventually moving Ron in with me and Ebony.

I should have thought twice when I found out about his true age. That happened after I won six tickets from a radio station contest for this popular 21 and over club in Sandy Springs. I also invited this lesbian couple living in our complex that we'd previously befriended. When we arrived at the club, Ebony and I were both surprised that Ron was denied entry because he was still only 18 years old.

After we returned to the apartment, I expressed my disappointment to Ron that he wasn't honest with me about his real age in the beginning and that it did not sit well with me that I was almost five years older than he was. I was very upset that he lied about his age. However, his saving grace was that his 19th birthday was the following June. Yes, only after checking the birth date on his real license did I let his sweet-talking charms persuade me into forgiving him for his deception.

Ron started to regularly escort me to the club and I was flattered by his protectiveness and reactions to other guys whenever they approached me! After one guy hugged me in front of Ron to offer congratulations after a performance, Ron immediately pulled me away from the embrace and whispered into my ear that I belonged to him and that he did not want any other guys touching on me even if they were gay fans or not.

You talk about cautionary red flags and alarms going off that I should have paid attention to. That night, I was just excited about working in the show. I performed "Smooth Operator" by Sade and Tara performed "Giving Up" by Jeane Carne.

If I recall correctly, it was maybe a couple of weeks later that, out of the blue, I received a phone call from Shawn one afternoon when I was alone in the apartment selecting costumes for that upcoming weekend show.

I was surprised; I had not expected to ever hear from him again. All I could do was reply after hearing his voice, "Where are you and why have you not responded to any of my messages Shawn?"

He replied."My father died and I had to go back to Kansas, babe."

My heart dropped because I didn't expect that answer as I replied, "I am so sorry to hear about your father, Shawn. Why did you not tell me?"

He replied, apologetically, "I'm sorry, babe, but I really needed some time away from everything to get myself together."

My past experiences with a predominantly heterosexual guy who's been in a relationship with transsexual women saying he just needed time away from everything usually means that their most likely challenged with their attraction to girls like me.

Those of us who are attracted to masculine men aren't exactly surprised at their abrupt change of mind about the relationship that they are in with someone who is viewed by most in society as disposable garbage.

Personally, it's very difficult to express your heartfelt love to a person that you've allowed yourself to develop strong feelings for and then realize that they have had second thoughts about being with you only because they're afraid of what society would have to say.

So, in response the guy might suppress his feelings for you and then suddenly disappear from your life without warning. It occurred to me during that afternoon conversation with Shawn that, in addition to dealing with the death of his father, I felt he was also probably experiencing a change of heart and conflict over our relationship that he was not able to express to me, which is what may have also contributed to him not even attempting to communicate with me while he was away.

Although I understood his independent nature, I believe that he should have made an effort to let me be there for him during such a heartbreaking time in his life. I truly regretted not being mature enough to wait and receive closure before getting involved with Ron so suddenly after Shawn disappeared.

As the old saying goes," look for the positive in the negative". So, the good that I received from that unfortunate experience has taught me one of the most valuable lessons that I will ever need to know about relationships. Never start another relationship with anyone else until there is definite closure from the previous one.

During our conversation that day on the phone, it was confirmed that I was more in love with Shawn than I'd realized, and I also felt really guilty about the feelings that I had developed for Ron.

I was torn about my feelings for two totally opposite guys and that experience would be unmistakably one of the toughest lessons for me to learn about what the consequences of not making wiser choices. I had no idea that the day that Shawn finally contacted me would be the time when my existence would become chaotic and unsettling.

I'd mistakenly thought that I had started to successfully move forward from the hurt and confusion that I felt after continuously attempting to contact Shawn after his abrupt disappearance. But, after hearing his voice on the phone, something deep down inside was uncontrollably happy that he had finally contacted me!

As our conversation continued, I dreaded telling Shawn that I had moved on with another guy, but I had to tell him about Ron. I wasn't able to delay the inevitable any further after accepting his apology for not returning my calls.

It was extremely hard to inform him that I was living with another guy as I proceeded explaining, "Shawn, I was very confused and disappointed that you never responded to any of my messages, and I didn't understand why you never tried reaching out to me to let me what was going on with you."

He remained silent as I continued buying time, "I just couldn't figure out what was going on with you, especially after the amazing weekend that we shared together."

I then hesitantly revealed the full truth. "I am so sorry Shawn, I didn't know what was going on with us after I wasn't able to talk with you so in an attempt to protect myself from being hurt, I became involved with someone else. Although I knew that it was too soon to do so, I did anyway."

Shawn calmly replied, "Babe, I'm sorry that you were hurt and I know that you did what you had to do to protect your feelings, I will always have love for you and I want the best for you no matter what."

I was relieved that he didn't judge me for my actions as he continued reminding me about our previously scheduled photo shoot at Lake Lanier and expressed that he would love to still take me to shoot my promotional head shots.

When Ron arrived home from work later that evening, I immediately informed him that Shawn contacted me earlier that day, and that he wanted to still take some promotional photos that we'd previously scheduled. To my surprise, Ron agreed to the outing only after he and Shawn met face-to-face to have a conversation about the ground rules for the shoot.

During their conversation in our living room the following afternoon, Ron made it clear that he was only agreeing so that there would be closure between Shawn and me. With all that was going on, I had forgotten that February 14th was Shawn's birthday, and the day of the shoot.

I awoke early the morning of our photo shoot to apply make-up and prepare myself before leaving to walk up the street to Lady Fabian's apartment for her to style my hair before Shawn was scheduled to pick me up.

When we arrived at the lake, instead of me giving Shawn a birthday gift, he surprised me with a romantic picnic! The energy between us was, regrettably, strangely unconnected and strained throughout the day, which was very different compared to how connected we were the last time that we were together.

There remained an uncontrollable pull to Shawn. During our entire time at Lake Lanier that Valentine's Day, I remained torn and confused about our current circumstances.

For a moment the affection that still existed between Shawn and I made it seem as if he had never left. I struggled as time progressed that afternoon, catching sunrays, posing for the right promotional headshot and then sitting on a blanket overlooking the sparkling lake.

The fact that this was the first time that I have ever been torn between two guys before, I didn't possess the knowledge or tools to deal with the situation in a mature manner. It was extremely hard being with Shawn on his birthday, struggling to resist and fighting against the familiar magnetic energy field that engulfed us.

Although I regretted my contributions to the awkward situation that we were in because I had gotten involved with Ron so soon, I was determined to not make a bad situation worse, so I tried to responsibly deal with the current situation at hand in order to not cause any more heartbreak and damage.

Regardless of how drawn to Shawn I still remained, I was going to remain faithful to Ron and not lead Shawn on. As the day progressed, I was proud that I maintained control over my emotions.

However, all good things, as they say, must come to an end and the predetermined time that I'd agreed to with Ron to return home closed in on us. So while Shawn packed away his camera and cooler, I folded the picnic blanket before we started our drive back to take me home.

After Shawn dropped me off at the apartment, I was even more conflicted about seeing him again and I tried tricking myself into thinking that Valentine's Day provided closure and marked the end of the relationship between us.

When I walked into the apartment, Ron was sitting on the couch dressed in his uniform waiting for me to arrive home before leaving for work and he, unexpectedly, seemed okay with me spending the day with Shawn.

After Ron kissed me on the lips and walked out the door to leave, I felt that I was effectively dealing with the guilt and conflict that I continued to wrestle with being torn between two sweet guys.

I moved forward with thinking that I was doing a good enough job controlling my feelings and emotions until several weeks later on the night that Shawn appeared in the audience at my shows. Wham, bam! I instantly realized upon sight of him sitting there smiling so handsomely that the unrealistic day of closure that he and I shared at Lake Lanier did not do anything but reignite the passion and flame that still blazed between us!

At that time and up to that point many weeks after our last encounter, I had resisted the temptation to cheat. However, it was foolish of me to start thinking that I could have my cake and eat it too, so I willingly gave in to temptation on a night that Ron worked the late shift managing at Domino's Pizza.

My head-first leap into trying to love two was also during the time I had just recently been given a great opportunity by Tina Divore to join a newly formed group called "The Diamond Girls Review" at club Lipstix!

It was after a show at Lipstix one night that everything changed. Shawn and I were free to become secret lovers on the nights when Ron worked the late shift. Looking back to this period, I really didn't know what the hell I was thinking trying to be a wannabe playgirl, leaving with Shawn after my shows and going dancing or ending up at his apartment.

We'd successfully gotten away with our secret rendezvous and deception for a little while until that unforgettable, explosive night that Ron unexpectedly decided to surprise me and show up at the Lipstix show.

It all unfolded when I was at my station just after performing "I Miss You Much" by Janet Jackson before starting preparation for my last number of the evening, "Everything/Real Love" mix by Jody Watley.

Since I had previously borrowed Asheley Kruiz's down-to-the-booty-long, Chrystal Gayle wig, I just knew that I was looking hot as I anticipated being with Shawn after the show! At one point during the night, I noticed when my other cast member, Paula Sinclair, looked over at me as if she had just seen a ghost as I reached to grab my hairspray that she had borrowed from her make-up station.

When I looked towards the direction that held her gaze, my heart skipped a few beats. Ron was entering the dressing room looking furious as he walked towards my station. First, he stopped and asked Paula for a cigarette and after using her lighter he turned to me and asked, "What the hell is Shawn doing out there in the audience, Tracee?"

I lied and pretended that I was not aware that Shawn was present. "Ron, I didn't know that Shawn was in the audience."

Ron wasn't buying my lie so he pointed his finger at me and commanded, "You, come follow me." At first, I hesitated to follow him out of the dressing room because I knew that he was going to confront Shawn, but I knew that this was not going to be a pretty scene if I had not done exactly what he demanded me to do.

I didn't know what to expect as we approached Shawn sitting at the very top of the stadium seating in the audience nor do I recall the exact conversation, but I do remember that it was a hot mess. Those two guys were arguing and almost coming to blows like the "Clash of the Titans!"

Thank God the music was loud and the audience seemed oblivious to the activities occurring right behind them. I tried to intervene and calm down the situation, but the tension escalated to the point that they both refused to back down until I literally placed myself in between them, begging them to break it up.

The only way that the incident was going to end was if I gave in to Ron and once again emphatically tell Shawn that the relationship that we'd previously shared was over, but deep down inside I still wanted Shawn.

At the rate they were going, I feared that they would become physically violent with each other if I did not comply and convincingly reassure Ron in front of Shawn that we were once and for all finished.

I also had to convince Ron that I would never see Shawn again if I stood any chance of finally separating two men with their chests flared in preparation for battle. Totally embarrassed after doing all that was in my ability to extinguish their short, fast-burning fuses, I turned to walk away from the scene hoping to diffuse the situation.

Before I could get away, Ron grabbed me by my arm, almost snatching the wig off my head, and forced me once again to reiterate to Shawn that our relationship was done. When he released me I returned to the dressing room humiliated and worn out with my desperate attempts to pull myself together before my final number, which was so excruciating to get through. I was dazed.

After the show, inside the truck was the first time that I had ever seen such extreme rage coming from Ron. He started recklessly driving at high speeds with no regard for our safety..

He ignored the red lights and stop signs along the way as he repeatedly back handed slapped me with his free hand and threatened, "I will kill us both before I let you make a fool of me Tracee!" All I could do was hope that a cop pulled us over.

I feared for my life and all I could do was beg and plead with him, "Please slow down Ron before you crash into someone!"

He ignored me and I then silently started praying to God, promising that I would never cheat again if he saved my life! I anticipated the next backhand after the third puff of his cigarette, so I tried shielding my face while profusely apologizing for what I had done as I caressed his leg and pleaded, "Ron, I am sorry, please slow down, you are going to crash into something!"

I thought that I would kiss the ground when we finally arrived at the apartment in one piece! I was also grateful that Ron didn't follow through with his threats to drive off a bridge and kill us both.

After he slammed the car into park, he immediately pulled me out of the truck through his side as he exited and proceeded to literally carry me as if I'd had no feet and legs into the apartment straight to the bedroom.

Once inside our room, he slammed the door shut and started yelling. "What the fuck are you doing still seeing Shawn, Tracee?"

All I could say was, "Ron, I am so sorry for hurting you and I promise that I will not see Shawn ever again!"

I was really sorry for what I had done after seeing the explosive repercussions of my actions, but it didn't matter how much remorse I'd expressed because nothing that I was saying registered with Ron.

He seemed possessed and overtaken by rage. As time slowly ticked by, he ended up restraining me on the bed whenever I tried to leave the room and continued yelling. "Look what you've made me do Tracee. It's your fault that I'm so angry. I will kill you before I let you leave me!"

Even though I was at fault, I was not going to just continue sitting there and letting him repeatedly slap me in my face, so I started fighting back after the second hour of enduring his rage.

It seemed like the more I resisted and fought back, the more enraged and out of control he became. I felt helpless when he wouldn't allow me to leave the bedroom because he was much stronger than I was straddled over me continuing to scream, "See what you have done! I will kill you, Tracee, before I let you go!"

It felt as if I was having an out-of-body experience and flashing back to the time when I was around 3 or 4 years old when my mother was violently beaten by her live-in drunken boyfriend.

I will never forget that horrific night, with my brother and me standing with my mother's fake friend, Jill, while our mother was being beaten down in the streets in front of our house at 110 Dent St in Sumter, South Carolina.

I remember Ma putting him out of the house because he'd come home drunk and later that evening she was on the ground with him straddled on top of her beating her with his fist like she was a man.

I didn't understand why no one was doing anything to help my mother, so I went over to pick up a big stone next to the fence that was almost bigger than I was to hit him with it and stop him from beating my mother.

When I picked up the stone, Jill made me drop it back down on the ground and I became angrier that they were all just standing around watching and Jill wasn't doing more to help my mother.

I've recently concluded that if Jill had let me use the stone to help Ma, I probably would have harmed her even more because her back was on the ground with him on top of her.

I was relieved when the cops finally arrived and took him away in handcuffs. The end result was that my beautiful mother was beaten to the point that she was almost unrecognizable to me. I remember her wearing large dark shades for days after to cover her black-eyes and the purple and blue bruises that distorted her beautiful face.

Amazingly, I seemed to have been shocked back to reality before I'd completely passed out from Ron choking me in our bedroom and it occurred to me that the more I continued resisting him, the more aggressively violent he became.

So, I stopped fighting him and when I looked into his dark and glazed eyes to get his attention, I didn't recognize the person staring through me because that sweet person that I knew just 24 hours previously was gone and replaced with a nightmare.

Since I could not leave the bedroom at any point, I submitted to his will and he then removed his hands from my throat continuously repeating. "Look at what you made me do, Tracee!"

As he continued blaming me for his rage, I reflected back to him telling me about witnessing his father beating his mother and I felt sorry that I had hurt him in that manner. I was thankful that I'd managed to have eventually calmed him down by gently stroking and caressing his face.

I continued apologizing for betraying his trust and promising to never hurt him in that way again because I didn't know what else to do except reassure him over and over again that I would never see Shawn again.

I thought that I could make up for all of the mistrust that I'd caused between us by not betraying Ron ever again. I also reassured him that he was the only guy for me and I justified the violence and abuse by blaming myself for cheating and causing him to become so angry that night.

The next morning I mistakenly thought that I could make things better by giving in and being intimate with Ron after all of the violence, which started another unhealthy pattern of having sex to make up and reassure each other that we were still committed to staying together.

I awoke later that next afternoon covered in purple and blue bruises around my neck and his Merlot shaded handprints imprinted in my arms. As I stood there looking into the bathroom mirror trying to figure out how to hide my shame, I really didn't have a real clue about what I had gotten myself into.

Fortunately, Ebony was there with me through it all. We supported each other through some crazy drama-filled relationships back in the day! When I walked into the living room, he was sitting on the couch watching television, so I snuggled next to him, knowing that he had heard the violence the night and morning before. I didn't even try to hide my bruises from him when he asked, "Honey, are you okay?"

Convinced that he knew I was far from okay I replied."Not really, but I have my cocoa butter and make-up to help hide these bruises so that I can go to work." I proceeded to share with Ebony, "Girl, Ron cried last night and promised that he would never hit me again."

I tried to convince myself that he would not hit me again, yet was only fooling myself into thinking that the physical violence could not have gotten any worse because I had no idea that his issues went a whole lot deeper than I was mature enough to have understood.

At the time, I honestly believed that my actions caused Ron to become so violent and I thought that if I totally committed to him and did not cheat again, he would see that I really regretted what I had done.

Ebony empathetically offered, between Justice League commercials, "Sister Sue, you know that I am here for you and I support your decision if you decide to stay with Ron or not."

Trying to ease the tension, I replied, "Thanks, honey. I know that you support me and I also know that I should take heed from the train wreck experience with Hilton and run for the hills, but since it was my fault that Ron caught me cheating with Shawn, I need to make amends for what I have done."

Ebony shared, "Honey, I hoped that Ron didn't catch you still seeing Shawn because I knew that considering how he feels about you, he was going to act a plum fool once he found out you've restarted your relationship with Shawn."

I regrettably replied. "Girl, I don't know what I was thinking trying to be some kind of player, seeing two guys at the same time, which will never happen again, that's for sure."

Ebony affectionately concluded in her concerned sisterly manner, "Girl, in addition to the fact that you were on the rebound from being hurt by Shawn disappearing, I also know it's that cute ass six foot something body and those boyish charms that he's throwing on you."

As we laid on opposite ends of the couch wrapped in a fluffy comforter watching "I Love Lucy" reruns, I justified to myself the abuse by thinking that if Ron really didn't care for me, he would not have gotten so angry about Shawn and I still seeing each other.

Since I admittedly really fucked up that time, I was committed to making things right if it was the last thing that I did because, as compared to Shawn, Ron had showed that he really wanted us to build a home together.

After the incident at Lipstix, things were not good between Ron and I. He refused to talk to me and he'd often leave the room or the apartment to avoid direct contact.

His rejection was extremely hard to handle, so I became someone that I didn't recognize, doing almost anything to atone for what I had done. I didn't think that things could have gotten any worse moving forward than they were until almost a month or so later when Ebony informed me that he was resigning from his job and moving back to North Carolina to live with his mother and regroup from his personal challenges.

That revelation took some wind out of my sails due to being caught off guard and really disappointed that my best friend was leaving. I knew that Ebony had to do what was required to deal with the demons that he continued battling, so I didn't judge him for his choices.

Looking back, it made a whole lot of sense to me that Ebony was having challenges because when his alter-ego, Tara Holiday, came out to play, we partied from dusk to dawn!

Sometimes Ebony would go home after our night at the club, shower and go straight to work! If I had not witnessed him drinking it up all night long and then going to work immediately after leaving the club, I would not have believed that it was possible.

Those were the days during our single lives when the men were gentlemen, not all jerks or strung out on drugs, and they'd treated you like a lady. A girl could go out and have a really great time without all of the drama!

During those days before live-in boyfriends, after me and Ebony finished paying the bills and bought groceries, we'd usually have just enough money to pay our way into the club. Once inside, Tara didn't have to worry about cocktails because due to me not drinking, whenever a guy offered to buy me a cocktail, I ordered whatever she drank and secretly passed it to her.

I'm not sure if they were aware of what we were doing or not, and if they were, they never stopped buying the cocktails.

As far as the adventures of Tracee and Tara, I vividly recall some really juicy stories that occurred over the years during our single days. However, since I don't want Ebony to kill me, I'll just stick to one of the most tamed memories.

We spent the few weeks before his departure curled up on the couch watching his favorite cartoons and reminiscing back over our years together. I vividly recalled the time after one of our marathon nights of partying at the Marquette, when for some strange reason, we lost track of time dancing the night away having a great time in the club!

When we were finally ready to leave, unaware of the time, we were greeted by the hot sun beaming down on us as we walked outside to go home. After adjusting our eyes to the sudden brightness and questioning aloud how we were going to get home. We'd declined offers to be driven by several of the guys in the club, because we knew that they were expecting a lot more than just giving us a ride home.

Since none of the decent guys were still around when we were finally ready to leave the club, we had no other choice but to take MARTA home. Now, I want you to just imagine the three of us Tara, Miss Darrell and me, looking like ladies of the night sitting at the back of the train on the last seat trying to stay out of view of the other passengers as much as possible.

Miss Darrell was tore up from the floor up in a pair of tight, shredded Daisy-Duke jean shorts practically up to her ass crack and a tight Tshirt that she'd intentionally ripped to reveal her bare-chest and nipples. She'd worn a weave down to her ass and a pair of combat boots, looking like she had just stepped off the whore stroll.

Topping it all off was a thick five o'clock shadow that erased any traces of foundation from the lower portion of her face. She was a hot mess! Who knows what other kind of recreational drugs that Miss Darrell was consuming in addition to drinking hard liquor straight from the bottle through a straw without any chaser?

Tara most likely had on a pair of my skintight stretch jeans and a sheer black laced body blouse and five inch pumps with her black Tara hair. She was also torn up from the floor up from drinking her usual cocktails throughout the night.

Although I've never been a alcohol drinker, I did however climb "Trees" before going to the club during those party days! I'm certain that I was also a hot mess after sweating on the "Quette" dance floor. I recall wearing a tight black zipper on the front of my miniskirt with a red sheer top that revealed my black pushup bra and breasts, black fish-net stockings with four-inch, knee-high leather boots! Of course my crowning glory was most likely my Vanessa Williams-bobbed honey-blonde wig!

Once it was determined that public transportation would be our mode of getting home, we brushed our wigs and touched up our makeup with personal compact powder as much as possible, trying to tone down the club illusions before we started walking up Martin Luther King Jr. Boulevard to the train station.

I am certain that we must have been one strange sight walking up the street, trying to not look like hookers, except for Miss Darrel because she loved the attention! Thankfully, it was early enough in the morning that there were not too many people on the subway and the bus ride to Buford Highway!

We all instinctively filed to the very back of the bus and prayed that nobody would bother us. I was so relieved that we made it home safely after traveling on the train and two buses without incident. After that experience, I declared and promised myself that a situation like that would never happen to me again.

There were many more wonderfully crazy memories to follow that Ebony and I shared leading up to that excruciatingly painful day that I watched by best friend leave for North Carolina.

Although I knew that he was doing what he had to do to address his personal challenges, I missed having his support. Especially, during the madness that was occurring between Ron and I after my indiscretion.

It was a dark day for me when Ebony's mother and uncle drove down from North Carolina to assist him with loading up his things onto the bed of their truck and after they'd completed loading his possessions, we hugged and promised to stay in touch.

When I went back into the apartment after they'd departed, I felt an intense sense of emptiness and loss, knowing that I would not have my friend to lean on for moral support through my current trying times.

For the first time in unnumbered moons, I was on my own without my sister, unsure if things would ever get better with Ron.

As time passed after Ebony's departure, I continued living up to my commitment to not see or sneak around with Shawn anymore and things seemed to slightly improve between Ron and I for a brief moment.

I thought that we were getting back on the right track. However, I was totally caught off guard the day that he suggested that in order to save money, we should move in with this queen named Lloyd who was a mutual acquaintance and lived in the next apartment complex over from ours.

Since Ron and I were both working and could have afforded our apartment, I didn't understand why he was proposing that we give up our very own place to move in with someone I barely knew.

My first thought was to refuse to move in with Lloyd, but the guilt that I still felt about cheating with Shawn, and wanting to make Ron happy, prompted me to reluctantly agree to leave our apartment and move in with someone that I had only ever conversed with at the mailbox.

I blindly moved in with someone whom I much later found out that was in collusion with Ron to start a crack dealing, drug distribution partnership together. After becoming intimate with Ron's new career choice, I couldn't fathom that I had overnight unwillingly become a drug dealer's girlfriend who was no longer in control of her life, or so I thought at the time.

I really didn't recognize the person that I had become, nor did I know how to stop my high- speed descent deeper into what seemed like the pits of hell because I was under Ron's control and he knew exactly what buttons to push to make me do whatever he wanted me to do.

I'd never been exposed to that type of environment before, where drugs were often prepared for distribution and used by strangers that were supposedly Lloyd's friends. Fortunately, Ron never asked me to participate in distributing the drugs or indulging in them.

I looked forward to the weekends when I wasn't working my day job, which allowed me to get away from it all at the clubs during my performances! I had convinced myself that everything would be okay, but I did not comprehend the reality and consequences of the situation that I was in until a few short weeks later when I arrived home after a show and walked into the apartment to a familiar odor that almost gagged me as I inhaled.

I recalled the distinct smell of marijuana laced with crack cocaine from the time Hilton smoked it. I knew that Ron occasionally "Climbed Trees," However, I had no idea that he also resorted to lacing it with crack.

When I walked in on them smoking laced weed, I didn't know how to respond to what he was doing in the smoke filled kitchen with a gay guy we called Ms. Lilly.

My only reaction to Ron and Lilly was to walk past them and open a window, completely stunned beyond measure to find that they were actually cooking crack on the kitchen stove and smoking it!

I turned around without saying anything to either of them and went into the bedroom, followed by Ron closing the door behind him then sitting down on the love seat next to me. Before he could say anything, I angrily asked, "Ron, what the hell is going on in here? Why are you smoking crack with Ms. Lilly?"

He put his arms around me and, obviously stoned out of his mind, replied "Baby, we'll get more for the money by making the product ourselves."

Looking into his dilated eyes, I replied. "I thought that you were just going to sell the stuff to make money, not smoke it Ron."

"Baby, Ms. Lily was just testing the quality of the product for me. I didn't smoke anything but weed."

I knew that he was lying so I pushed him away, yet being cautious to not go too far and piss him off as I turned and replied, "Ron, although I agreed to you selling drugs on a temporary basis to do what you feel that you need to accomplish, I'm not going to continue living like this with you now using crack."

"Baby, you don't have to worry, I got this!" He leaned in closer to me and continued, "I promise I'm not smoking crack and nothing is going to happen to me or you, Tracee."

He then kissed my forehead, took another puff of his cigarette and walked out of the bedroom, leaving me sitting alone and feeling like I had just entered some sort of sixth dimension.

I couldn't help but wonder what the hell had I gotten myself into and how I could escape from the hell-ride? I guess that I could have just left if I really wanted to, but it was as if I was brainwashed and afraid that Ron would have reacted violently if I attempted to leave him.

After I was caught cheating with Shawn, I willingly allowed Ron to control me emotionally and physically in a way that I have never allowed myself to be handled by any other guy before.

Immediately after I accused him of resorting to lacing his "Trees" with crack, he became more controlling and possessive, treating me like a trophy that he would only take off the shelf, polish off and insist on me posing on his truck to impress his boys whenever they played basketball at the public court.

Although Ron would never really let any of the guys get close enough to interact with me, I overheard one of his flunkies complimenting him on having a light skinned girlfriend with green eyes.

Recalling this period in my life, it disappoints me extremely to have allowed Ron to have psychologically manipulated me the way that he did due to my guilty conscience.

After a period of time, I grew concerned about Ron staying out all night with strange characters whom I would never have associated with. One day he suddenly appeared out of nowhere, pulling up behind me in his truck when I was walking from the mailbox back toward the apartment, and started chastising me because he felt that I was switching a little too hard and drawing unnecessary attention to myself from other men walking and driving by on Argonne.

Honey, as petite and tiny as I was back then, I really didn't have anything to switch. Anyway, his jealousy and insecurity caused him to resort to instructing me on how to wear my make-up, hair and the clothing on and off the stage.

I purposefully avoided having ongoing conversations with other guys who approached me in the club or on the streets in our neighborhood because I wasn't sure if Ron was somewhere lurking around spying on me.

I also suspected that Ron was taking me through a series of tests to see if I had resumed seeing Shawn again, but I had not. I felt that I had no choice but to do whatever was necessary to please him because I never wanted to see the kind of intense rage that I'd previously witnessed after he'd caught me cheating.

As one sunrise turned into another sunset, it didn't take very long for me to see that Lloyd had other interests in Ron more than just their amateur drug dealing partnership. I wasn't threatened by Lloyd because I knew that Ron was attracted to full-time transsexuals that looked and lived 24/7 as women, not someone like Lloyd who only dressed up and became Tangy when he went out prostituting on Ponce De Leon.

I'm not judgmental about decisions others make in regards to their lives and personal choices. However, I have never been a prostitute and never ever considered becoming one. I'd chosen not to associate with those that I knew to be confirmed prostitutes because I didn't want to be negatively influenced by them to go for the easy money, selling my body and risking my life on the streets from one John to another. I wasn't raised to take the easy route out; I was raised to work hard for what I wanted and to have self-respect.

Lloyd unsuccessfully tried hard to conceal his feelings toward Ron from me and I didn't doubt for one moment that his resentment towards me was overwhelmingly strong, and if Ron had given him the opportunity to be with him, Lloyd would have taken it in a heartbeat.

Instead of fulfilling his fantasies regarding Ron, the coward pretended to be my friend in order to gain my trust, but I knew better and I didn't trust him as far as I could see him.

I undoubtedly knew that if presented with the opportunity, Lloyd would stab me in my back without a second thought in hopes of gaining Ron's affections.

I was afraid to insist to Ron that we move back into our own place, and I wasn't sure about how to effectively deal with the circumstances that I had entered into with both eyes wide open.

This was unknowingly a fork in the road, a turning point in my life that has taught me many valuable life lessons. Just one wrong move could have had a long-term devastating effect on the rest of my life if I did not proceed with caution.

I was smart enough, no matter however conflicted I was about my current situation, to not call Shawn and start that vicious cycle of turmoil all over again.

Although I missed the closeness and affections that Shawn and I once shared together, I focused on work and exerting my energy on finding some joy by evolving and experimenting with some very eclectic music choices for my performances, like "Three Hundred and Sixty Five Days" by Anita Baker, "I'll Always Love You" by Taylor Dayne and "Nothing Compares to You" by Sinead O'Connor.

There were many restless nights when I did not know if Ron was hurt or arrested and I foolishly hoped that he would start to show me the tenderness that he had previously shown.

As time moved on, I spent many nights wondering where Ron was, what was he doing and with whom he was spending his time. In hindsight, why did I not just leave then? Fear, maybe. I was afraid to leave with no definite plan and not sure where I would go if I left because Ron promised that he would kill me if I ever tried leaving him.

I felt that I had no other choice but to do almost anything to get him to love me the way he once did before things went all awry. I now question if he really loved me or was he just infatuated with being involved with a transsexual female. I do believe that the latter might have been the case.

It seemed that I was entranced and engulfed by a dense fog that consumed my entire being, which restricted me from clearly seeing a way through to walk into the light away from my dysfunctional darkness.

In addition to going back to South Carolina never being an option, I did something that I had never considered doing before in my state of desperation when I sought counsel from a spiritual advisor acquaintance of Lloyd's named Miss LoRay.

Currently, it's ironic that of all people to have consulted with about my problems, I chose to confide in someone who was acquainted with my enemy Lloyd.

There was something familiar about Miss LoRay during her visits (she regularly traveled from Alabama to meet with her clients in Georgia). Whenever she consulted with Lloyd I often voluntarily left the apartment because I did not want to take part in what they were doing.

However, when I was informed that she'd be returning for another consultation with Lloyd, I figured that I had nothing to lose since I didn't have anyone else to go to for moral support. Since she was available, I felt that it couldn't hurt to also meet with her to see if she could advise me on how to deal with my current situation.

Mother, father, God and universe ensured that I was unexpectedly alone in the apartment on the morning that Miss LoRay was scheduled to arrive, because Lloyd was detained at work while Ron was out doing who knows what.

I'd already figured that I would have to come up with another plan if this spiritual advisement thing didn't work out, when I heard the knock on the door. I knew that it was most likely Miss LoRay!

After first peeping through the security hole and confirming that it was her, I opened the door to greet she and her male traveling companion. I informed her that Lloyd called and asked me to relay that he would be arriving a little later for their appointment because he was being detained at work.

She replied, "Oh, good, because I was hoping to get to talk to you alone, due to being very concerned about your mental and physical well-being living in this environment."

I responded somewhat surprised at her bluntly stated comment! "It's interesting that you are saying what you just said to me, Miss LoRay, because I have also wanted to talk with you about those exact issues and concerns."

Miss LoRay placed her wise hands over mine before continuing, "I already know what one of your problems is, and I have also warned Lloyd that if he's interested in your man, he's wrong for that."

As I listened to her continuing to speak, I could not deny any longer what was staring me right in my face. Lloyd was using voodoo rituals to sabotage my relationship in hopes of gaining a chance to have Ron.

Miss LoRay continued by warning, "You are in the midst of deceit and betrayal and you really should make some serious decisions about changing your living situation very soon if you want to have any chance of making your relationship work."

It was interesting to me that she was Lloyd's personal advisor, yet she had reconfirmed that living with Lloyd was bad for my mental and physical psyche. As I sat there analyzing and absorbing the information she was providing me, she told her companion to go to their car and retrieve a gallon milk jug that was inside the trunk.

As he was leaving to obey her command, I wondered what was in the milk jug, knowing very well that I was not about to ingest anything that she'd prepared and stored in her trunk.

When Miss Loray's companion returned from the car, I observed that the jug was filled with tea-shaded liquid in which floated various green leaves and herbs. I continued waiting patiently to see what she was about to tell me to do with the jug of brown liquid.

She reached over touching me gently on my shoulder and directed, "Go and get your Bible dear." When I returned with my Bible, she continued. "Turn to the 27th Psalm."

I figured that her suggesting that I read a Bible verse was not too suspiciously farfetched, so I read the verse. Afterwards, she continued to explain that the contents in the jug were a guidance and direction potion of herbs and that I should run a nice warm tub of water, pour all of the contents of the jug into the water and visualize what I wanted my life to be as I soaked and read the 27th Psalm.

After she briefly prayed with me and reassured me that everything would be revealed to me in due time on how to proceed with making the changes that are necessary in order to obtain my happiness and sanity, I didn't have a problem with paying her for the consultation.

My curiosity was piqued when she didn't even wait around for Lloyd to arrive for his consult, leaving immediately after my consultation concluded.

I decided to take a bath. At first, I was very reluctant and hesitant about immersing my entire body into the unknown contents in the jug, so I sat on the floor for almost 15 minutes or so with one arm immersed in the mixture to make sure that it wouldn't irritate my skin.

After becoming comfortable enough that the mixture was not harmful, I sat down in the warm water and started reading the 27th Psalm several times and then closed my eyes and visualized moving out of Lloyd's apartment.

The water was warm and comforting as I reclined, hoping that I would be able to successfully move forward from my current circumstances. Right before I completed reading the verse for the final time before getting out of the tub, I heard someone come into the apartment.

Before I could get all the way out the water, Ron entered the bathroom and closed the door behind him after he saw me in the tub. He then sat down crossed-legs in Indian position on the floor beside the bathtub. He proceeded to apologize for the way that he was treating me because he felt that I still harbored feelings for Shawn. He was now convinced that I was sincerely sorry and regretful for cheating with Shawn.

After seeing familiar eyes reflecting back at me, I did not put up any resistance because there was no denying the electricity between us! I also suspect that the vulnerable position that I was in made it easier for me to not put up too much of a fight.

I did manage, however, to resist long enough to inform him, "Ron, in order for us to forgive each other and heal from the situation that we are currently in so that we can move forward with our lives, we first have to move out of Lloyd's apartment into our own-- number one. And then you have to get a job, and, lastly, you have got to stop hanging out in the streets all night long selling and using crack, if that's still the case."

He replied to my statement with no objection. "Now that you've convinced me that you're not seeing what's his name, I can live with those conditions, Tracee, and we can start looking for an apartment whenever you are ready!"

He continued before allowing me to speak, "I will also reapply for my management position at Domino's today and once I get rid of the remaining supply, I will not re-up."

He shifted position, kneeling on one knee and continued, "I will do whatever I have to do to make things better for us, baby."

It was the way he said baby that got me! After mutually committing to making an honest effort to improve our relationship and immediately change our environment, I believed that he would live up to his promises to me. I believe Wendy Williams said it best: "Stupid and dumb twenty-something-year-olds."

Anyway, I could no longer resist Ron so I climbed out of the tub to retrieve a condom from my bag and returned, proceeding to give in to his passionate kisses as I helped him to remove his clothes and shoes, before us both climbing into the water and ultimately unleashing the uncontainable explosive passion that still boiled for him, erupting like a volcano!

That sunny afternoon in the tub with Ron, I once again gave into his charms and seemed to have completely turned my soul over to him. The following day I was so excited about starting to look at prospective apartments and submit rental applications!

On our second day looking at apartments we placed a deposit on a nice one bedroom, full kitchen, bath, living room with tenant parking that was located on Buford Highway! We were planning to move as soon as possible once we had gotten the word from the apartment leasing agent the following week about whether our application was approved or not!

Things seemed to have been back on track until over that three-day weekend period, beginning early evening Friday on into Sunday morning. All of a sudden my dreams and hopes came to an abrupt halt. It felt as if I had crashed head on into a huge plantation oak tree that was suddenly hit by lightning, causing it to fall on the train track right in front of me.

I was horrified that all of my long overdue hopes of finally breaking free from the black widow's web that I had been entrapped in for the last several months were instantaneously derailed in a snap of a finger it seemed.

My joy started unraveling after a full moon night when I arrived home from working at Crazy Ray'z somewhere after 2 that morning. I was slightly taken by surprise when I walked through the apartment door and found Ron sitting alone in the living room and smoking a cigarette, waiting for my arrival.

I had expected for him to been out getting rid of the remainder of the drugs so that we would start afresh. His presence caused me to also hope that he'd completed getting rid of drugs, thusly concluding his drug dealing days earlier than expected!

I joyfully placed my costume bag on the floor beside the couch and sat down next to him and attempted to hug him, but he pulled away from me and without saying a word handed me a large opened manila envelope that was addressed to me without a return address.

It was obvious to me that he was angry about what was inside the envelope, so I reluctantly pulled the contents from it. They were semi-intimate photos of me posing in lingerie that Shawn had taken when we were sneaking around with each other.

I was completely devastated as an arctic chill flushed my body and I instantly knew that the trust that I had managed to rebuild between Ron and I was shattered into a thousand jagged pieces by an envelope full of photos that were taken months ago.

I suspected that Lloyd was intercepting and opening my mail, and that he had given the pictures to Ron. I also knew that there was no way that I would be able to reassure Ron that I had not seen Shawn since the last incident at Lipstix club.

It seemed pointless for me to try and convince Ron that those photos were taken months ago, but I didn't have anything to lose so I tried explaining anyway. "Ron, these pictures were taken months ago. I have not seen or spoken to Shawn since then."

Ron stood without saying a word in response to what I'd said to him and he then walked out of the room, leaving me there alone once again wondering how this could have happened after all of my efforts walking the straight and narrow.

I had forgotten about that photo shoot with me in lingerie before old ugly Murphy's Law had my past mistakes reappear to threaten my future. I've since realized that maybe Shawn was hurt by what I had done moving on with another guy and sending those photos in the mail was his way of dealing with his feelings.

Although I never made any assumptions about our relationship, there were no other guys because I only dated Shawn in the beginning before Ron entered the picture. I've wondered why he never verbally expressed to me that he wanted our relationship to progress to the next level? If that's what he wanted, I believe that he should have treated me as such by communicating with me about his concerns and pain during his father's passing.

As I sat alone after Ron exited, flipping through those intimate memories of Shawn and I --36 printed shiny images from within the manila envelope – it seemed that I was once again ushered right back into that oh-so-familiar dark cloud fog rolling in without warning.

Also, I found myself once again behaving irrationally, sitting outside of the apartment of the lesbian couples who were mutual friends of ours like a little puppy waiting to talk to Ron in hopes of getting him to believe that I had not recently been with Shawn.

I needed for him to know that I had not been unfaithful again, but he would not give me a chance to explain. Finally, after being rejected and told over and over by him that our relationship was over, I decided that I was not going to continue humiliating myself any longer. I'd finally felt that I deserved better because I was telling the truth about not cheating again.

For once in a very long time the eastern winds blew in and rolled out the fog just as I had finally arrived at the point where I was not going to continue allowing myself to be treated so horribly when I knew that I was faithful.

I figured that his mind was made up that I had cheated again and that it was a futile waste of energy trying to convince him otherwise, so I reconciled that it was really over between us and that I needed to go on with my life without him.

I considered immediately leaving the apartment, but since I had already paid my portion of the rent, I decided to take advantage of the time to formulate my plan to finally leave that potentially explosive environment.

The following morning, I felt a little like my old self once again, thinking clearly and back in control, even though I was still hurt by the unfortunate events that had unfolded over the last couple of days.

I was determined to get my own place and start rebuilding my life as soon as possible and I'm sure that at one point Ron noticed the changes in my attitude, no longer running up behind him trying to convince him that he was mistaken about when those photos were taken. Instead of focusing on him any further, I directed my attention on making new living arrangements and then, all of sudden, that Sunday afternoon when I was sitting alone in the living room watching television and circling more affordable studio apartment ads in the classifieds that I was intending to visit, I noticed that Ron had stayed in the apartment instead of leaving to avoid me as he had been previously doing. I was taken aback when he casually strolled into the living room where I was sitting, sat in the chair next to me and then reached for my hand, asking, "Can I talk to you, Tracee?"

I pulled away from him and angrily replied. "What is it that you want to talk about, Ron?"

"I want to apologize to you, Tracee," he replied.

At that point, I was done and ready to get off the nauseating rollercoaster ride with him. "Ron, your apology is not enough this time," I said.

I felt slightly empowered as I continued, "You were wrong for not hearing me out because I did not do anything to give you any reason to think that I was cheating again and you treated me like in the summertime outhouse shit and maggots when I tried to explain those pictures."

He replied, "Tracee, I am sorry for not believing you when you told me that those pictures of you and whatever his name is were taken months ago."

Unconvinced, I replied. "What is it that finally made you realize that I was telling the truth from the beginning, Ron?"

He interjected before I could continue. "I am sorry that I allowed other people to influence my thinking, Tracee."

Since I still blamed myself for the drastic change in Ron's personality due to my infidelity, causing him to turn from the loving, trusting person that I once knew into someone with no heart, I stupidly felt that the only way to make amends for what I had previously done was to forgive as I wanted so desperately to be forgiven.

We both committed to moving on from Photo Gate and later that early evening slightly before sunset, I was in his truck looking for my Sade cassette tape to perform at the club that upcoming weekend!

As I reached underneath the seats searching around for my music, I pulled out some photos of a biological girl in a cheerleader uniform hidden underneath his seat.

After taking the photos upstairs and confronting Ron about the cheerleader, he told me that she was just a girl that he'd dated in high school. He also revealed that during our separation he had reconnected with her, taking her and some of her friends out to dinner that past Friday evening before we got back together.

Of course I was furious about him taking another girl and her friends to dinner because he had never taken me to dinner like that before. After I ripped the photos into pieces, I held my composure and did not fly off the handle right away because I recalled how I felt during my photo incident.

So, I gave him the benefit of the doubt and believed that the dinner with his high school girlfriend was during our break-up, however, I warned him that if I was to ever find out that this was an ongoing relationship, he and I would be finished.

Naively, I thought that we were making an honest effort to move forward with our plans to start over after receiving word on that following Tuesday that our apartment application was approved, and we scheduled an appointment for the following Wednesday to go and pay the first month's rent and deposit balance before signing the lease and moving in.

Later that afternoon after returning from the basketball court with Ron, I retired to watch television in the living room and he went into the bedroom to watch a boxing match. All of a sudden Lloyd, of all people, came tipping into the living room breathing like a black bull and whispered to me, pointing towards the back room, "LeRon is on the telephone talking to some girl!"

I carefully picked up the receiver in the living room and started eavesdropping on the conversation and I was hurt as I listened to him making plans to take her out again. I suspected that she was the girl in the photo and when I could not stand hearing how sweetly he was talking to her the way that he used to talk to me, I snapped and interjected, "Who are you talking to, Ron?"

He remained silent and she asked, "Who are you?"

I replied to her question, "I'm his girlfriend that he currently lives with. Who the hell are you?"

I didn't wait for an answer, slamming down the receiver, not knowing what possessed me when I went into the bedroom and saw Ron reclined on the chair with his legs casually crossed, still nonchalantly talking to the cheerleader all casually.

Without saying a word, I dove on him like Rick Flair in a contested battle for the wrestling title take-down match. It was as if I briefly blacked-out when I started hitting him like a crazed woman, and as I attacked, I no longer feared what his response was going to be.

I was enraged this time, continually and uncontrollably beating Ron, calling him every name in the book. I released all of the pent-up anger and frustration on his head as I recalled all the extra mess that we had been going through since we've moved into that apartment from hell, living with Satan's spawn!

Amazingly, he didn't react as violently as he'd previously responded whenever I fought back during physical altercations, because he knew that he had been caught in the act of cheating after promising me that he was not still dating the cheerleader.

Finally, after a few seconds I grew tired of whaling on him and since I'd also realized that my actions were pointless, I let him up and walked out of the apartment to take a walk up the street to calm my nerves.

When I returned to the apartment parking lot almost 15 minutes or so later, I saw Ron sitting inside of an ambulance being treated by the paramedics with an ice pack on his eye looking like he had just been attacked by a leopard that left scratches and claw marks all over his body.

I felt so sorry for attacking him in that manner and seeing him in the ambulance. I don't know where I had gotten the courage to attack him like that. What I did know was that continuing to live in that environment one moment longer was not healthy for me and that I had to get out immediately.

As I walked back upstairs after making sure that Ron was okay before entering the apartment, Mr. Smith, who was this really nice elderly neighbor across the hall opened his apartment door and commented to me, "I don't know what it is about that apartment, but it always seems that all of the guys that have ever lived there have at one time or another ended up sitting inside an ambulance being treated for injuries."

All I could do was respond before entering the apartment, "Mr. Smith, you're probably right and one thing for sure is that I am getting out of this abyss as soon as possible."

That Friday night at work I didn't know where I was going to end up after Ron's ambulatory incident, but I did know that immediate change was in my future! My song selections and performances usually reflected the mood and state of mind I was in, so that weekend at Crazy Ray'z the first number I performed was the crowd pleaser "Is It A Crime" by Sade, which by all intentions reflected my personal deep pain.

Even though I didn't discuss with the cast members the details about my current situation, it was obvious to them that something was wrong with me. They kept expressing their concerns and asking throughout the night if I was okay.

Since I've always been private about my relationships and I only discussed my personal challenges with those very few people that were close to me that I trusted, I continued lying and telling them that I was okay.

After the incident with the cheerleader on the phone I was officially done with trying to make something out of a destructive relationship that seemed destined to fail from the very beginning and as far as I was concerned, we were no longer in a relationship.

I had finally come back to my right mind to move on! I also took my Crazy Ray's co-worker up on his offer to temporarily move in with him until I was able to find my own place after securing my portion of the deposit that we'd previously placed on the Buford Highway apartment.

Thinking back on those volcanically eruptive transitory days in my life in All Girls Village, I have often questioned why I did not just leave in the beginning when all the drama started to unfold and why was I not strong enough mentally or physically to end that tumultuous relationship a lot sooner than I had.

I now know that I'd mistakenly assumed that I had the power to make things better and turn the negative around in a positive direction. Also, I've currently comprehended that there was absolutely nothing else that I could have done except for what I ended up doing, which was to use the power that I was still in control of to briskly walk away with purpose before it was too late.

On Saturday after performing my second number, "Hold On" by Wilson Phillips, at Crazy Ray'z that weekend, I went back to the apartment and immediately started packing my things in preparation to load them onto my co-workers' boyfriend's truck come the following Tuesday morning.

It seemed like one bad event right after another continued happening before I was able to leave that hell hole. The craziness started earlier that Sunday afternoon when this strange white couple came beneath the apartment window and started shouting really loudly for Miss Lilly.

When I looked out the window and informed them that Lilly wasn't there, they refused to believe me and insisted that Lilly had stolen their drugs.

Just a little background on Miss Lilly before we proceed, he was this tall and really skinny dark-skinned gay guy who was a stone cold crack-head. He had smoked so much crack that his skin was dried out and flaky white from the drugs in his system.

The saddest part of it all was that he had just recently inherited hundreds of thousands of dollars after his mother's death that he spent all on crack cocaine.

Okay, back to the weirdly acting white couple continuing to yell for Lilly to come outside and give them their drugs that he'd supposedly stolen from them.

After I threatened to call the police, they finally left. Later that ominous evening the weirdness continued when Ron unexpectedly arrived at the apartment and joined me in the living room trying to smooth things over.

He'd futilely tried convincing me to stay with him. No matter how apologetic he seemed, my mind was made up that I was leaving without him-- period. After 20 minutes or so of telling Ron why our relationship was over, we were interrupted by a loud, continuous banging on the door.

I heard a voice commanding to open the door and that they were Atlanta Police Department! I didn't know what to think, so I peeped through the security hole and saw that they were police officers before unlocking and then opening the door to inquire about what was going on.

One of the officers asked to speak to Lilly and when I informed him that Lilly was not there, they stormed into the apartment and started searching the back bedrooms, closets, kitchen and stairwell!

Even though I didn't have anything to hide, I knew that a warrant was required to search a residence like that and after I requested to see a copy of their search warrant, the detective informed me that they had an arrest warrant for the person that went by the alias Lilly and suggested that if I knew where he was, I should call him at the number on the business card that he handed me before they left.

Whew, talk about pure madness! I did not know what Lilly had done, nor did I enquire about whatever came of their search for him. Frankly, I didn't care because I was out of there!

Tuesday could not have come soon enough for me, and when it finally came, I awoke early that morning anticipating escaping from the apartment of horrors! It occurred to me later that Lloyd had been missing in action during the raid and he was present on the morning that I was scheduled to leave.

At first, he stayed out of sight, lurking around in his bedroom the whole time because he had been recently fired from his housekeeping job at the Marriott after he'd proposed to give a male guest a blow job in the guest's room, which was also why he was delayed from meeting with Miss LoRay that day they were scheduled for a consultation.

I found it strange that day when he called to ask me to lie and say that he did not live there if anyone from his job called. Karma is a bitch!

So back to my liberation Tuesday, Lloyd and I were the only two in the apartment that afternoon and as I stood at the window keeping watch for Billy to pull into the parking lot, I wasted no time carrying as many bags as I could carry down the stairs when he finally arrived and placed them neatly on the ground to be loaded onto the truck. Billy got out of the truck and asked, "Is there anything else that needs to be carried down and loaded, Tracee?"

Overjoyed that he was there, I replied, "Hello Billy, thank you for helping me move. All that's left to be loaded are my loveseat, chair and three wardrobe trunks, which are the only big ticket items that need to be carried down!"

Billy followed me upstairs to help bring down my furniture and clothes and as I was dragging the last wardrobe trunk out over the threshold, I turned to grab my shoulder bag off the couch, unintentionally displacing the carpet at the apartment entrance.

When I reached down to straighten the rug back into place in order to close the door, I found several photos of Ron and I underneath the carpet that had previously and mysteriously disappeared from my bag.

When I picked up the photos, I noticed that there were some strange markings on each of them and instinctively knowing that this was Lloyds' sick and twisted effort to use witchcraft to lure Ron into becoming sexually interested in him, which was not going to happen with me in the picture or out.

Although I was done with Ron in my mind, the one and only thing that I knew for sure and can give him credit for is that he'd informed me whenever a couple of the gay guys who'd befriended me to get close to him went as far as proposing to give him up to a thousand or more dollars just to sleep with them, which never happened due to Ron's attraction to transsexuals!

Ron loved femininity not masculinity, so Lloyd and the other gay guys that were not living as a full-time female who were on hormones never stood any chance of being intimate with him.

So, after finding the pictures beneath the carpet, I wrapped them in a scarf and placed them into my shoulder bag to destroy later. Turning to leave, I relished the fact that moment would be the last time I would ever cross that path or step inside that hell's pit ever again!

Right before closing the door for the final time, I saw Lloyd slithering his way out of the bedroom with his hands on his hips and snorting around like a razor-back hog with those soup-cooler lips sticking out like a rabid baboon.

Guilt was written all over his ugly face as he bee-lined it towards the door and grabbed it before I was able to slam it shut and then stood at the top of the stairs as I was leaving my nightmare on Argonne.

I felt his demon eyes piercing my back like daggers as I walked down the stairs thanking God that I was moving on in one piece and that there was nothing that he could do about it but watch me walk away.

Right before I took my last step out of the apartment complex entrance, he yelled down the stairs after me. "Bitch, you forgot something!"

When I turned to see what he was yapping about, I saw that he was holding the beautiful antique retro tangerine colored glass table ornament that Shawn had previously given to me for my birthday that I had mistakenly left on the floor beside the door to carry down last before becoming distracted by the photos underneath the carpet.

He then dramatically threw my cherished gift down the stairs shattering it against the wall and when I looked down and saw the reflecting sun through the broken pieces that covered the cement floor, it took everything within me to not run back up those stairs and choked the ugliness off of Lloyd!

I didn't respond in the manner that I'd suspected he wanted because it was not worth it. I remained calm, cool and collected although I was hurt by what he had done. I was not about to give him the pleasure of seeing me angry over material things or let him know that he had gotten to me.

However, I had to show him that I wasn't intimidated or afraid of him, so I took a step back up one stair and stated, "I can always replace the vase and, oh by the way, I found my pictures that you'd stolen and placed underneath the carpet and it really doesn't matter how much witchcraft you use, Ron will never be sexually interested in someone like you, so, try as you may it will never happen ugly beast!"

After my final words to the Creature from the Black Lagoon, I knew that turning my back and walking away infuriated him. So, I let the apartment entrance main door slam behind me as I walked away, leaving him standing up there with a cracked face.

As I got into the truck with Billy, I imagined Lloyd pacing around his den of drama as usual, looking like the fool that he was, trying to figure out how he was going to replace my contributions to his rent now that he had been recently fired for being inappropriate at his job.

I felt a great sense of relief and my spirit became more at ease as I watched through the passenger side rear-view window All Girls Village shrink out of sight after the light turned red, signaling right of way onto Ponce De Leon Avenue.

Almost three days after moving into my Crazy Ray'z co-worker Gabe's spare bedroom, I accepted his invitation to become his new roommate because his old roommate had permanently remained in his home state due health issues.

I was determined to make it on my own so I continued working part-time in the Kmart Apparel Department and regularly performing in the shows! It suddenly seemed like I had a just-broken-up-from-my-boyfriend announcement tattooed on my forehead, because the guys started approaching me left and right, but I avoided the advances of those guys trying to hook up with me so soon after my separation.

Instead of dating, I directed my attention on obtaining outside bookings other than just Crazy Ray'z in order to supplement my income. As time progressed however, there were brief moments that I was tempted to call Shawn, but I did not call because I knew that calling him would not have been fair or healthy for either of us.

I wasn't mature or secure enough at that time to not think the worst of Shawn for not responding to my attempts to reach him during the time that he was taking care of his business with his family, and my one regret is that I didn't handle things differently with him during that time.

Moving forward, I so desperately wanted to change my life and break the destructive cycle of choosing the wrong men -- like Hilton and Ron.

One afternoon during my self-reflective and re-evaluation period as I watched television alone in my room, I felt that I needed an all-around fresh start after receiving an inspiration when I saw this beautiful little African-American girl in a toothpaste commercial named Destiny!

As the little girl's name kept popping into my head I was also anticipating a bright future for myself in both my personal and professional career, so I immediately decided that I would start by changing my stage name to Destiny!

Weeks had passed and I was finally starting to feel that I was successfully moving on with my life, until Ron started to unexpectedly appear at my jobs. One night he showed up bare-chested in the middle of winter driving a Jeep with the cover off.

Another time our neighbor and Crazy Ray'z bartender friend Robert told me, during one of our regular Sunday afternoon gossip sessions, "Miss Destiny, when I arrived home from the club this morning with my new boyfriend, Luke, I saw Ron lurking around the apartment security gate shirtless in the freezing cold with a huge stick looking for you girl!"

I hadn't expected to hear that he'd seen Ron at our apartment so all I could do was respond, "Oh, really?"

Robert questioned, fishing for dirt, "Girl, he must be on some serious drugs to be out there in that cold barely dressed like that."

I deflected and deliberately avoided directly answering his question, instead responding, "Who knows what he is out there doing? What I want to know is how the hell did he find out where I live?"

I became even more concerned about my safety after Robert suggested and warned, "Honey, that man is stalking you; you better buy some pepper spray or something and you need to watch your back girl!"

Robert obviously had traces of whatever he'd been snorting the before still in his system, causing him to become more animated as he continued. "Girl, just think if you had come home with another guy from the club this morning, who knows what he would have done with that big ass stick he was carrying, Miss Destiny."

Robert was known for usually overly exaggerating things. However, I knew that he did not have any reason to overemphasize what he'd observed that time. Since I wasn't sure of what Ron's intentions were towards me, I was also concerned that he might have resorted to stalking me to see if I had resumed seeing Shawn even though we were broken up.

The following Saturday night at Crazy Ray'z when I was in the dressing room after the show packing up my costumes and preparing to go home, the club manager, John Fox, came and informed me that Ron was outside in his truck requesting to talk to me.

I'm sure that the fear of talking to him was all over my face, although I agreed to hear what he had to say because I knew that I would be followed home if I did not. John insisted on standing and observing our conversation from the restaurant entrance.

I was glad that John wanted to make sure that I was okay, and when I walked outside of the club/restaurant, I saw Ron sitting in his truck looking pitiful. I cautiously walked up to him, stood next to the truck and asked, "Ron, why are you here?"

Before responding to my question, Ron threw the cigarette that he was smoking outside the window onto the ground, then he replied, "Tracee, I just wanted to see you and talk to you."

I replied in a matter-of-fact manner, "What else do we have to say to each other, Ron? I believe you said it all when you chose to continue the relationship with your cheerleader girlfriend and then lied to me about it."

He responded in an innocent boyish tone that always seemed to have made me want to not make him suffer any longer. "Baby, can you please get inside the truck so that I can talk to you?"

I turned to see if John was still keeping watch and after confirming that he was, I reluctantly walked around to the passenger side to an open door. After climbing inside the truck I intentionally left the door ajar due to not knowing what his intentions were.

Once I'd gotten settled in the truck, Ron reached over and turned on the preset car stereo that started playing softly in the background what used to be our song, "Ready or Not" by After Seven.

He then began looking remorsefully and longingly into my eyes as he continued. "I miss you, Tracee, and I am so sorry that I lied to you."

Before I could respond he reached for my hand as he continued, "Please reconsider giving me another chance to make this right with you, baby."

As I sat there listening to him plead for my forgiveness, I reflected back to immediately after I'd left Ron. It took me awhile to not hurt whenever I thought about him living with the cheerleader or some other girl.

I spent several weeks after our separation hoping that after a period of time I would be able to move on from thinking about him living with some other girl. I continued hoping that after a period of time I'd find contentment with not seeing him again.

As previously mentioned, Ron knew exactly what buttons to push so my seeing him in such a vulnerable position, practically begging me to take him back, played out exactly as he'd planned by beginning to remove the wall of protection that I'd built.

Before moving in to take a bite of the bait, I tried to leave the truck, but he asked me to please stay and talk to him a little longer. Although I should have ended the conversation not too long after sitting there with him and immediately running for the hills, I responded as if I was no longer in control.

Due to him looking so pitiful and broken it was as if he'd possessed some kind of magical powers that he used to stop me from putting up any further resistance to his requests to come back to him. I couldn't help but feel sorry for him and ease his obvious pain, so I asked, "Ron are you still selling drugs and living with Lloyd?'

Ron quickly replied, knowing that the well-baited hook he'd set had been doing its job to lure me in. "No, baby. I'm back managing at Dominos again and staying with my Dad until I get it together."

He then took my hands into his and convincingly continued, "Tracee, baby, I know that I fucked up, but I am working on my issues and I really hope that you would please give me another chance to make things right with you."

Vacillating in the wrong direction, I don't know what I was thinking even considering his proposal so soon after all of the black eyes, bloody lips, purple and blue bruises all over my body that he caused trying to control me.

For some unexplainable reason, I was still drawn to him after all the mental and physical abuse. Shamefully, I admit to responding, "Ron, you were wrong for not believing in me." Ron continued looking pitiful and silently, waiting for me to continue. "Since everybody deserves a second chance to make amends for their mistakes, because I have certainly made my share, consider this your second chance, but if you are not serious about wanting to turn over a new leaf please do not make any false promises to me that you are not able to keep."

Ron successfully reeled me in. When I returned back in the club after our conversation, my cast members and management were surprised that I had agreed to leave with him that night, but their discontent didn't matter to me, because I was going to take advantage of the opportunity of getting another chance to start over with my man. I know what you're thinking: stupid, stupid, stupid.

Although I respected and appreciated my cast members' opinions and concerns for me, I was headstrong in my misguided determination to prove all of the naysayers wrong by making my relationship work that time!

Writing about Crazy Ray'z at this current moment in my life and recalling those personal circumstances during that period has caused me to recognize that being in that physically violent relationship with Ron really did negatively impact both my personal and entertainment career no matter how much denial I engaged in during those days.

Since I'd always been a stickler for being on time, I was really challenged by the constant tardiness to work due to regular obsession- and possession-driven arguments that lasted for hours, which usually elevated to Ron physically restraining me from going to work.

Let's not forget about the emotional effects of having to wear extreme makeup applications to hide my live tattoos that additionally negatively affected my appearance no matter how successful I felt that I was with a little highlighter, foundation, loose powder and bronzer.

Although I did not think that the decreased Crazy Ray'z bookings were fair then, I now understand that management did what they felt that they had to do. Oh, well.

I wasn't mature enough at that time to comprehend their concerns for my safety back then, however, I am confident that I now know better and wouldn't tolerate that type of relationship ever again in this or any other incarnation!

It's unfortunate that I can currently relate to those other people that continue to get back on those physical and emotional rollercoaster rides in relationships with abusive people. Also, through my own personal experiences I, unfortunately, somewhat understand their motivations for being drawn back to their abusers like what I can only imagine is like a crack-head to the crack pipe.

I've also since learned from those personal experiences that no matter how much our family members and friends try to intervene to convince us that we deserve more than just being abused by someone who claims to love us, we will not usually get it from them because we have to make up our own minds to believe that we deserve better than what we are getting. I deserve much better!

In my situation back then, I carried the guilt about cheating and contributing to the negative events that took place which initially started my downward spiral, so I kept going back in hopes of atoning for my transgressions.

Not long after we started seeing each other again, Ron and I were invited to dinner by some friends of mine from the club named Vince and Elvis to check out their apartment complex to see if it was a place that we would like to consider living.

That evening after dinner, Ron and I shared a romantic romp alone for several hours in one of the four large, heated swimming pools on the premises. The deceptive closeness that I experienced with Ron frolicking around as we became one while sister moon's light danced on the warm water would soon be revealed for what it really was, an illusion.

Two weeks later, after our application was approved, we moved into a beautiful new apartment located outside of the city limits on Indian Trail Road way out off I-85 North in hopes of putting some distance between the previous haunting memories and our new beginning!

Our new home was in a really nice gated community, miles away from Ponce De Leon and the beast of the East. Things went great for the first month or so after we finished moving into our new place and furnishing it with some beautiful antique furniture that we got for a good price from a friend's aunt.

However, the inevitable happened. My perceived new beginning at happiness screeched to another halt the night that Ron was supposedly going to be working the late shift at Dominos, with me expecting for him not to return home until the following morning.

The following morning when I awoke, Ron was nowhere to be seen. I heard nothing from him for the next several days. When I called his job looking for him, I was informed that he had quit a week earlier.

I was concerned because I didn't have any other alternative way to get to work at the club that weekend. Elvis and Vince were had already left. Since there was absolutely no way that I was going to call and ask them to leave the club in order to give me a ride to work, because I really did not want them in my business, I called off from the club that weekend and concluded that I could not depend on Ron. If he really wanted to let me know where he was, he would contact me.

Sitting in our modernly decorated living room and meditatively gazing at the pine trees through the floor-to-ceiling windows, I thought back to when Ron showed up that night at Crazy Ray'z asking me to give him a second chance just as I had started to move on from him.

I never suspected for one moment that he was strategically plotting and succeeding at isolating me from my sources of support. I admit that he had done an excellent job implementing his plan because I had no idea of what was really going on in his mind until it happened.

Although I could not read his mind, I knew exactly what was going on in mine, which was that I was finally sick and tired of the emotional roller coaster ride with him, and that I needed to seriously concentrate on being totally dependent upon myself.

For whatever reason, I felt that Ron was on a mission to physically and psychologically permanently break me. So, I also decided during those meditative moments to not spend anymore of my time worrying about his true motives or trying to change that which was unchangeable.

I was also most certain that he would re-appear sooner or later, and when he did show up, I was determined more than ever to show him that I was once again strong enough to make it on my own without him.

So, I used the time with myself to assess and evaluate my situation. Realizing that there wasn't any reliable transportation from the apartment to my job in Sandy Springs and not wanting to become unreliable for my shifts at Kmart (in addition my independent spirit that would not allow me to become dependent upon Elvis and Vince), my plan was to get a job closer to the apartment.

I started with laying out some interview appropriate clothes because I knew that if I spoke with a manager that day, I would most likely be hired. I then set the alarm clock for early that following morning to take a short cut through the woods near the apartment complex to the main highway to fill out employment applications.

I submitted my first application for a waitress position at Sonny's Bar B Q restaurant and, as planned, I interviewed with a really nice African-American shift manager named George whom hired me on the spot to work the lunch schedule the following day!

Exactly three days after training at Sonny's, I submitted my two-week resignation notice to Kmart and I was really excited about having cash in my pockets everyday from the great tips that I received after being assigned to work my own station to serve.

That following Wednesday one of the second-shift servers called in sick, so I worked both lunch and dinner shifts for extra money and afterwards all I wanted to do was to go home to soak my tired body in the Jacuzzi and sauna to relieve the pains and stresses of the last year.

After closing out my station that evening, I went straight home to shower and change into my bathing suit anticipating how good the steam room was going to feel! I was very pleased when I arrived at the facilities that there was no one else there!

After spraying the eucalyptus and water mixture that I'd purchased at an aromatherapy store in the plaza next to Sonny's during my lunch break on the hot rocks, I then relaxed and contemplated what I was going to do whenever Ron returned home.

Once I'd finished detoxifying in the steam room, I then reclined with my eyes closed in the sauna. Spending some much-deserved quality time in the pool room alone contemplating my future was interrupted when a girl and two guys whom I had never seen before came into the pool room with a six pack of beer just as I was preparing to get out of the water.

After greeting each other and brief small talk about the temperature of the water as they finished settling into the Jacuzzi, I then politely excused myself to leave and just as I rose to exit completely out of the Jacuzzi, Ron walked through the door.

When I looked into his eyes, I recognized that oh so familiar look that I had hoped was gone forever. I noticed that he'd changed clothes and was obviously high on something. When he saw me, he puffed his cigarette before flicking the butt outside as he walked over to where I was standing almost frozen in shock by the sight of him.

As he got closer, my expectations were that he was just coming over to address me as I composed myself to greet him, but without saying a word, he reached down, grabbed my arm, and snatched me out of the water like I was a rag doll left behind in the pool by a child.

After feeling the sting of his backhand that seemed to come out of nowhere, he then threw me up against the wall asking, "What the hell is going on in here Tracee? Are you cheating on me with a white boy now?"

Since Ron was the one missing in action, I had not expected for him to have responded in such a violent manner. In addition to being beyond embarrassed after managing to gain my balance, I immediately grabbed my keys and towel from the bench, wrapping it tightly around my body before running out of the pool room horrified.

I quickly exited the pool room because I knew that if I'd resisted him or attempted to defend myself in front of those strangers, the scene would have been much worse than it was as he followed me outside and continued interrogating me asking."What the fuck are you doing in there with those guys, Tracee?"

Angry, hurt and in a state of disbelief I responded, "Ron, all I wanted to do was to just relax after working a double shift at work today."

I used the end of the towel to blot the blood from my swollen lip before continuing, "I don't know those people, they're strangers to me who just walked into the pool room less than five seconds before you arrived."

He ignored me and commanded, "Just get in the damn truck Tracee, I will get to the bottom of this when we get home!"

Since there was no way in hell that I was going to get into that truck with him that night, I ignored him, turned and started walking toward the apartment leaving him standing there alone before he then started slowly following behind me in his truck.

As I walked away from another embarrassing physically violent domestic situation, rubbing the bruises imprinted on my arm and purposefully taking the long route back to the apartment in order to have time to gather my thoughts about what I was going to do next, all of the lies and abuse that I had endured from him over the brief time that we'd been together played out like a scene from a melodramatic movie in my mind.

I recalled that before we'd moved into our new apartment together, Ron wept crocodile tears and profusely promised to never hit me again if I took him back. I was steaming that he had the nerve to be violent with me after he'd just shown up out of the blue after being gone for days at a time doing who-knows-what with whom.

At first, I felt stupid for going back with him and then I immediately became angrier at his nerves, thinking that he could just show up and accuse me of cheating or being dishonest with him. I decreed during my snail-paced walk to the apartment from the pool facilities that what I was currently doing was not working and frankly, it really did not matter what I did to try to make amends for the wrong things that I had done in the past; nothing would have been good enough to change the unhealthy circumstances between Ron and I.

I decided at that very moment, under that humid, star-filled sky, that too many boundaries had been crossed and I was not going to continue to give him permission to manipulate, mentally control and violently abuse me anymore.

With each step that I took back to the apartment, I felt his piercing eyes watching every move that I made as he continued following slowly behind me. I could tell from the voided look in his eyes that he was beyond the point of change and trustworthiness, so spirit and intuition placed upon me that I needed to get out of that situation with him once and for all in order to save my life.

I did everything within my power to avoid getting into a physical altercation with him on that occasion. I honestly believe that if we had gotten physical with each other after the Jacuzzi incident, I could have possibly ended up hurting him defending myself.

I was no longer going to tolerate the unjustifiable violence any longer; I could have ended up permanently scarred, maimed or even killed by him.

I also knew that just moving to another part of the city would not work because he would inevitably find me and, like a fool, I probably would go back to him to my demise, so I decided that I needed to put as much distance between he and I as possible by leaving Georgia altogether to completely sever all ties to him in order to keep my physical and mental well-being intact.

It seemed that I was energized by the answers that I received to all of my questions that were being showered down upon me from the universe on that clear balmy night! When I finally arrived at our apartment, I went inside and directly into the bathroom to take a long shower to allow for more time to really consider how I was going to successfully put my plan into action!

After showering, I applied cocoa butter to my wounds and took a deep breath before walking out of the bathroom wrapped in a terrycloth robe to do whatever I needed to do to survive that night.

When I walked into the bedroom, Ron was sitting on the bed smoking a cigarette and sipping on a 40-ounce malt liquor, watching me as I changed into my pajamas. You could have cut the tension in the room with a knife because I was not going to say anything to him first, so I waited for him to start the conversation. "So, I see that you are cheating on me again, Tracee."

I replied, "Ron, I am not cheating on you and as I've explained to you at the pool I have never seen those people before because they had just arrived just minutes before you walked in."

I didn't want him to suspect anything so I cautiously continued, "The important question at hand is what you have been doing for the last five days Ron?"

He puffed his cigarette before casually replying, "Tracee, I wasn't able to drive because the tags on my truck have expired, so I had to stay a few nights at Lloyd's so that I could get to work."

I replied, unconvinced, "Why did you not at least call and let me know what was going on, Ron?"

He replied, clearly agitated, "I was busy working, Tracee."

Since I knew that Ron was lying, I had a lot to say to him and if I had not vented it all at once I may not have had the opportunity or guts to have done so later. So, I inhaled from my diaphragm before releasing all of my pent-up frustrations into the atmosphere.

"You know what, Ron? I called your job looking for you and your assistant manager, Steve, told me that you'd quit … so what is the real story?"

I felt somewhat in control and encouraged about the direction of the conversation, perceiving all the while that I still had to proceed with caution, because I didn't want to push him into becoming overly defensive and angry.

I continued, knowing that if he became more agitated, we would have definitely ended up in a deadly physical altercation. "Ron, it has not yet been a good month since we've moved into this place and you have already gone back on your promises to stop hitting on me, selling drugs and staying away from Ponce De Leon."

I knew that if my anguish wasn't revealed all at once, it would never happen, so I continued. "I warned you that night in your truck at Crazy Ray'z and we both agreed that this was your second and final chance to do the right thing, but you've instead made the choice to throw it all away by going back on your word."

Before allowing him to speak I took another deeper breath and continued, exhaling, "Ron, I cannot go back to you beating on me again and wearing the heavy makeup to cover the scars and black eyes so that I can continue working."

He interjected, "Tracee, baby, I'm sorry that I didn't call and let you know what was going on and I am also sorry for hitting you, but it's just that when I walked into the pool room and saw you wearing a bikini in the Jacuzzi with those guys gawking at you, I just flipped out!"

That boyish charm and those fake tears were no longer affecting me, so I dictated to him, "Ron, I do not know what else to do because I'm tired and I refuse to continue to live like this with you anymore. You need some professional help and I just need some time and a little distance away from this whole situation to figure out what I am going to do about you breaking your promises to not hit me again."

I slightly hesitated before continuing, "I'm going to move out for a little while until you decide that you are going to get some counseling for your anger, trust and drug issues."

I could tell that he was not at all happy about me suggesting that I leave our apartment and after taking another puff of his cigarette he replied, "Tracee, I don't have a drug problem and you do not have to be scared of me, baby!"

"Ron, no matter what you say, I am literally frightened to death of you at this point to be honest." Continuing, as I raised my arm up to the light, "Look at your finger imprints tattooed on my arms."

I knew that if he had thought for an instant that I was leaving him permanently, he would have for sure became extremely violent, so I reassured him, "Baby, my moving out would only be temporarily and it doesn't mean that I don't still love you. I will be here to support you in every way possible. It's just that I cannot help you without first healing myself."

When I noticed that he was becoming more agitated, I coaxed him into lying back on the bed and then laid my head on his chest as I softly caressed his face and continued reassuring him that I was not moving out for good.

He reached over and dropped his cigarette butt into the beer bottle before asking, "Who are you thinking I'm going to let you stay with, Tracee?"

I tenderly kissed his lips softly responding, "Baby, I'm going to call Vince and Elvis to see if I can stay with them for a little while until you and I get it together."That night I could have won an Academy Award for Best Actress in a Drama due to ultimately being able to convince him that my intentions were to move back into the apartment with him immediately after he started anger management and drug counseling.

After ultimately committing to sex with Ron, I called Vince and Elvis to inquire if it would be okay for me to stay with them for a short period of time. Very much aware of the abusive situation that I was in, they inquired about my well-being and did not hesitate to let me stay with them for as long as I needed to.

Elvis asked, in his Southern protective voice, "Girl, do you need me to come over there and pick you up right now?"

I calmly replied, "No, honey, I'm okay. Will you pick me up in the morning?"

After being reassured that I was safe, he replied, "Sure, honey, I'll see you first thing in the morning and you be sure to call me if he starts to acting crazy again I will come get you no matter how late it is!"

I calmly and reassuringly replied, "I will, honey, thank you for being concerned about me." I hung up the phone and went back into the bedroom where Ron was lying naked under the covers and when I joined him in the bed, I didn't resist when he wanted to have sex again, because maintaining his trust and making him believe that we were going to eventually get back together was an important element to making my plan work.

The next morning when Ron questioned why I was packing so much of my stuff if I was planning to move back in after he'd started counseling, I also managed to have convinced him that I wanted him to know that I was serious about the only condition that I would return was if he started treatment and counseling.

Over the course of the next few days in an attempt to show me that he was trying to do better, although I've never met his parents in person, he took me to his mother's house where I met his little brother.

Even though I'd already moved out, I continued playing the game and allowed Ron to also later take me to his father's house for a visit. Although I continued to be intimate with Ron upon suggestion from him, I refused to spend the night all the while during work secretly planning my final escape from any future black eyes, bloody noses and swollen lips.

I knew that I had to get as far away from him as possible in order to succeed, so my choices were between Paris, France or California. After carefully evaluating both places, I chose Los Angeles, California, because it was far enough away from him and a short enough distance from my mother than France!

I also knew that I would need to save as much money as possible to successfully move to a state so far away on my own to live in a place where I did not know anyone or ever visited before.

In addition to serving barbecue, coleslaw and beans at Sonny's Restaurant during the day, I supplemented my income dancing at what I've since discovered through research was the first in Atlanta and one of the longest-operating biological female strip lounge establishments located in the basement of the Clermont Motor Hotel on Ponce De Leon.

At first appearances when I went in to apply for the job, I had no idea that the Clermont Lounge was a landmark historical spot, because it seemed to me like just another small hole in the wall neighborhood club with a single stage in the middle of the bar.

There was no DJ, so we selected our music to play on an old fashioned coin operated jukebox. I don't even recall what made me choose to take a taxi to that particular place to apply for employment, other than assuming that it would be easy to get hired since it was just a neighborhood hole in the wall.

During the interview at the lounge I was given the option to strip topless or dance fully nude, which contributed to the decision to go topless in order to make some quick money that would assist with my master escape plan!

Actually, I had no other choice but to only go topless when I applied for the job, since neither the female manager who interviewed me or her boss knew that I wasn't a biological female. They hired me on the spot.

Since I had no previous topless dancing experience, I just imagined that I was performing a show in a regular club and immediately started making great tips during my topless performances!

Additionally, I also made good tips whenever a customer offered to buy me a drink in between my performances. Since I was not a drinker, I made a secret deal with the bartender to serve me only club soda or something that resembled a cocktail and we later split the tips that I made from the customer drink purchases!

I was successfully pretending to be a biological female stripper for several weeks until one night after work when I was approached and solicited for sex and drugs by this regular customer who would always be very persistent in trying to cop a feel when he tipped me during my routine.

Little did he know that he was attempting to get a quick feel of a vagina which never existed, so I refused to let him touch my private spot during my routines by strategically repositioning my body, I didn't know that they were usually allowed more contact

When the guy later approached me that night as I was leaving the club, I declined his proposition to get a room at the hotel with him and walked away. The following weekend before my shift started, the club manager called me into her office and informed me that a customer had complained and questioned if I was a real female.

She then proceeded to tell me that she needed for me to show her my vagina in order to continue working. I knew that I did not have a vagina to show her, so I refused and left her office to never return again.

It really wasn't a big thing that I was found out, because I knew that performing topless was only temporary and I also knew that I was taking a risk from the beginning trying to work at a female strip club doing what I had to do in order to reach my financial goals.

In addition to the great tips that I'd received and stashed away during the brief time working there, I also befriended a costume designer in the process who traveled from strip club to strip club selling costumes that she'd created!

Since I don't believe in throwing away costumes, I still have a couple of the original pieces that she designed for me in one of my costume trunks!

Back on Indian Trail, since Vince sometimes had loose lips, I kept my extracurricular money-making activities a secret from them both and I only told Elvis about my plans to leave Georgia after Vince mysteriously had to move back to his home town to deal with some undisclosed personal issues.

Vince abruptly abandoned all of his furniture and personal items, leaving his leather wearing friend Billy, Elvis and I alone in the apartment. It was later reported that after Elvis and I left Atlanta, Vince's friend Billy packed his entire apartment onto the back of a pickup and drove through Midtown selling off Vince's things to the highest bidder.

After I felt it was safe to confide my plans to Elvis, he told me that he was also tired of his current circumstances and asked if he could go to California with me. I ecstatically welcomed the idea of traveling such a long distance with someone that I knew and trusted!

Elvis got money for his bus ticket from his parents and together we went and purchased our one-way tickets to Los Angeles, scheduled to depart two weeks before I was supposed to move back in with Ron.

While Elvis arranged for his mother to drive us to the bus station the morning that we were scheduled to leave, I booked and performed "Is It A Crime" by Sade, "Dreamin/Right Stuff" mix by Vanessa Williams, and the always crowd-pleaser "Don't You Want Me/Looking For A New Love" Jody Watley mix for my farewell performance at the always dependable Backstreet club!

The show was advertised in Etcetera magazine as "a special farewell performance by that Faboo entertaintress Destiny"! Fortunately for me, Ron never read any of the gay publications, because if he had, all of my carefully laid plans would have been exposed and then all hell would have broken out!

Also, I managed to book my last show at Crazy Ray'z the weekend before our scheduled departure, choosing to perform "Friends" by Jody, because I felt betrayed by someone at the club that I had previously grown close to and considered a friend.

I also recruited Elvis to learn the guy's rap in the song to perform with me and we wrote down the lyrics for him to study during regular practices and created the choreography in the living room in preparation for the show.

We were both excited and ready to perform the night of the booking. We incorporated a portable black lounger that I reclined on dressed all in sheer black, and when we started performing, the fans loved our production and showed their appreciation for our number by tipping fives, tens and twenty dollar bills!

I'd purposefully chosen to only perform that one number because I wanted to make a statement by showing them that I am a survivor and that I was not dependent upon them for my livelihood.

After our performance, we gathered up our props and walked off the stage directly to the car where we divided up the tips before leaving Crazy Ray'z for the final time! You talk about being mature? Oh, well!

Two nights before Elvis and I were scheduled to get on the bus for California, Ron and I spent the night together, which is when he informed me that his father had asked him to spend the week with his little brother while he was out of town.

My plan could not have come together any better because after his revelation, I was no longer concerned about him showing up unannounced and catching us in the act of leaving.

Elvis and I were scheduled for an early departure from the bus station, which required us to spend the night at his parents' house so that his mother could drive us to Greyhound for our departure.

The night before we left to go to his parents', Elvis informed me that I was going to be the first black person to ever spend the night in his parent's home.

I resisted asking him if I was the first black person to ever be allowed inside of their house, because I wasn't too concerned about how his parents would respond to me.

Due to trusting Elvis to not put me in any awkward environment which would not be good for my physical or mental well-being, I didn't think twice about changing our plans after his revelation. It really didn't matter to me in anyway how they may have felt about a black person sleeping in their home, because my tunnel-vision attention was on adhering to the escape plan.

I was determined to do whatever I had to do, so enduring being judged for my color by people that I was not going to ever see again really didn't affect me one bit moving forward.

The evening that I met his parents was more pleasant than I had expected, because they were very kind to me and his mother even gifted me two beautiful brand new night gowns! One was pink with white flower prints and the other was a leopard skin-printed, long elegant gown, which I still have!

Chapter Seven

1990: Do you know where you're going to?

It was sometime in August 1990. The next morning we awoke bright and early, and after breakfast Elvis' mother drove us to the bus station. I sat alone in the backseat bitter-sweetly peering out the window during the drive, immensely excited about the fact that I was one step closer to changing my life.

After arriving at the station and processing our tickets, we finally stepped onto the bus and I exhaled a sigh of relief, knowing that the ingenious plan to finally leave my abuser had worked out perfectly.

After the bus left the station, carrying us through cities and states that I have never visited before, I was grateful that my creator instilled within me the knowledge during that time to know that I had just made the right choice to leave the state rather than continuing to be a human punching bag for Ron to beat on!

During one of our frequent stops, this very muscular, handsome guy got on the bus and it seemed that he was immediately drawn to me like a magnet. After a few stops, we eventually ended up sharing seats together. It later occurred to me that by his demeanor he might have just been recently released from being incarcerated. Just a guess!

Although I wasn't interested in starting a relationship with a possible fresh out of jail or prison guy, it was somewhat comforting having him close just in case something broke off during our cross-country bus ride!

One perfect example of scary occurrences was when we broke down late in almost pitch-black Texas. It was horrible when we had to get off the bus in the humid, starless night to stretch our legs once the repair person arrived.

We had to wait outside while the repairman jacked it up to do what he had to do to fix the bus. As we stood there waiting, I was bitten by the most horrifying mosquitoes that didn't compare to the allergic reactions from the mosquito bites that I'd previously received growing up in South Carolina.

Those boogers were like Amazonian tribesmen pummeling me with needles blown through a blow-gun that instantaneously created itchy whelps rising and throbbing like Rudolph, the red- nosed reindeer.

Thankfully, my traveling companion draped his jacket over my shoulders! I've always been extremely allergic to fleas and mosquitoes, so when we were finally cleared to get back on the bus after an hour or so, I ran to my seat and started practically bathing myself in almost a whole bottle of green rubbing alcohol that I pulled from my carry-on bag.

The green alcohol eventually slightly relieved the excruciating pain and I was ecstatically happy several hours later once we'd left dreadful Texas! Once we entered into Mexico, I freshened up in the depot ladies' restroom before getting back on the bus with Elvis and our traveling companion.

Finally, after over five long, excruciating days traveling by Greyhound from the East Coast to the West Coast, enduring the inconvenient breakdowns, mosquitoes and having to freshen-up and shave every morning as much as possible in the tiny sink on the bus and depot bathrooms,.

I was awakened from catnapping by the voice of the bus driver over the intercom and announced that we were on the Hollywood Freeway and that we should be arriving at the downtown Los Angeles bus depot in about 20 minutes. On my Walkman the Mahogany theme song "Do You Know Where You're Going To?" was, ironically, playing on FM radio!

I was determined to savor the moment and sense of accomplishment to have finally broken free from Ron's charms and influence.

I also chose to turn the volume up and finished listening to my new theme song before waking Elvis and my seat-mate from their slumber. My heart fluttered with anticipation as I pressed my face against the window to see the crowns of the majestic palm trees and instantly fell deeply in love with the tall gentle giants lining the freeway, swaying in the wind and stretching toward heaven!

The palm trees seemed to reassure me that everything would be okay now that I was finally safely thousands of miles away from my abuser! After Miss Ross finished filling me with inspiration, I reached behind and shook Elvis from his coma-like state before nudging my traveling companion awake so that he would make his bus transfer.

When we prepared to exit the bus, I was unaware that my traveling companion was remaining on the same bus to continue on his journey. As we bid our farewells, he requested my phone number so that he would be able to contact me once he'd reached his final destination.

I explained to him that I did not currently have a number to give him because I was relocating to California to start over, so I suggested that he give me his number to call him after I'd gotten settled. After scribbling his digits and passing me the paper he asked, "Will you promise to call me after you get settled, Tracee?"

I took the number replying, "Sure, I will call you as soon as I get a phone number!" After we bid our final goodbyes and as I stepped down placing my feet on new ground, I knew I had no intentions of ever contacting him.

I felt no obligation to him because I was excited about my newfound freedom and filled with such gratitude to have possessed the strength to have finally broken away from Ron, so I was certainly not going to entertain even for a nanosecond of getting involved with the first strange guy that showed interest in me on a cross country trip to liberation from bondage.

After exiting the bus, Elvis waited with our bags while I walked over to the cabstand to hail a ride to a hotel and as I walked toward an unoccupied cab, I was filled with anticipation about the possibilities of what was awaiting me in Hollywood, California!

Upon approaching the taxi, I addressed the driver, "Hello, sir, would it be possible for you to take us to a safe and reasonably priced hotel in this area?"

He replied in a foreign accent, "Sure, young lady!" He then enthusiastically got out of the car walking over to assist us with our bags. After placing our bags into his trunk, he then opened the door for me and Elvis to climb into the backseat.

I was beside myself during our early evening drive through mysterious downtown Los Angeles! When we arrived at the Troubadour Hotel that from the outside appeared to be safe enough, he then retrieved from the trunk and placed our bags inside the well-kept hotel lobby.

I figured I'd not sugarcoat my next question to him, because if anybody knew where the female illusionist entertainers worked, a cabdriver would, so I asked as he placed the last bag. "Sir, do you know the part of town where female impersonators perform?"

"Sure!" He again excitedly continued as he turned and pointed to a bus stop across the street from the hotel! "Just take the number 200 bus to Santa Monica Boulevard and just make a request to the bus driver to drop you off at a club called "Peanuts."Good luck, young lady!"

"Thank you, sir!" I replied, paying and generously tipping him for being so helpful to us before checking into our new digs. After providing Identification during check-in, I paid three weeks in advance for the room, which I figured should be enough time for me to get a job somewhere and then start making other living arrangements.

We received the key to our extended stay hotel room that had one queen-sized bed and a private bathroom .After entering the room, I was pleasantly surprised that it was very clean and after disinfecting it with a can of Lysol that I always have in my carry-on bag whenever I travel, I then selected and ironed an outfit to wear for my gainful employment inquiry the next day.

Later that evening in a quaint little Chinese restaurant across the street from the hotel, we plotted and devised the master plan for taking advantage of the opportunities that would be presented in C-a-l-i-f-o-r-n-i-a!

Over shrimp fried rice and egg rolls, we mapped out our plan of action, which was to take the designated bus to "Peanuts" the following morning in order to inquire about a club booking so that at least one of us would have a regular income coming in, because Elvis really didn't have any prospects for a job.

As a matter of fact, I don't recall Elvis ever going to a job since I've known him. Anyway, I knew that it was my responsibility to make sure that we would not be out on the streets, so I was determined to make a good impression on whomever I'd be interviewing with at the club!

After dinner that evening, we returned to the room and turned in early, anticipating our first full day in California! It was a clear morning when we awoke early to get dressed and appropriately made up for our bus ride on the number 200 to Santa Monica Boulevard with the intentions of me securing a job.

When we stepped onto the bus I greeted the driver, inquiring, "Good morning, sir, does this bus go to Santa Monica Boulevard?"

"Yes," he replied.

"Would it be possible to let us off at a club called Peanuts?"

"Of course I'll let you off; just have a seat behind me, dear!"

We sat in the seats right behind the driver and I made sure that I was able to clearly see the various streets, neighborhoods and estimate the amount of time that it had taken for us to travel from downtown to Santa Monica Boulevard.

When we turned onto Santa Monica, it seemed to be an ordinary and unassuming street all the way up to our destination. The driver then gave us a two stop warning before opening the doors to let us off one block from the club.

Once we'd exited the bus, the butterflies really started fluttering around in my stomach as we crossed the street to approach Peanuts! We walked through the front door, turning a corner before approaching a lady behind the bar stocking the coolers with bottles of beer and liquor.

I took a deep breath and nervously introduced myself. "Hello, my name is Destiny would it be possible for me to speak with management to inquire about auditioning for your show?"

She stopped filling the cooler and responded, "I am the club manager, Michelle. Where do you currently perform, Destiny?'

I enthusiastically replied, "I've previously performed in Atlanta, Georgia, before recently relocating to Los Angeles, which is why I'm here to inquire about booking an audition for your show!"

She smiled and replied, "Well, Destiny, you are in luck because we're currently auditioning for the Friday night late show, so if you're interested, bring two high-energy numbers on this coming Friday night. The show starts at midnight and we will see what you can do then."

Gratefully, I replied, "Thank you so much for this opportunity, Michelle. I will see you bright and early on Friday night!" We shook hands. Elvis and I left the club excited about the opportunity!

Since it was a beautiful, warm sundrenched afternoon, we decided to walk back up the street to an eatery called Astro Burger that we'd previously passed on the bus to have a celebratory lunch.

It was surreal sitting underneath a clear blue sky on the outside patio toasting our arrival to California with fountain drinks, French fries and burgers!

In between sips of his soda, Elvis inquired. "Are you excited about Friday night or what, Tracee?"

I was smiling ear to ear while raising my soda to toast replying, "I am so excited Elvis. I have really got to get this job!"

"What are you going to wear and perform?"

"I know exactly what I'm performing and wearing!" I replied, excitedly. "I'm going to open with my Paula Abdul "Cold Hearted Snake" extended mix with the sexy 60s-style sheer black-fringed top and wide-legged bottoms that Miss JonVille gifted to me after a show that we worked together in Atlanta!"

As I continued speaking, I visualized the choreography to each song. "I'm stripping down to a two-piece fluorescent lime green, Day-Glo bikini that I wore during my short stint at the topless stripper club back in Georgia!"

Laughing aloud, he replied in surprise, "Girl, when did you dance at a stripper club?"

"Remember when I used to always arrive at the apartment really late during the weekdays back in Georgia and you would always question where I was?"

"Yes!" He replied with a puzzled look on his face.

"Well, I was taking a cab to topless dance at this lounge on Ponce De Leon for extra money!"

"Why did you not tell me, Tracee?" He replied, bugged-eyed!

"I did what I had to do in order to have as much money as possible for this trip. I'm sorry for not telling you Elvis, but I didn't want anyone to know because I needed to make sure that Ron did not find out what I was planning."

"Girl, I knew you were being suspicious and sneaky back then; I would have loved to have seen you topless dancing in a fish club!"

He continued, after sipping his drink, "What about your second number, you little she-devil?"

"For my second audition performance, I'm doing the always dependable crowd-pleaser -- the Jody Watley "Looking for A New Love/ Don't You Want Me" mix with an oversized black leather jacket, a red bustier with the short black petticoat along with fishnets and my new boots and black laced gloves that I wore in our 'Friends' production at Crazy Ray'z!"

"You are going to knock them dead, girl. I wish that I didn't have already scheduled my date with Troy on Friday night. Should I cancel and go with you?"

Unaware that he even knew anyone in California, I questioned, "Where did you meet Troy, you little sneak?"

Smiling his devilish grin before replying, he said, "We met at Crazy Ray'z last year when he was visiting Atlanta for Black Pride. We hung out doing what we did and promised to keep in touch. You know, girl, the usual!"

Since I had never previously met any of the guys that Elvis dated before, I replied, surprised, "You little tramp. I will be okay; go on your date and have fun!"

Shamefully covering his face, he said, "Girl, I really need to see Mr. Troy because Mama needs some money!"

Understanding exactly what the deal was, I replied, "Honey, go and get your coins; I am sure that there will be other shows that you can attend!"

After finishing our lunch, we walked several blocks back up Santa Monica Boulevard to further explore the area before getting on the bus for the ride back to the hotel so that I could begin organizing and transferring my costumes for the show into my show bag.

While on the drive back to our room, I obtained an updated bus schedule from the driver and scouted out some interesting little shops and department stores downtown close to the hotel where I could purchase hairspray and other essentials that I needed for my audition.

I was all set when Friday morning arrived and alone in the hotel room after Troy picked Elvis up, which allowed me to mentally prepare for what was ahead without any distractions.

The alone time enabled me to really concentrate on the task at hand, mapping out the time needed for makeup application, double checking that everything that I'd needed for the show was packed in my costume bag!

After reconfirming the bus schedule to be assured that I was on the 8 p.m. bus to

Santa Monica Boulevard with the intent on accomplishing my mission to secure a job, I then enjoyed an early quiet dinner at the Chinese restaurant!

Upon completing the tasty Chinese food, I returned to my room to relax for an hour or so before starting to apply makeup. During my earlier strategic planning evaluation, I figured that it was necessary to go as incognito as possible for the bus ride to the club due to not wanting to draw any unnecessary attention to myself.

I'd chosen to wear an oversized, black 70s-style cap, dark shades, a lace-centered black jumpsuit covered with an oversized black leather biker jacket and knee high flat black boots that were perfect for the bus ride.

It has always worked out better for me to apply most of my makeup prior to going to a performance because you never know what kind of lighting will be in the dressing room, and you're really lucky if you even get a dressing room at some venues.

I figured that I'd apply lip gloss, stage hair and touch-up my makeup at the club before changing into my first costume. After completing painting my mug and dressing, I grabbed my show bag, put on dark shades, pulled my hat as far down as possible to conceal the dramatic stage makeup and lashes before hurrying to the elevator for the ride downstairs to catch my bus!

I expected that riding the bus on a Friday night with Fire & Ice ruby red lips and highlighter almost as bright as the moon would be a harrowing experience. However, after entering the almost empty bus, I found the ride to be a relaxing experience.

I felt fortunate to not have been harassed by any of the other passengers, in addition to being happy that I had taken the earlier bus, because when we turned onto Santa Monica Boulevard, the traffic was backed up for miles moving at snail's crawl pace.

Although the traffic was slow moving, the nightlife energy on Santa Monica as compared to the daytime ride was quite different. It was simply electric and I inhaled every possible bit of the energizing, flowing currents!

As the driver intermittently stopped in the bumper-to-bumper traffic stretching blocks upon blocks and once we'd crossed LaBrea, I was amazed at the large number of half-naked transgender ladies of the evening from every walk of life walking back and forth on the stroll. The tricks contributed to the traffic congestion as they stopped at the corners to proposition the girls working their beat.

Being a country girl from South Carolina and Georgia, I've never seen anything like that before. The half-nude trans girls wore five-inch stilettos and thigh-high boots as they sashayed and yelled catcalls at the johns while competing with each other to be the next to get a date!

Finally, when the bus driver announced my stop, I secured my show bag closely to my body as I exited the bus and as I stood waiting for the traffic light to cross the street, several guys pulled up in their Escalades, Mercedes Benzes and fancy sports cars to the curbside, offering to take me where I was going.

Of course, I declined their offers and crossed the street, citing a quick prayer to myself before walking up to the two extremely intimidating muscular bouncers in black T-shirts standing at the entrance.

After jovially smiling, presenting them with my identification and explaining that Michelle had invited me there to audition for the show, they cleared me for entry into the club. The music was thumping as I stepped through the black drapes into the carnival atmosphere, with lights flashing to the beat and reflecting on a few corporate-dressed ladies peppered in amongst even more half-naked girls and their suitors jammed tightly on the dance floor.

I thought back to the little hole in the wall club Romey's that my friends and I used to hang out in back home in addition to the clubs in Georgia, which had nothing on "Peanuts"! The girls were edgier and the guys wore designer suits and swarmed around like hummingbirds searching for just the right nectar to taste!

It was as if I had finally arrived to where I was supposed to be. I didn't mind too much that some of the guys were cruising for a bruising when they'd intentionally rubbed up against me to cop a quick feel as I struggled to make my way through the crowd with my show bag in tow to find Michelle.

Once I'd successfully navigated through the predators, I found her once again behind the bar serving up cocktails, and when she saw me, she walked from behind the bar, shook my hand complimenting me as she escorted me to the dressing room. "You're here almost two hours before the show."

She then turned and smiled, continuing, "Hopefully, you will rub off on some of the other girls that rush in here at the last minute!"

Following Michelle from the front of the club through the billiards room was almost like squeezing through sardines in a can, due to a majority of the guys seeming as if they were in some sort of a hyper zombie-like trance fumbling around from one girl to another attempting to look cool and suave.

When we finally made it through the crowd and entered the large dressing room, Michelle stated as she handed me three drink tickets, "First come, first served at the dressing stations."

I took the tickets, replying as I scanned the room for a corner station, "Thank you, Michelle!"

She asked, "Would you like a cocktail now, Destiny?"

I replied, as I sat my bag on the chair to hand her a ticket, "I would love a Coke-Cola please, thank you!"

Obviously surprised that I had requested a Coke, she declined the ticket, responding before returning to the bar, "Tatiana is the show director tonight. She will open and then you will follow her. Just give her your music and break a leg!"

The dressing room was a huge space decorated with really cool fluorescent futuristic semi-nude erotic space figures painted on the walls. After a server returned with my Coke, I was the only one in the dressing room for almost an hour or so touching up makeup, securing my stage hair on with extra bobby pins and changing into my first costume before the other girls started to file in.

When the first cast member walked in looking as if she could have been Madonna's twin sister, with an entourage in tow, she introduced herself, extending her hand to shake mine. "Hello, I'm Diva and you must be Destiny. Michelle told us that you would be auditioning for the show tonight. Welcome, girl!"

I stood and took her hand replying, "Thank you, Diva, Yes, I am Destiny and tonight is my audition for the show!"

"You look great, girl, and Lord knows that we need some more pretty people of color on this damn cast!"

I found Diva to be a genuinely down-to-earth person whom I instantly connected with after being introduced to her entourage of five or more before we both retreated to our mutual stations to make sure things were in place before the show started.

The rest of the cast eventually started arriving just minutes before the show started briefly greeting me as they rushed to their stations and hurriedly ripping off their clothes to get ready to perform.

I nervously waited in the dressing room for the overture to start and when Tatiana started performing, I peeped out of the dressing room to determine the amount of time that was required to maneuver through the congested congregation of people in the billiards room to hit my mark.

Sitting back at my station, I sipped my Coke for a little caffeine boost in anticipation as the butterflies that I'd felt earlier started really uncontrollably fluttering around in my stomach.

I re-checked in the wall-to-wall mirror to ensure that everything was still in place before going to stand at the dressing room exit and excitedly wait to be introduced. When Tatiana finished her number and then welcomed the audience, continuing in broken English, "Ladies and gentlemen, put your hands for the new girl in town auditioning for the cast tonight. Show her some love if you like what you see. Welcome to the stage, Destiny!"

After hearing Tatiana announce my name and my music start, the butterflies began to settle down somewhat. I stood off stage waiting for the musical cue to enter the show room and when I exited the dressing room it seemed that the sea of people in the billiards simultaneously cleared a path, watching every step I made. I was feeling it, and the sound system was right on, pumping throughout the entire club. Immediately upon stepping into the showroom on stage, captured by the spot light from the right angle, I called upon all of my energy from within that seemed to transport me into a zone slightly out of my control!

I strongly believe that all of the advanced preparation I always invest in allows me to freely express on stage what I visualize during the process of choosing what songs and costumes I use for each individual performance.

Patting myself on the back, I admitted that I really worked those numbers, and the audience also loved both performances, showing their appreciation with applauds and fists full of ten and 20 dollar bills!

As I exited the stage through the audience, I thought that I had missed a tip when a professionally dressed guy approached me with a 20 dollar bill extended from his hand. I took the tip and thanked him for his generosity before he commented, "For a good time, there's plenty more where that came from, Destiny!"

Deeply offended by his remark, I turned to him and replied as I handed him back his tip, "No, thank you, I make my money performing on the stage, thank you very much."

Obviously surprised that I'd returned his money, he sarcastically replied."Pretty new girls just in town like you usually end up on Santa Monica Boulevard eventually, so why not let me break you in the right way?"

Before turning and walking away from him, I leaned close enough to discretely respond with authority, "The only thing that will be broken in is your face, if you don't get out of my way, asshole!"

After the show, Michelle came into the dressing room passing the cast checks and then showed her appreciation to me when she also unexpectedly handed me a folded check for $100 and then welcoming me to the Friday night cast!

You talk about being ecstatic about having a job and also getting paid for an audition. That would be an understatement! After securing my costume back in a corner underneath the bar in the dressing room, I then took the drink tickets to the front bar and purchased another Coke Cola. After tipping the bartender, I then sat on the empty barstool sipping on my chilled Coke, celebrating my victory and watching the action and antics on the dance floor.

As the morning progressed, Diva invited me to join them for breakfast at Yukon Restaurant, which was the popular 24/7 social hang-out spot on Santa Monica Boulevard that was the breakfast destination of the performers, club patrons and anyone who wanted to meet a transgender person.

It was crazy driving into the parking lot sitting in the backseat of Diva's entourage member's car, watching some of those that did not get a date at the club trying desperately to snag someone at the last minute by trolling the parking lot! It was a pure mess seeing the working girls off the stroll skirting from one car to the other, turning tricks in the lot!

Thank goodness the restaurant was decent enough, because if it was not I believe that I'd only would have ordered coffee, maybe! During breakfast, sitting at the largest corner booth, which accommodated Diva's entire entourage and the new girl on the scene, I kept being congratulated on my performances by random girls approaching our table.

While eating wheat and nut pancakes, turkey sausage patties and scrambled eggs with cranberry juice, I knew, judging by the positive response I'd received on stage, that Los Angeles was the very best choice for me to begin anew since she was thousands of miles away from the drama in Georgia!

After breakfast with Diva and her crew, I took a taxi back to the room and since Elvis spent the night with his boyfriend, I took advantage of the time alone with myself and unwound in a long candlelit, bubble bath while I reflected back on my night.

I was filled with immense gratitude for all of the blessings as I soaked in the warm water reviewing the show in my head and also planning the music, costumes and choreography for the following weekend.

Several weeks after arriving in California, I felt reasonably secure with my new job. However, not wanting to rest on my laurels due to being the only one with a steady income, I was determined to find a day job to supplement my income.

It became obvious to me that Elvis wasn't used to working regularly, because for whatever reason his previous roommate, Vince, worked and paid all of their bills. It was also obvious that he wasn't very motivated to find a job.

Inevitably, it became financially challenging for me to be the only one feeding two adults and paying our room rent on my own, although managing to do so. It was also extremely difficult for Elvis to find a job when he finally started showing serious interest in getting one after much encouragement from me to do so that he could contribute to our everyday needs.

I honestly believed that in addition to not having any luck with getting a job due to inexperience and lack of skills, Elvis also became homesick, so I wasn't surprised when he informed me that he was going back to Georgia.

We mutually agreed that his decision was probably the right one for him, so he called his parents and asked if they would purchase him a bus ticket back to Atlanta, and he then arranged for his boyfriend, Troy, to drive him to the bus station three days later.

Even though we remained sisters on the morning of his departure, I suspected that I'd probably not see my friend again.

After Elvis departed, I was on my own and happy to be regularly booked to fill in on the Saturday night shows at Peanuts whenever someone called off. I was quickly building up my own group of followers.

I knew that most of the guys patronizing the club were tricks looking to get their freak on. However, there were also those who were fans, so I remained cordial and approachable to those whom respectfully approached me after my performances.

A few times, I'd walked into one of the four restrooms in the club to find them in compromising positions actively engaged in sexual acts with some of the known hookers. It was a trip!

There were also the men who were probably living out their sexual fantasies, trolling around the club enchanted and cheating on their wives, girlfriends in order to have an intimate or otherwise experience with their favorite transgender, transsexual and gender non-conforming person!

Neither was I naive to the fact that most of the girls patronizing "Peanuts" were ladies of the night, your wish is their command. I have never judged people for the choices they've adopted in order to survive or in some cases just for the thrill of it. However, I did not want anyone to ever think that I was a prostitute for sale to the highest bidder.

After my performances, I mingled with the fans that came to see me in the show, thanking them for their support, and if the music wasn't jumping to my taste, I usually made my exit to most likely hang out with Diva and her crew at Yukon or we'd carpool to The Palace in Hollywood, The Roxy that used to be on Sunset Boulevard or some other cool, eclectic clubs to dance the morning away.

Whenever we were not performing at the clubs, Diva also introduced me to some amazing Hollywood memorabilia conventions where you could purchase the rarest collectibles of your favorite celebrities.

Additionally, after I'd gotten settled into my own place, we all usually crashed back at my apartment after a show or night out! I really enjoyed those simple moments shared between a group of friends from various cultural and racial backgrounds, sharing varying personal experiences and stories! Some stories were pleasant experiences and then there were those too painful to recall.

Walking through the club after performances and observing the girls in the corners snorting drugs with others and allowing those creepy men to disrespect them, I vowed that I would never be disrespected in that manner or allow myself to become a victim of the fatalistic lifestyles that most transsexual women feel they have no other choice but to engage in.

I feel that some girls have fallen victim just because they've been wrongfully conditioned to believe that prostitution, drugs, alcohol, physical abuse and the rock-bottom-inducing porn industry are the only options available to us.

From my perspective, the truth is that if we take more initiative and stop making excuses, there are so many other opportunities and paths to take that would assist with surviving the ongoing systemic discriminatory adversities placed upon us, including, but not limited to, the high rates of violence, unemployment, unfair housing and injustice that's still prevalent within our modern-day society.

I also personally believe that since transgender and gender non-conforming people were created in the image of our Creator, I've personally chosen to stop subscribing to the misguided notion that I was born inferior.

I'm also grateful for the realization that it's up to me to remain conscious that there is karma and consequences when I intentionally chose to release negative thoughts, vibrations and energy into the universe, so I'm happy to report that walking the streets prostituting myself was never an option for me!

Ever since arriving in California, my focus remained on getting established and working as much as possible until the night that this very masculine and mysterious guy named Dwayne started to regularly appear on the scene at the club.

Dwayne was usually hanging out observing the action with another respectable, elderly guy named Curtis whom was always a gentleman to me whenever I occasionally joined him between numbers to chit-chat about the madness that was going on in the club.

Curtis always stood at the end of the second bar in the billiards room in order to see the stage while also trying to catch one of the unsuspecting girls in his net. Up to that point, I didn't intimately know any guys yet, nor had I dated anyone since my arrival, so finding myself attracted to Dwayne caught me slightly off guard.

I'm sure that my attraction to Dwayne was fueled by his mysterious swagger as compared to the other men in the club. I'm also positive that his Barry-White, melodically smooth voice contributed to me accepting his invitation when he'd finally gotten up the nerves to ask me out after weeks of just silently observing my conversations with his friend Curtis.

Since Dwayne seemed to be a nice enough person during our initial conversation with each other, and I didn't see any harm in going to Yukon with him for breakfast later that morning after the show riding, in his classic BMW to the restaurant.

During the drive up Santa Monica Boulevard, with the usual working girls stomping the pavement, I observed that Dwayne was even more attractive, as his immaculately groomed beard glistened in the light from the street and headlights reflecting inside of the car.

When we arrived at the restaurant, I was impressed that he insisted on opening the door to help me out of the car before walking into the restaurant, where we were escorted to an intimate booth in the back of the diner.

After placing our beverage orders, we started to engage each other in a general conversation about me being new to Los Angeles and where I was from.

After placing our orders, all was going well during the small talk until he switched the conversation, asking in a velvety deep voice some really strange questions about a former performer that was in the show at "Peanuts" named Grace Jones who preceded me on the cast.

"Destiny, I had a good understanding with Grace and all of my girls, I'm sure that we will also develop a good understanding and arrangement as well."

What? Hold on! I had no clue about what he meant by us developing an understanding and arrangement, because all I knew about Grace was that before my appearance on the scene, she'd mysteriously skipped town to New York after allegedly killing someone in the dressing room during a drug deal gone bad.

When it finally registered to me that he was actually interviewing me to become his next drug dealing, bottom bitch, transgender prostitute turned out on the streets of Hollywood to replace Grace Jones, I responded, disgustedly, "Dwayne, you really have me mistaken for someone else. I am not interested in being one of your drug-dealing anything and if I decided to sell my body, I certainly do not need a drug-pushing pimp like you to collect the money after risking my life on the streets."

I was happy that since I've never left my costume bag unattended and it contained my coins from work, I could reach down and grab her in preparation to make a Betty Davis exit! I was fuming that he'd even assumed that I had such low value.

Dwayne was speechless after I excused myself from the table and once outside of the restaurant, I hailed a cab, then stopped by Ralph's Market for a few staples before going back to the hotel.

On the elevator ride to my floor, I was still furious over him suggesting that I become a tragic statistic, risking my life, strung out on Santa Monica Boulevard and selling my soul to make money to pad his pockets. I don't think so!

I questioned what was it about the way that I was presenting myself that gave him the impression that I would even entertain his proposal to sell his drugs and prostitute my body for his financial gain. Not in this lifetime or any other would that ever happen.

I didn't think that my morning could have gotten any worse, but then my grocery bag bottom busted, spilling apples, oranges and bottled water all over the hallway in front of my door. As I gathered the fruit and water, this somewhat well-dressed, African-American stranger appeared out of nowhere and started scooping up the fruit from the floor and then offered to give me a hand with my bags.

After placing my other costume bag in the room on the floor near the door entrance, I turned to thank him for helping me with my runaway groceries. He then commented, passing over my fruit, "You have the most beautiful eyes. Would you like some company tonight, baby?"

I instantly suspected, since his eyes were familiarly dilated, that he was probably high on something, so I walked inside the room, responding with the door slightly ajar, "Thank you again for your help and the compliment, but I'm expecting my boyfriend to arrive in a moment now, so I have to decline your invitation. Thank you, though."

Just as I attempted to close and lock the door, he pushed his way into the room, causing me to stumble backwards to the floor, stunned that he was actually forcing his way into my room. I instinctively knew that I'd have to protect myself from this crazed stranger as I was literally power-lifted from the carpet and then slammed onto the bed. "Your man won't mind if I warm you up a little bit for him right quick!" he said.

Frightened as he ripped my top open, I replied, hoping that playing on his sympathy would help, "Please, you don't have to do this!"

I pleaded with him to stop attacking me, all along reaching under the mattress for the hammer that I'd previously hidden for protection after Elvis left. After I managed to place a knee in his groin causing him to curl up in pain grabbing his crotch, once I finally located the hammer and quickly pulling it from underneath the mattress tightly grasping the handle and swinging like a wild woman screaming, "You sick, perverted motherfucker, all you are going to warm up is this hammer over your head!"

I called upon all of my strength continuing to bash him until he bolted out of the room, trying to escape the wrath of a pissed-off showgirl! I wanted to teach him a lesson when I grabbed the robe from hanging behind the door to cover myself before running after him up the hall also yelling, "Come on back you coward! You think that you can just go around attacking people without there being any consequences?"

I tried hitting him again, but I missed and just as he opened the stairway door to run away a security guard grabbed him asking, "What's the problem here?"

You talk about being thankful that the security guard arrived when he did to apprehend that creep! After catching my breath enough to inform him, "This asshole just attacked me as I was entering my room!"

After the security guard got a closer look at the attacker he replied. "We've actually been on the look-out for this guy for burglarizing and attacking women in other hotels." He then removed a pair of handcuffs from his utility belt placing them on the attacker with both hands behind his creepy back continuing, "Ma'am I apologize for any inconveniences. But I am going to need you to come with me to the office and file a report."

I replied, gladly!"Sure, officer, no inconvenience at all, I just need to change into something more appropriate."

He replied before leading the rapist to the elevator, "Sure miss, take all the time you need. I'll meet you downstairs in the hotel manager's office."

After gathering up my groceries and placing the perishables in the mini-fridge, I quickly changed into a pair of jeans and a sweatshirt.

When I stepped into the lobby, the cops were already on the scene arresting the perpetrator for assault and attempted rape. If only he knew. Oh, well. As they were taking him away, once they'd obtained my written statement, I overheard them chuckling with the security guard that he would not be attacking anyone else anytime soon!

Later that night after being reassigned to a different floor, I lit some candles to calm myself in a hot bubble bath while also reflecting on the insane events of the most miserable night and morning.

The following weekend, in the dressing room at "Peanuts", I shared with Diva and a couple of the other girls the details of what happened to me that night. Of course, Diva said, in her usual blunt manner, "Girl, I told you that Dwayne motherfucker was trouble, with Grace selling drugs for his ass during the time when that guy was killed right here in the dressing room last year. And as for that robber son of a bitch who attacked you, I bet he'll have flashbacks whenever he sees another hammer!"

We were all cracking up when one of the only other African-American cast members that I'd previously befriended named Mahogafish walked into the dressing room and learned that I had been attacked in my hotel.

She generously and really unexpectedly invited me to move in with her until I was able to get my own place! I never expected that she'd approached me after the show saying, "Girl, these men are crazy so if you want to stay with me until you are able to get settled, you are more than welcomed, honey."

Surprised by her offer, I replied, "Thank you, Mahogafish. I promise I will be out of your hair as soon as possible!"

After moving in with her the following Monday afternoon, we seemed to have develop a close sisterly relationship and she also took me around, introducing me to some of the other shows in town!

At first, it was just she and I staying at the apartment overnight. Then her boyfriend, fresh out of prison, started spending the night more regularly and often insisting that I go with them every time that they went out somewhere.

Overtime, it was heartbreaking witnessing him being emotionally abusive towards her and knowing from experience that there was nothing that I would be able to say to convince her that she deserved better than the way that he treated her.

It didn't make any difference in the outcome after I shared my personal story of abuse with her so that she would know that I understood what she was going through loving a man that showed his so-called love by making her cry and physically abusing her.

Since my words didn't work, I figured that for her birthday show at the "Horizon" one of the clubs that she'd introduced me to, I'd dedicate my "Girlfriend" routine by

Pebbles to let her know that I was concerned about her and that I cared.

After a certain point, I started insisting that I had other plans when they invited me to join them wherever they were going, because I knew that it would have been just a matter of time before Mahogafish's boyfriend eventually started to aggressively come onto me sexually.

I was prepared for him whenever he and I were alone in the apartment, so after he made his first blatant move I explained to him, "Mahogafish is my sister and I'm not going to betray her by sleeping with her man."

After several unsuccessful attempts at seducing me, he began to make it intolerable to be in the same room with him and it was obvious to me that Mahogafish suspected that he was coming onto me. But it seemed easier for her to remain in a sense of denial about what was really going on right under her nose.

Since I didn't know Mahogafish well enough at that point to predict how she would respond to me telling her about the advances that her man was making towards me, I intentionally made myself invisible by leaving whenever he came over to visit her if he hadn't spent the night.

Due to appreciating Mahogafish for inviting me to stay with her so that I would be able to save up enough money to get my own place, I definitely wasn't about to mess it up by stabbing her in the back with a dog in heat.

I would never have shown my appreciation by sleeping with her boyfriend. As a matter of fact, messing around with other girls' men, especially someone that I considered to be a sister and friend has never been my style because I don't want other girls' sloppy seconds. I want a man of my own that has not been intimately familiar with all of the other girls.

The escalating hostility that her boyfriend displayed towards me ultimately required Mahogafish to approach me one afternoon when we were alone with questions about his sudden attitude change.

I explained to her that he was angry with me because I was not receptive to his sexual advances whenever he and I were alone. I also reassured her that she did not have to worry about me sleeping with her man, and that I was even more determined to get my own place as soon as possible so that I would not cause any conflict between her and her boyfriend.

The following evening, he spent the night, making it obvious that they were having sex, which would not have been a problem with me if her apartment was not a studio.

Almost immediately after my revelation to her, the relationship between Mahogafish and I became strained, which contributed to my determination to get three jobs if necessary so that I could get my own place sooner rather than later.

In an effort to avoid him, I left the apartment early the following day to go shopping at Hollywood Costumes and Frederick's of Hollywood, purchasing new pumps and supplies for the show that upcoming weekend.

After leaving Frederick's (once I'd found the perfect black pumps to match my new Toni Braxton outfit), I stood waiting at Cherokee and Hollywood for the traffic light to change I was just standing there minding my own business when a fairly handsome and tall Caucasian guy that resembled a sexier Jim Carey stood next to me at the crosswalk and asked my name.

I replied, not to be rude, "Joy, what's your name?"

He replied, "Hello, Joy, I'm Jim and I noticed you shopping earlier so I was hoping that you would consider joining me for lunch at the Hollywood Café?"

At first, I was reluctant to continue engaging this stranger from out of nowhere. However, on the other hand, I wasn't in any rush to get back to the apartment. Furthermore, since the restaurant was right across the street, I saw no harm in going to lunch with him in a public place, so I accepted his invitation to lunch.

As we crossed the street, I hoped that by the time we'd finished eating, Mahogafish's boyfriend would be gone. After ordering club sandwiches, fries and beverages, he proceeded to share with me that he was looking for an office manager for his company. "I own a computer company and I'm looking for an office manager to help operate my business. You look like you would make a great office manager, Joy!"

I replied, fascinated by his proposal, "I've recently relocated from the South and I'm definitely looking for another job to supplement my income so that I can move out of my friend's apartment and into my own!"

After enumerating the responsibilities of managing the four-member office staff, scheduling contracted service calls, ordering all equipment that were necessary for the technicians to build and maintain computer systems for large corporate contracts, I felt that I'd be able to handle those responsibilities with no problem.

However, before accepting his job offer, I explained to him that I'd given him a fake name because he was a stranger approaching me on the streets and although slightly suspicious about his proposal, I told him my real name, figuring that I didn't have anything to lose.

He unexpectedly responded with a chuckle, "I understand why you felt the need to give me a fake name, Tracee, and I can appreciate that you've just moved here trying to get settled into your own place, so I would like to help by giving you an advance on your salary just to show that I am really serious about you working for me."

I was pleasantly surprised that he'd voluntarily offered to give me money before I had even started doing any work, because getting money on a job that I have yet to complete would have helped tremendously toward moving out of Mahogafish's apartment a whole lot sooner!

After Jim pulled out his check book from his back pocket, removing the pin from the bill tray and endorsing a check before passing it to me, I was just expecting a $100 or maybe $150 dollars at the most. However, when I looked at the check and saw that it was for $300, I almost screamed out loud inside the restaurant!

Once I composed myself, all I could say was: "Really, thank you so much, Jim. This is more than generous of you!"

He replied, placing his credit card on the bill tray and handing it to our server, "You seem like a nice person, Tracee, and I just want to help you out."

I suspected that he had other ulterior motives for wanting to help a stranger that he'd just met on Hollywood Boulevard and I also knew that he was expecting something from me in return, something more than just being his office manager. However, I didn't refuse his generosity because I was confident that I'd be able to deal with his additional expectations as they'd arrived.

Nothing really mattered to me during that time except coming one step closer to my goal of leaving Mahogafish alone to deal with her relationship before something crazy happened that I wanted no part of!

Jim also wrote down the address and directions to his office in addition to giving me his business card to call if I had any problems getting there on the following Monday morning. After lunch, I thanked him again and then headed back to the apartment to find Mahogafish in tears after an altercation they'd had after she found out her boyfriend was cheating on her with another postoperative transsexual.

I knew better to try and intervene after seeing too many beautiful and talented transsexual showgirls remain in domestic violence relationships with guys that inevitably ended up permanently maiming or, even worse, killing them. We had our example in a mutual showgirl acquaintance named Jasmine.

Jasmine was another cool person I'd befriended who briefly lived with me after she left her boyfriend, whom eventually knocked out one of her front tooth during their many crack-induced physical confrontations. It was so painful seeing a beautiful person inside and out resorting to using pieces of white Ivory Soap to create an illusion of having all of her front teeth.

Unfortunately, Jasmine went back to her abusive boyfriend and later we were informed that he'd killed her. As for Mahogafish, my experiences have taught me that some girls possess a need to learn the hard way and that there was nothing that I could do to influence her to leave, so I attempted to ease the tension by telling Mahogafish about the encounter on Hollywood Boulevard with Jim and his job offer.

Although I'd figured that Jim was expecting much more from me than just being his office manager, I never considered that he might have been a complete phony until Mahogafish suggested that there are all sorts of fakes running around Hollywood making promises to unsuspecting, gullible girls.

Since I didn't really have any way of confirming if the check Jim had given me was legitimate or not on a Saturday afternoon way after the banks had closed, I let Mahogafish slide with the underhanded read, considering her state of mind.

I'm not sure why it never occurred to me to cash the check at one of the many check cashing places on Hollywood Boulevard instead of waiting for the bank to open on Monday. Oh well, at least I didn't have to sleep with the man for anything.

I had nothing to lose if Jim was a fake due to my eyes remaining on the prize. I was determined that living with Mahogafish was only going to be temporary, so it really did not matter if the check bounced or nor because I was going to get another job regardless. With that attitude of self-confidence that I would accomplish my goals, I called and scheduled an appointment to look at an apartment in Silver Lake.

Later that afternoon I took the bus to Silver Lake to see the apartment and instantaneously fell in love with the studio containing a separate kitchen, full bath that was conveniently located near public transportation on Sanborn Avenue!

I filled out an application and used the savings that I'd made from performing to place a deposit, holding the apartment upon approval of my application and prayed that I'd qualify for it while hoping that I would have the remainder of the deposit once approved.

That weekend at Peanuts in addition to my salary, I made some pretty good tips performing "The Right Stuff" by Vanessa Williams and "The Men All Pause" Klymaxx mix. It was more than enough to pay the final deposits on my apartment.

My corporate clothes were pressed and ready to go when I got up really early that following Monday morning, hours before getting on the bus to go and start working at Dolan Micro Consulting, because I wanted to be one of the first people at the bank to confirm if the check that Jim had given me would bounce like a basketball as Mahogafish had suggested.

The moment of truth arrived after endorsing and handing the check along with my identification to the bank teller then shallowly breathing until she asked, "Would you like large bills or would twenties be okay?" I requested large bills, relieved that the check had not bounced like a toy jacks ball and then securely tucked them away into my wallet before walking across Hollywood Boulevard to get onto the bus to begin my first day at the computer company!

I was alone in the office vibrating with uncontainable anticipation during my lunch break later that afternoon no longer willing to further delay dialing my prospective landlord Alva's number to enquire about the status of my application. Upon Alva replying that I had been approved, I jumped for joy when she'd also informed me that all I had to do was pay a pro-rated move-in fee to take possession of the apartment!

After scheduling an appointment to meet with Alva the following afternoon on my lunch break, I went through the rest of the day as if floating on a cloud, having no idea at that time Alva would soon become another guardian angel who would be there for me in my time of need!

I was happy that Jim allowed me to take an extended lunch break the following afternoon to go take care of my business. After taking possession of my first apartment on Sanborn Avenue and moving my things from Mahogafish's apartment, I loved exploring the majority Latino neighborhood, eating the Mexican baked desserts and shopping at the eclectic retro consignment stores and boutiques for costumes!

I also took the bus back to Broadway Street downtown in order to shop for other costumes and groceries at Union Station Market where there were all kinds of unique produce and strange animal parts with heads, eyes and ears still intact. In the corner of the large bustling marketplace there was a small stage consisting of straw spread all over the dirt floor where Latina transgender performers performed Latin music!

Strangely enough and, unbelievably, shortly after moving into my new apartment, although I'd had ample opportunities to meet and date other guys, I'd started to really think about Ron and fantasized about the possibilities of us starting over together in a new state.

I don't know what came over me to even consider being with Ron again after all that I'd previously been through with him. I wish I can explain my thinking, but I couldn't at that time. If I had to guess why my thinking shifted, I'd attribute it to the one very handsome guy in particular named Joey whom I met in the club as I was leaving after the show.

Joey was a lot of fun and he treated me like a lady on our dates to my favorite seafood restaurant Gladstone's in Malibu for lunch or dinner overlooking the ocean.

After several weeks of going out with Joey, I started spending nights at his condo following many nights dancing and having fun at the club on the weekends. I was caught off guard when he eventually asked me to paint his face and dress him up like a woman the second time that I attended Halloween festivities in West Hollywood.

When Joey made that unexpected request to dress him up in hair and makeup, I knew that if I had beaten his face with makeup and dressed him in drag I would no longer make out with him, because I was not attracted to men who wore makeup or cross-dressed even though they didn't consider themselves to be gay.

Well, needless to say after I finished painting myself, I then moved in to get started on Joey's face, knowing that my work was cut out for me because he refused to shave his moustache.

He also insisted that I make him look Whitney Houston, so I did the best that I could with what I had to work with, which was very challenging, might I add. Later that night, we had a great time on Santa Monica Boulevard in West Hollywood celebrating Halloween!

Moving forward, I never saw Joey in the same light again and we no longer made out because he also requested to start wearing female clothes during the process, which was not happening with me no matter how masculine and fine he was.

There was no way that I could psychologically or emotionally get into making out with a man who was dressed in female clothes. However, we remained close friends and party buddies!

Just for re-clarification, when I refer to making out with a guy it means just kissing, bumping and grinding, not intercourse.

After resolving that Joey and I were like brother and sister, I also believe that my shift from sane thinking into an insane mind frame may have been additionally attributed to being disappointed a month or so later after this well-dressed guy whom seemed to have it all together approached me in the grocery store check-out line and asked me out to dinner.

Since he was a charming and attractive person, I accepted his invitation and agreed to have dinner that following evening. During our conversation at dinner he seemed to be a well-rounded, educated person until he went overboard trying to also impress me later with an invitation to meet his sister and her kids.

Although I was taken aback by the sudden invitation to meet his family, I agreed to meet them anyway, not wanting to be rude or disrespectful. After arriving at his sister's apartment and when it was clear that they were conveniently not there, it immediately occurred to me that he had had other intentions from the start of that evening.

I really wasn't familiar with where we were so I played my displeasure off ,deciding to go with the flow as long as he remained respectful, having no intentions of doing anything other than conversing with him.

During the conversation sitting on the sectional couch, it came out that he actually lived with his sister and he claimed that he was staying there to help them out financially since her divorce, which did not bother me because I knew that I would never see him again after that night.

However, I was beyond bothered and agitated when he pulled a vial of cocaine out of his blazer pocket, offering it to me. That was it! I told him that I didn't indulge and then requested him to please drop me off at the nearest taxi stand, which he did without objection. I guess he could read the disdain written all over my face.

That dating thing had not worked out so well for me up to that point and I wondered if all of the men in California that were attracted to girls like me either had drug and alcohol problems or possessed weird freaky fetishes that were all turn-offs to me.

I also questioned if I would ever meet someone that was at least halfway "normal" after those experiences. However, I knew for a fact that I was not about to go the route of looking for a man the way some of the other girls chose to – in desperation going to hang out in areas where they'd meet the cute-built guys who were recently out of jail, prison or strung out on drugs.

According to a friend who was also a performer and show director at Horizon club named Mother Rose, it was a habit of some girls to get guys off the streets and take them home to clean him up and then designate him her "husband" after a wedding ceremony at Horizon as Mother Rose had done.

I will never forget her telling us to wear all white for her ceremony on the dance floor, nor will I ever forget the time several weeks earlier when Mother Rose asked me if I wanted to go "slumming" with her. Although I didn't immediately comprehend what the term "slumming" meant before her explanation, I was down for the adventure!

I should have put two and two together. Oh, well! It never occurred to me that slumming actually meant going downtown to Skid Row where the homeless and drug addicts created their own little city, with some of them sleeping in cardboard boxes on the sidewalks, openly smoking crack and shooting drugs intravenously.

I had never seen or experienced anything like that except for depictions of zombies in a horror movie. I was amazed when we went to a park just to sit and hang out for hours where the crack-heads and drug dealers were all over the place like flies.

I really didn't see the purpose or the thrill of being in that sort of environment. However, I understood why others "slummed." Taking a guy off the streets just was not my cup of tea or choice for a relationship, and hanging out with Mother Rose on Skid Row was a once-in-a-lifetime experience that I did not care to ever repeat again.

After those crazy dating experiences, my thoughts kept going back to Ron, craving for the familiar because I was concerned that I wasn't going to meet any quality men. Disillusionment became my middle name. I wrongfully and prematurely thought that those extremely kinky or hard-core drug addicts were my only choices.

Another thing I could say without a doubt is that Ron never asked me to paint his face and dress him up in my clothes. Unbelievably, during one of those moments of weakness, after spending most of the holidays alone, I broke down and called his father's house to inquire if he was there. It was almost five months after making my escape from Georgia.

I know what you're thinking – what!? I agree with you, however, please give me a moment to explain my reasoning as I dialed the number, not expecting Ron to pick up the phone. I was happy to hear his voice on the other end, boyishly answering in a sweet tone:" Hello."

I took a deep breath before responding. "Hello, Ron. It's me, Tracee."

Ron seemed genuinely excited to hear from me as he enthusiastically replied, questioning, "Where are you, Tracee, and why did you just disappear?"

I responded in a soft tone, "Ron, I'm in California."

He remained silent a few beats before replying, "I miss you, baby, and I looked everywhere to find you!" I remained silent as he continued, "Why did you leave me here alone, Tracee?"

Although I was happy to be talking to him, I had to let him know how I had really felt during our time together. "You know Ron, I'm really sorry that I hurt you when I left town without telling you, but I felt out of control and not myself being with you, so I needed to get away from the drugs and drama that was going on with us in Atlanta."

"Tracee, I understand why you left and I don't blame you for leaving baby. I admit that I was out of control, but I've started counseling for my anger."

I inquired about the pink elephant head-on. "Are you still dealing and doing drugs, Ron?"

He replied in almost one breath, "No, baby, I'm living here with Dad and my little brother Richie until I get it together, but most of all I'm missing you, Tracee, and I am so glad that you called me. Baby, can I come to California to be with you?"

Lonely for his affections I replied, "I've missed you also Ron and, yes, you can come here to be with me as soon as you're able to!"

After a moment of slight hesitation, he replied in a calm voice. "Tracee, I want to tell you the truth about everything and there is something very important that you should know about what happened after you left Georgia."

"What is it, Ron?" I inquired and then held my breath as he explained that after I left Atlanta, he had sex with a biological female who'd previously come to the apartment when we were still together on Argonne Avenue.

After I answered the door one afternoon she'd unknowingly handed me a love letter that she'd written and requested for me to give it to Ron. She'd obviously didn't know who I was and I did not immediately tell her, until after she'd handed me the letter, and then I warned her to never come to that door again looking for Ron. After closing the door in her face, I read the letter in which she professed her undying love for and desire to be with Ron.

Now Ron told me, "Tracee, I had unprotected sex with her after you left and contracted an STD, which is being treated with medication that I got from my doctor."

I recall wanting to move on from the mistakes of the past and since it felt so nice hearing his voice on the phone again I desperately wanted to believe that we possessed the potential for things to be different with a fresh start in a new environment,

Go ahead, you can say it again, and looking back on those days from an objective and more mature point of view, yes. I agree 100 percent that I was really stupid. But back then I didn't regret my decision to call him and reassuringly replied after hearing what the sexually transmitted disease was, "Ron, as long as we are cautious and don't have sex until your infection completely clears up, and continue having protected sex, I'll be okay. I'm just happy that you don't have HIV or AIDS!"

He confidently replied, "I've been tested for HIV and I'm negative, Tracee!"

There's no doubt now that I was certainly in a deep state of denial about Ron being in counseling, which at the time was okay with me as long as he was telling the truth about his medical challenges.

I called Ron because I'd really wanted to try one last time with him, so after hanging up the phone, I remained hopeful about a better future together being away from the negative influences in Georgia.

You can also say that I absurdly thought that we'd really have a fair chance at being together in a more positive way and take advantage of the almost limitless opportunities that the new beginning presented to both of us!

After our conversation, I started counting every minute of each hour slowly ticking up to the five days or so that were required for him to arrive in California while preoccupying my time with work and shopping for a new bed, leather sofa and matching love seat to decorate the apartment, which made it feel so much more homely.

On the evening that Ron was expected to arrive, I patiently and excitedly tidied up the apartment, then prepared his favorite smothered chicken dinner in anticipation of his arrival.

When I heard the knock on the door, I knew that it was him and after seeing his face for the first time in almost six months, I embraced him tightly and observed that he appeared to be healthier than he was when I saw him last in Atlanta.

We spent the evening after dinner rekindling the passion that I never thought I would ever experience again with him and things were going well after his arrival

One night several weeks after Ron's arrival, he accompanied me and some lesbian friends of me and Mahogafish to a ghetto fabulous show. It was a show that Mother Rose had previously booked for me at the Horizon, which was this hole-in-the-wall club located in the hood on Washington Street that I would not have ever chosen to perform at if I had not felt fairly safe. I'd previously performed there with Mahogafish during her birthday show and Mother Rose's wedding to the crack-head off Skid-Row.

Also performing on the show that night was one of Mahogafish's friends, Le'Monica, whom I had met once at Mahogafish's apartment. Le'Monica had been recently released from incarceration for credit card and check writing fraud.

Le'Monica had made it very clear to me from the beginning that she did not like me; I suspected that she was probably threatened by my presence and friendship with Mahogafish.

Later that night after the show had started, Le'Monica and I were alone in the dressing room when she suddenly decided to take a piece of tissue that she'd used to blow her nose and tried to intentionally throw it in my face.

Here we go again, with another queen mistakenly taking my kindness for a weakness. After successfully blocking the tissue from hitting my face, I did everything that I could possibly do to not immediately start beating her down, because my performance was next and she knew it.

It always seemed that the cowardly girls always chose right before my performance to see how far I'd let them go with me. However, I was not in the least intimidated when I informed her that I would be seeing her after my number.

After pulling myself together and once I was introduced, I went out and performed "Everything/Looking for a New Love" by Jody Watley as if nothing had happened in the dressing room.

Even though the audience was enjoying my number, I was anticipating the end of the song because I was angry that Le'Monica tried to throw used tissue in my face right before my performance.

Immediately after finishing my routine, I went back into the dressing room to look for her and when I saw that she was not there, after placing my tips into my bag I then went into the back lounge area to see if she was back there.

Upon spotting Le'Monica sitting on the couch in the corner, holding court and bragging about what she'd done to me in the dressing room, the only words that I spoke to her were, "Bitch, don't never try to throw shit in my face ever again!"

I dove on top of her like Christmas paper on a present and after we clashed, the whole room immediately erupted into a full-out brawl when some of her friends jumped into the fight to try and double-team me. But Ron and our two lesbian friends DJ and Lou-Lou had my back and did not hesitate to come to my defense after her friends got involved!

We tore up that lounge, battling it out from one side of the room to the other before eventually being ushered out by the club security onto the dark streets out front where the battle continued!

At one point, Ron managed to separate me and Le'Monica, then made me stand on the opposite side of the street while he tried to calm down the situation. As I stood there alone waiting for our friends to retrieve their car from the parking lot, Le'Monica tried to sneak up on me in the dark to get a sucker punch in from behind.

What she didn't know as she tried tipping up in the dark was that I had already taken off the steel buckled black leather fringed belt that I'd worn during my performance and securely wrapped her tightly around my hand for protection.

So, since I'd kept my eyes on her the entire time, I was ready when she'd unsuccessfully attempted to swing at me and unexpectedly received a loud and clear final warning to back the fuck off me after I introduced her head to my cold solid steel belt buckle.

"Come on, bitch, I got more of where that one came from," I said. "I told you that I'm not the one to be threatened by you!"

Although I was poised to give Le'Monica one last warning if necessary, it only took that one pop. She yelped as she stumbled backward and grabbed her head in shock!

Then in a flash, she high-tailed it behind a parked car still holding her head and running her big fat mouth making idle threats. It was clear to me that she'd been trying to pretend that she wasn't in obvious pain while remaining at a safe distance until after we'd all gotten into the car and sped off from Horizon to never return again!

When she'd initially violated my private space out of pure jealousy that night in the dressing room, I felt that I had no other choice but to stand up to her because Le'Monica had the well-known reputation for giving the new girls on the scene a really hard time, according to Mahogafish.

I knew that it was going to be just a matter of time that I'd have to stand my ground after previously during random conversation being informed by Mahogafish that the weekend before Le'Monica and some of her crew members jumped on this other new girl, beating her to the point that she was rushed to the hospital in an ambulance.

I've always disliked bullies with a passion since most of the ones that I've personally encountered usually attempted to be disrespectful and shady just to see how far I would let them go with me.

I knew upon initially meeting Le'Monica that she was an insecure Bully whose bark was probably worse than her bite, and I also knew that if she'd ever built up the false courage to come for me, I'd have to let it be known from the get-go that I was not intimidated by her in the least.

Although the night concluded with Ron being really mad that I'd gotten into a physical altercation with another queen, I experienced pleasure after my buckle met her forehead when she'd tried to sneak attack me on Washington Street in the hood that night!

That incident became my very first physical fight with another queen in California.

Unfortunately, several years after our altercation, Mahogafish told me that Le'Monica and some of those same members of her crew were hanging out, sitting on top of a car belonging to a friend who was inside the apartment arguing with their boyfriend.

After the guy ran out of the apartment and jumped into the car quickly peeling off at a high rate of speed, instead of Le'Monica immediately jumping off the car with the rest of the crew, she stayed on top, dramatically showing off in front of the spectators that were watching the events unfold.

Le'Monica was ultimately thrown off the car as it turned the corner. She remained in a coma for several months.

She was not the same person after coming out of the coma. Her hygiene, speech and mobility were completely impaired, causing me to empathize with her whenever I saw her on stage trying to perform in the condition that she was in, so I set aside my previous disdain by helping her to get dressed in the dressing room and then tipping her whenever we performed on the show together at "Catch One" club thereafter.

Meanwhile, back on the home front several weeks after the throw-down in the hood, the reunion with Ron seemed to be still going well considering his jealousy gene remained. He seemed to have adjusted to my work schedule and even compromised on not attending any more of my club appearances in order to manage his anger towards the attention that I'd received from the clientele.

His jealous responses to the attention I got whenever he was in attendance made it necessary to quickly set boundaries pertaining to my security and job.

As the days turned into weeks, Ron became noticeably frustrated about being left at home alone while I worked both jobs, and he also stopped making an honest effort to get a job after only three weeks of filling out employment applications.

Instead of persevering until he got a job, he chose to stay at home and sleep all day while I worked, expecting me to buy his cigarettes, beer, and his Big Daddy Kane and Jimi Hendrix cassette tapes, so that he'd have something to occupy his time while I was out working to pay all of the bills with no help from him.

One afternoon after work, I arrived home to a dark apartment and responded by immediately pulling the shades to let some sun light into the stench-blanketed room. I was devastated after removing the cover from my pet parakeet Charlie's cage and finding him dead on the bottom of the cage.

Angrily, I picked up the shoes, books and empty beer cans that he'd used to torture my pet bird to death, asking only after containing myself, "Ron, what happened to Charlie?"

He remained with his head still tucked underneath the covers nonchalantly replying, "That damn bird would not shut up making noise all day and keeping me from getting any sleep."

As I replied, beyond pissed off that he didn't show any remorse for killing my bird," "Ron, it doesn't make any sense that you have just given up entirely on getting a job. You have managerial experience from Dominos. Why have you not applied there until you can find something else later?"

Ron adjusted the pillows, sitting up and lighting a cigarette before replying to my question about him getting a job. "Tracee, I told you that I don't want to go back to flipping dough all damn day again!"

Proceeding cautiously, I replied, "So Ron, you'd rather sleep all day instead of getting a job and contribute to paying some of our bills?"

He was clearly irritated by my questions as he sat on the edge of the bed, replying after puffing his cigarette and then placing it into the ashtray. "Tracee, I am doing the best that I can right now, so that should be good enough until I can do better."

The undeniable awareness that I should not continue agitating him any further caused me to delicately as possible diffuse the conversation, replying, "Ron, I do not want to fight with you. I just don't like seeing you giving up on accomplishing your goals of getting a job so soon and I know that you will get it together, but right now I have got to bury Charlie."

I grabbed a white scarf from my vanity top drawer, wrapped Charlie in it, and left Ron alone in the apartment while I buried my bird in the flower bed beneath the apartment window.

As I shoveled dirt over Charlie, I beat myself up questioning whether I had made the right decision to contact Ron. It was clear to me that he was rapidly resorting to his old ways, and I would have to proceed with caution in order to immediately get myself out of the old, familiar suffocating environment.

As I walked back into the apartment, I truly regretted that I had foolishly placed myself right back into the same position that I'd successfully escaped from back in Georgia, pretending that things were okay when I knew that it was not.

As I tidied up and opened the kitchen window and turned on the ceiling fan to blow the smoke out of the apartment, that fear that I thought was left in Atlanta started to rear its old, ugly head.

However, that time as I listened to him profusely apologize, promising to get it together, I was not the least influenced by his sudden remorsefulness, because I'd become numbed to him after burying Charlie.

I knew that I'd have to handle the situation like a surgeon with a steady hand in order to strategically figure out the best way to respond.

The following weekend I didn't put up any objections when Ron announced that he was going to escort me to the club on Friday night. I knew that it was going to be really challenging having him there with me; I don't even recall my music selections that night because I was so consumed with not doing anything to provoke him.

I intentionally stayed in the dressing room from the time that we arrived at the club, and immediately after performing two routines, hurriedly changed out of my costumes as fast as possible to leave the club through the back entrance, thusly avoiding altogether exiting through the crowd.

That following Saturday night was a completely different story, because Ron reverted to being insecure and demanded that I stay home. I was slightly astonished at my ability to convince him that I needed to work so that we'd be able to eat and pay the rent!

Several hours passed as I reasoned and reassured him that I would be coming straight home after my last performance before he allowed me to leave the apartment alone to go to work without incident.

I was mentally and physically stirred and shaken that night at the club, although I managed to pull it together alone in the dressing room before the other girls arrived for the show to perform "You Can't Deny It" by Lisa Stansfield and the "Smooth Operator/Is It A Crime" mix by Sade, reflecting my mental state of mind!

My intention after the last number was to rush into the dressing room and change into my street clothes before going to obtain my check and then hurrying to catch the next bus home in hopes of preventing any unforeseen possibility of arriving later than I was expected.

My wish was to avoid an argument and accusations from Ron that stemmed from his fear that I might be persuaded to leave him for one of the guys at the club.

I was happy about my schedule panning out just as planned on the way from picking up my check from the front bar until I was intercepted in the pool room by one of the girls, Amber, excitedly informing me that she had a friend who wanted to meet me!

Since I didn't want to be rude to any potential fan, I agreed to meet him and then allowed her to lead me by hand over to this very attractive guy that she introduced as Tevin. After our introduction, she left the two of us awkwardly standing there alone, exchanging small talk for about 20 seconds or so.

I recall him complimenting me on my performances and I also recall remaining suspicious during that brief conversation that he was interested in more than just his admiration for my performance.

I don't know what caused me to go into such details about my business with him, but I immediately explained to him that I was in a relationship. I also, for some insane reason, revealed that although my boyfriend and I were currently going through some challenges, the thought of going out with another guy at that moment was not an option for me.

Immediately after his response, which I don't recall, I politely excused myself from the conversation then went into the dressing room to grab my show bag and leave to catch the next bus home!

On the ride home, I reflected on how painful it had been when I made the mistake in Atlanta to choose getting involved with Ron before resolving the relationship with Shawn. The consequences of cheating were still fresh in my mind.

No matter attractive a guy like Tevin was, I was not going to even consider going there because I was determined to learn the lesson from those painful past experiences and not repeat them.

Since I didn't know what state of mind that Ron would be in when I finally arrived home, I mentally prepared myself for Jekyll or Hyde. When I walked through the door arriving home no later than usual from the club, he was in a reasonably calm disposition and it turned out to be a pleasant night for a change.

The following Monday on my bus ride to work at the computer company, I was filled with gratitude that I did not have to stay up all night long arguing and fighting with Ron! I also continued questioning some of the really stupid decisions that I'd made over the last few months.

Ugh! I felt really stupid that my choices once again thrust me right back into the same old pathological patterns that I'd fought so hard to leave back in Atlanta, Georgia. Although I'd beaten myself up during the ride to work, I fortunately realized that I needed to finally forgive myself for cheating on Ron with Shawn so that I would be able to finally let go of the guilt and stop trying to fix an unfixable situation.

Additionally on that 8a.m. bus ride up Westmoreland that morning, I finally became content that I had done all that I could possibly do to atone for my actions back then. I was wrong to have contacted Ron and I knew that I would have to responsibly proceed with finding my own personal solutions for dealing with the consequences that I'd created for myself before the unthinkable occurred.

After arriving at DMC, Jim introduced me to his new girlfriend, Rose, who was visiting from Kansas. When I saw her it confirmed for me that he was attracted to African-American women, I knew that I'd have a fairly easy day at the office after being informed that he was going to be out of the office for the rest of the day after lunch with Rose.

For the week that Jim's girlfriend remained in town, the technicians took advantage of Jim's absence by staying out of the office after their service calls were completed. I was happy that he had met someone; that took the pressure off me always having to professionally maneuver my way around his obvious flirtatiousness!

Before Rose arrived on the scene, whenever we were alone in the office Jim often questioned me about the status of the relationship with my boyfriend. I pretended that things were great between us because I did not want him knowing that we were having really serious problems.

I was grateful that I'd managed to make it through the remainder of the week without incident at work or at home. After work that Friday afternoon, when I arrived home and found Ron doing his usual idle sitting on the couch, smoking cigarettes, drinking beer and watching television, I was still thankful he didn't have a problem with me working at the computer company during the weekdays.

It was an entirely different story when it came to me working at the club on the weekends. After resting and dinner later that evening, I packed my costumes for the show and showered before sitting at my makeup dresser to start painting for the show.

It wasn't out of the ordinary for Ron to watch me the whole time, drinking a six-pack of beer and chain-smoking a pack of cigarettes. As I applied my face, I observed through the smoke-filled room that his attitude and body language had changed as he quietly continued watching me.

He patiently waited until after I was finished applying L'Oreal Fire and Ice red lipstick, and had reached for my costume bag, jacket and hat before telling him that I was leaving for work and that I would be home right after the show. Just as I walked over to kiss his forehead, he asked. "Where you think you are going, Tracee?"

I don't know why I was bewildered by the question considering his regular mood changes, but he very well knew that I'd be working at the club every weekend. I could only reply, "Ron, you know that I'm booked to work at Peanuts on the weekends. Do you want to come with me?"

"Tracee, you know I hate going to that club just to sit around watching how those guys gawk after you."

Annoyed that he'd waited until I'd finished applying makeup to question where I was going, I replied, fighting to keep my emotions in check, "Ron, you know that performing for me is just a job. I am not interested in any of those men at the club."

I placed my bag on the floor and sat down on the couch next to him and began negotiating with him, "Baby, if I expect to be successful at making some money to support us, I am required to be pleasant to the club clientele, which does not mean that I want to be with them. Do I not come straight home to you after work?"

He insisted, "Tracee, I know that eventually one of those guys tipping and admiring you during your show will take you away from me with their money."

I hoped to diffuse the tension in the room by gently replying. "Ron, if I wanted to be with any of those guys in Peanuts or anywhere else, I would not have never called to let you know where I was, would I?"

Without saying a word Ron rose from the couch, walked over to the door and removed my set of keys from the double-bolted lock. He then turned to me replying, "Tracee, I am not going to let you ever leave me again."

I feared what was going through his mind, so I reminded him, "Ron, you know that if I don't work this weekend, we will not have enough money to pay our upcoming rent and eat."

He replied. "I don't give a fuck about no rent or food right now, Tracee. You're not going anywhere, because I want you to prove to me that no other guy is going to take you away from me."

As he rose from the couch facing me, déjà vu all over again washed over my spirit as I looked into his hauntingly dark and emotionless eyes. Since I'd been there with him before, I reluctantly replied. "Ron, you know that there's no other guy for me but you and I thought that I have already proven that to you over and over again. What else do you want me to do?"

He reached for my hand and gently pulled me close to his chest, whispering softly in my ear, "Stay home with me tonight, baby, and let me make love to you without a condom. That's how you can prove that you love me and you are not going to leave me again."

I was shocked he'd actually suggested that we have unprotected sex considering we'd never gone there before without using a condom, and the fact that I was not sure about what other sexual partners he might have been with. After all, he'd had unprotected sex and contracted a sexually transmitted disease during the almost five months since my departure.

I knew that having sex with him without using protection was not going to happen no matter what. I was also resolute that if I was not able to persuade him to let me leave the apartment, my life would be in danger.

So, understanding that I'd have to urgently change his energy, I pressed my breasts against his chest, and caressed his erected penis through his jeans with one hand. I then whispered into his ear after gently applying pressure to his lobe with my teeth. "Baby, let me go and make this money and when I get home from the show, I will leave on my makeup, hair and costume so that you can do whatever you want to do to me."

All along I knew without question that once I was allowed out of that apartment that night, there was absolutely no way I was ever going to return while he was still there. But, he was not having it, he grabbed my shoulders with both hands and pushed me back against the couch replying, "Take off your clothes, Tracee."

I refused replying, "Ron, I'm not taking off my clothes because I have to go to work!"

"Tracee, if you don't get undressed now, I will do it for you!"

I begged pleadingly. "Ron, please, don't do this."

Ron continued ignoring my pleas and ripped my top completely off then threw me across the room onto the bed. After he dived on top of me and continued to remove the rest of my clothes, I struggled to free myself from his grasp, but he was much stronger than I was.

He wrapped both hands around my neck and then spat in my face before pressing his face against mine, screaming, "I will kill you before I let you leave me again, Tracee!"

In between gasps for air I continued trying to caress him, hoping to calm him down and for a brief moment, I thought that I was getting through to him after stating, "Ron, I am not going anywhere. I love you!"

"That's what you said to me before in Georgia and you left, Tracee!" His grasp around my neck got tighter as he continued constricting like a boa constrictor angrily, yelling over and over. "You not going to leave me the way my mother left our family, Tracee!"

As his grip progressively became tighter around my neck, I felt that I was going to pass out if I didn't breathe in some air so I continued trying to remove his hands from around my neck, feeling that he was really trying to kill me. I called upon every last bit of strength I had left using my legs to get him off of me, but the more I fought, the stronger and more violent he became. He threw me off the bed onto the floor then, straddling me, violently slammed my head against the floor, yelling, "Look what you made me do, Tracee!"

Just as I felt myself blacking out, I heard a continuous loud knocking on the apartment door, allowing me to catch my breath. When he finally loosened his death grip from around my throat to walk over and peep through the security hole. I jumped up from the floor and ran into the bathroom locking myself inside as I heard him ask. "Who is it?!"

When I heard a voice respond, "LAPD, open the door, sir!" I knew that I would be safe after the door opened and I heard the voice of a male officer informing him that they were responding to a domestic violence report.

I was certain that seeing the condition of the apartment, particularly the warm, splattered blood still dripping down the white wall beside the entrance, it would be obvious to them that everything was not okay.

The officer asked, "Sir, what's your name?"

"LeRon Goodard."

The officer further inquired, "Who else is here with you, Mr. Goodard?"

Ron replied, "My girlfriend, Tracee, is using the restroom."

When I heard the knock on the bathroom door followed by a female voice commanding that I come out, I thanked God that they were there as I opened the door to walk out.

After exiting the bathroom I did not have to say one word when the officers both saw my bloody face supplemented with fresh crimson bruises around my throat. The male officer without hesitation commanded to Ron, "Turn around and place your hands behind your back, Mr. Goodard, you are under arrest for domestic violence."

I was relieved when he placed the handcuffs tightly around Ron's wrists then inquired if I needed medical attention. After reassuring them both that I'd be okay after they'd taken Ron away, the female officer reassured me, saying, "He will most likely be in jail for the rest of the weekend, so you should make sure that you go and press charges against him if you don't want this to happen again."

Before they took him away, she gave me a business card to contact them about pressing charges, but I knew that I was not going to press charges on him because he was so far away from his family.

I was extremely grateful that they'd arrived when they had! I also knew that I needed to immediately find somewhere else to live for awhile until I was certain to never see Ron again.

I called in sick from work that night and then called my friend Ashley to tell her about what just happened with Ron. Without hesitating, she invited me to stay with her for as long as I needed if I didn't feel safe at my apartment.

After I finished talking to Ashley, I called Ron's father at his house and informed him that Ron had been arrested for domestic battery and that I had reached my limit with continuously being beaten by his son.

I also shared with him that I had done all that I was capable of doing to help Ron with his anger and drug issues, so he needed to make arrangements to get his son out of jail and provide him with a ticket back to Georgia. He thanked me for calling him and apologized for his son's actions after assuring me that he would make arrangements for LeRon to return to Atlanta.

We concluded our conversation after Ron's father also shared with me that Ron had an early history of selling drugs, which contributed to him being kicked out of his dad's house.

Immediately upon ending the conversation with Ron's father, I didn't waste any more time packing enough clothes, music and costumes to last for several weeks, then I called a taxi and anxiously awaited its arrival. I had no intention of returning until I was 150 percent sure that Ron was gone for good!

Later that morning after Ashley and I finished gossiping on the couch in her living room about the craziness that occurred the previous weekend at the club, I resigned to the guest room, gasping in disbelief as I applied antibacterial cream to my wounds.

I scanned my entire body and gently rubbed cocoa butter over those bodily bruises and then I focused on figuring out the best way to hide the purple eye and the handprints around my neck.

I stood dressing my wounds and my almost broken spirit seemed reflected in the mirror. It was then that I received an epiphany. I realized that while I had been constantly telling Ron that he'd needed counseling for his issues, it occurred to me that I needed some professional help also!

One of the important questions that I needed to further explore was why I'd let the good guy get away? I also wanted to figure out the reasons that I'd allowed myself to become a magnet for both mentally and physically abusive guys.

Up to that point, my attraction to the bad boys had become like an addiction to a drug that I could not resist for some reason. However, during those battered and bruised moments I didn't need a therapist to tell me that the bad boys weren't good for me. I'd clearly gotten that message once and for all.

Although I was done with the so-called bad boys, I really wanted to obtain a permanent cure for the addiction to them so that I could also change whatever it was about me that attracted abusive men into my life.

So, I flipped through the yellow pages in search of an affordable therapist and came upon the phone number for the Gay and Lesbian Center that was on Highland Avenue at that time. After writing down the number and address, I decided that I would call them the following Monday morning to schedule an appointment to speak with a domestic violence counselor and also take a precautionary HIV/AIDS test.

I remained low-key for the rest of that weekend other than occasionally walking Ashley's dog Mr. McGuinness outside to potty. Early the following Monday morning I called and scheduled a Wednesday morning appointment to speak with a domestic violence counselor and also to be tested for sexually transmitted diseases.

I awoke early on Wednesday morning to be on time for my appointment before going to work, managing to conceal the black eye and scars as much as I possibly could with makeup, a chiffon scarf and dark eye shades before leaving the apartment.

Going in, I knew that I had to be truthful with the counselor in order to really heal, so I opened up to him about the abuse that I'd experienced in my relationships with Hilton, Ron and in my childhood, in addition to also sharing the feelings that I'd felt as a child helplessly witnessing my mother being brutally beaten by her boyfriend.

I explained to my counselor that I really wanted to know what was it about me that I needed to change in order to not continue to repeat the same old destructive cycle that I've grown so accustomed to.

My counselor was very empathetic and engaged as he listened to my concerns and circumstances. It was nice that he wasn't judgmental about the situation.

He made me feel better after suggesting that I deserved a chance to live a fulfilled and happy life regardless of my past experiences. He also suggested that I was associating love with abuse, quite possibly because the first person that I loved most of all was my mother, who was physically abused by someone that supposedly loved her and who was also physically abusive to me because she did not understand my gender identity.

When the counselor suggested that in order to begin really healing and moving forward, I needed to have a conversation with my mother about the things that occurred during my childhood, I explained to him that I was not really comfortable with having that sort of conversation with my mother face to face.

As when most good counselors become aware that Plan A may not be the best option, he then suggested Plan B, which was that I write my mother a letter to purge myself of the guilt that I was feeling about who I was, and to also tell her how I felt about her contributions to the abuse that I'd experienced growing up.

I was more comfortable with the letter suggestion and before our session ended I promised that I'd give him an update at my follow up appointment. Thereafter, I started attending Agape Church that following Sunday morning for some spiritual fellowship!

Later that morning when I arrived at the computer company, I lied to Jim and the other employees telling them that I had gotten caught up in between a fight involving two other girls in the dressing room at the club.

I am most certain that they did not buy my story, however they respectfully chose not to press me for further details about my battle-wounds. Later that afternoon Jim took me to our favorite Thai restaurant on Westmoreland Avenue for lunch.

Even though I'd long suspected that he wanted more from me than my office management skills, I hadn't expected for him to reveal his attraction to me during the conversation. He suggested that if things were not working out between my boyfriend and me, he hoped that I would give him a chance to show me how I should be treated.

Jim's direct revelation took me by surprise, because I thought that his girlfriend Rose was still in the process of relocating to California to be with him, so I inquired, "Jim, what happened to Rose moving here in three weeks?"

He nonchalantly replied, "Rose and I broke up, Tracee."

I was flattered that Jim liked me in that way, but I knew that going there with him would be a big mistake. I couldn't even think about getting involved in another relationship with, of all people, my boss, who may not have been aware that I was transsexual.

Since he seemed so sincere, I didn't want to hurt his feelings by telling him that I wasn't attracted to him in that manner so I continued with pretending that I was still committed to my boyfriend, replying, "Jim, things are not fully finished with Ron yet and I really need to remain focused on resolving those issues without further complicating an already complicated situation."

He placed his chopsticks on the plate, replying, "Tracee, take all of the time required to do what you need to do with your boyfriend. I am not going anywhere."

I do not feel that I have to immediately inform every single guy I meet that I am transsexual, nor was I interested in a relationship with Jim, but I knew that he'd continue flirting with me in the office and professing his feelings no matter what happened between me and my nonexistent boyfriend.

I was concerned that he'd eventually accuse me of deceiving him since he'd acknowledged his attraction to me, so I decided to inform Jim of who I was and hoped that my revelation about my gender identity would not cost me my job.

Even though I wasn't sure if he would fire me on the spot, I figured that if he did, I could always get another job, so I discretely shared with him that I was born a transsexual woman. After explaining to him that I was a pre-operative transsexual who had chosen to not have gender reassignment surgery, I saw the color in his face turn almost beet red in shock!

He seemed to recover from the initial jolt associated with what I had just told him after a couple sips of his frosted beer. Then he said, "I do not believe you."

I replied, after sipping my Thai iced tea through a straw, "I have no reason to lie to you. It's the truth, Jim."

After Jim paid for lunch and we got back in the car to go to the office, it was almost as if he wanted me to prove to him what I'd just told him informed him over spicy curry chicken, brown rice and spring rolls was the truth. I just shrugged off his disbelief and was thankful that I had not been fired on the spot!

Back at DMC, I went on with my daily managerial duties as if the conversation had never taken place, and for the rest of the day I mentally prepared myself for the unexpected at the end of the day. I also observed Jim out of my peripheral vision from time to time just staring at me from across the room with an expression of disbelief still all over his face.

I was happy that I still had a job at the end of the day.

Later that evening, lying across the bed alone in Ashley's guestroom, I took up a pen and pad and started to pour my heart out in my "Dear Ma Letter."

When I began writing down my feelings and thoughts, I didn't want to sugar coat my experiences growing up, so I chose to be honest as I informed Ma that I needed to begin healing some of the open sores that remained infected from my childhood, and that she could help me by acknowledging the pain that her actions contributed to those festered sores.

As I continued pouring my heart out, I feared that she might choose to not respond to my letter because I'd never before directly expressed to my mother that it felt as if something died inside of me the day that she told me the following after finding out that I was still dating guys:

"My brothers are not that way. Sometimes I wish that you were never born." In addition, I discussed the anger that I'd felt about the beatings that I endured from she and her boyfriend Singleton just because I could not be the boy that she so desperately wanted me to be.

After completing the letter, I was hopeful that she would acknowledge her contributions to my pain and despair. Then I immediately started to have second thoughts about sending it to her.

So, instead of continuing to procrastinate I got up and immediately walked down to the post office up the street and deposited the letter into the night slot before I changed my mind.

As I walked back to the apartment, I thought about how leaving Ron in the manner that I had was the third time I'd left everything that I had worked so hard to obtain, including furniture and priceless costumes in order to get away from a destructive relationship.

When I got back from the post office, I called the apartment to see if Ron would answer, and when he picked up the phone I asked, "Ron, I thought that your father was sending you a ticket back to Atlanta. Why have you not left yet?"

"Tracee, I know that you don't trust me anymore, but if you just let me know where you are, I will prove to you that this time I'm serious about getting help. I promise that if you come home, baby, I will get a job, counseling and never hit you again … if you please give me just one more chance to prove to you that I love you and I can change!"

I was not buying the load of crap that he was peddling, nor was I falling for the fake tears anymore because my mind was made up when I informed him, "Ron, you have gotten all of the chances from me that you are going to get ever again, so you can forget about getting another opportunity at extinguish my life, because I am not telling you where I am and I refuse to return back to that apartment until I know for sure that you have gone back to Georgia."

He continued attempting to play on my emotions with threats of suicide. "Tracee, I'm going to kill myself if you don't come home."

Unconvinced that he would have resorted to such an extreme measure I replied, "Ron, you are not going to kill yourself, nor am I coming back to the same stupid shit that I thought we'd left back in Atlanta."Without giving him an opportunity to reply, I immediately hung up the phone.

After a little over three weeks of randomly calling the apartment Ron eventually stopped answering the phone, but I still wasn't convinced that he was gone so I waited two more weeks because I did not want to risk running into him.

Finally, after deciding that enough time had passed and that it should be safe enough for me to take the chance and go back to the apartment, I first stopped by my landlady Alva's apartment to talk with her about the domestic incident.

During our conversation she told me that on the night Ron was arrested she had heard him threatening to kill me and, out of concern for my safety, she went around to the apartment window and was able to see him strangling me on the floor through the half drawn blinds. She then immediately called the police.

She also empathized with me, because she was once in an abusive relationship with her former husband. I didn't feel safe living in the apartment any longer, she'd allow me to break my lease without being penalized for early lease termination.

I thanked God that she was there to assist me in my time of need and I was filled with gratitude that she was so understandingly supportive. I hugged her and once again thanked her for saving my life!

After leaving Alva's apartment to see what damages Ron caused in mine, I and could not believe what I saw! At first I thought that the red writing on the wall was his blood until I realized that he had written in my red acrylic nail polish, "Bitch, I am going to kill you!"

On that same wall behind the couch was also my dried blood still splattered all over it from the night that he'd attacked me before he was arrested.

Ron also took a hammer and smashed the other fingernail polish bottles into pieces all over the carpet, and he'd used a butcher knife from the kitchen totally destroying all of the new leather furniture that I'd worked so hard to purchase before his arrival.

As if that was not enough, he then took all of my photos ripping them into tiny pieces and placing on the couch individual fragments that only had my face and eyes on them. I gasped for breath and went into the bathroom to find my costumes and outfits all torched in the bathtub.

The destruction in the apartment and the thought of the cost to replace my work costumes overwhelmed me for a brief minute, but I was sure that overtime I would be able to replace all of those material items that were destroyed during his rage with something comparable.

Most of all, I was just thankful that I'd remained physically intact and that he was finally gone for good!

I took several calming deep breaths before starting to clean up the mess, first trying unsuccessfully to wash my dried blood from the wall and then cleaning up the rest of the mess to the best of my ability.

As I cleaned, I was startled by the sound of the ringing telephone! I tipped over to the phone desk hesitating to answer because I feared that it might have been Ron calling, so I screened the call by letting the answering machine field the call.

I did not answer until I heard Ashley's voice leaving a message. "Tracee this is Ashley. I'm just calling to see if you are okay, girl."

I picked up the receiver, replying, "Hey, Ash, I'm okay. Ron destroyed the apartment and torched all of my costumes in the bath tub, however, he is gone and I still have all of my teeth and life so I am better than okay!"

"Do you need any help cleaning up?" She asked.

I replied, not wanting anyone else to view my shame, "No, honey, I can handle it myself. Thanks for offering to help, though."

She replied, "Well, girl, I know that you are going through some things right now, but I have a friend of mine on hold that wants to meet you!"

I interjected, "Ashley, I am really not in the mood for meeting anyone right now, honey."

She responded, almost insisting, "Tracee, I know that you may not want to meet anyone right now, but you are going to want to meet this person because he is a really nice guy and he might be just the distraction that you need right now, girl. Just talk to him!"

Hesitantly, I asked."Who is it this guy that wants to meet me, Ashley?"

She replied, "He's one of your other favorite actors that you previously commented on liking. Hold on, girl, I'll click him on the line!"

Since he is still a very popular screen star to date and in consideration of his privacy, I will just refer to him as Mr. Debonair. While I waited for her to click over to the person on hold, I wondered who could this celebrity have possibly been on three-way waiting to talk to me ?

After Ashley clicked over, I heard a deep, masculine, sexy and slightly familiar voice on the other end saying, "Hello, Tracee, this is Debonair, how are you?"

Once assured that we were connected, Ashley announced before hanging up her extension, "I am going to leave you two to get acquainted!"

After she hung up the phone, my initial thought was that this was some kind of joke and that I really was not in no mood for jokes at that moment, but instead of immediately hanging up the phone, I decided to play along. "Who is this really?"

"This is really Debonair. Ashley was telling me about your current situation with your boyfriend, so if you are willing, I would love to meet you and take you out to get your mind off everything negative that you're dealing with you right now."

Although I was still unconvinced, I continued playing along just to see who this really was pretending to be Mr. Debonair and since I trusted Ashley not to put me in a dangerous position, and because he sounded quite convincing on the phone I decided to distract myself with an adventure, replying, "Sure, why not be adventurous and take you up on your invitation to go out with you Mr. Debonair. What do you have in mind?"

He laughed his very familiar chuckle and alluringly replied, "How about dinner on Tuesday evening at Seven. I will pick you up in front of Ashley's apartment if that's okay?"

I replied, "This Tuesday evening at 7pm in front of Ashley's would be perfect!" Although I was still unconvinced that he was whom they claimed he was, I really needed a distraction to take my mind off my current situation.

Once again, I stepped out of the ordinary to meet this person who claimed to be and convincingly sounded like one of the entertainers that I admired. He was right up there with my celebrity crush Lawrence Fishburne, who by the way is only second to Numero Uno fantasy man Dorian Harewood!

As for Mr. Debonair, he responded, "I know that you are taking care of your apartment right now and I don't want to keep you from your business. I will see you on Tuesday evening and I'm really looking forward to meeting you, Tracee!"

After hanging up, I immediately called Ashley back, asking, "Ashley, is this some sort of a joke?"

She replied reassuringly, "Tracee, girl, you know I wouldn't play this kind of joke on you. That really was Mr. Debonair you were just talking to. He asked me to introduce him to a nice girl and you were the first person that came to mind!"

It never occurred to me that Ashley was a prostitute when we'd initially met at the club and upon finding out that prostitution was her chosen occupation after becoming roommates, I never judged her for those choices.

It really didn't matter to me what Ashley's occupation was as long as she did not try to recruit me into the game with her and she respected my choices for not participating in selling my body to those creeps.

She was a nice person to me, so that was all that mattered at the time because I liked her personality and still remained her roommate even after she'd failed to initially disclose that her boyfriend Eric would be living with us when she'd first asked me to become her permanent roommate.

Although Ashley's occupation wasn't a big deal to me, overtime I grew concerned because her boyfriend Eric whom did not have a job and all of the responsibilities of paying our $1,300 a month rent plus utilities were solely on Ashley and me.

When Tuesday evening arrived I was still not completely convinced that I was going out to dinner with Mr. Debonair, so I really did not put too much of an effort into what I was going to wear, dressing casually in a pair of white chino jeans, a pink cotton blouse and my favorite comfortable pair of black loafers.

When I walked outside of the apartment, I saw a shiny black Mercedes Escalade parked on the curbside in front with dark tinted windows and at first I was not sure if it was him until after he'd flashed his high beams several times to signal to me that he was there.

Reluctantly, I strolled over to the truck and as I got closer the window slowly rolled down enough for me to see that it was really true, I was actually going on a date with America's leading box office superstar Mr. Debonair!

He reached across and opened the door for me to get into the truck and after I was securely inside, I didn't want to act star struck because he was so damn fine in the flesh! I played it cool, keeping my composure as we re-introduced ourselves to each other. I thought that I should pinch myself to wake up from the dream that I never imagined would ever be happening to me!

I could have melted all over his shiny, black, soft leather seats when he looked at me, flashing the most beautiful, pearly white smile and then asking in a very seductive voice, "Are you hungry, Tracee?"

"Yes I am!" I replied girlishly.

"That's good, because I have planned something very special for you!" He turned on the ignition and almost glided away from the curb. I enjoyed the various neon lights illuminating the electric currents vibratory flow as we drove around the city.

It didn't register to me until later that Mr. Debonair was intentionally driving around to see if there were any paparazzi following us until he shared with me that they were the only down side to celebrity and fame, because he was not able to have a private moment without them invading his privacy for photos.

Finally, when he was comfortable enough that we weren't being followed, he turned into the lot of L'Ermitage Beverly Hills where we were greeted by an elderly African-American bellman who was obviously awaiting our arrival.

He walked over to the passenger side to open my door and then escorted us to a private entrance! I had not expected that dinner was going to be in a private suite, so when we arrived at the entrance and Mr. Debonair opened the door, I was surprised that there was a preset candlelit dinner and a bottle of expensive Dom champagne chilling in a silver decanter on a table overlooking one of the most amazing views of the skyline,

Since I wanted to keep my faculties and wits about myself, I chose to drink only sparkling water. I was also pleasantly surprised during our dinner discussion that he was honestly concerned about the emotional transition that I was currently going through with my recent break-up.

I also found it refreshing to be conversing with someone that was expressing concern about my well-being for a change! After dinner, we resigned to have coffee, continuing our conversation on the couch in the living area!

During the initial conversation before our date I'd shared with Mr. Debonair that I was scheduled to do a photo shoot for some promotional head shots after he'd inquired about my future plans and requested for me to bring my portfolio to share with him!

I was honored that he was interested and when he turned to the page of the most recent proofs, he removed them to take a closer look and complimented me on my book! He continued viewing the current proofs and then pointed out his favorite photos, suggesting that they were his favorites because I had on the least amount of makeup.

The photo that he liked the most is currently my 2013 Facebook profile picture that I decided on a crazy whim to post, because I felt that I'd quickly needed a new attitude on social networking! I was really surprised at how much positive feedback that I received after posting a photo that was taken in early 1991. Make-up artist extraordinaire Adam West, whom you will hear more about later, did my makeup for that photo shoot!

On my unexpected fantasy evening with Mr. Debonair, we talked for what seemed to have been hours until I eventually rose from the couch and then walked out onto the balcony, admiring how brightly the stars were twinkling in the clear sky above!

He followed and embraced me from behind jokingly commenting, "Please don't jump, Tracee. Your boyfriend isn't worth committing suicide over!"

I turned to face Mr. Debonair, replying, "I'm not thinking about my former boyfriend right now. I am just really enjoying this fantastic view!" When I turned back to continue absorbing the magically laced night energy, he pressed his muscular body up against mine and his strong embrace sent a shiver up my spine weakening my knees, almost causing me to collapse into his arms.

His strong arms kept me from falling to the balcony floor as he gently kissed the back of my neck and then, taking my hand in his, he led me back into the suite. Once inside, he gently removed the hair clip, causing my hair to cascade in slow motion onto my shoulders.

His masculinity and kisses really turned me on, but I felt that we would cross the line of no return, if I allowed him to continue breathing his sweet warm breath on my neck and kissing my earlobe.

I knew that I would not feel good about myself in the morning if I allowed this to go any further so I explained, "Please don't misunderstand me, Debonair, you are so irresistible to me right now but, since I'm in a very vulnerable period, I don't want to further complicate my life while in this emotionally fragile frame of mind by doing something with you that I may regret later."

Mr. Debonair replied, pulling me closer, "I understand what you're going through right now Tracee. There's absolutely no pressure to do anything that you are not comfortable with doing. I am enjoying just being able to spend this time getting to know how special you are."

We sat back on the couch, passionately caressing and making out with each other totally dressed for several more hours until we both observed that it was getting very late. I interjected in between the kisses, "Debonair, I can do this with you all night, but I have to be at work very early for mandatory inventory."

He continued kissing me before responding, "I know, I also have an early production meeting myself, but it's really hard for me to take you home so soon!"

I unassumingly replied, after kissing his sweet lips, "Well, I don't usually have to go into work early every day, so maybe I will see you again soon?"

He replied, "I hope that I'll get to see you again sooner than later, Tracee!"

"You have my phone number, Debonair!"

"That I do. I better have the car brought around before we change our minds about leaving!" After a long, strong embrace and final kiss he phoned down to inform the bellman that we were on our way down, and before leaving the suite, I gathered the roses and book of matches from the table as souvenirs for my scrapbook!

After exiting the private elevator, the bellman greeted us and opened my door, taking my hand to assist me into the truck and after I was securely fastened in, he then walked around to Mr. Debonair's side of the truck and received a wad of money for a tip!

When we arrived at the apartment, Mr. Debonair asked if he could see me the following weekend before leaving for three months to start filming his latest blockbuster movie and I told him of course I would love to see him again!

Then he proceeded to remove an envelope from his console saying, "This is just a little something to help you get settled, Tracee."

Since I did not go out with him for money, I replied, "Thank you for your concern and generosity Debonair, but I can't accept your money because that's not why I agreed to meet you."

Then I exited the truck with my apartment door keys and souvenirs in hand as he sat watching until I was safely inside of the apartment building. To be honest, I thought that I'd probably never see him again after that encounter, so I focused on moving forward with my life after Ron.

Immediately after going into the room to undress and shower, Ashley knocked on the bedroom door before excitedly entering, lying across the bed, and then asking, "So, how was it?"

Replying, as I put on my robe, "Girl, he was just simply amazing!"

She confidently replied, "I told you that he was a nice guy!"

After securing my robe and sprawling across the bed with her, I said, "I still didn't believe that I was really meeting Mr. Debonair until I saw him waiting for me in his shiny black Escalade and then taking me to a very romantic dinner in a huge suite at L'Ermitage Hotel in Beverly Hills!"

"Girl, he has always been very generous with the girls as I'm sure he was with you!" She said.

"When he dropped me off he tried to give me some money, but I told him that I was okay."

Surprised that I did not take the money from Mr. Debonair, she replied, "Girl, you mean to tell me you didn't take the money. What the hell is wrong with you, sister?"

I was content with my decision to not accept money from Mr. Debonair, so I replied, "I just didn't feel comfortable taking money from him and I don't want to give him the wrong impression about me even though I'm sure that's what he'd expected when he asked you to set us up for a date."

Clearly annoyed, Ashley replied, "Wrong impression? Girl, you are crazy. Well did he ask to see you again?"

"Yes, he said that he would call me to go out before he leaves for Canada to film his new movie!"

Laughing, as she responded, "Girl, if he offers you money the next time, you had better take it and if you don't want it, bring it to me. I'll show you what to do with it!"

I was curious about how they'd met so I inquired. "How did you meet Mr. Debonair, Ashley?" Smiling a wide grin, she replied, "Well, girl, I met Debonair many years ago when I was working the stroll on Santa Monica Boulevard!"
"What was he doing cruising the stroll?"

"Tracee, Mr. Debonair, as well as a lot of other big-time celebrities, have been picking up girls off the stroll for years because they just love the girls!"

Surprised and amazed that such a high-profile celebrity was actually cruising the stroll for prostitutes, I responded, "Well, I like his movies and he is fine as hell, but I am not interested in being with someone who is known for picking up girls off Santa Monica Boulevard."

Rising up from the bed and replying. "You don't have to have sex with him, he just likes the company. Oh, girl, before I forget, here's your mail!" She pulled the letters from her robe pocket, handing them to me, adding before leaving my room, "Girl, let me get back to Eric before he starts tripping!"

After Ashley left me alone in the bedroom digesting the events of the evening and as I flipped through the insignificant mail, there was a letter amongst the others from my mother dated May 30.

My heart skipped several beats as I read the five-page response, which I've only chosen to paraphrase on the following page, because her full correspondence to me remains a private blessing and gift that I do not want to put on full blast:

Hi Tony,

I hope that things are going all right for you, my son. I do worry about you and the difficult life you are living. Life is hard enough when you are straight and more so for you, my baby. I only want you to be happy, yet I am so afraid of losing you to this deadly disease

AIDS because I want you to meet your nephews, nieces and the twins soon to be born. Yes, we have been abused, neglected, and all the things that Singleton has done to us is being done to him. He is getting his and having a really rough time right now. I am only concerned about you. I love you and the reason that I said that I wished you were never born was because I was hurting because you did not develop into the little baby boy that I had such high hopes for who was born on that cold night on January 20, 1967. I wanted to hurt you like you were hurting me, baby. It hurts me deep down in my heart when I think about my past life, growing up was so very painful. I wanted a life for you that was less painful and less complicated as compared to mine. I gave birth to a beautiful male child that January night. I can only see my boy child that I named after Frederick Douglass. You are not a mother, you will never be a mother, so there is no way you will ever know how my heart feels and aches for my son. I do not love you any less because you are gay. I just do not know how to deal with the things that people are always saying about gay people. It hurts very much because those people do not know that my son is gay also. This is your way of being and if I could change it I would, because I want my son back. I am praying to God to change you because it is never too late. Baby, I am not going to be here always. If I could hold my son again it would be worth all the pain that I have endured in my lifetime and only God knows how deep the pain goes.

Mom Always,

Lots of Love.

After re-reading the response from my mother recalling the details during that time, I am mature enough to understand and empathize with the hurt and pain that she felt in regards to my gender identity and I also acknowledge the pain that I've caused her after I eventually legally changed my name.

However, though I recognized her feelings, I really wanted my mother to know that I was not one of those gay people that her acquaintances were negatively referring to during their hateful and bigoted conversations.

Hurting my mother was the last thing in the world that I would ever set out to do, so I was conscious that I didn't become one of those loud and rude transsexual persons that are always doing stupid things to draw unnecessary attention from others.

I assume that our letter correspondences were most likely during the time when she must have read the obituary of my previous boyfriend, who had died from AIDS. She was rightfully concerned about my HIV and AIDS status.

I thank God that Gerome and I never had intercourse! I am also grateful that Ma acknowledged the physical abuse that I'd experienced at the hands of her and her boyfriend, Singleton! I'm not sure if I received any satisfaction knowing that Singleton served time in jail after being convicted of possession and distributing narcotics.

Additionally, I know that Ma was only concerned with my mental and physical well-being when she'd said those hurtful words to me about wishing that I was never born. I am also blessed beyond measure that a channel of open and honest communication had been opened between my mother and I!

I'm happy to say that our line of mutual respect endures to this day, because her response to my letter began the process of healing and closing those old wounds that once caused us both such deep pain!

After being validated by my mother, I was empowered to continue my transition both metaphysically and literally. The following Thursday evening I was pleasantly surprised when I answered my phone and heard Mr. Debonair's voice on the other end."Hello, Tracee, this is Debonair. Are you still free to have dinner with me again?"

Excited that he'd called as promised, I replied, "Sure, Debonair, I would love to go to dinner with you. What time should I be ready?"

"How is seven this Sunday evening?"

"Seven this Sunday evening is perfect, I'll see you then!" I replied enthusiastically and proceeded to tell him about my day and inquire about his before concluding our conversation. This time I wanted to be sexy for our next date!

So, I went shopping at the Beverly Center, splurging on purchasing a spaghetti-strap, little black lace dress and red, five-inch stilettos. I planned to flatiron my hair for our date.

Not necessarily recalling the songs for my performances that weekend, I am however certain that they were more energetic and upbeat as compared to previous shows, because I was anticipating my second date with Mr. Debonair and the final burial of an unhealthy relationship!

Sunday evening began with me walking outside of the apartment draped in a black silk wrap with clutch in hand as Mr. Debonair waited, this time in a jet black Porsche 911 Carrera. He looked sexy as hell dressed all in black!

After I got into the car and fastened my seatbelt, he stated, "Wow, you look great!"

Smiling, I replied, "Thank you, so do you!"

Once again Mr. Debonair strategically drove around to ensure that we weren't being followed by paparazzi and when certain that we were not, we were once again at the L'Ermitage being greeted by the same elderly gentleman who parked Debonair's car as before .

Mr. Debonair took my hand, escorting me to the suite where another romantic candlelit dinner awaited us.

I still didn't want to feel cheap and easy, so after dinner and stimulating conversation we did not have sex. However, we did have fun concluding the evening with exploring each others' bodies! His "huge ego" and muscular silky smooth body were irresistibly gorgeous!

After that second encounter with Mr. Debonair, I wasn't naïve to think that the experience would become anything but the once in a lifetime opportunity that it was, so eventually after that date with Mr. Debonair, I started to go out on other dates, attempting to move forward with my life.

I didn't want to fool myself into thinking that there could be something more with him than what we were sharing. I also became more selective about the kinds of guys that I'd considered getting emotionally involved with.

Back then when I was single, my personal definition of "dating" was just going out to dinner or movie. Now I've learned that the current widely perceived meaning of "dating" is having sex for money or drugs. So that there's no misunderstanding, during conversations amongst my girls, I am very conscious of the verbs that I choose when discussing my past with guys.

I feel now, as then, that just because I'd gone out with a guy it didn't necessarily mean that I had been intimately involved with him. One of many such relationships was with this very handsome Middle Eastern guy named Bahadur who also approached me while shopping at Ralph's Market.

Since he was charmingly respectful upon his approach, I accepted his dinner invitation. I enjoyed just spending platonic time with Bahadur, because he'd treated me like a lady on our strolls on the beach at Santa Monica Pier and during candlelit dinners.

I was not looking for any long term commitments during that time, because I was having fun just going out with him so it didn't matter that we never made-out, kissed or that I never visited his residence.

However, one day he just disappeared without any warning. Several weeks later when I was in my bedroom choosing music and costumes for my next performances, Ashley knocked on the bedroom door, informing me, "Tracee, Bahadur is outside asking to see you."

Surprised that he'd reappeared out of the blue, I replied, "Bahadur? I haven't seen him in weeks. What does he want?"

As I walked from the bedroom to greet him, I really was not in the mood to start playing that game where guys cut communication and disappear only to suddenly reappear at *their* pleasure.

Although there were no strings attached to our courtship, it was a matter of respect as far as I was concerned. It's as if he expected me to just drop everything with no questions asked and pick up from where we'd left off upon his reappearance. Not this girl!

By the time I'd made it to the apartment entrance, I knew that I was not letting Bahadur in until I was sure if I wanted to see him or not. So, when I opened the door seeing him standing there looking creepy, I walked outside, closing the apartment door behind me.

"Hello, Bahadur. Where have you been for the last several weeks?"

He replied, as he gently kissed the back of my hand, "My love, I had to return back to Iran and visit my family and take care of some business."

Removing my hands from Bahadur's, I replied, "You know, Bahadur, I don't know anything about you, like whether you are married or not, which I assume you are. And the disappearing for weeks at a time without any communication just doesn't work for me, so I will not be able to see you again."

He insisted, "My dear, I can assure you that I am not married. Please let me take you to dinner to convince you that I want to be with only you!" Unmoved by his efforts of persuasion, I replied, "I'm really sorry, Bahadur, but I've just recently ended a very tumultuous relationship and I am certainly not ready to get into another one, so I have to decline from going out with you."

Before I turned to go back into the apartment ,he pulled me tightly against his muscular chest, disappointment written all over his cute face as he kissed me on the cheek and jokingly replied in his hypnotic Persian voice, "I should kidnap you and take you with me, baby!"

Joking or not, he was very strong and if he was serious about kidnapping me, I would have had to put up a good fight to get away from him, which I was prepared to do if he had acted stupid, but he released me and I never saw him again.

Although he seemed to be a nice guy, I wasn't going there with no married man or someone that mysteriously disappears and expects me to be there anticipating his return. Absolutely not!

After going back into the apartment, locking the door and peeping through the curtain and blinds to make sure that he was gone, Ashley came out of her room inquiring, "Girl, what's really going on?"

Continuing peeping through the curtain I replied, "Bahadur is crazy if he thinks that he can just disappear and show back up when he feels like it!"

She replied, "Girl, he reminds me of one of those terrorists that I saw on the news!"

I replied, closing the blinds and double checking both locks on the door, "I don't know what he is and sexy as all get up or not, I am not going to see him again so if he comes back just tell him that I've moved."

As time progressed, although I remained open to going out with other guys, I wasn't planning to immediately start a relationship or be intimate with them. I just was not going to be a desperate fool dating someone that could have very well been married or otherwise committed to someone else.

A month or so later after Bahadur, this other handsome guy approached me at an old school concert that I remember fondly because Curtis Blow's record started skipping during his performance, revealing to the audience that he was not really singing at what was supposed to have been a live concert.

The really tall gentleman who approached me and insisted upon paying for my refreshments didn't seem crazy, so I later accepted his dinner invitation after he'd asked permission to hang out with me for the duration of the concert!

On the night of our date when he arrived carrying a bottle of wine in one hand and his tooth brush sticking out of his shirt breast pocket, I just assumed that he was compulsive about his dental hygiene, so I didn't think anything further about it, proceeding to the Olive Garden for dinner.

At first he had seemed to be a nice guy, but during dinner, in addition to practically slurping up his food like a pig feeding at a trough, he was also annoyingly possessive. He kept saying that the server was inappropriately flirting with me while taking our orders and then returning to check on us too many times during the meal.

We managed to get through dinner okay and when we returned to the apartment it became obvious that he had been expecting to spend the night with me, but it was not going to happen.

I explained to him that I had an early day at work the following morning and that if he called me, we could schedule another time to get together when I was off from work.

After the glutinous hog left, I knew that his behavior was inappropriate and unacceptable considering that we had just met, and I also knew that I would not be answering the phone whenever his number showed up on the caller identification. I felt comfortable not seeing him again due to our apartment management recently hiring a security guard, so I did not worry about him just showing up unannounced.

It didn't matter to me if either of those guys were or were not aware of my gender identity, because I had no intentions of going any further with them other than casually going to dinner or a movie.

You may question why I seemed to have only gone out with guys who were not associated with the venues where I worked. My answer is that I'd consciously committed to myself during those days that I would no longer date any of the guys from the clubs where I'd worked.

I also developed a keen eye for spotting the frogs that had no potential of being anything other than the self-absorbed perpetrators possessing their own self-aggrandizing agendas for showing interest in transsexual showgirls.

I was definitely not going to just sit around waiting by the phone hoping that Mr. Debonair called as he'd promised. I was clear about him having his own thing going on with his big-time public career. I pressed on with the knowledge that I would never be anything to him other than just another one of his secret transsexual conquests.

Don't get me wrong; I had my own thing going on also! In addition to continuing to enjoy receiving a reliable source of income from my day job at the computer company, I was also blessed with some great successes in establishing a professional reputation and working relationship with the other club entertainment bookers that regularly booked me for their shows.

I even managed to accumulate a reliable following of loyal fans and supporters during my time on the entertainment circuit. Almost three months had passed since I last saw Mr. Debonair and I was once again pleasantly surprised when I answered my phone and heard his voice on the other end saying in a very sexy tone, "Hello, Tracee, this is Debonair, how are you?"

Once again surprised that he'd called, I replied, "Hello, Debonair, I am very well. How are you?"

Continuing to speak to me alluringly, he said, "I am much better now!" He briefly paused before asking, "Did you think about me while I was away?"

Taken aback by his question, I replied, passing the ball back to his court, "Yes, I did think of you while you were away. Did you think of me?"

Chuckling, he replied, "Of course I thought about you, Tracee. I was just coming out of a production meeting and all that was on my mind is to see you this week if you're not busy."

"Sure, Debonair. I would love to see you!"

"Are you free at 7 p.m. on Tuesday evening?"

"Sure, I am free at 7 p.m. on Tuesday evening, Debonair!"

"Okay, I will see you on Tuesday. Stay sweet until then!"

This time he drove another classic sports car to pick me up on that following Tuesday evening for our third date. There were evasive maneuvers before we arrived at L'Ermitage.

Once again we were greeted by the same elderly bellman and we enjoyed a delicious grilled chicken, risotto and mixed vegetable dinner in the same luxurious suite.

After dinner, we retired to the living area of the suite and sat on the couch. During our conversation, he proceeded to gently kiss my neck, and I did not put up any resistance when he reached behind and started to slowly unzip my dress as he caressed my earlobe with his lips.

Before I knew it, Mr. Debonair and I were in the bedroom naked caressing and affectionately kissing each other on the lush comforter, but not going any further than just making out!

I admit that I really once again enjoyed every inch of his beautiful, muscular body. However, I was still not so delusional that I thought he would be my knight in shining armor or that he'd risk his box office career in order to be something more to me than what he was.

I also remained aware that this man was undoubtedly involved with leading ladies in Hollywood, so I had no expectations that what we were doing was nothing more than two consenting adults living out our fantasies with each other.

After mutually coming to an orgasmic explosion, we showered together before getting dressed and conversing the rest of the evening on the living room couch about his latest movie and my current endeavors.

As he picked up the television remote control, turning on CNN he informed me, "I shouted you out in my latest flick, Tracee, I hope you like it!"

Surprised and flattered that he'd mentioned my name in his latest movie, I replied, "I will be at the theater on opening day to check it out, thank you, Debonair!"

Several hours later, we both observed that it was getting late so we gathered our things then left the hotel in the awaiting car after exiting the private elevator.

After he pulled to the curbside in front of the apartment, I turned to him stating, "Thank you, Debonair, for such a lovely evening. I had a great time!"

He affectionately replied, "So did I, Tracee, I hope that you will let me see you again!"

I replied, preparing to exit the car, "Sure, Debonair. I would love to see you again!"

Before I exited completely out of the car, he reached into the glove compartment and once again retrieved an envelope, handing it to me. "What is this?" I inquired.

He smiled, replying, "It's just a little gift for you to treat yourself to something nice!"

At first, I was slightly offended, feeling that he was still treating me like a prostitute and even though I could have used the money to begin to start replacing some of the costumes and clothes that Ron had destroyed, I informed him, "Debonair, I've told you before that I am not a prostitute. I'm just a country girl from South Carolina living out an unexpected dream of being with someone I've admired for a very long time."

He asked, "Please, Tracee, get back in the car and let me talk to you for a minute." After I sat back in the seat and closed the car door, he proceeded to explain, "I know that you are a classy lady and not a prostitute. I have money and I just want you to buy yourself a nice dress or something. I will be offended if you don't allow me to do this for you."

Reluctantly, I took the envelope from Debonair and immediately stuffed it down into my evening bag before exiting the car. When I got upstairs to tell Ashley what had happened on the date and informed her about the envelope that he had given me, she excitedly asked, "Miss Tracee, what did he put in it?"

"I don't know, it's still in my purse!" I replied, before retrieving the purse from my room and returning back to the living room. There was $2,000 in crisp $100 bills inside!

"I told you, girl. It's not about prostitution with Debonair. He's just a rich and generous guy who has been giving random girls on Santa Monica Boulevard money to help them out for years now. Are you going to see him again?"

"He said that he'd call, so I guess so. Here girl, take $500 for yourself and buy that dress you were lusting so hard over at the Beverly Center the other day!"

I went on to explain to her that he was a nice distraction, but considering that a recent rumor surfaced connecting him with one of my favorite female performers, I was not fooling myself that he'd risk his career or reputation to be with me.

Neither was I interested in getting emotionally involved with someone whom I would have to sneak around with whenever we were together.

Until I met someone that didn't have to dodge paparazzi, I went on with my life, working at the computer company during the weekdays and performing at Peanuts and making various special appearances at other clubs.

As time went on, I kept my ears open for other financial opportunities to book more shows, so when I overheard the Latina girls in the show at Peanuts talking about a show at Plaza I was curious about it. I decided to attend one of their Saturday night shows to check it out and observed that Plaza was a Latino club on LaBrea and Melrose with an all Latin cast and a predominately Latino clientele. They really knew how to have fun, and they also appreciated the entertainers performing on the humungous center stage!

I knew that I wanted to be on that cast after seeing the large sums of money the performers were being tipped!

After the show, I spoke to the guy at the front door named Carlos, inquiring about auditioning for the show. He told me that he was dating the manager and that he'd introduce me to him right then and there if I liked.

Upon meeting the club manager, I was invited back the following Saturday evening to audition and meet the show director.

After being introduced to the owner and hired for the show on the spot, I faced a brief dilemma after being informed that I would be working the Thursday, Friday, Saturday and Sunday night shows!

Thankfully, my dilemma was momentary because I was only committed to working on Friday nights at Peanuts and because the show was always after midnight, I would be able to go directly to Peanuts after my last number and final bows on Friday nights at Plaza, not having to worry about the other nights!

Not long after I was hired at Plaza in the early 90s, Jacqueline was fired from her position as show director, because the club management wanted another show director who would create more elaborate productions.

She was replaced with Tony Corpuz a couple weekends after I started working at Plaza. Plaza was the first club that I had ever made $100 tips on a regular basis. Especially whenever this alleged drug-dealing high roller group reserved a huge table front and center of the stage and always requested for me to perform "Smooth Operator" by Sade!

Along with the free flowing money at Plaza, there were also the cartelistic drugs and the always pouring alcohol being sent to the dressing room or invitations to join fans at their table for cocktails. I thank God that I have never developed the taste for alcohol, nor did I have a problem with ordering club soda whenever joining a fan for a drink. I've seen too many talented performers become alcoholics and take extreme risks because they just cannot say no to the free drinks and fatalistic drugs.

However, there were those few times that I indulged in a toast with champagne or a small Grand Marine' on holidays and special occasions. Yet, I never indulged in drinks that were sent to me from a fan by a bartender due to never trusting or feeling comfortable drinking or partaking in anything that I had not seen being poured or prepared with my very own eyes.

Working in that type of entertainment industry and environment, you always have to worry about someone – maybe a deceitful queen – putting a Mickey or something life threatening in your drink to sabotage you.

Once my ground rules were established in my new environment, I started having fun and becoming more creative with new routines. Plaza was also the first cast that I worked in where productions and rehearsals were emphasized, including some of my favorite productions where I performed lead in "Giving Him Something That He Can Feel" by EnVogue.

The four of us wore matching red fitted gowns and gloves similar to those worn by EnVogue in their music video.

Additionally, another of my favorite collaborations was with Melissa Del Jano, performing" Boogie Oogie Oogie" by the group Taste of Honey that I suggested for a Cinco De Mayo show. Another favorite production was a dance number performing lead with Tony Corpuz and Jaime as my back-up dancers!

Some of my solo favorite productions included, "You Don't Have To Worry" by EnVogue, "Mercedes Boy" and "Backyard" by Pebbles, "You Got To Be" by Desree', "Rush Rush" by Paula Abdul and many other popular artists.

I also really loved rehearsing for annual Cinco De Mayo celebrations and Christmas productions where I performed "What Child Is This" by Vanessa Williams solo.

Usually whenever I left Plaza at the end of the night, there would be this homeless person sleeping in the alley whom I'd always given money to. One morning on my way to my car after the show, I noticed that they were bundled up on the corner of the club in their usual spot. I could not tell if they were male or female.

They'd always be covered completely up in dirty blankets and clothes from head to toe with a shopping cart filled with their personal stuff parked right next to them.

I've always felt blessed that I was financially stable enough to take care of my responsibilities and if not for the grace of God I could have been homeless on the street! I also gained an understanding earlier on that in order for prosperity to abundantly flow throughout my life I had to give in order to continue receiving personal daily blessings.

In gratitude for my blessings, I always tried to pass on a blessing to someone else without expecting anything in return except the joy that I'd feel being able to touch others in a positive way.

One particular morning when I reached down to hand them some money, they surprised me by reaching up and handing me a beautiful pink silk rose that I still have in my cedar chest! I never expected for them to have taken what little they may have had in order to purchase a gift for me that I will always cherish!

One afternoon before rehearsal at Plaza, I decided to grab a spicy polish sausage at the world famous Pinks hotdog stand right next to the club on the corner of Melrose and LaBrea. As I stood in line waiting to place my lunch order, listening to a new Latino production song "Las Chicas" on my walkman, I observed a sleek Cadillac pull close to curbside driven by a slick looking guy trying to get my attention, but I pretended not to notice him.

The guy in line behind tapped me on the shoulder informing me that the guy in the Cadillac was trying to get my attention and when I turned to see what he wanted he asked, "Hey, baby, can I buy your lunch?"

"No, thank you," I replied to the guy in the Cadillac before turning and replacing my headphones back over my ears. From the sound of the tires and rubber being burned speeding off, I thought he had gotten the message that I was not interested in anything he had to say.

Right after I sat down to enjoy the spicy Polish sausage and French fries that I'd been craving all day, he walked over to my table in this green pair of fake leather shoes, wearing a lime green three-piece suit in the middle of July.

He had the nerve to stand over me with a tooth pick hanging from his lips, flashing his gold-covered teeth and slicking back his processed Super Fly hair before asking, as he pulled the chair from underneath the table to sit down next to me, "Hey, pretty lady, can I talk to you for a minute?"

I was embarrassed and annoyed that the time-warped pimp thought that I wanted to be bothered by him, so I sarcastically replied, "No, thank you. I'm waiting for my boyfriend."

Ignoring me, he positioned his chair closer to mine and said, "I could not help but to notice how beautiful you are when I spotted you from my car. What is your name, sweetness?"

After previously being propositioned by a drug dealer to sell his drugs, I could spot a pimp in his pimp mobile from a mile away. I once again sarcastically replied. "Thanks for the compliment. My boyfriend tells me how beautiful I am everyday!"

The pimp replied. "Is your man making you happy?"

"Yes, he is and he's also very jealous. He would not be too happy if he walked up to see you as close as you are to me right now!"

He replied, standing and placing a card on the table before strutting away, "I see. Well here is my number if you should ever become unhappy with your man and want to make a lot of money, call me!"

I wasn't sure if he knew that I was a transsexual or not when he'd approached me and it really did not matter to me if he was aware of my gender identity, because I had no interest in what lies he was selling. I crumbled the card with the wrapper from my sandwich and threw it into the garbage can with the other trash before going to my first all-Spanish language production with Paloma, Carmella, Melissa and Angela Shelby.

Once the lyrics to "Las Chicas" were translated to me, I quickly picked up the essence of the production really, having a lot of fun learning Jaime's choreography to the song.

Several weeks later when I was leaving Venice Beach with a friend, I saw the same pimp who had approached me at Pinks sitting on a bench in the hot sun waiting for a bus, wearing a dirty plaid suit with nappy hair looking like a homeless person that had just crawled from under a bridge.

As for Plaza, their clientele's appreciation of the show was beyond my expectations, so I worked very hard on presenting quality illusions and performances whenever I stepped onto the stage. My efforts were acknowledged, appreciated and richly rewarded!

There were other girls in the cast who in the beginning pretended to be my sister, but soon became envious, jealous and deceitful about the attention that I started receiving when the High Rollers once gifted me with two beautiful sequined gowns.

They'd gone as far as trying to sabotage my performances by moving my production costumes from the designated area. They then pretended not to be ready when it was their turn to perform, which meant that the next girl on the line-up became rushed and pressured to perform out of place. But I was ready for anything once I got to know who they really were.

Also, there was this one tweaked-out Latina girl that was a guest performer named Vicki who was consumed with envy and jealousy that I was hired for the cast instead of her. She started making her disdain for me quite obvious during the show in the dressing room. She was obviously high and drunk when she tried to intimidate me with a pair of scissors that she pulled from her bag threatening to stab me with them.

Since I felt threatened when she pulled out her weapon, I told the show director that I was not going to hesitate to protect myself with the dressing station chair if she even came anywhere near me with those scissors.

When the sketched-out Latin queen saw that I was not cowering or intimidated by her threats, she quickly came to her senses, placing the scissors back in her bag. Of course, I kept a close eye on her to ensure that she stayed her distance from me for the remainder of the show and after the owner was informed about her actions, she was never invited back as a guest performer again during my time there.

I give the owner and show director Tony Corpuz credit, because they did not play when it came to putting on a quality and professional show to entertain our audience. I thought that the queens from Atlanta were messy and caddy, just imagine what it was like for me having to deal with the drama and being talked about in Spanish as if I was not there.

After a period of time, I picked up on the language, starting to understand it whenever they talked about me, so I let them know in no uncertain terms that I understood what was being said about me.

Once they knew that I was aware of what they were saying about me, they became more cautious of what was being expressed while I was still in the dressing room.

I was almost certain that they really dogged me out whenever I was not around. However, I continued ignoring the jealous girls that disliked me for no reason. I ignored them because I was there to make money and I fed them with a long handled spoon as long as I didn't feel physically threatened by any of them.

I remained focused on my goals and representing myself in an appreciative manner during show breaks whenever I left the dressing room to mingle and dance with my fans and audience. It was a great way to get away from the alcohol- and drug-induced mess in the dressing room while also learning the hottest Latin dances to incorporate into my routines.

Several months after being hired at Plaza, Ashley informed me that we were both invited to fly to Portland, Oregon, to appear in an annual, highly anticipated show put on by a friend of hers named Brown Sugar.

Ashley only performed every blue moon and her stage name was Sade back then. She and I stayed three days and four nights with Miss Cee Cee in her upper-class penthouse high-rise containing a rooftop indoor heated pool. Ashley, Cee Cee's young boyfriend Joey and I waded around in it, posing for pictures and working out in the private gym!

Joey was a naive blond kid that was cute and sweet as he could be, but he did not have a clue about what was really going on. I really connected with Brown Sugar and Miss Cee Cee, because they did everything with class and style starting out with our all expenses paid flight and accommodations.

Although I was looking forward to doing more updated songs, at the sold-out show on April 19, 1991, I was simply amazed to be presented with special requests to perform "Real Love" by Jody Watley and "Dreamin" by Vanessa Williams. The audience went out of control, forming one of the longest tipping lines that I have seen in a very long time.

Although I was having a great time on my first trip to Portland with Ashley, all good things come to an end and I had to get back to Los Angeles to work at Plaza and Peanuts the following weekend.

Significant time had passed since my last date with Mr. Debonair and, quite frankly, I did not expect to ever see him again. But after the Plaza show one Saturday night after toning down my makeup, Ashley and I got all dolled up to go to Peanuts for a girls' night out.

As we were riding in the taxi on our way to the club and checking out the girls on Santa Monica diligently working their beats, Ashley commented, "Tracee, girl, is that Mr. Debonair following behind us in that blue Lamborghini sports car?"

I turned to try and see if Mr. Debonair was really following us, but although I saw the sports car, I was not able to get a clear view of the person driving.

Ashley told the cabdriver to turn onto a secluded street near the club and the sports car turned also, following closely behind us. He then pulled up next to the cab where I was sitting and I could clearly see his face when he rolled down the slightly tinted window asking, "Where are you ladies going?"

"We're going to Peanuts for a girls' night out. Where are you going?" I replied.

He greeted Ashley, replying, "I was on my way home when I spotted you lovely ladies in the back seat!"

"Really?" I replied somewhat sarcastically.

He inquired, "Are you in a hurry to get to the club, Tracee?"

"No, I'm not in any hurry. What do you have in mind?" I inquired.

"I would love to talk with you. Can we go for a drive somewhere?"

"Sure!" I grabbed my clutch from the seat and told Ashley that I would meet her at the club.

She replied, "Okay, see you there!" She then turned her attention to Mr. Debonair, warning before pulling away. "You better take care of my sister, Debonair!"

I slinked into the car with Mr. Debonair and after he drove around enough to be sure that we were not being followed, we parked on a one-way street, allowing him to see who was coming and going from both directions.

When we exited the car, Mr. Debonair leaned up against the front end and pulled me close to him after I walked around to where he was standing. "Damn, you look sexy as hell!"

I could tell that he was excited when I felt and saw his erect "Big Ego" through the blue and black tight spandex biker shorts hugging his body like a glove. "Thank you, you look sexy also!"

He flashed that beautiful Hollywood smile, embracing me tightly with his strong arms and inquiring, "Are you getting settled into your new place okay with your new roommate?"

"Yes, I am getting settled in okay. How have you been?"

"I've been just a little busier than usual, but I will not complain, especially now that

I see you!" He flashed that bright smile once again, continuing, "Do you really have to go to the club tonight?"

I replied, knowing that Ashley would understand if I decided to not meet her at the club, "No, I don't have to, but since I told Ashley that I would meet her there, I think that I should keep my word."

Mr. Debonair and I stood there tightly embracing each other for almost an hour or so as he continued trying to convince me to go with him.

Although Mr. Debonair was irresistible, I did not want to be seduced into becoming something that I was not, so I was determined not to go with him that night. I could tell that he was becoming nervous about being out in the open for so long, so I suggested that we should leave, and as we got back into the car, he jokingly remarked, "I don't want to be offensive again, but I would love to buy you something really nice and sexy to wear!"

I replied, "Mr. Debonair, you don't have to give me money every time I see you, but if you insist on being generous, I'm not going to offend you by refusing your generosity!"

He reached into the side panel of the car handing me an envelope. I did not look to see what was inside before stuffing it down into my clutch. When we arrived, I was okay with him dropping me off at the French Quarter one block away from the club, but he insisted on driving into the club parking lot to make sure that I was okay.

That was the last time that we were together. The following week, I watched news coverage on Entertainment Tonight and every other entertainment show covering his marriage to a beautiful model.

When his movie finally opened, I was extremely flattered and excited about him mentioning my name in one of the opening scenes! I was not surprised that he had gotten married and I was happy that I was smart enough to know that he and I could not have ever been anything more to each other than what we were.

However, it was my choice not to allow the allure of making easy money from emotionally unavailable rich men who only want to see you because they need a fix to satisfy their hidden addiction to transsexuals living their female gender identity.

I later heard stories of another transsexual that may have been involved with Mr. Debonair who tried committing suicide after his marriage announcement. Unbelievable! I was just grateful for the unforgettable experiences that I shared with him. I went on with my life, relying on brain and talents to make money, not selling my body and soul to the highest bidder.

I've chosen to neither deny, nor confirm his true identity or the identity of another high-profile hip-hop performer that I had an insignificant intimate encounter with, so don't ask.

Some may ask why I've chosen to reveal the encounters with those celebrities and my response is that I write about those high-profile entertainers not to "out" them. To the contrary; I personally understand why they're forced to deny their desires, attractions and who they are.

I strongly believe that "coming out" should be their personal decisions. My intention for discussing my celebrity encounters is to bring awareness and illuminate the fact that since we've started documenting and misinterpreting our history, we have been conditioned by society to think that transgender people are unacceptable and undesirable freaks of nature.

Yet, there are those from all walks of life, backgrounds and cultures whom strongly desire us just like those high-profile entertainers that I've personally encountered.

However, they're afraid of what society will say about them, so, unfortunately, whenever the conversations arise about human rights and public acceptance of those that are perceived to be contrary to "normal," it's usually deny, deny, deny to protect their careers and reputations.

After my unforgettable encounters with Mr. Debonair, I knew that I deserved to be with someone that did not take me for granted and worked hard to earn my affections. I really wanted to break the bad habits that were pulling me to emotionally unavailable men.

I felt that however tempting it was to go with him that night on another secret rendezvous, I'd made the first step in the right direction toward not becoming comfortable with the heartache of dating someone as unavailable as Mr. Debonair. It was a bridge leading to nowhere.

My second positive step was to truly start embracing and totally accepting who I was so that I'd be able to attract the positive situations and people into my life that would not be ashamed to publicly be with me.

Lastly and as importantly, during that time I received another moment of clarity from the realization that I have always been in one relationship right after another with very little time in between to understand the reasons that they were not working out in my best interests. So I committed to start spending more quality time delving beneath the surface becoming more acquainted with my true self!

Going back to our childhood and adolescence, it was a requirement that we regularly attend church on Sundays and although I also attended church as an adult, I still found it challenging to reconcile my personal beliefs with my Baptist upbringing. I continuously questioned why God would create something in her image and then condemn that creation to hell for being human? I also questioned why some sins were greater than others.

Most people usually turn to the religion in an effort to finding answers to their questions, seeking spiritual inspiration and guidance to help them deal with the innumerable challenging situations that they may be confronted with in their daily lives, however, as a result of being so beaten down with the Holy Bible as a child, I do not consider myself a religious person, preferring to be labeled spiritually-minded. I truly believe that there is a big difference.

I also strongly believe that the various religions have more in common than they differ. They just constantly battle about whose God is mightier, in my opinion. Overtime, I've chosen to incorporate elements of those various life-affirming religions into my daily life, receiving a true gift in the realization that I do not have to go through a third person to commune with my Creator!

Upon developing those strong connections with my Creator and my mother, I felt that I could do anything I focused my energy on! Most importantly and conclusively, during that time I also consciously opened myself up to experiencing and receiving grace, love, mercy, knowledge, wisdom and understanding after developing a personal relationship with my God that has nothing to do with damnation, judgment and criticism about who I was created to be.

For the first time since my puppy-love relationship in Job Corps, I was really enjoying my independence and not dependent upon a man to validate me! I also started cherishing getting to know me and becoming more aware of the special person that I was created to be. In doing, I chose to become celibate during that time, which meant no sex or even making out with any guys for a period of time!

I also became a vegetarian for over a two-year period, but since I started to look like a walking skeleton I had to put meat and limited dairy back into my diet. In addition, I felt that I finally found some very valuable tools, immediately incorporating them to assist me with obtaining the qualities within myself that I desired in a mate!

In addition to my own newly developed and direct connection with my Creator, I also started attending Deepak Chopra wellness seminars and conventions, purchasing books like "Creative Visualization" by Shakti Gawain, "Meditations For The Tenth Insight" by Salle Merrill Redfield, and "Journey Into Healing" by Deepak Chopra. And although it wasn't my desire to bend a spoon with my mind, I also incorporated "Mind Power" by Uri Gueller!

Additionally, I immersed myself into reading the "Celestine Prophecy" by James Redfield, which validated my innate connection with nature!

Over the years, I've incorporated those various metaphysical meditations and prayers into my daily life. These practices have supported me through some very hard and lonely times on my journey to self-awareness and self-acceptance.

I even found inspiration from a spiritual book I received one day on Hollywood Boulevard. I was walking home from work when all of a sudden this white stretch limousine pulled to the curbside next to me. The window rolled completely down, and out popped the face of Little Richard, motioning for me to come speak with him about the love of the Lord!

I could not believe that Little Richard was actually being chauffeured around in a white stretch limo passing out spiritual booklets to random people on Hollywood Boulevard and that I would be one of those people to have received that blessing. Wow!

All of these events and more led me to truly believe that there is something much more to our purpose for being here that is on a spiritual and quantifiable level connecting us with our universe, planet, nature, animals and each other on a deeper level than we have realized.

Another true blessing for me was that I'd begun to understand that there is much more to life than just what we've been almost brainwashed to believe. I am aware of the misinterpretations and contradictive translations that are associated with religion and our environment that is continuously spoon-fed to our society in high quantity as truth!

As for relationships with prospective mates, I was not ready for a serious one at that time. But I knew that when I was ready, I wanted someone that would not be insecure about accepting and loving me unconditionally.

I envisioned him being kind, loving, giving, passionate, supportive, emotionally and physically available, considerate, affectionate, not abusive mentally or physically, responsible and trustworthy! I did not want someone that I'd have to sneak around to be with because he was more concerned about his career and conflicted about being monogamous with someone who is a transsexual woman.

Throughout my spiritual quest, I began developing and learning to metaphysically use my "Third Eye" to see the future that I desired for myself. I visualized that the next man I chose to give my heart to would be someone who would desire me the way I observed the interaction and affection between this lesbian couple that I lived with for a brief time during one of my childhood runaways from home back in South Carolina!

To me, they were a real couple that respected and supported each other and who were also unashamed to be seen together in public. I hoped to meet someone like that who would accept, respect and treat me the way that I knew I deserved to be treated and loved!

Also I visualized that my future long-term mate would be mature, masculine and secure with his manhood, understanding that in order to be with me being possessive and obsessive would not be tolerated at all for one moment in our relationship.

After several months, that living arrangement just did not continue to sit well with me anymore so I decided to wait for the most appropriate time to discuss it with Ashley and to suggest that we start splitting the bills three ways.

As far as their relationship, all I knew was that they had some sort of weird arrangements. Whenever she brought home a trick from the club, Eric usually left the apartment and he would often be outside waiting until she finished turning her trick when I arrived home from working at the club.

On one Saturday morning I shall not soon forget, after arriving home from Plaza, I suspected that Ashley was entertaining someone whom she'd met at Peanuts, so I went into my room closing the door because their arrangement was not any of my business. However, the straw that broke the camel's back was the frightening incident that followed around three in the morning.

I finished showering and removing my makeup and had settled underneath my comforter in bed, flipping through the channels unwinding alone, when all of a sudden I heard Ashley screaming, "No Eric, get off him!"

I jumped out of bed quickly throwing my robe on and stepping into my slippers to go see what was going on and when I opened the bedroom door, I saw Ashley trying to separate Eric and a trick and they were both covered in blood, trying to massacre each other in the hallway!

After she finally broken the fight up, the trick immediately bolted out of the apartment leaving Ashley and Eric arguing that he did not like what the guy was doing to her!

Eric then stormed into the bedroom, leaving Ashley and me staring at each other in disbelief. Seconds later, he abruptly and excitedly left the apartment, slamming the door behind him.

I asked, "What the hell is going on, Ash?"

Obviously high on something other than just "Trees" and covered in blood, she pulled her robe tightly shut explaining, "Girl, Eric asked if he could hide in the closet instead of going outside in the rain while I turned my trick and because he had gotten jealous about what we were doing, he jumped out of the closet attacking Bob!"

"What?"I replied and cautiously inquired, "Girl, whose blood is that all over you, are you bleeding?"

"I'm Okay, this is Eric and Bob's blood." She replied, motioning for me to follow her into their bedroom, which looked like a silent but deadly earthquake had pinpointed the room. I carefully stepped over the splattered blood on the floor and sat at her makeup station chair.

Ashley walked over to the closet, removed her robe starting, to dress in jeans and a sweater and continuing, "Girl, I have to go and find Eric because he took the money from my purse to buy crack!"

It became clear to me at that moment why he never had a job and contributed to any of the bills the whole time that we were roommates, so I replied, "Crack!"

I looked around the room at the mess and further inquired. "Ashley, how long has Eric been smoking crack?"

She replied after zipping up her jacket. "Tracee, let's just say that this is not the first time Eric has stolen my money to go buy drugs."

After she left the apartment to go after Eric, I went back into my bedroom closing the door and digesting what seemed to be an ordinary experience for them.

Several months after joining the Peanuts cast, Ashley approached me after the show, extending an invitation to her apartment for dinner. On the evening that I arrived at their apartment, I was surprised that her "husband" was a guy who had recently approached me while I was shopping on Hollywood Boulevard for pumps and accessories for an upcoming show..

He'd persistently followed me from store to store, asking for my phone number. Finally, after becoming tired of being pursued by him, I gave him a bogus phone number just to get rid of him.

I wonder what he was thinking when we were introduced, realizing that their dinner guest was someone that he'd recently propositioned on Hollywood Boulevard? What I do know is that I was not interested in him because he just was not my type at all.

Later that evening after dinner, while Ashley was in their bedroom on the phone (most likely scheduling a date with a client), he had the nerve to sarcastically comment, "So, Tracee, you gave me the wrong number, huh?"

I was disgusted that he was still trying to push up on me, so I replied, "You know what, Eric, Ashley is a really nice person, so let's just pretend that the day you approached me on Hollywood Boulevard never happened."

That whole scene was surreal.

When Ashley and I initially discussed living together, the plan was that it would be just the two of us moving into the new townhouse together, splitting the rent and utilities down the middle. But when we moved, Eric tagged along with her, creating the catastrophe that contributed to my decision to get my own place and live alone after the bloody trick and Eric fought!

Although I cared for my friend Ashley, I knew that I would not be able to continue living in that type of environment. Almost immediately after that incident, I told Ashley that I would have to begin looking for my own place. I didn't tell her that I had already secured an elegant studio apartment with a separate full kitchen and balcony on Whitley and Hollywood Boulevard for $600 a month.

I was happy that I didn't need a roommate in order to afford the rent. I was done with roommates!

Needless to say Ashley was not happy at all about my decision to leave, and we even got into a physical altercation after she stormed into my bedroom insisting that I continue arguing with her about my decision to move out!

After Ashley angrily forced her way into my room and attempted to attack me, followed by Eric who held my arms to keep me from defending myself against her, although he pretended that he was trying to break us apart.

I was able to break away from his grip and back her off me with a statue from my dresser and I then called 911. Finally, after the police officers arrived, I explained to them that she was angry about me giving her notice that I would be moving out into my own apartment after a violent incident between she and her boyfriend.

Once the officers determined that she and I were the only ones on the lease, all they were able to do was warn us to stay away from each other until I moved out of the apartment and during the conversation, Eric was ultimately arrested for being disorderly and high on crack.

I wasn't sure when Eric would be returning after his arrest, so I was determined to be gone that day. Since I didn't know anyone with a truck that I could call at a moment's notice, I left the apartment in hopes of finding someone that I could pay to help me move my stuff.

When I exited the elevator in the parking garage, I spotted a utility guy reading the meters with his flatbed company truck parked close to where he was working and, without hesitating, I approached him to explain my desperate situation and asked if I could pay him to use his truck to move my things.

He was a really nice guy who asked, "Are your things here at this complex?"

Encouraged that he had not said no from the offset, I quickly replied, "Yes, they're on the third floor!"

He asked, as he shoved the screwdrivers into the utility belt compartment, "Where are you moving to?"

"I'm moving right up the street to Whitley and Hollywood Boulevard," I replied, somewhat still encouraged.

He turned to look me in my eyes, responding, "Well, this is my last job so you are in luck. I will help you move."

"I can pay you for helping me!" I replied, hoping that it would not be more than $100 or so.

"It's okay because you seem like a nice young lady that's in a tough situation right now, so we'll consider this to be my good deed for today." He locked and secured the meters, continuing, "I'm not going to charge you anything; now show me where your belongings are."

I excitedly replied, "Thank you so much! I don't have a lot to move, there are just the things from my bedroom!" I pressed the button to call the elevator in disbelief that he had actually agreed to use his company truck to help a stranger move on the spur of the moment without charging me anything. Another guardian angel!

When the elevator opened on my floor, he followed me to the bedroom and started dismantling the bed while I grabbed my wardrobe trunks and duffle bags to start filling them with everything that could fit!

Ashley remained in her bedroom for the entire time that it took to pack up all of my possessions, and it took less than 30 minutes for us to load and secure all of the items onto the back of his truck. Eric arrived back at the apartment right before we took the elevator to the garage and pulled away into the light heading towards my new apartment!

After parking in my new apartment garage, he helped me to unload and carry my things from the back of his truck up to my apartment. After we finished I offered, "Please excuse my manners … my name is Tracee, by the way, and I really appreciate you helping me out today!"

He reached out to shake my hand, replying, "I'm Tom and it was my pleasure to be of assistance to you, Tracee." He reached and pulled a card from his breast pocket continuing, "Here's my phone number if you should ever need any help in the future!"

I took his card and jokingly replied."Thank you so much again, Tom, but I am not planning to be in that sort of situation ever again!"

He replied before turning to walk back toward the elevator to leave, "Well, I had better get going to turn my truck in. please don't hesitate to call me if you need anything."

I never saw or spoke to Tom again after that day and I was just grateful for the random kindness of a stranger in my time of need! A few weeks later, I felt that living on Hollywood and Whitley was very convenient and after I got settled into my new apartment, an acquaintance that I had recently met named Nikki was standing with me inside the apartment lobby waiting for the elevator when we were approached by a high-profile actor/comedian that was on a very popular sketch comedy television show at the time inquiring if we knew where he could score some crack.

Several months later, I figured that I would wade back into the water and give the dating scene another try after several months of choosing not to be intimate with anyone. I'd broken my rule once one Friday night after the show at Peanuts after meeting and dancing the night away with a really nice military guy!

While we were dancing, I scanned his finger for a wedding band before agreeing to have breakfast with him after the club.

During breakfast at Yukon later that morning, I felt that I should further investigate and question him about his current relationship status, because a lot of guys removed their wedding bands before entering the club.

I was pleasantly surprised that he was honest enough to disclose to me that he was married with two children!

The military guy also informed me that he and his wife were both fans and both became interested in meeting me after they'd previously seen my show!

I was shocked that his wife did not have any problems with his attraction to transsexual women, and that she'd actually encouraged it. I informed him that I did not date married or committed men.

However, I was really curious about an African-American woman from North Carolina encouraging and supporting her husband's attraction to transsexuals. The following weekend they attended the show together and afterwards, we were introduced.

If I had seen them together on the streets, I would never have suspected that they were in such an open relationship, because they seemed like an average couple that you'd encounter every day.

Later that morning over breakfast at Yukon, she invited me to their house for the upcoming Thanksgiving holiday. When I agreed to join them for Thanksgiving dinner, I had no intention of being intimate with either of them and my curiosity would not allow me to decline their invitation to spend Thanksgiving Day with them at their house on the military base.

So, he picked me up early Thanksgiving morning for the drive to Santa Ana to spend the day with them and upon arrival at their military housing on base, I was introduced to their two daughters, who reminded me of my little cousins back in South Carolina!

The girls and I played kickball and jumped rope outside before dinner and later that evening her husband eventually retired to their room to watch football. After the girls later went into their room to play, leaving their mother and I alone in the dining room clearing the dishes from the table, she informed me, "Tracee we have a bedroom all ready for you!" She continued, questioning, "You are going to spend the night with us right?"

I wasn't really surprised by her question due to her husband already broaching the topic during out drive earlier that morning after he'd picked me up for the drive to Santa Ana. California. I replied, "No, I will not be able to spend the night because in this short period I've come to view you as a sister-friend and I adore your daughters!"

After delicately placing the plates in the sink, I continued, "I am really not comfortable with your proposal of sleeping with your husband, because I want a man of my own that I don't have to share with anyone else."

She replied, "I understand and respect your decision, Tracee. I hope that you continue to be our friend because the girls adore you also!"

I concluded that conversation, happy that we'd reached an understanding, "Your family reminds me of my family back in South Carolina and I would be honored to continue getting to know you!"

I was comfortable with them respecting my decisions, which contributed to us becoming closer, and before they were deployed to another state, I spent other holiday weekends with them overnight without being expected or pressured into sleeping with her husband. They all often hung out at my apartment in Hollywood!

My moral values just would not allow me to knowingly become emotionally or

physically involved with a married or committed man, because it would only end up ugly

in the end.

Chapter Eight

Lights, Camera, Action: My First Featured Acting Role!

My decision for choosing Los Angeles as the place to make my great escape was not because I harbored any big dreams of becoming the next leading lady or anything of the nature. LOL!

Even so, I did get approached by folks recruiting for something or the other. Once I was shopping at Thrifty Drug Store and this sweet, fragile elderly lady passed me a phone number that she'd handwritten on the back of an envelope and enthusiastically insisted that I contact her son who was a casting agent at Central Casting to register for commercials!

Then there was this other lady who approached me when I used to work part-time for a special events staffing agency that was hired to staff a cast lawn party for "The Mark Curry Show" at one of the executive producer's massive estate. She suggested that I should be a star, not serving them steamed vegetables!

Although I was flattered to have my potentials for acting and modeling acknowledged, I never took them seriously because my main intention for going to California was simply to save my life, not to become a movie star.

However, once again, fate had additional plans for me! My first encounter and one of two other requests for autographs was with my favorite male Hollywood actor during that time when he happened to have been filming his latest movie on Hollywood and Cahuenga right in front of the infamous Golden Touch hair salon.

Previously after a hair appointment, my hairdresser and the proprietor of establishment, Nolan, offered to take me to the Catch One club with him for my first time to see the new Monday night show and inquire about bookings.

I was filled with anticipation, excitement and nervous energy following my appointment that afternoon making every effort to keep myself occupied until Nolan was finished with his other clients! I busied myself reading the latest salon hair style books and celebrity magazines.

Another dream come true occurred later that early evening after I'd finished reading almost all of the latest celebrity gossip and then stood at the salon entrance window stretching my legs and watching a film crew setting up to begin shooting a blockbuster movie that I soon realized was starring my second celebrity crush of that era, Larry Fishburne!

I later learned that I'd watched him film a pivotal scene from his breakout movie "Deep Cover"! I was beyond excited about being within reach of his masculine aura, which captivated and mesmerized me as I observed him working his craft that is unlike any other, in my humble opinion!

Eventually, I walked outside and stood on the sidewalk, leaning up against the salon to get a nonintrusive better view.

I could not believe it when he came and stood within arm's length of where I was standing, then he leaned against the wall, and lit a cigarette during a break in the filming.

I just couldn't resist not taking a once in a lifetime opportunity to ask for Larry Fishburne's autograph! At first, I was so nervous to approach him, but I quickly gathered up my nerves while rushing to ask Nolan for a pen and piece of paper and then going back out. I demurely asked, "Mr. Fishburne, I don't mean to intrude in your break. However, I love your work and would be honored if you considered giving me your autograph."

He was very gracious, although I had interrupted his cigarette break, nor did he hesitate for one second to take the pen and index card from my hand, responding, "What's your name, dear?"

I excitedly replied, "My name is Tracee, Mr. Fishburne!"

He then signed his autograph and then said as he handed back to me the pen and autographed index card, "Thank you, Tracee, for being a fan. I hope you continue to support my work!"After thanking him for his time and seeing his beautiful smile up close, I morphed into a giddy little school girl. Elevated onto cloud nine, I floated back into the salon to show Nolan and the others the autograph from my dream man!

The wait was very worth it after Nolan finally finished his last client and we arrived at Catch One. I was not expecting to be asked to perform "Dreamin" by Vanessa Williams on the spot for my cast audition after being introduced to the show director, Cabrini!

Thankfully, the DJ had the song and after the show that evening, Cabrini invited me to join their Monday night cast. Several months later, I was in the dressing room when fate started to weave her magic again. I was approached by the club manager, Carlton, after performing the Jody Watley "Everything/Don't You Want Me" mix.

I was blown away after he told me that a casting agent friend of his was currently auditioning for a movie about the Jackson Five family and he asked if I would be interested in auditioning for an Apollo Theater scene.

Carlton went on to inform me that this would be a paid featured role and that I needed to meet the director the following Tuesday on July 1, 1992, for casting at the Ambassador Hotel, which is the hotel that I later learned, was the hotel in which Robert Kennedy was assassinated on June 5, 1968.

Although I've never really seriously thought about being in movies, I figured that this would be a unique and quite possibly amazing experience for me, so the following afternoon I met the director, Karen Arthur, at the Ambassador Hotel on the day she was shooting Holly Robinson Peete performing as Diana Ross in concert.

I should preface the remainder of this experience with the fact that since I didn't have an agent or a mentor teaching the ins and outs of the movie making industry, nor did I grasp the magnitude of what I was doing until one of the production assistants told me that I could meet Vanessa Williams in between scene set-ups.

I was excitedly standing to the side, watching the production and waiting for my opportunity to meet Vanessa Williams with my little business card in hand and prepared for any opportunity that may have presented itself to be in one of her videos or something! Do not judge me, because I did not know any better then.

Finally when the assistant escorted me and introduced Ms. Williams, instead of requesting her autograph, I gave her my business card and told her that if she needed anything, extras or stand-ins, to please call me.

That experience makes me cringe every time I think about it, because I have since learned that if you are fortunate enough to ever meet a celebrity that you admire on a movie set, it is extremely inappropriate to give them your business card, photo or anything else.

Thankfully, she was nice and gracious after realizing that I was an inexperienced star- struck fan!

On August 30, 1992, I arrived for an early call-time at the historic downtown Los Angeles Orpheum Theater to begin shooting my historical appearance as the Snowflake Girl in the balcony scene at the Apollo Theater the very first time that the Jackson Five ever performed and won the amateur contest at the Apollo.

I've always made it a habit to arrive as early as possible to work and on that day I was honored to have met and spent one-on-one time with our choreographer Michael Peters, who also played the character Sandman and swung on a rope from the balcony!

Michael Peters was also famously known as the premier choreographer who created most of Michael Jacksons' signature moves, and I've recently learned that he'd choreographed Diana Ross for her "Live In Central Park" concert in 1983.

That morning I later observed one of the other main stars, Lawrence Hilton Jacobs, standing in the background watching our taping. The cast of characters included Candace, two other girls and I whom were cast to play the historical group of transsexuals and transgender people that were a very popular attraction at the Apollo Theater on August 13, 1967, seven months after my Birth.

I guess that because I'd exuded so much energy during rehearsals, I must have caught the attention of the director, because she moved me to the front of the other girls for my featured nose- pinching and booty-shaking scene!

Between takes, I went to the restroom and upon returning back to set to take my place, the director jokingly asked, "What restrooms do you use, Tracee, the men or ladies?"

I replied in a matter-of-fact manner, "I use the ladies restroom of course!"

She chuckled at my response and then called, "Action!" It was obvious to me after finally seeing the movie that she was amused by me, because she'd given me the best camera time that didn't end up on the cutting room floor, and to date I am still surprised that so many people recognize me from that movie.

Once, while spending the night with my cousin Lynn who'd taken me out dancing in Columbia, South Carolina along with a friend of hers from work whom asked, "Are you the person shaking her booty at the Apollo in the Jacksons movie?"

I remain surprised to date that after so many years have passed that bio-pic has inspired generations!

I'm still amazed that I am often asked whenever I go back home if I am that person in the balcony dressed in all white jamming out. Maybe it's because almost every other weekend for quite some time the re-broadcasts still airs.

During that time I usually had Vanessa Williams' "The Comfort Zone" album on constant rotation playing on my stereo as I unpacked my costume bag and reminisced about the antics occurring at the club that weekend!

When the phone rang, I turned the volume down low enough to continue listening to "Still in Love" playing softly in the background before answering. On the other end a familiar voice from my past said, "Hey, babe. It's Shawn. How are you doing?"

Although Shawn and I never officially committed to exclusively dating only each other when we met back in Georgia, up to the point of my cheating indiscretion, I'd chosen to be exclusive with him when we were dating. I was really hurt and confused when he abruptly left town without responding to my phone calls and messages.

Back then, in the late '80s. I was saddened when he later told me that his disappearance was in association with the death of his father, and even more disappointed with myself in the way I chose to handle the situation.

I was happy and slightly discombobulated to be talking to Shawn after our previous history together, so I managed to respond as I sat on the bed, "I am doing very well Shawn. I was just unpacking my costumes before going to the club for rehearsal. How are you?"

Shawn's voice was sweet and comforting as he said, "I am doing great, babe. I'm still producing music for C.A., currently living in Sacramento, California, and missing you immensely!"

I was excited to be talking to him again replying, "I've missed you also, Shawn!"

"Well, babe, I'm driving to Los Angeles next week and I would love to take you on a road trip to San Francisco for a weekend getaway!"

"Of course you can come see me next week, and I'm sure that I won't have any problems getting off from work to go to San Francisco with you!"

"Okay, then, I will let you go to your rehearsal and I'll see you on Monday afternoon!"

I replied, before hanging up the phone, grabbing my rehearsal bag and almost floating on air out of my apartment to go to Plaza for rehearsal, "I will see you on Monday afternoon, Shawn!"

Monday afternoon seemed so far away after finishing tidying up the apartment and going through the motions at work that weekend anticipating seeing Shawn again!

Finally after returning home from my day job that Monday afternoon when my door bell rang, I knew that it was most likely Shawn! I wasn't sure how to respond once I opened the door and saw him for the first time in such a long!

I recall him standing at my door looking good and carrying what seemed to have been thousands of red roses and birds of paradise bouquets! I grabbed my face in shock, asking, "Shawn, what did you do?!"

Sweetly smiling from ear to ear, he replied, "You know me, babe, I will do anything to make my favorite girl smile!"

I was almost in tears as I grabbed and squeezed him tightly, kissing his sweet lips."I thought that I would never see you again, Shawn!" I then took some of the bouquets from his hands. "Let me give you a hand with these. They're so beautiful, Shawn. Thank you so much!"

"Anything for you, babe, and just so you know, I always knew that I would see you again!" He lifted me from the floor with a firm embrace!

Although I don't recall how he found out that I was living in California, I do remember that after we'd finished bringing in his luggage and the hundreds of roses that filled my entire apartment, we sat for hours talking and catching up with the events that had lead us to that moment.

We spent the next several days making up for lost time. We left early on that Friday morning for my first exciting and adventurous visit to San Francisco, where we visited Chinatown and danced the night away at Finnochio's club.

I was grateful that I'd received a second chance to make amends for the hurt that my previous actions had caused us, and on the way back from our adventure-filled San Francisco excursion we spent a beautiful day in Sacramento sightseeing and taking pictures in the park.

We also spent the night at the mansion of former Sacramento Kings NBA player C.A, who Shawn was still writing and producing music for. I strongly believe that I'd never really considered Shawn to be the guy that I had been visualizing about being with forever due to him having his own life in Sacramento producing music.

Since I did not think that his career would have allowed for him to unconditionally accept and love me the way that I envisioned being loved, I didn't have the nerve to directly ask him if this was something that he was interested in, so I just focused on enjoying the time that we were currently spending together.

After Shawn returned to Sacramento, I auditioned and was hired to join the cast of "La Cage Aux Folles" in Beverly Hills, impersonating Diana Ross and Whitney Houston.

I found it ironic that before the audition I had only performed a Diana Ross song once, at Loretta's in Atlanta.

After scheduling my audition date for "La Cage", I was concerned about looking like Miss Ross because I had never attempted to do so before. Now Whitney Houston was a different story, because I had impersonated her before and felt comfortable performing her music.

I was very nervous about the audition because previously I'd driven all the way to Las Vegas and auditioned for the "LaCage" show there and was rejected because I lived full-time as a female on hormone therapy with real breasts.

I feared that "LaCage" Beverly Hills would also reject me due to my breasts and the fact that they'd preferred their performers to live as men. I hoped that they'd look pass the physical and instead focus on my talents during the audition!

Previously, I shared my concerns with my Peanuts cast member Diva who was also a "LaCage" cast member, a featured Madonna impersonator at the time, and she encouraged me to audition regardless of my apprehension and fears.

The day of the audition, my costumes were all ready to go, but I still had no idea of where to begin to apply makeup to make me look like Miss Ross, so I arrived several hours before the scheduled audition and asked a guy named Tim Dunn to help me with the Ross makeup.

Tim Dunn was a white guy on the "La Cage" cast that spot on impersonated Dionne Warwick and since he was so convincing to me, I figured that he would be able to help with creating a Diana Ross illusion.

Later that afternoon in the dressing room after showing me how to apply his exaggerated version of Miss Ross makeup, I auditioned for the management, performing the medleys "I'm Coming Out/Ain't No Mountain High Enough" and Whitney Houston's "I Wanna Dance//I will Always Love You."

Considering the makeup Tim Dunn taught me was so hideous, I was once again in the right place at the right time, becoming less than a handful of transsexuals living full-time with real breasts were asked to join the exclusive, world-famous "La Cage Aux Folles" Beverly Hills, California cast!

Thankfully, several weeks later, Adam West, makeup artist to the stars, taught me the right way to apply my stage makeup to create what looking like Miss Ross is all about!

In addition to the assistance of the makeup session, I had a video of Adam applying cosmetics and walking me through the process before posing and for the photo shoot, evolving from just Destiny into Destiny (Your Mistress of Illusions)!

I'm very appreciative that Adam West came to the rescue to generously introduce me to the tools and supplies that were required to continue transforming my image to reflect someone that I've grown to respect and admire once I'd consumed every bit of her history, photographs, music, movies and live concerts.

"La Cage" was the crème de la crème of success for professional performance artists and she provided me with a very generous weekly salary, which was more than enough to take care of my obligations. I was also blessed with the ability to pay cash for my very first used car that I purchased from the sister of a security guard from Benin, Africa, whom was posted at my place of employment and also smitten with me!

Although my two-door, sky-blue Pinto had some rear end body damage, she got me from point A to point B without any challenges! The "La Gage Aux Folles" rehearsals and show commitments required me to eventually resign from Plaza and Peanuts, but I made sure not to burn any of those bridges as I left.

I adjusted very well to my new job and routine, so when I wasn't working or rehearsing, I spent my free time on the beach or meditating at the ParamahansaYogananda Lake Shrine Fellowship in the Pacific Palisades where some of Mahatma Ghandi's ashes are enshrined. Lake Shrine Fellowship also features the most colorful koi-filled lake and Dutch windmill surrounded by a lush and tranquil garden.

That same year I appeared at the annual Las Vegas Comdex Computer convention where I was booked to mingle with the guests impersonating Diana Ross at Caesars Palace Nevada.

I cringe when reminiscing about my most embarrassing experience while in Vegas. After everything had gone smoothly during the convention and once I finished my shift of photo-opts and engaging in casual conversations with the guests, the Cher impersonator and I were invited by one of the handsome production engineers to attend the VIP after party with them later that evening in the ballroom.

Since we had several hours before our flight was scheduled to depart, we decided to go dancing with the guys after rushing up to our dressing suite to change out of our costumes into something more appropriate for dancing!

I wore a sexy, black-lace body suit that accentuated my figure and I also decided to wear a long Sade braid for affect! Instead of taking the time to make sure that the braid was firmly secured, I rushed in order to get back to the cute engineer!

Later that evening the handsome engineer and I were on the dance floor having a great time with me thinking that I was fierce, slinging my long braid to the beat of the music. All of a sudden, I went to swing her and she kept going, flying off my head onto the dance floor.

I was so embarrassed, but the engineer was so sweet and unaffected by what just happened as he reached down to pick up my pony tail and calmly handed it to me. I thanked him for retrieving my hair then pinned her securely back on my head and we continued having a great time!

Afterwards, the guys tried convincing us to change our flight departure to the next day so that we could spend the night partying with them, but I had a show that following night back in Los Angeles so I was not able to stay.

However, the handsome engineer and I exchanged phone numbers, agreeing to stay in touch with each other and possibly get together in the future! Although we communicated off and on by phone for a week or so after my return to Los Angeles, I'm sure that due to the distance between he and I was why we mutually never really made the effort to see each other again.

Immediately upon my return from Vegas we started prepping and rehearsing for my very first city-to-city tour with "La Cage." Then out of the blue, Shawn showed up at my door battered and bruised.

Although I was enjoying my single life dating whenever I wanted to and his appearance was unexpected, I was absolutely not going to never turn him away in his time of need, considering all of our history together.

He told me about the physical altercation between he and the pro ball player's relative, thus ending his music-producing arrangement. I didn't find it necessary to press Shawn to disclose all of the details contributing to their physical altercation, because I was just happy to have been able to be there for him.

As the days went by, when I noticed that he was sleeping a lot seeming somewhat depressed about the situation between him and the ball player, I wanted to cheer him up! Because I believed him to be the most talented music producer and singer that I'd ever dated up to that point, I tried supporting and encouraging him by arranging an interview with an artist and recruiting representative from Sony Records that I'd met during one of my second jobs at Thrifty Drug Store on Santa Monica and Labrea.

After Shawn's meeting with Sony, he was understandably disappointed that he was not signed because the A&R rep compared his music and style to Prince, which they weren't in the market for his similar musical style at the time.

I really didn't understand the depth of what Shawn was going through, because I was more focused on preparing for my first major road tour. Unfortunately, the day that I left to begin the tour things were strained between us and we did not depart on very good terms.

I knew that Shawn was disappointed with me, because when I returned from the tour he was gone, leaving behind all of the cards, letters and photos that I'd given to him over the years.

I was really enjoying my freedom, spending time getting to know me for a change during my very important mental and physical transformation during that time when Shawn unexpectedly showed up at my door to live with me for the very first time since we'd known each other.

Even though I was really happy to see Shawn, however, we never discussed the possibilities of us living together and I also started resenting his expectation that my life was placed on hold for him.

Thankfully, a few years later Shawn and I reconciled after he purchased a plane ticket for me to visit his hometown, Wichita, Kansas, for a weekend.

Although I loved Shawn, I did not want to lead him on so I'd suggested that we sleep in separate bedrooms during my stay at his family home, because I was in a place that I needed to continue re-establishing a different kind of relationship between him and me.

The fact that we were not intimate during my visit did not stop me from having a great weekend with Shawn, going out to the local clubs, sightseeing and taking pictures like we've always done together in the past.

After that weekend with him, we continued to support and communicate with each other on a regular basis up to the point when, many years later, I informed him that I was engaged to be married. I've since accepted that I was growing and discovering who I was at that time and I remain okay with making the wisest decisions that have led me to where I am.

A year or so passed before the management and owners of "La Cage" began to express their financial challenges. Alleged drug abuse and embezzlement charges brought up against one of the co-owners eventually contributed to the permanent closing of the landmark celebrity look-a-like performance artist club "La Cage Aux Follies" Beverly Hills.

Another landmark event occurred during that time when in 1992 the acquittal of police officers accused of excessive force against Rodney King sparked riots in South Central Los Angeles.

Out of concern for our physical well-being, we were let off early from work that day from my day job to go home and prepare for what was to occur next. Later that evening, I called the club to inquire about the show and was told that because of fires, rioting and lawlessness on the streets, the show was cancelled.

I stayed safely inside my apartment alone for the rest of the weekend, watching from the window the plumes of smoke and flames billowing and illuminating each burning building in the distance. The frightening illuminated night sky caused me concern that my neighborhood might be next to go up in flames. Thank God the violence, looting and fires never reached my neighborhood.

A few months later, after tensions were beginning to somewhat de-escalate from the rioting and burning to a sense of calm, an acquaintance that I met through Ashley named Donna approached me on Hollywood Boulevard to inform me that Eric recently sold all of Ashley's furniture and personal possessions after she'd attempted suicide in response to contracting AIDS-related pneumonia. Ashley eventually died in hospice care.

I was saddened by the news and I could not understand why she'd tried to take her own life, although I could, unfortunately, relate to why she'd chosen to stay with her abusive crack-head boyfriend.

A couple of short years later when I was once again costume and hair shopping on Hollywood Boulevard, I was approached by Eric trying to get me to talk to him, but I ignored him as if I didn't hear him calling my name and attempting to remind me of who he was.

I replied as I kept walking, disgusted by him, "I know who you are, Eric."

Also the inevitable occurred when I had to resign from Dolan Micro Consulting because the environment became unbearable as a result of not reciprocating the feelings of affection that my boss Jim was expressing towards me.

Since I was making a pretty comfortable living performing at night, when the environment at the computer company became hostile, I stepped out on faith willingly, leaving a security blanket day job to work full-time on stage.

Shortly thereafter, I was contacted by Cabrini, whom I had previously worked with at the Catch One before she left the show. She invited me to join a new cast that she was producing at The World club in the Beverly Center.

I also went back to regularly booking Love Lounge, Rage, Plaza, Robbie's in Pomona, and Catch One, thanking goodness for not demolishing those bridges as I moved up the ladder to work for "La Cage". A memorable performance at Catch One that I recall was doing "The Sweetest Days" by Vanessa Williams with her music video to the song being projected on the large screen on-stage behind. Many years later, I was complimented on that performance from a random person in Georgia!

In addition to performing in the clubs, not long after my resignation from the computer company, I also received an opportunity to apply for another day job. I was approached at Catch One by a lesbian in between shows whom suggested that I interview for a new program at P.A.M.

P.A.M is an acronym I've chosen to reference an organization that provided HIV and AIDS social services to people of color! After interviewing and being hired at P.A.M my responsibilities were to establish and manage their first-of-its-kind transgender outreach program for people of color.

The reason that I've chosen to discuss those experiences at P.A.M is because there was a well-publicized vindictive effort by my then-superior, whom I will call D.P., to unjustifiably defame and besmirch my character. D.P. was resentful about me standing up for what was not only right for me, but for the health of the clientele who were vulnerable to the policies P.A.M incorporated during that time.

Also, my desire to reveal this story is my opportunity to set the record straight to my former colleagues, because they were facetiously mislead about the reasons that my contract was not renewed.

I had no idea of what I was walking into upon accepting the job and later learned that there was another transgender sister named Vanessa Chancellor whom was expecting to get the job.

Vanessa was understandably furious that she was hired as my subordinate, and she displayed her venomous discontent by making it a living nightmare to establish an effective social services program that would serve the most underserved and at-risk people of color trans community members.

I didn't have the support from my immediate supervisor D.P. to deal with Vanessa's issues because he was the one who had led her to believe that she was a sure-in to fill the position. It was only after a few one-on-one heated conversations between Vanessa and I about who was in charge that we managed to successfully launch the program!

It was my personal labor of love to finally introduce the program to the community at an "Introduction to Something Different" event at Catch One. We selected Catch One for the program launch event because the owner, Jewel Thais Williams, had always been very supportive of me personally and she was also a staunch supporter and ally to the transgender community, employing some of the girls to entertain in her show.

Although Vanessa was resentful that she didn't get the management position as promised, I respected her potential feeling that we had more in common than not, so I made an effort to work with her in the antagonistic environment that I often endured.

Vanessa and I were both Aquarians, so I also somewhat understood where she was coming from. Occasionally, after the program was officially launched, we continued butting heads because I was not going to apologize for getting the job that she'd thought was hers, and as far as I was concerned, it was not personal due to it being about business as usual in the corporate world.

For the most part, Vanessa and I respected each other and we've remained good acquaintances to date whenever our paths cross in social environments! During my employment at P.A.M, I quickly learned the dynamics and the inner workings of a non-profit organization.

Then there came a time when I felt that I had to literally fight for my life while working for P.A.M, because some of the other employees were accustomed to chain-smoking in the tiny office spaces, which presented a problem for those of us that were non-smokers.

Considering the building was small and unventilated with usually five to six employees in a small, windowless office, it seemed that the ones whom smoked would have been a little more considerate of others. I've never been a smoker (nothing against those who do), however, when their choices compromise my health, I have to speak out about the conditions.

My reactions were in response to the overwhelming studies during that time about the effects of second-hand smoke and the fact it just was not fair to struggle to type a curriculum and required reports through the strangulating, stagnant smoke in order to meet program and funding deadlines.

In addition to the second-hand smoke, I was pissed off about my clothes and hair constantly smelling like I'd been at a bar all day whenever I left the office for offsite appointments and engagements during work.

The smear campaign started after I spoke out against the smoking in the workplace during a management meeting. After all, P.A.M was an environment where sick people with compromised immune systems visited everyday to receive social and health services.

They were coming to P.A.M for testing and other medical needs, and it felt immoral to me that they should not have to endure inhaling the smoke from cigarettes being smoked by those individuals empowered to provide them with help alleviating their pain and suffering.

I also felt that it was my basic right to work in a smoke-free corporate environment, especially when the law prohibited smoking in the workplace and other public facilities were passed in that state. I'm sure the rest of the management team was caught off guard when I raised my concerns about the constant chain-smoking taking place in our offices.

I knew going in that voicing my objections would most likely jeopardize my job, but I did not care because I felt strongly about my health, and it was also the principle of the matter.

After much debate over several days following the meeting, the non-smoking ban in the workplace was enforced by the executive director, which resulted in most of the program managers and some of the other employees resenting me for causing them to have been forced to go outside to smoke their cancer sticks.

I understood their resentment and expected the backlash, and as predicted, my contract was not renewed the following year. However, I did take issue with the excuse that was given to others by my supervisor D.P., which was that I had written some sort of grievance letter to the funding sources making strong objectionable accusations against P.A.M, which was a blatant and outright lie.

I would have never put the Agency in jeopardy of losing their much-needed funding by complaining to the source funding the only program providing social services resources to people that needed HIV and AIDS risk reduction, prevention, education, testing and life-saving tools to people of color.

The undeniable and irrefutable truth was that during my time at P.A.M, my supervisor at some point must have received a letter from the funding contract manager commending me on the great job that I was doing with the program. I still have a copy of the letter in my personal files!

I was required by contract to submit regular reports and updates to the grant manager, and I am pleased that under my leadership, the program was often highlighted by that manager. Unbeknownst to me, the complimentary letter was sent to my supervisor D.P., but in response D.P. attempted to unjustifiably assassinate my character and negatively impact my future job search.

His efforts worked for a brief period until I was confidentially informed by a prospective employer and acquaintance during an interview that my previous supervisor was giving misinformation whenever he was contacted for a job reference.

I'm certain that D.P. may have felt some sort of vindication in response to the nonsmoking band, because he smoked up to two packs or more a day of those cheap, stinky cigarettes in his office and during staff meetings.

After removing P.A.M from my resume, I didn't have any further challenges with obtaining other gainful employment! I was recently informed by a former P.A.M employee whom I currently keep in contact with and who still lives in California that D.P. had died from lung cancer, God rest his soul.

I now know that I was placed at P.A.M for a specific purpose and if it was getting them to enforce the state legislation on the smoking ban in the workplace, it made the end result worth the sacrifice of losing a job. I must be honest and also admit that the knowledge, wisdom and experiences that I received during my employment there has been very valuable to me both personally and professionally.

My time wasn't wasted at P.A.M because I became a certified HIV/AIDS pre- and post=test counselor, in addition to learning so much about HIV/AIDS and educating myself and others about how to protect themselves from sexually transmitted diseases. It amazes me that after all of the senseless loss that's being experienced in society due to the onset of HIV/AIDS that there are still so many people whom should know better, yet still insist on not protecting themselves during sexual intercourse.

If I had a million dollars for each guy that has tried to convince me to have unprotected sex with them, I would almost be living like Oprah Winfrey. Mind you, I did say almost!

I vividly recall each of those idiots going back to when I'd previously lived in Atlanta. In 1998 where I briefly dated this guy named Isaiah and after several months of dating during what was supposed to have been our first all- the-way intimate experience, he tried to slip the condom off right before penetrating me.

My habit is to always be sober and observant whenever I choose to just make-out or go all the way with a guy. Once I saw that he'd intentionally done something as reckless as that, I called him on his attempted deception that could have put my life in jeopardy.

At first, Isaiah tried convincing me that the condom was too small, although it was a magnum size, and when that lie didn't work, he started professing his undying love for me, so much that he wanted to make love to me raw. No matter how many times he apologized, promising to never try that with me again, the trust factor was gone, thusly and abruptly ending that courtship.

Several years later in California there was Tommy, whom had insisted, and I quote, "I never wear condoms with my lovers."

I could not believe it! My response to him was "no glove, no love, baby," which also concluded that brief affair. Another interesting experience with grown-ass, stupid men who did not want to use a condom during intercourse was several years later in 1994 with this sexy Latino guy named Mynor, whom insisted in his hypnotic, foreign broken accent that his Catholic faith forbade him from using condoms and other contraceptives. Resulting in another one biting the dust!

I cannot fathom the fact that there are still so many people in this day and age who've not developed the tools and skills for being able to successfully negotiate rules and regulations for sexual engagement with others.

During my employment at P.A.M. and as a former member of the church, I regularly visited other church members at the Carl Bean Hospice who were dying from AIDS. The drawn, gaunt, twisted condition they were in was very heartbreaking and prevalent in my mind in regards to my personal dating habits.

Usually after those visits, I reaffirmed the personal vow that I'd made to myself to never forget what I had witnessed on those deathbeds, because my life is more important than satisfying ignorant men so that I can feel so-called love and acceptance by someone whom doesn't show any concern for their own lives.

It was also interesting to me that whenever they tried to persuade me to have unprotected sex with them, they never even inquired about what my status was. Utterly and unbelievably amazing!

Also, I've come across those people in my line of work whose state of mind is that since they're already infected, they don't have to use condoms. Wow! That way of thinking is also ignorant and misinformed because, although you may already be infected with HIV, you might have a weaker strain of the virus that may not cause the onset of AIDS as fast. But if you continue having unprotected sex and possibly re-infecting yourself with more aggressive and deadlier strains, you're risking dying sooner than necessary.

To make things worse, we must not forget those criminals who feel that since they're infected, they're going to take as many people out with them as possible.

Later when I started working at Lexi International, I did not inform any of my current or previous co-workers at my day jobs of what I did during my evenings and I was okay with their assumptions that I was a part-time model and actress in my spare time.

I became a sales representative for one of the largest telemarketing firms in California at that time after this lesbian photographer that I met at Catch One approached me in the middle of the dance floor asking me to shoot some publicity shots in Griffith Park for her photography book.

During the course of the photo shoot the following Sunday afternoon, between poses and set-ups, she told me about this great money-making sales opportunity where she was presently employed, selling long distance services to callers.

After applying and being hired for the position that following week, I believed that I was successful at not spreading personal business concerning my gender identity during the regular office water-cooler gossip and chatter sessions.

But later, this really tall and, yes, fine co-worker of mine named Lewis asked me to go out on a dinner date and movie with him! Since I really did not feel like revealing to him that I was a transsexual (and then having to explain what that entailed), I declined his invitation at first.

I didn't want to possibly put my job in jeopardy if my revelation to him went haywire and all wrong, so I kept putting him off because I knew that he'd probably expected more than just going to dinner.

As time progressed, I pointlessly tried evading Lewis so that I wouldn't be seduced by his charisma and the constant attention he was showering upon me even though his sister also worked with us. Lewis was very persistent in always inquiring about my lunch plans to ensure that we'd be together.

One day during lunch when Lewis and I were sitting in my car sipping on nutritional fruit shakes, he finally wore me down. He looked directly into my eyes and asked, "Why will you not go out with me, Tracee?"

I was trapped and cornered in the car and I could not continue brushing him off, so I replied. "Lewis, I haven't agreed to go out with you because I am a transsexual woman and I do not want my business spread all over the office."

His frank response was, "Tracee, I already know that you are transsexual, everybody in the office knows your business because your photographer friend Lenore already told us everything about you before you started working with us!"

My jaw dropped after his revelation that the whole office knew that I was transsexual, and I was pissed that Lenore had spread my private business without consulting me first to inquire if I wanted others to know my personal business.

Just a quick note to those people like Lenore, if you are not sure what personal information that you may or may not reveal that's private and may be off limits to discuss with others about transsexuals be it at work or not, please ask first because you would not want anyone discussing your personal and confidential business with strangers, would you?

As for Lewis, since the cat was out of the bag, I gave in and went out with him several times, until I found out that he was into some really kinky stuff in bed using pizza cutters and other freaky devices. I really could not get down with that, no matter how fine he was, and who knows who he'd used those sex toys on?

As for my job, thankfully, one of the owners of the company was openly gay in addition to my immediate supervisor, so I did not have any problems in regards to my gender identity and job.

Respect is also due to Lewis, because he was very mature about the whole situation and he was also proud that he was the only guy in the office that I'd ever gone there with!

Actually, during our new recruitment orientation meeting, during a motivational speech given by one of the heterosexual owners, who was not aware of my gender identity, came on to me very strongly in front of a room full of new hires. Can we talk about embarrassing?

Oh, well, I guess my gender identity didn't stop a couple of other guys in the office from unsuccessfully pursuing me for whatever reasons they may have possessed. I didn't go out with those other guys because I was very discerning about who I dated because of my desire to absolutely not become the good-time trans-girl, jumping from one guy to another.

Chapter Nine

Mother Chinue: Spiritual Mother, Rest in Peace

I am blessed to have had guardian angels come into my life along the way that have individually had a positive effect on the person that I currently am! During my escapades in Georgia and then California I've also met some really good people whom have become extended family members and were there for me whenever I could not be with my own family!

There included, but was not limited to the Tysons, the Mudds and Mother Chinue, who are all precious people that the Creator gave to me while I lived in Los Angeles! I distinctively recall the first time meeting another California guardian angel Mother Chinue on a night when I was performing in The World club show at the Beverly Center in California.

That night I recall performing "The Right Stuff" by Vanessa Williams and "The Men All Pause" by Klymaxx, seductively seducing an audience with legendary celebrities such as Brock Peters. There amongst them sat an elegantly dressed, magnetic elderly lady, regally adorned from head to toe in a tailored, vibrant African ensemble.

During my performance, she tipped me with a designer bottle of the most aromatic essential oils, so after the show, I introduced myself, thanking her for the beautiful gift! She then informed me that she'd personally blended the oils for protection and prosperity purposes, which intrigued me even more then concluding our conversation with exchanging phone numbers that night.

Before long, Mother Chinue adopted me as her spiritual daughter, teaching me how to blend aromatherapy oils that I still use to date. She also gifted me my African name, I'mani (pronounced Eye-Mani), which represents faith in Swahili!

I was drawn to her spunkiness and independence. She didn't take any crap from anybody! Before meeting her, I had never personally known an elderly person whom was so comfortable with their sexuality. When we first met, I would never have guessed that she was a lesbian and after her revelation, I was really surprised!

It never occurred to me that she was lesbian, due to her being so elegant and classy, unlike some of the butch lesbians that I'd personally met who were a bit too aggressive and hard-core for me. I guess the fact that she was also a former member of the church that I'd attended should have given me a clue. Oh, well!

She'd left the church right before I joined and one year she returned to participate in one of the reverse role shows, an annual fund-raiser that I'd produced and coordinated for P.A.M, when the men performed as women and the women performed as men.

I really enjoyed spending those years together because she brought a more experienced and wiser perspective to gender identity and expression topics than what I was taught as a child!

During one of our many conversations, Mother Chinue also shared with me about the physically abusive relationship with her husband, which contributed to their divorce. She'd also shared with me that she'd been estranged from her family due to her being lesbian, which explained why she'd adopted other outcast people as her children.

I admired Mother Chinue because she would have given her clothes off her back to someone in need, and she also cared for those who were disowned by their family members just because they were transgender, lesbian, gay or HIV/AIDS infected.

I was inspired by the strength and courage that Mother Chinue displayed in the face of dealing with her personal challenges with melanoma cancer. It was heartbreaking that even though she'd worked for most of her life, paid into the insurance system, she faced unlimited barriers and roadblocks dealing with the insurance companies and the high cost of her prescriptive medications.

Since it was very challenging whenever Mother Chinue became bedridden or was not feeling well enough after chemotherapy, especially during the holidays or her birthdays, I ran errands for her during those tough times, making sure that she had the daily things that she needed.

Several years after meeting Mother Chinue, I was introduced to her estranged son and one of her two daughters. After that introduction, according to Mother Chinue, she never saw any of her children again.

To make things worse, before his disappearing act her son borrowed money from her that he never repaid and he then ceased communicating with her, although he'd claimed he was a deacon at one of the mega-churches on Crenshaw Boulevard.

I was empathetic to the fact that Mother Chinue's biological children had chosen to not have a relationship with their mother, which is unthinkable to me.

Although at that time the relationship between my mother and I had begun to become much stronger than it previously was, discussing my intimate relationships with her was something that I may never feel comfortable enough to do, so I was grateful that I had another mother figure in Mother Chinue with whom I was able to discuss my boyfriends and dating challenges!

I really appreciated that even though Mother Chinue may have seen that my then boyfriend Kedrick was not good for me, she allowed me to see it on my own. I believe that her wisdom and experiences had taught her that if she attempted to intervene in our relationship, I would have most likely rebelled and been drawn to him even more just to prove her wrong.

Once, Mother Chinue and I attended an indigenous Indian sweat lodge ceremony in a teepee. We were required to wear all white, write down our dreams, desires, prayers and hopes for ourselves on paper, and then make a fire offering, burning them in the fire-pit while meditating on those hopes and dreams.

I will never forget that although I identify as female, this was an all biological female ceremony, which caused me to feel a little apprehensive about participating, because I was not born a biological female. During the ceremony, Mother Chinue affectionately took my hands into hers and whispered in my ear, "You belong here. God created you in her image for a specific purpose."

I will always cherish Mother Chinue's words during the sweat lodge ceremony, because intuition must have told her that I needed to hear those exact words at that exact time to elevate my spirit! It occurs to me that it was during those moments in the sweat lodge that I finally stopped feeling inauthentic about whom I was created to be!

After leaving Los Angeles, I continued visiting and helping Mother Chinue whenever we were in town and I spoke with her every Sunday on the phone. Several years after I left California, she informed me that she was scheduled to have surgery to replace her knee that was deteriorating due to cancer,

I was very concerned about whether she was strong enough to endure surgery, considering her fragile physical state. However, I also knew that her independence was very important to her. I'm also sure that the challenges with her knee, which had rendered her disabled in a wheelchair, contributed to the reason that she'd chosen to undergo such a dangerous surgical procedure.

During our regular phone conversations, she'd also reveal to me her concerns about being placed in a hospice after her surgery, so she wanted me to know her wishes for after being released from surgery.

Unfortunately, Mother Chinue also suffered from bipolar disorder, which made some of her decision-making questionable. She was concerned that if she went into surgery, her doctors would send her to a convalescent home afterwards, which in her mind meant that she would die there.

So, after her surgery, Mother Chinue discharged herself from the hospital against the advice of her doctors and went home alone. She seemed to have been recovering from her procedure, but she fell a few times at home, causing her knee to become infected.

I called her daily, checking on how she was recuperating. At one point, I was not able to reach her on the phone no matter how often I called. My concern grew when she did not return any of my phone calls after almost three weeks of trying to contact her.

I knew that she had a caretaker coming in during the day to care for her and I hoped that she would get the messages that I was leaving on Mother Chinue's answering service and return my calls to let me know what was going on.

I left messages that if anyone was receiving her messages, I was concerned for her well-being and I hoped that she would let me know where Mother Chinue was and how she was doing.

When the caregiver finally returned my phone calls after several weeks, I was told that Mother Chinue had been readmitted into the hospital. Because she'd checked herself out after her initial surgery and because the cancer had not been monitored and treated, it had returned with a vengeance. In addition to the infection in her leg, the doctors were not able to bring the cancer back under control.

It still bothers me that Mother Chinue's nightmare became reality when she was admitted into the hospice. The worst part of this story was that the caregiver also informed me that she did not know what facility Mother Chinue was currently in, because her estranged sister did not want any of the people who cared about Mother Chinue to know where she was.

By the time the caregiver finally found out where she was, Mother Chinue had reached a critical point where she was not able to effectively communicate and express her wishes. There were so many people who loved and cared for Mother Chinue who so desperately wanted to be advocates on her behalf to make sure that she was cared for in the manner that she'd previously expressed.

Her selfish sister refused to allow anyone else to assume responsibility for Mother Chinue and, according to one of the social workers at the facility whom I managed to have confidentially spoken with on the telephone, they were continuously asking her sister if she was making inevitable funeral arrangements for Mother Chinue. But apparently the sister had no intentions of making any burial arrangements for her sibling.

Also during another off the record conversation, according to the hospice social worker, once Mother Chinue was admitted into the facility, her sister changed her personal phone number. The authorities eventually had to go to her job and force her to take responsibility for her ill sister, because they were not able to reach any other family members to handle her affairs.

We wanted to make burial arrangements for Mother Chinue, so we all tried our best to convince her sister to add our names to the visitors roster and let us make burial arrangements, but she'd refused to speak with us. I wanted so much to go to Los Angeles to be with Mother Chinue, however, legally I was not allowed to even visit her without the permission of her wicked sister, so I continued calling Mother Chinue on the phone everyday to let her know that I wished that I could be there for her and that I loved her.

During previous conversations with Mother Chinue, her voice was usually a childlike whisper which was challenging to understand. However, during our very last conversation when I told her that I loved her and if I could be there I would be, she seemed to be her old self for a brief moment, clearly replying as she'd always referred to me, "Dear heart, I know that you would be here if you could and I love you, too, I'mani."

Mother Chinue made her transition the following day and, according to the caregiver, after she died, her sister did not care enough to dress her so that she could be seen for the last time by those who loved her.

I found it unthinkable after being informed by the social worker Mother Chinue's sister told the hospice staff to just wash her face and pull the sheet up to her neck.

It was also unbelievable to me that Mother Chinue had all of these beautiful custom-made African outfits, and her sister didn't even have the compassion to choose one of numerous dresses to dress Mother Chinue in. It made my heart ache.

I never wanted to see Mother Chinue in a manner contrary to her elegant and regal nature, so I've instead chosen to remember her as the beautiful, compassionate, feisty, independent angel in heaven whom I met and loved for more than 12 years.

As for her sister, God don't like ugly, so I would hate to see her biological family members, when the time comes, to reap what they've sown. My feeling is that it's not going to be pretty.

I was blessed to have been able to bring some joy into Mother Chinues' life on days that I was off from work and we'd often collect seashells in bare feet in the ocean at Venice and Malibu beaches. And we both loved to meditate in the hidden Virgin and Child garden at the Lake Shrine Fellowship!

Although I am not able to communicate with her in the manner that we used to before her passing, I'm reminded of her whenever the wind ruffles through the trees, and I am comforted with the knowledge of having another angel who's guiding and watching over me from up above!

Rest in peace, Mother Chinue

Love always,

I'mani

Chapter Ten

Another Chapter

My first major earthquake experience in California occurred on January 17, 1993, when the

Northridge Earthquake shook the earth collapsing bridges and devastating communities.

Early that morning, when the shaking woke me from sleeping, I just said a prayer for

protection to God, turned over and went back to sleep.

When I woke up later to start my day, I was unaware of how much real damage had

been done, because all I was thinking about was the fact that I'd received gift certificates

during my birthday party at work for I. Magnin and Saks Fifth Avenue on Rodeo Drive.

I was excited about going shopping for my favorite Opium bath crystals and some

new accessories! However, after turning the television on, the news coverage was on every

channel, documenting the fallen bridges, mass destruction and devastation all over the city.

It bummed me out that instead of going shopping, I celebrated my birthday alone

because during that time, I was off again with an on and off again boyfriend, Kedrick,

whom I first met in the check-out line at Thrifty Drug Store in Culver City after working at

my then current job at RPA Advertising Agency.

Kedrick was a customer service cashier that I'd previously briefly conversed with

during check-out who finally built up the nerve asking me to go out with him! He was not

the usual bodybuilding, athletic type of guy that I was typically attracted to, however, he'd

possessed an endearing smile and comedic sense of humor that drew me in.

Since I wasn't dating anyone and because he'd exposed himself to the possibility of

being rejected in front of the other customers in line after he'd asked me out, I felt that it

would be harmless to go to a movie or dinner with him, so I took his phone number. I

waited three days before calling to schedule our first official date at Aunt Kizzie's Kitchen

in Marina Del Rey.

After sitting for dinner, I continued wondering throughout if he'd known that I was

transsexual upon asking me out. However, I didn't think that a popular soul food eatery

was the appropriate place to be assured that he'd known my gender identification.

Since I had no initial intention of sleeping with him when I'd accepted his invitation to a movie and dinner, that evening I kept the conversation general, disclosing that I worked for a popular advertising agency during the day and I was also a performance artist on weekends.

He disclosed that, in addition to his day job, he was a student working toward a marketing degree. After finishing dinner so that we would not be late for our movie, he paid the check and we gathered our things in preparation to cross the street in anticipation of seeing one of Will Smith's blockbuster movies that year.

But that movie was sold-out, so we ended up seeing "The Last of The Mohicans" with Daniel Day Lewis.

After the movie, we sat in my car talking for hours just getting to know each other and I found out we were both Carolinians. He was from North Carolina and played the keyboard in his free time!

Since I'd felt safe with Kedrick up to that point, I figured that before we went any further with whatever outcome he'd been envisioning for us, those secure moments in my car was the best time to reassure myself that he knew that I was a transsexual woman.

It was very challenging focusing on the conversation as I simultaneously in my head went through the scenarios of how he'd respond, while also calculating the best time to interject and just let him know for sure what was really going on.

I did consider not even telling him since it wasn't my intention to do anything but dinner and a movie, however, he seemed to be a nice, motivated guy that I wanted to possibly get to know. He gave me a perfect opportunity to ease into the revelation after he further inquired about my night job!

The floodgates opened after I explained that weekends and sometimes during the week I moonlighted at night performing on stage as my alter ego Destiny (Your Mistress of Illusions) in local clubs! I noticed a puzzled look in his eyes but, he chose not to ask me to clarify what kind of performing I did, probably thinking that I was a stripper or something like that.

Experience had taught me that in situations like this, where I knew that a heterosexual guy was attracted to me on a date, honesty was the best policy if I'm also attracted to him, and as long as I feel safe, number one.

Kedrick didn't seem threatening to me and I l was attracted to his down-to-earth personality, so I told him that I was a transsexual woman. After explaining what a pre-operative transsexual was for several more hours, it was obvious to me that he was still really attracted and turned on by me, regardless of what I had just revealed to him!

Although he did his best to contain the surprising level of attraction, he was uniquely challenged with concealing his uncontrollable level of excitement when we hugged at the end of the date, which concluded with him asking me out again!

I was planning to purchase a ticket to see Sade in concert at Universal City Studios, so I thought it would be a nice gesture to buy him one, too, for our second date. It was an interesting evening since people who'd seen my stage shows came up and spoke!

For our third official date, Kedrick insisted on preparing dinner for me at his place and when I walked into the apartment the mood was set with Michael Franks, Will Downing, Patti Austin, Najee and Babyface softly playing on rotation in the background, setting a romantic ambiance!

I had decided to wear a black, sheer lace jump suit and black thigh-high, leather five-inch boots to satisfy Kedrick's curiosity about the kinds of costumes that I performed in on stage!

When he removed my trench coat, he was obviously once again turned on by what I was wearing! He managed to remain composed during dinner, expressing to me that he still really was attracted to me and that he was not convinced that I was anything other than a biological female.

After dinner he proceeded to inform me that he'd always seen transsexuals on television, but he's never seen anyone like me! He seemed slightly entranced as he continued telling me that he didn't want to be insulting, but asked if I would remove my clothes and show him that I was telling the truth, because in his opinion he really didn't believe that someone as beautiful as I was could have been born a male.

I've seen this move before starring guys who have never been intimate with a transsexual and they want you to become their first experience, which may be pleasant for them or it could end really ugly. Some guys really are not able to deal with being torn about their uncontrollable attraction to transsexual women, so they may act violently due to their associated guilt that they feel after the fact.

No matter how comfortable you are with a guy, you're never sure of what direction the experience may go until it happens, so I've resisted being intimate with guys that have never been with someone like me before.

It's personally not worth potentially being in a life threatening altercation with someone who's confused about their feelings. Who needs the unnecessary violence? Also, I don't want to be used by guys to fulfill and satisfy the sexual fantasies they may have about transsexuals.

However, I was physically attracted to Kedrick and since I also felt safe with him, I agreed to take my clothes off on one condition, which was that he had to remove his clothes also. He enthusiastically agreed, so we seductively proceeded undressing each other as the smooth jazz played in the background.

I was pleasantly surprised that the experience with him was different, because there wasn't the usual awkwardness of being with a rookie and it did not seem to me that this was his first intimate experience with a transsexual. He also surprisingly seemed comfortable and engaged in the experience from beginning to the conclusion!

Afterwards, he didn't start tripping out, expressing guilt and regret about being intimate with me so we continued dating, switching nights at each other's apartments! During lunch at the pier one afternoon I was caught off guard when he told me he was experiencing some financial challenges and that he'd probably have to drop out of school and move back to North Carolina.

I was contently living alone several blocks away from Venice Beach off Venice Boulevard in Culver City, near Abbott Kinney and loving being able to walk up the street west several blocks to the beach! If I may digress slightly, one thing I really miss about not living on the West Coast is not being able to go to the ocean.

Even though I liked the idea of dating a guy with his own apartment, I didn't want to see Kedrick drop out of school after seeing how much time he'd committed since we'd first started dating. I figured I would be helpful to him by inviting him to move in with me, sharing the rent and other expenses in order for him to continue his education.

I guess I was still somewhat naïve and gullible back then, because it never occurred to me at the time he moved in with me that he had been planning his move the entire three months that we'd dated.

Anyway, after almost three years together, I realized that Kedrick was aspiring to be a womanizing player like his best friend, Robert, who was married and cheating on his wife with multiple women.

I was introduced to Robert after arriving home from work one afternoon as he was leaving our apartment from visiting with Kedrick. I must admit that even though our introduction was brief, I did observe that he was a very handsome man.

Kedrick and Robert were mutual friends with this lady called The Duchess who managed her sons' aspiring rap group and other hopeful artists in search of a recording contract. After being introduced to The Duchess and her business partner Vernon, they hired me to coordinate and supervise the musical acts appearing in their weekly showcases.

Several weeks after I started working with their production company, Kedrick warned me that Robert was going to be at an upcoming showcase, cautioning that Robert loved pretty women and that he'd previously commented to Kedrick about how attractive he thought I was.

After our introduction, I noticed that Kedrick made extra effort to make sure that Robert and I never met again up to that point, but he had no control over his friend attending one of their other friend's showcases.

On the night of the show, before leaving the apartment, Kedrick joked to me. "Tracee, you should know that Robert is going to try to come on to you even though he knows that we're together. Most girls cannot resist him, so don't fall for his charms, Tracee."

After putting on a sparkly black and silver jacket just before exiting the apartment, I reassured Kedrick, "You should know well enough by now that I am not interested in married men, Kedrick."

When I arrived at the venue, I wasn't sure if Robert recognized me from our previous introduction, but if he did he didn't care that I was in a relationship and living with his friend, because after the show he immediately started overtly flirting with me as Kedrick had predicted.

He waited around after the showcase and then offered to walk me to my car and when he saw the car that I was driving he stated, "My homeboy was recently driving that car. Are you the Tracee who is dating Kedrick Pippins?"

I replied playing along, "Yes, I am the Tracee who's dating your friend Kedrick,

Robert."

Wow, you look a whole lot different than when we first met!"He replied.

Okay, he really expected me to believe that he didn't know who I was, so I continued playing along, responding and unlocking the car door at the same time. "Well, we only met briefly, speaking to each other that afternoon, and I do look quite different during the day after work as compared to a social evening event like this one tonight."

Also as Kedrick predicted, Robert proceeded boldly laying on the charms even though there wasn't any doubt that I was dating his friend. "You have the most beautiful eyes that I've ever seen, Tracee. I sure would like to look into them while making love to you!"

I was not falling for his swagger and undeniable attractiveness. There was absolutely no way that I would ever consider going there with him, so I replied, "Thank you for the compliment, Robert, but there is no way that you and I would ever be in that position with each other."

After helping with my car door and once I'd gotten settled in, Robert leaned over, sticking his head inside the window, attempting to kiss me on my lips. I quickly pulled away from him, asking, "How would your wife feel about you trying to kiss up on another woman, Robert?"

He nonchalantly replied, removing his head from inside of the car, "I won't tell my wife or Kedrick if you don't, nor will what they don't know hurt them."

"Well, I'm in a relationship with your friend Kedrick and I'd feel really guilty about cheating on him with you, so let us just not even go there, Robert."I then started the car engine to leave after turning off the inside light, which I could not find the switch to operate it since my car was in the shop being serviced. I wasn't very familiar with the rental that was provided, so I twisted and pushed in every knob or switch in sight trying to turn that damn light off, but nothing worked. Robert opened the door, leaning inside the car attempting to help find the switch that operated the light, but he was not able to find the light control mechanism either and after becoming really aggravated I interjected, "I'll just have to drive home with the light on."

Are you sure?" He asked.

At that point it was late that following morning after the showcase concluded, and I was frustrated beyond measure and ready to go home, so I replied before driving off with frost on the windows. "We've both unsuccessfully tried to find the switch to turn it off, it's getting late and I have an early day at work this morning. I should be okay. Thank you, though, for helping me!"

When I arrived at our apartment, I immediately informed Kedrick about what occurred with his supposedly best friend, Robert. He laughed, replying, "I told you, Tracee, he was going to try to push up on you!"

Smiling, he continued, obviously surprised that I did not swoon all over his friend taking a bite off the bait," I honestly didn't think you were going to be able to resist him, Tracee, he always gets the girls that he goes after!"

I confidently replied, "Kedrick, yes Robert is cute, but you should know by now that I've never been interested in married or committed men."

After almost the third year of dating, Kedrick informed me one day out of the blue that he needed to return to his home state North Carolina for six months to establish a relationship with his son. Although his revelation caught me by surprise because he'd never once previously ever mentioned that he was considering moving back to his home for any purpose after we'd moved in together, I never tried dissuading him from doing what he needed to do as far as his son was concerned. I supported his decision while also suspecting that there was something more to his trip.

Pondering back to that time, Kedrick was very secretive leading up to revealing that he was going back to North Carolina. I had also become suspicious about his intentions towards me when he would not allow his mother's request to visit us in California for Christmas, even though she knew about our relationship due to us previously speaking by phone several times.

During that time, I was also concerned and resentful that he felt that I was good enough to play house with, but refused to allow his mother and I to meet each other in person. Once I became hip to his game (no longer being the complete naïve person that I used to be), there was no way that I intended to tolerate being a fool for a man that perpetrated to care for me, but was ashamed of me.

So, I decided that on the evening that I drove Kedrick to the airport for his departure flight to North Carolina that I would suggest that we bid our final good-byes at that point.

That suggestion caused us to get into an argument about something else that didn't have anything to do with what I was really feeling about him suddenly being gone for six months.

In my mind, I thought that I would not see him again, feeling that our relationship was once and for all concluding, because I did not want to become anymore emotionally involved with him than I already was.

However, Kedrick and I stayed in contact with each other by phone during the time that he was gone and he promised me that he would fly back to Los Angeles to spend Thanksgiving with me.

When Kedrick did not return to California for Thanksgiving as promised, I inquired why he'd chosen to tell me that he was coming back to California when he very well knew that he had no intentions of following through with his commitments. Believe it or not, his explanation was he didn't want to hurt me by telling me that he was not going to be able to return for Thanksgiving.

My emphatic response was, "You know what, Kedrick, I would rather that you had told me the truth than to have purposefully lied to me." I was infuriated that he pretended to be so clueless about what he was doing in his nonchalant response, so I furiously continued, "How do you think I felt that you are once again being an inconsiderate, selfish liar?"

Continuing, intentionally not letting him off the hook, I said, "I spent unnecessary money purchasing groceries to prepare a special dinner for the two of us so if you had been considerate enough to have told me the truth, I could have saved some money and spent Thanksgiving with my friends."

As you're aware by now, I was not at all happy that Kedrick felt that he was protecting me by telling a blatant outright lie and, most of all, I felt that he was trying to insult my intelligence, which made me not trust anything else that he told me.

After that conversation, I took everything he said with a grain of salt. He returned to Los Angeles almost six months later, asking if he and his son could move in with me until he was able to find their own apartment.

I didn't see anything wrong with letting them stay with me as long as he paid their way, so I allowed them to move in with me and things were very different between Kedrick and I due to him sleeping on the couch with his son. I slept in my bedroom alone.

Although there was no intimacy between us during that time, I babysat his son during the days that I wasn't working, while he worked. He was a little bratty spoiled 6-year-old that thought he did not have to listen to me whenever he did something he wasn't supposed to be doing.

I never expected when I told him to stop misbehaving that he'd respond by stating that his daddy said that I was not his mother and he did not have to listen to me. I explained to him that I never suggested I was his mother and as long as he was in my care during his father's absence, he had no choice but to obey my rules.

Later that evening, I asked Kedrick if he told his son that he did not have to listen to me whenever he was in my care. He said that his son's mother would be really upset if he told her that another woman was telling him what to do. I reminded Kedrick that they were living in my apartment and that if the mother had a problem with her child listening to another adult that was charged with caring for him in his father's absence, then maybe he needed to find another place for he and his son to live.

I was not going to let some child and his mother who was thousands of miles away dictate what went on in my household. I would have never put my hands on their child, but if he was acting out the way that little Damien "Omen" child behaved and his father was telling him that he did not have to listen to me, they both had to go.

Also, it occurred to me that Kedrick was perpetrating a fraud, testing the limits to see how far I would let him go. I was finished being taken for granted and used by him.

A few weeks later Kedrick made other living arrangements and chose to wait until I wasn't at home to move their things out of my apartment. When I returned home from work that evening, I discovered that the locked box where I kept my journals were gone.

I felt that he'd taken my journals and diaries to spite me, because he was the only other person who knew where I kept them. The violating and disgusting effects of him stealing my diaries caused me to stop journaling for several years because I was hurt that he'd taken something that was so personal to me.

I figured that he might have taken my journals because he wanted to know what I was doing while he was away, but there wasn't anything out of the ordinary written in my journals. I'm not that stupid.

It wasn't because I felt some sort of commitment to Kedrick while he was gone, because I had no idea what he was doing or with whom he was doing it while he was away for the six months in North Carolina.

After the finality of the relationship with Kedrick, I really wasn't as prepared as I thought for dealing with the disappointing emotions following the final separation from him after spending almost three years together.

I imagine that not being human without a heart would have been the only way to justify not feeling something over the dissolution of a relationship, however unexpected those feelings were. I managed to resiliently move forward from those sentiments once I realized that Kedrick did not have my best interests at heart and that he just was not the man that I was destined to be with.

Immediately upon closing that chapter, my friend Diva told me about this guy named Patrik Whitbeck, also known in the fashion design industry as "Shooting Star," who was producing an all-celebrity impersonation exclusive event at the El Rey Theater on Wilshire Boulevard.

Diva suggested that I meet Shooting Star to be in his show, scheduled for December 10, 1995. I could not have predicted that on this date someone else would enter my life who would contribute immensely to my successes and entertainment career.

I met Patrik "Shooting Star" for the first time the night of the show in the dressing room. I performed an extended mega-mix version of "Love Hangover" by Miss Ross in his sold-out showcase along with Diva also bringing the house down with her spot- on Madonna performance!

When Shooting Star and I were being introduced to each other, there was an instant creative and spiritual connection. It seemed we were destined to join forces to create some of the most magical and amazing moments on stage, moments that I will always cherish!

Patrik eventually became my personal manager, and his original costume designs were incorporated into my shows. They really helped me elevate my stage performances to a whole new level! In addition to being a producer extraordinaire during those years, Patrik was also a costume and design illustrator for the legendary Bob Mackie!

Mr. Mackie, whom we all know as the ultimate designer to Diana Ross, Cher, Tina Turner and many other Hollywood icons, showed his support to Patrik and I by allowing us to borrow costumes from his Elizabeth Courtney Costumes collection for special

engagements and personal appearances.

Chapter Eleven

1996 – The Year that Transformed My Life

Several months or so after resolving my feelings around being single again, I was directing all of my attention and energies on career advancement opportunities! I continued working part-time at the Advertising Agency during the day and continued entertaining in the clubs on the weekends.

A couple months after Patrik and I started our whirlwind collaboration, I received a phone call from him. He mysteriously said, "Destiny, darling, you will never guess what I have to tell you."

"What, Patrik?"

"Are you sitting down?"

The joy and excitement in his voice informed me that he was calling with a major proposal so I could only keep responding as he continued torturing me, "What is it, Patrik?!"

He finally replied, "I scheduled you an appointment to audition tomorrow afternoon with veteran music video producer Marty Callner to be a back-up singer in the new Diana Ross music video "I Will Survive," which is being used to promote her latest album!"

I could not believe it! All I could do was scream really loudly, asking, "Are you serious, Patrik?"

"Honey, I am serious!"

After grabbing my appointment calendar from my purse, I asked, "What is the place and time of the audition, Patrik?

After confirming that I'd pick Patrik up so that we'd arrive together at the audition at least 30 minutes early, I hung up and collapsed on the couch in gratitude!

As I relaxed there for several minutes, I felt that in a way this opportunity was what I really needed to celebrate my new-found freedom! I was overjoyed with overwhelming excitement about the possibilities of meeting Miss Diana Ross and working on one of her videos! You talk about a dream coming to fruition right before my eyes! T.U.M.F.G.U.!

Patrik and I arrived at the casting office early on the day of my audition and I performed an "I'm Coming Out/Aint No Mountain High Enough" medley! According to Patrik, I was booked on the spot to appear in the video because the camera guy did not want to stop filming due to being mesmerized by my performance!

Soon after my audition, the most surreal moment for me up to that point occurred on January 17, 1996, three days before my 30th Birthday. It was then that it hit me at my core: I had just spent hours filming a high-profile music video with a living legend that I have been inspired by since starting to impersonate her many years ago at "La Cage Aux Folles" Beverly Hills!

I believed it when Patrik informed me that it was a very rare occasion for Miss Ross to use impersonators in her shows and videos. If I'm not mistaken, she has not used impersonators since the "I Will Survive" video.

I really did not comprehend the historical relevance of being chosen to have participated in such a monumental event and not to mention the positive affect that the experience has had on my professional career at the time!

The morning after my audition at the studio in Hollywood after reconfirming my set call time for the video shoot with Patrik, I recall from that time forward consciously savoring every single minute of the experience!

It began with packing almost three weeks before the production after repairing my best silver sequined gown, which was hand-sewn for me by Crystal. I accessorized the ensemble with a pair of silver Frederick's of Hollywood pumps and polished rhinestone jewelry most likely purchased at one of costume jewelry places on Hollywood Boulevard.

On the day of the most amazing music video shoot that I've experienced to date, I didn't want to take any chances of getting stuck in the unpredictably crazy Los Angeles traffic driving from West LA to West Hollywood or whatever other unforeseen event that might cause me to be late for my call time.

So, I arrived on set almost three hours before my scheduled time, claiming a prime corner spot in the dressing trailer that the back-up performers were assigned. After checking in with the production assistant, I had plenty of time before rehearsals to take a stroll on a little side street that I was familiar with by the club Rage to "Climb a Tree" for a little energy boost! Later that day, after Patrik joined me on the set, I was selected by one of the video producers and video director Marty Callner to stand-in for Miss Ross at dress rehearsal for the video opening scene. It was such an honor and privilege to have been chosen to rehearse her scenes!

Later that evening the energy was extremely elevated almost beyond the stratosphere on Santa Monica Boulevard as we launched into "A Night of A Thousand Dianas"! A portion of the longest street in the entire city was closed off to traffic due to it being filled with thousands of admiring Diana Ross fans rivaling the West Hollywood annual Halloween celebrations and parades!

The fans were patiently anticipating her appearance onto the float and erupted into loud applause when the four features lined up to be ushered onto the float by our choreographer for last minute rehearsals. But before we were allowed on the float, M. David, a self-proclaimed ultimate Diana Ross look-a-like was informed by the production assistant that Miss Ross did not promote wearing fur, so he was not allowed to take a huge fox tails stole onto the set.

Shortly after that brief delay and rehearsals, when Miss Ross finally made her royal appearance on the float to join us, the crowd erupted into ear-piercing applause and cheers! The paparazzi were yelling for pictures with the back-up performers and Miss Ross, so we all clamored to stand next to her!

Once again, I was in the right place at the right time, taking advantage of an opening and not wasting any time getting a prime spot right next to Miss Ross for photos! Simply amazing!

I'd previously met RuPaul when we were initially introduced by Diva and photographed together in the dressing room a couple weeks after I first joined the cast at Peanuts upon my arrival to California, so it was an honor to have received another opportunity to work with him for the first time on such a massive level.

Once RuPaul made his appearance on the float several minutes after Miss Ross, the crowd continued cheering loudly. Since the energy level from all of those Diana Ross fans was so electrifyingly energizing the whole night, it didn't matter that we'd spent hours upon hours shooting and reshooting the video!

We shared intimate moments during the breaks in filming for resets, all sitting at the top of the float next to Miss Ross massaging each other's feet! I felt privileged to have helped glue her false nail back on and later unexpectedly having Miss Ross grab and pull me forward to the front saying, "Pose, girl!"

I was so taken off guard and entranced by her grabbing my hand, I was not able to pose due to almost being frozen by what she'd just unexpectedly done to me of all people. However, I made up for it later with a memorable pose after I ascended up the stairs toward the huge martini glass on the float.

Later, Miss Ross unbelievably spontaneously dove off the float into the awaiting arms of her adoring mega-fans causing most people to think that the stage-dive was staged! Some refuse to believe that she really dove off the float into the audience, but I am here to testify that it was not staged and she actually leaped off the float into the crowd twice, being caught and held up by her surprised fans both times!

Miss Ross also had a very observant and vigilant personal security person who made sure she was safe at all times during the entire filming until after 3 that following morning. When I think back to being Featured in a Diana Ross music video with another diva sister, RuPaul, all I can do is be thankful and filled with extreme gratitude for a once-in-a-lifetime experience that I never imagined would happen to me. Another precious gift and blessing!

During those exciting times, I had been single for almost seven months or more, and because I would often just go home, staying in after work, I started realizing that I needed to change my routine just a little.

I had no idea that on August 19, 1996, I would once again meet the man of my dreams almost five years after being introduced to him.

I was scheduled to perform a birthday guest of honor special request, "I Want Your Love" by Jody Watley and "Smooth Operator" by Sade, one evening at Catch One.

After the performance, I wasn't ready to go home, so I settled on going to Peanuts to catch their show! As I walked into the club a showgirl acquaintance of mine named Linda, who regularly booked me for her show at Robbie's club in Pomona, was performing "Candy Man" by the Mary Jane Girls.

After tipping her and then standing on the side with the rest of the audience watching her performance, I noticed this guy across the room making his way to stand next to me and attempting to get my attention with a stupid pick up line: "Can I be your Candy

Man?"

Talk about a total lame turn off, so I gave him a no, thank you, smile and immediately refocused on the show. Once Linda finished her number and the other performances concluded, I politely excused myself to go say hello to my friends.

I was side-tracked as I entered the billiards room heading towards the dressing room to say hello to Diva and the other girls that were in the show. I became intrigued by this very attractive guy sitting alone on a banquette with his head held down and rubbing his eyes, looking quite bored!

I have never been one to approach guys first no matter how attractive they are, but I was uncontrollably being drawn to this person like a moth to a flame and I was determined to at least meet him.

So I discretely and slowly moved in to get a closer look, becoming impressed that he was not cruising from one girl to another like the other guys who were hanging out near the dressing room door with hopes of picking up a showgirl, which is another turn off to me.

Since I didn't want to be obvious that he was on my radar, I played it cool, sitting on the other end of the banquette next to him, nervously commenting. "You look rather bored."

He stopped rubbing his eyes and seemed to perk up a little bit, replying, "I was bored and just about to leave the club, that is until you arrived. I'm not bored anymore!"

"I've got to admit that I was just going into the dressing room to speak to my friends before going home."

He quickly replied, "You don't have to go anywhere now. We can keep each other company!"

Tevin and I talked for an hour or so that night, and I broke all of my personal dating rules. I'd never approached a random guy in Peanuts or anywhere else. Proceeding to strike up a conversation was the second taboo broken, and then eventually inviting him back to my apartment after we ran out of small talk in the club. "The music is really loud," I said. "Would you like to go somewhere so that we can hear each other speak and continue our conversation?"

He excitedly replied! "Sure!"

Another rule breached.

Later that morning, I spotted the guy that previously offered to be my Candy Man watching us with a disapproving look on his face as Tevin and I passed him, exiting the club. Once across the street to where we were both parked, I remembered that I was out of bottled water so I said, "I just have to go into 7-Eleven to pick up a couple things; would you care for anything?"

"No, thank you," He replied. I don't recall if he went inside with me or not. All I remember is after purchasing the water, we got into our cars that were both parked on the street next to 7-Eleven and then he followed in his car to West Los Angeles to my apartment.

When we arrived, as we were walking through the apartment gate, I asked, "Did you see that guy following us from the club?"

"I saw him when he pulled behind us leaving Peanuts. Are you sure that you're not being stalked by a crazy boyfriend with a rifle or something?" He jokingly inquired.

Replying reassuringly, "No, no stalker boyfriend, but it's not unusual for guys to try following me home from the club and I've even had to drive through yellow lights right before it changed to red to lose them whenever I noticed that I'm being followed. I've also resorted to keeping pepper spray in my car and costume bag just in case!"

After inviting him in and placing my costume bag in the closet next to the front entrance, I made hot tea and we sat in my living room talking for what seemed like hours! During our conversation I shared my background with him and I learned that he was originally from Chicago and his family of three other brothers and one sister moved to California with their parents when he was a teenager in order to get away from the gangs and violence there.

Tevin also revealed to me during our engaging conversation, "I noticed how beautiful you were when you first walked into the club, looking so exotic in black hair, dressed all in black, looking sexy with those green eyes reflecting across the room like a dream when I looked up and watched you almost glide on air toward me followed by your entourage!"

I replied, not wanting to brag about appearing in a Diana Ross music video, "I've never had an entourage always traveling with me. I was alone upon arriving at the club that night and those other girls were just fans saying hello and congratulating me on a recent performance!"

Tevin replied, "Upon looking up and seeing your face, I thought that there was no way I would get to meet such a beautiful person like you, but I was determined to try, so when you sat next to me, I knew that you weren't getting away before talking with you to at least get your name."

I blushed at his compliment, replying, "Really!"

He continued, confessing, "I was really nervous when you sat next to me and I didn't want to say anything stupid or offensive that would have scared you away!"

In response to his concerns I replied, "Well, Tevin, I must say that you were cool, calm, collected and, to your credit, you didn't say anything offensive to turn me off, which is one of the reasons that I'd felt comfortable enough inviting you back here with me which is something that I usually never do!"

I continued, "To be quite honest, when I first saw you, I thought that you were so fine and hot, I just knew I would also have to at least say hello to inquire if you were a jerk or not!"

Almost two and a half hours into our conversation he revealed, "I cannot get over how beautiful you really are and I must confess that while we were in the club talking, I was really turned on by your sexy hands!"

I held my hands out in front, inspecting them while asking, "What turns you on about my hands?"

He gently took my hands into his replying, "They're so elegantly shaped and complimented by your sexy red nails!"

I replied, unzipping my boots, "Thank you, but I really don't feel so sexy right now because these boots are giving my feet the blues."

"I give great foot massages, if you are interested?"

"Sure, that sounds great!" I replied, hoping that my feet didn't stink and only after rubbing both feet with my hand to be sure that there wasn't any foul odor coming from them did I allow him to gently place them both on his lap and he started to tenderly massage my aching feet.

As he caressed my achy feet, I suddenly came to the realization that he was the person from all those years ago whom was so attracted to me and insisted that a mutual acquaintance named Amber introduce us after one of my earlier Peanuts performances!

Of course during that previous introduction, Amber made it seem to him like she and I were best friends forever when he inquired about who I was. Recalling that introduction, I said, "I remember you from that first encounter thinking you were very attractive then!"

I continued before he responded, "I recall telling you all of my business during that brief conversation, revealing although I'd been going through personal challenging times, I was still in the relationship with my former boyfriend with there being no way that I was going to go any further than just meeting you that night."

Tevin responded, surprised that I'd remembered him, "I often thought and fantasized about you after we met that night and I regularly went back to Peanuts when I was off from work hoping that you would be there!"

After several more hours of talking about our initial introduction, the sexual tension and energy between the two of us had reached the boiling point! I didn't see a ring on his finger and feeling that we were both single, consenting adults I excused myself to shower off the sweat and makeup from that night's earlier performance at Catch One.

After showering, I walked out of the bathroom wearing a silk lavender robe and proceeding to take him by both hands, pulling him up from the couch and seductively escorting him into my bedroom without saying a word!

After lighting an aromatherapy candle on the dresser, he swept me up in his arms, pressing his masculine, muscular body against mine with just the right amount of pressure, ensuring that I felt his rapidly beating heart!

It was as if he was looking right through, me gazing into my soul as I pulled his polo shirt over his head and began to gently caress the hairs on his chiseled chest! We continued passionately kissing as he gently laid me across the bed before removing my robe, which resulted in the mattress from my bed being displaced onto the bedroom floor!

We were awakened by the bright sunrays peeking through the sides of the blinds and curtains later that afternoon! After Tevin finished getting dressed, preparing to leave, he helped replace the mattress on the bed, informing me, "I'm flying to Arizona tomorrow to visit my family for about a week. If you write down your phone number, I will call you when I return."

Although I really didn't expect to ever see him again, I gave him my phone number anyway, walked him to the door and after bidding our farewells, I went back to bed for some more sleep.

Later that afternoon when I awoke feeling that there was something special about him beyond just the lust and physical attraction.

The thought that I had brought back home one of the perverts from Peanuts was the last thing on my mind due to us being grown adults practicing safer sex during our night of no strings attached passion!

However, between each call at my desk during work the rest of the week following our rendezvous, I found myself hoping that he was not one of those guys with a girlfriend or wife who secretly patronized Peanuts to fulfill their sexual fantasies of spending a night with a transsexual whenever their significant others were out of town or whatever.

When Tevin contacted me after he returned from Phoenix, we spent as much time with each other as our work schedules permitted and on some rare memorable occasions, we shared numerous precious evenings talking and getting to know each other until the sun rose the following morning!

Recently, whenever he and I discuss guys taking advantage of girls on the first date, he often brags and teases that he was able to take me to bed on our first night together. However, I beg to differ, because I recall picking him up from the club, then luring him to my lair and proceeding to take advantage of him! Talk about stepping outside of your box, I did and am beyond happy that I did so!

During that exciting new chapter in my life, my personal appearances and performance schedule was in full force! I didn't think that it would get any better but almost seven months later on August 27, 1996, I was featured in a Shooting Star Production, "Ultra Lounge Revue," performing a song from Diana Ross and The Supremes' unreleased album "Boy From Ipanema"!

Believe it or not, a Latina Miss Coco and a white girl name Nina Manhattan rounded out our Supremes trio! It was very interesting pulling that one off and, as usual, I had a fantastic time! Soon to follow was another featured role in the second Patrik Shooting Star Extravaganza "Candy Girls a Go-Go!"

The fantastic bookings continued. On October 22, 1996, Patrik Shooting Star revealed a strong desire to potentially take my stage show to another level, concluding that a great way to challenge and test my abilities would be to produce my very first solo engagement, entitled "Call Her Miss Ross"!

My first solo show was scheduled to premiere at the Love Lounge in West Hollywood. We mixed and recorded my song selections on Shooting Stars' home stereo, chronicling Diana Ross' distinguished career, beginning with the Supremes, throughout her films "Lady Sings the Blues" and "Mahogany," up to her current solo career.

During the planning process, I had no idea that the show would be a great success, filling every seat in the house with others packed shoulder to shoulder in the overflow areas! "Call Her Miss Ross" was a highly anticipated engagement promoted to be the break-out performance specifically designed to showcase my talents as an entertainer and performance artist!

I was both nervous and excited about the show, working really hard to create something that was both memorable and entertaining! During the process, Shooting Star and I had daily conference calls whenever I was on tour, which consisted of finalizing music arrangements, costumes and estimating the amount of time necessary for four costume changes, and group productions.

Once when I was on a break between shows at the Palm Springs, California, Riviera Resort, while unwinding in my suite, the telephone rang on time for one of our regularly scheduled conversations!

Upon hearing Patrik's voice on the other end, I'd suspected by his mysterious tone that he was calling with some exciting news.

"Destiny Dear, I have got a big surprise for you to wear for your "I'm Coming Out" opening number!"

Since he was sounding very coyly, I knew that whatever it was, it was going to be fantastic, so all I could do was respond excitedly, "What is it, Patrik?!"

Patrik proceeded, informing me, "Well, Bob saw your photocopies that I was making on my desk at work today and he has offered to let us borrow a white, full-length ostrich feather, Swarovski jewel-encrusted coat that's perfect to wear for your opening number!"

"Are you serious, Patrik?"

"Yes, and guess what else, honey?"

"What, Patrik?"

"It's rumored that Miss Ross may have worn this coat some years ago in a photo shoot!"

"Wow, that is beyond amazing, Patrik!" I replied.

He inquired, "How do you like the new Billie Holiday mix?"

"I love it, it's absolutely perfect and I am going to put it in the second half of the Riviera show tonight to test it out on the audience!"

"Good, honey, I'm glad you like it. When will you be back in town?" He inquired.

"I'll be back on Monday afternoon and I will stop by your place later that evening when you get off work to try on that ostrich coat!"

"Okay, break a leg tonight, drive safely and I will see you on Monday to show you this fabulous coat. Honey, you are going to love this!" He chuckled.

"I cannot wait, see you on Monday, thank you for everything, honey!" I replied before hanging up the phone. Later that evening I performed my new Diana Ross "Lady Sings the Blues" medley on a show, also featuring a live Temptations Revue and a dead-on young and sexier Elvis Presley impersonator.

We concluded the show and then in addition to posing on stage, we also all posed for pictures on the Riviera grand stairs. That following Monday morning, after checking out of the suite and on my drive back from Palm Springs, my energy level was really low and I was not feeling quite right, which contributed to me stopping more frequently than usual to use the restroom.

Soon I was deep into the reality of how much work was required. I had to rehearse with my back-up performers and have final costume fittings, all while traveling to Palm Springs almost every other weekend for the entire month to appear as Diana Ross at the Riviera Resort, and keeping up with my local performances. It all seemed to weigh me down during the drive back to Los Angeles.

Ever since I'd first left home when I was a teenager, I'd been accustomed to working two or sometimes three jobs at a time to make ends meet, so I didn't think twice about scheduling a back-to-back travel schedule such as the one that I had during that time.

I had no idea that my schedule would contribute to me being admitted into Cedar Sinai Hospital for food poisoning and dehydration two weeks before "Call Her Miss Ross" was to premiere.

As I lay there in the hospital bed receiving intravenous rehydration medication, I was afraid that we'd probably have to postpone the show if I was not physically well enough to complete rehearsals and costume fittings. The fact also weighed on me that I did not want to let Patrik, Miss Kiwi, Miss Alana and everyone else who was involved with the show down.

During my time at Cedar Sinai Hospital, I became even more determined to not cancel my show. Therefore I spent those two days resting and still diligently practicing my mixes on the Walkman cassette player that Tevin brought to the hospital during one of his visits.

Incidentally, the photo that we used for marketing the event was taken in my dining room on a sunny, beautiful Sunday morning by Shooting Star a day or so after I was released from the hospital.

The night of "Call Her Miss Ross" brought out all of my extended family and friends living in Los Angeles to show their support! I especially wanted Tevin to be there to dedicate "The Man I Love" medley to him from the Billie Holiday segment in the show!

Although I tried resisting it, I had fallen head over heels for Tevin by then! He went into work later that evening in order to be there to support me on my special night. As for the show, we'd previously watched any and all VHS video copies of Diana Ross and the Supremes and choreographed our steps either in my living or on the outside deck.

Since we had the serious first portion of the routine down pat, Patrik and I thought that we'd make the "Some Day Well Be Together" song concluding the Supremes segment a comedy instead of being so serious.

I used my huge Chiffon Duster to block Miss Kiwi and Miss Alana signifying that I was the only star moving on to a higher level. The audience loved it when Miss Alana had to be restrained by Miss Kiwi after taking off a pump gesturing to beat me down with it!

It was so much fun being able to incorporate comedy into our show and then using some of the girls from the audience that were recruited by Patrik to join me on stage during the "I Will Survive" finale in their extreme costumes, hair and makeup!

After the show, Patrik and I discussed our favorite moments of the night over eggs and pancakes, with his being the opening, Supremes and finale and my favorites being the opening, Billie Holiday and Supremes segments!

We were later joined by others in attendance, wanting to celebrate with us at our after party in Jerry's Deli, where we were seated one table over from where former Los Angeles Lakers player Shaquille O'Neal and his crew sat.

Although there were a couple of comments made by some of Shaq's entourage when the other girls twirled in to join us at our table, for the most part the after party went smoothly and without incident.

My memory is that "Call Her Miss Ross" was an electrifying, sold-out, exclusive engagement! However, by the end of the "I Will Survive" finale and the after party, I was physically drained and required a couple of days to fully recover and come down from the natural high.

After a full recovery, I continued working nonstop and on November 2, 1996, Diva, Miss Alana, Miss Kiwi, Mama, Patrik and I were chauffeured by a hired limousine driver to Palm Springs for an exclusive milestone birthday celebration!

Our road tour Palm Springs hosts was this really rich gay couple that invited an elite audience of family and friends from various parts of the world to celebrate their special occasion under the stars. The celebrations took place in their beautiful, plush, backyard, where we felt like real stars performing on a specially built stage under a star-filled, breezy Palm Springs evening.

It had been arranged that I'd be dropped off home first upon our return from Palm Springs later that morning because I knew that some of the others were going to be dropped off various individual locations across the city pass my exit.

Up to that point, Tevin and I had been dating for almost three months and I still wasn't a hundred percent certain about his relationship situation. So, whenever time permitted, I tested him by visiting him unannounced and he liked it when I'd unexpectedly showed up at his job fully made up after my shows.

On another occasion when he was the only one working the graveyard shift, we adventurously engaged in some unmentionable crazy things together! I also recall another time we spent an evening just sitting in his car and watching the coyotes' glowing eyes in the dark pouncing around for prey in the adjoining fields!

Later that morning when I was ready to leave, my car would not start. Although Tevin didn't say anything, I knew that he was concerned about his supervisors arriving the following morning to find a car broken down inside the gated and secured facility. Fortunately, Tevin discovered that it was just a dead battery, which was recharged with his jumper cables.

As time passed, I grew to recognize the distinct sound of his car muffler waking me from my sleep whenever he cruised up our street! I'd anticipate him holding me in his arms and showering me with sweet kisses upon hearing the sounds of footsteps in his Harley Davidson boots on the wood porch whenever he came over in the mornings after working overnight to spend the day with me! I loved our long romantic hot bubble baths together.

I'm not sure why I never directly questioned Tevin about his relationship status, but I did continue putting him through a series of tests designed to reveal if he was in a relationship or not.

I knew that if he made any excuses for not being able to spend the nights on special occasions, or holidays with me, those were very clear signs that he was married or committed to someone else. If that was the case, he would not have been the type of person that I was interested in continuing to be with even in a casual, no-strings-attached manner.

As time progressed, I was impressed by Tevin's commitment to me and for passing my tests with flying colors! The fact that he wasn't playing those typical games that were being played by those perpetrating, fake Hollywood playboys pulled me even closer to him!

After spending more time together, I saw that Tevin was also sincere and trustworthy and I felt that I would be safe with him because he had my best interests at heart! Even though I did not expect to fall absolutely in love with him so quickly, I did!

However, I consciously resisted moving too fast too soon, because I wanted us to really get to know each other. I felt that he was the "One" and I wanted to really get it right this time. Also, even though I had developed very strong feelings for Tevin by that time, I'd learned a very valuable lesson from past experiences about jumping from one man head on into another without really getting to know him first before living with him.

Since I wanted to do as Percy Sledge suggested in his song "Take Time to Know

Her," I took heed in his lyrics and took time to know Tevin.

As the months turned into years, Tevin revealed to me that when we'd met for the second time, he was still recovering from a divorce from a biological woman that had ended before we met again.

He also shared his appreciation for the mental and physical support that we'd given to each other during our regular visits to the Lake Shrine Fellowship, meditating and praying in the Hidden Virgin & Child garden.

Fate would have it that we were a source of comfort and support for each other through some emotional times we both experienced after our recent break-ups with others. It was fun just walking hand-in-hand with him through the magnificent gardens in the Palisades, communing with nature surrounded by nothing but peace and tranquility.

We never missed an opportunity to lounge on the plush green grass by the lake underneath the majestic Lake Shrine Dutch Windmill contemplating what the future had is store for us, and observing the beautiful multi-colored koi fish swimming around in the sparkling water.

As time passed, I learned that Tevin's previous relationships have primarily been with biological females and after divorcing his wife, he had decided that he would not continue denying his strong attraction to transsexual women.

However, the challenge, according to him, was finding one that was not a prostitute or the typical porn star that he'd met at Peanuts and other places. Also, Tevin shared with me that on the evening we'd met for the second time, he was discouraged about not meeting any quality transsexuals who were not strung out on drugs and possessing the "What can you give me?" attitudes.

The fact that Tevin was strongly considering moving to another state right before we'd met reconfirms to me that fate intentionally brought us back together on that fateful night in 1996.

However, our relationship wasn't all peaches and cream because I recall one occasion when we first started dating when he probably thought that he'd also test me to see what I would and would not allow him to get away with.

The unexpected pop quiz occurred after we previously made plans to go to Venice Beach on one of our rare days off. I was really looking forward to going to the beach, because the rolling waves in the ocean always took away the stresses and strains of the day.

Earlier that afternoon, Ebony had stopped by on his way home from work and we were sitting in my living room talking when I received a call from Tevin, who nonchalantly proceeded to inform me, and I quote, "We're not going to be able to go to the beach today. I'm going to hang out with my cousin for a little while and I will call you later."

I couldn't believe Tevin had the nerve to call me just minutes before our scheduled date to inform me that he'd made other plans. Since I didn't want to tell him off in front of my guest, I immediately excused myself from the living room and went into the bedroom closing the door to respond to what he'd just told me.

My quote: "Tevin, I don't have a problem with you hanging out with your cousin if it was not for the fact that I'm sitting here waiting for you to pick me up, but you've chosen to wait until the last minute to inform me that you would rather hang out with your cousin."

I continued before he could respond, "You go right ahead and do what you need to do." I then hung up the phone again without giving him a chance to respond, thinking what nerve he had to think that I would be okay with his inconsiderateness.

At that point in my life, I was not desperate for a relationship and I was definitely not going to allow another man to take me for granted. Yes, he was cute, but not that cute. Neither was I going to just sit around my apartment waiting on him to call me whenever he was ready, so I called my sister-friend Nikki to see if she wanted to ride with me to the beach.

Of course, Nikki was always down with going to Venice Beach to flirt with the cute guys playing basketball and working out on Muscle Beach.

After Ebony left to go home, I gathered up my purse and keys in preparation to go pick Nikki up and, as I prepared to walk out the door to leave, Tevin appeared, standing outside the screen door peering in.

I invited him in and he apologized for being inconsiderate. I restated, "As I said earlier, I understand and do not have a problem with you hanging out with your cousin, but for you to just disregard our plans as if they're not important to you is unacceptable and will not be tolerated."

As far as I was concerned, there was no compromising about being disrespected by a mate because I knew that once the cycle started, it's usually more difficult to end the pattern if you buy into the notion of that's just the way it is.

I emphatically did not want Tevin to ever get into the habit of thinking that he could just disregard my feelings on a whim, because I've also learned that we teach people how to treat us.

To his credit, Tevin continued profusely apologizing again for taking me for granted and has never tried to run that game on me again, confusing me with one of his former groupies. I don't' think so!

After getting that bit of important business out of the way, our afternoon proceeded with the three of us at the beach, with Nikki aggressively flirting with a popular actor during that time. The poor thing had to almost run away from Nikki, traumatized!

After a period of time dating, there was no doubt in my mind that Tevin really respected me and made it unequivocally clear by his actions that he wanted to exclusively be with me when he'd eventually relocated from the high desert to be closer! This enabled us to spend more quality time together building on a solid foundation for our future.

After Tevin finished relocating closer to the city, there was no question in my mind that his intentions were genuine as far as I was concerned. His unsolicited actions were the fuel that enabled me to allow myself to feel and hope that just maybe I had finally found a man whom knew exactly what he wanted.

His adult decisions also affirmed to me that he was secure enough in his manhood to not trip out about dating and possibly falling in love with a transsexual woman.

Before I met Tevin for the second time, there were two other suitors vying for my affections that were not able to pass the tests I'd implemented.

Their failures contributed to them both miserably falling by the wayside when I found out that one of them was actually married and suggesting that he would leave his wife and child to be with me.

He'd never taken into consideration that I would have been stupid to trust that he would not later cheat on me with someone else the same way that he'd cheated on his family.

The other guy also flunked out due to him being a big flaky and undependable, self-absorbed individual who wanted to play little stupid mind games with me. On the other hand, Tevin was different and I'm extremely grateful that I made the wisest choice -- the good guy for a change!

It was pleasurable for me to inform those other suitors that I was committed to a special man who has become my immediate future, so I would not be able to see them again whenever we encountered each other.

Of course, they were not happy that I'd chosen Tevin over them, but they really had no say so or choice in the matter but to accept my decision to exclusively commit myself to Tevin. Tevin was also honest enough to tell me about the other women that he'd been seeing before we committed to each other in addition to expressing his delight that he had also chosen me over them, so it all unfolded in divine order!

As the sands flowed through the hour-glass, one day when I was home alone in the apartment, I received a call from an acquaintance named Caprice whom I previously hired to videotape my "Call Her Miss Ross" solo show at Love Lounge.

"Destiny, girl," she said, "I was showing my copy of "Call Her Miss Ross to a producer friend of mine from Portland, Oregon, and he would like for you to contact him about performing in his HIV/Aids fund-raiser!"

I enthusiastically replied. Her phone call was a pleasant surprise and blessing, and I did not hesitate to consider the producer's proposal, replying, "Really, thank you Caprice for the hook-up, because anytime that I can use my talents to give back, I am always excited to do so!"

Since I recalled previously in the early'90s falling in love with Portland when my former roommate, Ashley, and I were guest featured performers in the Brown Sugar Extravaganza, I found the crisp and refreshing Oregon winters invigorating!

After hanging up, I immediately called the producer to confirm receipt of his proposal! Then once Patrik and I worked out the details and booked the event, we collaborated on my music selections and costumes.

On November 4, 1996, Shooting Star and I were on a plane for a very special weekend appearance in the Pacific Northwest to raise money for HIV and AIDS.

The adventure started at check-in when the airport staff tried convincing me to check my garment bag and wig box. That was not going to happen. There was absolutely no way that I was going to risk them losing my costumes and hair on my special return to Portland.

Thankfully, the stewardesses conceded after I explained the circumstances around requiring that my costumes and hair remaining with me and they also agreed to store my garment bag near their station. I stored the wig box on the floor between my legs during the flight, ensuring that she'd be safe.

When we landed in Oregon, we were provided with a driver who picked us up at the airport and remained at our disposal for the entire weekend.

Later that evening on November 5, 1996, I made my second exclusive Portland appearance in "Ready to Live Dress for Life," which was a Parisian-style fashion event sponsored by Saks Fifth Avenue and Cascade Aids Project.

I performed my "I'm Coming Out/Ain't No Mountain High Enough" Diana Ross medley wearing a Shooting Star Design and David Hawkins original silver sequined gown with an almost seven foot train he'd created for me for another exclusive performance.

I topped the ensemble off with a Shooting Star designed red and fuchsia chiffon "Super Nova" floor-length duster that made me look like I was being engulfed by a giant energy cloud.

The arena was sold-out and when I appeared from the back of the huge showroom through the audience to make a grand entrance onto the stage opening the show. I heard a roar of applause and cheers from them that I had never experienced before that was exclusively for me.

Their uproarious energy caused an instant rush of electricity running from the soles of my feet up my spine, seeming to transport me to another euphoric zone! I mean that audience soaked up every bit of what I had to offer, intermittently interacting with the audience! Unforgettable!

After the fashion show concluded, models rolled onto the stage disguised in huge Cirque Du Soleil latex balls and then simultaneously emerged, concluding with ripping the runway!

Patrik and I later expressed our overwhelming gratitude to the producer over dinner at an exclusive Five Star restaurant! I'd be remiss to not mention that I was chic and sharp in a beautiful satin, gold and black cocktail dress that Mr. Bob Mackie generously loaned to us for our elegantly magical evening in Portland.

Back in Los Angeles the following weekend after my Portland engagement, I received another epiphany the night that Tevin escorted me to a club appearance at the Fire House formerly located on Robertson Boulevard in West Hollywood.

Just for clarification purposes, before Tevin and I started dating, I was single for several months and slightly uninhibited about my stage performances. It was only whenever I performed sexier numbers in response to the energetic audience, such as when I did the Jody Watley "Looking For a New Love/I Want You" mix that night.

In my defense, it was due to the overwhelming number of gay guys that were in attendance. I didn't think anything of it that I was somewhat flirtatious with them. Tevin later disabused me of that notion after informing me that he'd felt disrespected and angry at how sensual I was being with some of the enthusiastic guys during my routine, causing him to walk out to calm down.

Up to that point, Tevin had never walked out on any of my performances, and later that night I knew that he was not happy when I got into the car and found him waiting for me when the show was over.

I figured that he would eventually tell me what he was upset about when he was ready, so I didn't push him to explain why he'd walked out before the show concluded. He remained calm and silent during the drive back home and later that night after calming down, he came into the living room where I was sitting watching television and said, "Tracee, I don't know how you are going to react to what I'm about to say, but I need you to just listen to me until I finish before you respond, please."

Since I knew that he was not happy, I remained quiet, listening intently without interrupting him as he continued. "I know that you are just doing your job performing on stage, but I really don't like or appreciate seeing you sitting on other guys' laps and letting them inappropriately touch on you as if you were a piece of meat. If we are going to stay together, I need for you to stop sitting on other guys' laps in that manner."

As I continued quietly listening and digesting what he was expressing to me, I agreed that I was somewhat overly seductive and slightly inappropriate during my performance that night, so I replied, after he asked if there was anything that I like to say in response, "I agree with you that my Jody Watley performance was somewhat inappropriate and your request for me to stop inappropriately sitting on other guys' laps letting them grope or caress me is fair. I am sorry about the inappropriateness and I promise to remember that I'm no longer single, requiring that I become more respectful toward you and myself on stage."

Moving forward from our conversation, I didn't have a problem with Tevin's request because his concerns were valid and reasonable, so after that conversation we kissed and made up!

During future sexier numbers, I remained more aware and conscious of my interactions with my fans during those performances, which made me feel more special that I was with someone who was concerned and protective of my reputation.

The very next test of our commitment to each other was a year later in 1997 when I received an offer from a prestigious Las Vegas production company that I just could not refuse to go on an extended six-month tour in Wendover, Nevada. Their proposal was for me to appear as Diana Ross and Whitney Houston in a celebrity look-alike showcase!

It was never a concern to me that upon accepting the contract I had to give up my apartment because I had to immediately fly to Las Vegas and meet the producer and sign official contracts.

Then there were the studio rehearsals with the cast and posing for the marketing promotional photo shoot. Afterwards, and upon my return to Los Angeles, I received plane tickets within three weeks and was scheduled to fly to Wendover to begin the tour,

Since I hadn't finished packing up my apartment when my departure date closed in, I asked Tevin and my sisters Ebony, Cookie and Erica if they would finish packing up the remainder of my entire apartment and put everything in storage until my tour was over.

I didn't hesitate to book the show, although Patrik was slightly miffed that I'd booked the event during rehearsals for my next Portland appearance. Since I felt that the experiences that I'd received booking that gig would be a priceless education and opportunity to make some money at the same time, there was no further heated discussions between my personal manager and I as to the reasons for choosing to tour once I'd explained my intentions with him!.

At first, Tevin wasn't too happy either about me going on tour right before our upcoming August anniversary celebration, because during that period in our relationship, we'd started celebrating our meeting for the second time at Peanuts as an anniversary every year.

However, Tevin also realized that the tour would be great for my resume, so we compromised by making arrangements for him to fly to Wendover for the weekend so that we'd still be able to be together on our anniversary.

Wendover, Nevada, is very unique due to it being established in the 1920's on the Bonneville Salt Flats, serving as an outpost of civilization in the midst of isolation where the B-29 bomb crews trained in preparation to drop the atomic bombs on Nagasaki and Hiroshima.

Incidentally and to my surprise, Wendover did not even have a Wal-Mart or an airport, so on the weekend of our anniversary after the last show I borrowed my roommate Phyl Craig's car and drove more than three hours alone in a snowstorm to Utah, Nevada, to pick Tevin up from the airport! Whew, what a drive in almost blinding slushy snow!

I didn't mind the drive at all due to being excited about seeing my "Pumpkin-head" after almost a month or so of being apart!

We returned to Wendover later that night in one piece to a beautiful suite that the State Line Silver Smith Casino Resorts entertainment manager provided for our anniversary! After a romantic dinner, we celebrated together in our elegant accommodations!

Our anniversary weekend began its conclusion during the drive back to Utah taking him to the airport for the flight back to Los Angeles. It wasn't too difficult watching Tevin board the plane, because we both knew that I had previously signed an agreement with the production company to pick up the tab for my return back to Los Angeles for three weeks to begin final rehearsals for my previously booked Portland engagement.

After returning to Los Angeles, I began to prepare for my Portland gig, which was scheduled for the weekend of February 4 to 6, 1997. I immediately jumped right into the final costume fittings and rehearsing routine in preparation for another HIV/AIDS fund-raiser due to the overwhelming positive response to my triumphant appearance the year before.

This time, Patrik and I recruited my friends and fellow showgirls Miss Kiwi, God rest her soul, and another fabulous multi-title winner performer that I'd worked with at Catch One named Rene Devereaux to star in a "DreamGirl" production with me leading the trio.

Although Patrik was concerned that the Nevada tour had taken away from the time that I needed for rehearsals and fittings before the big show, I had faith in my abilities to do what I needed to do, because before previously leaving for Nevada, Patrik had already designed and sketched our gowns.

Then the fashion designer extraordinaire to Hollywood stars Bob Mackie once again generously donated his assistant seamstress to create three of the most magnificent gold and red metallic "DreamGirl" and Supremes inspired gowns designed by Patrik Shooting Star!

We'd also previously gone downtown to the garment district purchasing the materials, pumps and other supplies that were needed, so all that was left to complete was the performance choreography.

Not to worry, because we'd also previously arranged after Patrik and I hired Rodney Chester, one of the most recent Noah's Ark Logo Channel television series and movie cast members to choreograph our routine. We'd also previously booked and blocked out rehearsal dates and times in a Studio City rehearsal dance studio to start choreographing and rehearsing the routine upon my return.

Ready, set, here we go! During one of our rehearsals, a guest attended with Rene whom I did not recall previously ever meeting when we were introduced at the studio! I was also happy that this was a very rare occasion that Tevin was off from work and he was able to attend rehearsal with me.

Over the course of the rehearsal that day, things were great because we were all excited about finally getting through the entire routine without messing up! Things were going well until afterwards when I noticed that Tevin was withdrawn and acting really weird when we got into the car to leave the dance studio.

I knew that something was seriously wrong with Tevin after the rehearsal by the foul mood that he was suddenly in, so I insisted on him telling me what the problem was that caused his attitude and energy to shift so drastically.

Tevin kept insisting that there was nothing wrong, but I'd known him long enough by that time to know when he was really upset about something. So, only after I continued inquiring about what caused his mood change, he finally told me the truth about what was bothering him.

I was floored and found it difficult to fathom that while we were rehearsing, this person that was a guest of Rene's approached Tevin outside of the studio and started telling him stories about recently seeing me with an Italian guy shopping on Hollywood Boulevard and also discussed personal things about himself that a stranger should not have known.

I was quite confused and pissed by the accusations that this person was making about me requiring an explanation to Tevin that I had previously dated an Italian guy named EnRico many years ago who had expected me to continue a relationship with him after he'd introduced me to his wife.

I had no awareness that he'd been married and found it interesting that he'd invited his wife and other members of his family to one of my shows at a popular restaurant on Melrose once after he'd returned from Italy a married man.

Since Enrico and I dated many years before I ever started dating Tevin, I didn't have any idea of why this person would have told Tevin that he'd recently seen me with any Italian guy shopping on Hollywood Boulevard.

At that point, I was furious that this stranger would come to my rehearsal and tell blatant lies about me to my boyfriend. I was even more upset that Tevin did not immediately inform me right then and there about the lies that this person had just told him about me before they'd left the rehearsal.

Obviously, that person had been deceitfully plotting against us for a while now and I was not going to let them get away with it that easily, so I sped through traffic up Ventura Boulevard trying to catch up to the car that they were riding in!

I was determined to confront the liar head on in front of Tevin to respond to the lies that he was spreading about me, but fortunately for him, I was not able to catch up with their car due to the red lights.

On the drive home, Tevin kept trying to convince me that he didn't believe the lies that were presented by the stranger and explained that he also did not tell me right then and there about what was said due to him not wanting to cause any disruption in my rehearsal.

Tevin was also rightfully so concerned about how I would have responded if he had told me right in front of the person, due to him also knowing me well enough at that point.

Even though I accepted Tevin's explanation for not immediately informing me of the liar in our midst, I was still fuming that he'd waited to tell me that someone I did not personally know was spreading inflammatory lies about me and to make it worse, he'd practically did it in my presence.

I understood and appreciated Tevin for being considerate of my rehearsal. However, I still should have been pulled aside and warned by him considering that guy came out of nowhere trying to create drama in our relationship.

After one of our long and intense conversations resulting in us both promising and committing to each other that if someone ever had anything to say about either of us whether we believed them or not, we would immediately tell each other what was discussed while that person was present.

We both agreed that rather than wait and be upset about some deceitful third party planting seeds of mistrust between us, we'd confront them head on to sever the snake's head. Then we filed that strange encounter as a learning experience contributing to future rehearsals being closed off to those whom were not directly involved with the production team.

Patrik had booked a show at the Love Lounge the weekend before our flight to Portland for a full dress rehearsal performance of our "DreamGirl" production to work out the kinks in preparation to take her on the road.

Ebony, his boyfriend and Scott along with Tevin were all in the audience while I was in the dressing room prepping for the show when Patrik hysterically rushed into the dressing room screaming, "Destiny, Tevin is beating some guy up in the club!"

I didn't have any idea of what was going on and my first thought was that some aggressive gay guy might have inappropriately approached Tevin, so I asked Patrik to tell Tevin to come into the dressing room so that I could inquire as to what was going on.

After Tevin got into the dressing room, he proceeded to explain that the same person that was at the studio rehearsal had aggressively approached him in the club with some more lies and started professing his love for him.

In response when the guy refused to leave after Tevin warned him to get away from him and stay away from his family before attempting to walk away, the guy became more aggressive and when he would not back off according to Tevin, he pinned the liar up against the wall threatening to snap him in half if he did not stay away from us!

As Tevin was explaining to me what had occurred, Patrik entered the dressing room informing me that the club management wanted Tevin to leave the premises because the guy complained and lied that Tevin attacked him for no reason.

I informed Patrik that neither he nor the club management had any idea of what we'd previously experienced with that person, because I did not initially tell Patrik about what occurred during rehearsals.

Therefore in response to the management requesting Tevin to leave the premises, I also informed Patrik to inform the club management that we'd previously had an encounter with that person spreading nasty lies about me at our rehearsal and if Tevin had to leave the club, I'd be packing my things and leaving with him.

There was no way that I was going to stay and perform in that show if Tevin was unjustifiably thrown out of the club for defending my honor against someone that was jealous and envious of our relationship. Nor was I going to just let anybody disrespect my man as if he was some loser off the streets.

Of course, Patrik knew that I was serious about leaving before my scheduled performances and not letting them devalue my relationship with Tevin, so he left the dressing room and only returned to give me a 20-minute cue without any further discussion about the response from the club management.

I assume that since our "DreamGirl" production was highly promoted and anticipated by all of West Hollywood and surrounding areas, there was not any further conversation about Tevin leaving the club amongst the club management.

Later that night Miss Kiwi, Rene and I performed in our one of a kind Shooting Star original designer gowns to a very energetic and enthusiastic sold-out audience ending immediately after the show with Tevin and I leaving the club together!

The following weekend we were in Portland to debut our "DreamGirl" production in another lavish Saks Fifth Avenue-sponsored fund-raiser entitled "Solid Gold Heart-Solid Gold Style" which was another amazing experience for me!

That time we also had a chauffeured limousine driver driving us to rehearsals and remaining at our disposal for the rest of the trip. Rene and Miss Kiwi wanted to go out for a night on the town after the show and dinner.

After dropping Miss Kiwi and Rene off at the club and reminding them that the limousine was scheduled to take us to the airport early the following morning, Patrik and I returned to the hotel. Upon saying good night to Patrik, I entered my suite and called Tevin to tell him about how great the show was.

After talking for more than an hour or so, I ordered hot tea from room service, took a long hot candle-lit bubble bath to bring my energy level back down to normal in response to the overwhelming love and stimulation that we'd received from the audience during our performance.

Once I finished soaking in the tub and saying my prayers, I climbed into bed flipping through the television channels until I was ready to fall asleep.

The following week, back in California, Tevin and I continued dealing with many other envious people throughout our relationship. It seemed as if they started crawling out from underneath every other boulder and proceeded to make futile attempts to break us up just because they didn't want to see us together

Included in the long list of jealous people was this former acquaintance that shall remain nameless who I suspected wanted Tevin for herself due to her unsuccessful attempt at playing the reverse psychological games on me during our interactions.

Her false perception was that she had some sort of influence on my personal life and after it was confirmed that Tevin and I were seriously dating each other, she offered unsolicited commentary about why I was wasting my time with Tevin.

According to her, "Black guys don't have anything to offer a girl."

I knew exactly what game she was trying to run, so I informed her, before abruptly ending the conversation about my personal life, "My dear just for your information, I'm not with Tevin for money or what he may or may not be able to do for me, because unlike you sister, I make my own money working and being self-sufficient, not sleeping with men for anything other than companionship if I so choose."

To add to the mix there was also this other queen whom I'd previously considered to be a friend who tried coming onto Tevin during one of the few occasions she was aware of my absence on tour.

I assume that she was jealous that I had a man who wasn't a crack-head like the numerous men that she'd always end up with. She just couldn't take it that Tevin was 100 percent committed to me and even questioned him about his decision to have allowed me to drive his car.

After she got heavily involved in the porn industry, she'd even suggested to me that Tevin and I could get paid for filming an adult XXX rated movie together for her producer.

I knew right then and there that Miss Thang could not be trusted.

It remains ironic to me that she made such a ridiculous suggestion, because when we first met, she was the one who was continuously berating the other working girls before she ended up doing exactly what she'd sworn up and down that she would never do. Hypocrite!

As a result of dealing with the best of those types of people futilely trying to come between our groove, Tevin and I have adopted standards of practice to immediately put in check those others to come and proceed to cutting them off at the root.

There's absolutely no way that I would have been able to regularly traveled alone out of town working or even visiting my family if Tevin didn't trust me, or I him because we'd consciously and verbally committed to being monogamous and exclusive.

I personally received great gratification resisting the advances and proposals from admirers during an engagement in addition to whenever I might be approached by a stranger or someone from my single days past.

I confess that I was slightly stimulated after rejecting them upon their approach for whatever reason that they may possess! It was wonderful for me to have informed them that I'm currently in a committed relationship.

Speaking of being approached by strangers or someone from the past, I'm reminded of the time in church during my uncle Isaiah's funeral when one of the funeral directors made it very obvious that he was attracted to me, which made me extremely uncomfortable considering my mother was present at her brother's funeral.

Before Uncle Isaiah died, he was known for not playing any games, causing people to think twice about bothering him with unnecessary drama and mess. I miss the Fourth of July celebrations when he would dig a pit in the ground to slow cook a hog overnight that they'd raised and slaughtered.

Once, when my cousin and partner in crime Marva and her sisters and brother were visiting for the summer, she and I decided that we'd sneak off and go to The Field while Ma was out for the evening with our other aunts.

Picture The Field actually being a huge open space way out in the country that was turned into an all-night after hour hot spot! All I know is that we were very precocious teenagers back then and although I don't recall how we even got there, I do remember later that night kicking up dust along with the adults seemingly oblivious to our little young butts dancing along with them to "Shackles on My Feet"!

Our good time abruptly concluded when all of a sudden, we were approached by Uncle Isaiah threatening that if we were not at home by the time that he gotten there, he was going to take the skin off our hides.

Like I said, Uncle Isaiah didn't play. As a result of knowing that he meant what he'd said, I don't remember how we got back home that night, but you best believe that we were there before Uncle Isaiah arrived at Grandma's house! I miss my Uncle very much. Rest in peace, uncle Isaiah.

Anyway, back to the stranger at the funeral. As I stood in the back of the church videotaping Uncle Isaiah's funeral, I was taken aback when Mr. Yarborough approached me asking if he could have my phone number and then inquired if I'd have dinner with him.

In response to his questions I replied that I was visiting from out of town and since I was also married I wasn't able to give him my phone number. He then persistently asked if I would take his number to call if I changed my mind.

Thankfully, I managed to resist telling Mr. Yarborough that his approach was inappropriate considering that I was attending my uncle's funeral and neither was I interested in getting his phone number. However, not to be rude and cause a scene in church, I took his business card with no intention of ever calling him.

Believe it or not, the very next day when my aunt Mae and I were shopping for items for an impromptu family gathering at Swan Lake the following Sunday, Mr. Yarborough unexpectedly turned down the same aisle that we were shopping on, walking in our direction.

Once again, not wanting to be rude, I introduced him to my Aunt and as we awkwardly stood there with her all up in the discussion. I concluded the conversation, informing him that I was really flattered by his invitation, but my husband would not appreciate me going out with another man, so I had no choice but to once again decline his invitation.

Before leaving town after the funeral during a visit with my friend Asia, I told her about how this guy who had approached me at my uncle's funeral. After telling her his name and the funeral home that he worked for, she reminded me that I had met him previously when I was younger.

It didn't' matter that I'd known him before when I was a teenager, because the trust that I was fortunate enough to have established between Tevin and I is much more important than a tryst with an old high school fling.

I've noticed in my experience that some guys don't expect for transsexual women, especially those of color, to reject them. It's also as if they think that we don't possess any discernment or taste about the type of person we prefer to be with.

Please don't get me wrong. Mr. Yarborough was a very attractive man, but I am totally committed to Tevin in that regard. However, I'm not insinuating that it wasn't previously required that Tevin and I have long and intense discussions about the no tolerance, ready to protect his territory stance that he'd assumed in response to a perceived invaders that may have mistakenly approached me in his presence.

I remember in the beginning of our relationship that I'd gotten so frustrated and angry with Tevin whenever he responded in such an aggressive ready to fight manner. Due to me feeling that he occasionally crossed the lines with various male fans or even admirers, we'd had several really serious arguments about him not trusting me.

It was important for me to have established with Tevin that no matter how strongly someone came onto me and due to having a mind of my own, he didn't have to worry about me being tempted to go there with them.

Overtime, it finally clicked with him that I cannot control what their individual personal agendas are for approaching me. However, I do possess control over the way that I respond to them.

Tevin was recently tested and passed with flying colors when we were together in the grocery store shopping. The discombobulating encounter with a stranger in the grocery store that evening also revealed to me just how far Tevin had progressed with managing his territorial-mindedness aggression.

Tevin actually found it very amusing observing the butcher basically stalking me down the aisles asking my name and then telling me how attractive he thought that I was.

I'm happy that Tevin and I shared trust from the beginning, which made it possible for me to have experienced out of town opportunities like entertaining audiences at the Saks Fifth Avenue HIV/AIDS benefit shows in Portland and other national appearances.

Immediately after returning to Los Angeles from Oregon, I was scheduled to return two days later to Wendover for the remainder of the six-month engagement! There wasn't a whole lot to do in Wendover but either work out at the gym with my roommate Phyl Craig or occasionally taking my limit of $20 to play a couple hands of blackjack with the other cast members.

There really weren't any other recreational activities to partake in after performing two shows a night during the week and three shows on the weekend, including a Sunday matinee with only Monday nights off.

It's sad that the only excitement and adventure we had was making a "Priscilla Queen of the Desert" adventure out of traveling over three hours back and forth to the nearest Wal-Mart almost every other week. Thank God there was at least a Kroger grocery store in town! I'm not complaining, just explaining.

Some of the other cast members seemed to really enjoy getting obscenely wasted on alcohol and other recreational drugs. We all made the best of spending the holidays away from our family and friends by coming together after preparing dinner for the entire cast.

Although it was admittedly somewhat bittersweet the preceding weeks and days leading up to the tour conclusion, due to the bond I had formed with my cast members, I was happy to leave cold, wet and isolated Wendover, Nevada!

After the Nevada tour officially ended, I returned to Los Angeles and continued exciting engagements. Patrik informed me that due to the overall success of the "Call Her Miss Ross" Love Lounge engagement, he was able to book a slightly edited version of my first solo show at another confidence builder!

It never occurred to me in my wildest dreams that I'd be offered a one month long run for me return and star in a one-woman show at The Comedy Store on the Sunset Strip starting on June 22, 1997.

The only real challenge for me during that engagement was when I had to leave an event early to prepare for show-time at The Comedy Store on the evening that Chaka Khan was scheduled to close out The Playboy Jazz Festival.

I was so disappointed about not getting to see Chaka Khan perform live at the Hollywood Bowl, but my show had to go on as scheduled!

A little history on the Sunset Strip Comedy Store: We had a brief run there (I don't recall the exact dates) when Patrik produced a celebrity look-alike consisting of a cast of about 12 unique personalities.

I do recall that during one of those rehearsals, I had to stand my ground and let some of the other cast members know that I wasn't a timid pushover after they kept insinuating that Patrik was showing me favoritism because he was my personal manager.

I'd grown tired of the non-stop jokes after the random comments. I felt that in order for them to cease, I would have to defend myself.

In response to the constant teasing, I rose from my seat, announcing to all of them that I was sick and tired of all the Destiny jokes and comments. I proceeded to inform them that I would appreciate that if any of them found it necessary to bitch about something they did not like, to not involve me in it.

That was that; there weren't any more Destiny jokes or comments, other than later when one of the male dancers whom danced backup in my "I Will Survive/Take Me Higher" medley had to be cut for time during one of the shows.

For whatever reason he thought that he'd take his anger out on me. I assume that he thought that I wouldn't mind his rudeness and disrespect after being informed by Patrik that since the show was running over schedule we were going to cut the number just for that night.

I personally didn't have a problem with Patrik cutting the number, because I was worn out from my other performances. However, the dancer stated for all to hear, "See, this is why I don't like working with drag queens!"

After the second drag queen remark he made, I calmly approached him in the dancers' dressing room and informed him, "You have a choice to either refer to me as Tracee or Destiny, but if you call me a drag queen again, you and I are going to have a really serious problem with each other."

He was stunned that I'd confronted him and left speechless. I continued, "Furthermore, if you have a problem with the song being cut, take it up with the show producer and leave me the hell out of it."

He'd really pissed me off, because there are usually always those self-absorbed gay boys who think they can be disrespectful to the girls just because we're wearing hair, makeup and dresses. My warning to him was a precautionary message that he should not take it for granted that I wouldn't go "Stonewall" on his ass if necessary! Better ask somebody!

My initial plan after the Wendover tour was to begin the process of looking for an apartment, but there was a delay once I signed The Comedy Store contract. I continued living with Tevin until the show was produced and finalized.

One day when we were both off from work and rehearsals, I informed Tevin of my intention to start looking for an apartment and we even looked at a couple of them together, which is when we were introduced to our first baby, Savannah.

It was a beautiful sunny day and we were walking up the sidewalk looking for a prospective apartment when this lady started walking toward us with a Shih Tzu mother dog followed by her babies in tow! We couldn't help but stop to admire them and when we turned to leave, the only little jet black one with white spots on her little breast and paws continued following us as we walked away, instantly hooking me with her little cute face!

Since Tevin and I had an appointment scheduled to view an apartment, we obtained the dog owner's phone number in order to contact her later about purchasing our baby girl. Later that evening we used some of the money from the Nevada tour to purchase our first born!

I named her Savannah after a previous alias that I'd used when I worked in the administrative office for an all-transsexual, transgender phone-sex business that connected incoming calls to girls from clients requesting their favorite fantasy phone-sex operators!

After securing our baby Savannah, I was unaware during the whole apartment hunting process that Tevin was harboring some anger at me because I had started looking for my own place and never considered permanently staying with him.

When I learned that he was very upset, I explained that I wanted to do things differently with our relationship because previously, I did not take the necessary time to really know who a guy was before living with them.

As a result, I'd vowed to myself that I would never live with another guy until we'd known each other for at least two years. During the conversation with Tevin, I saw that he was really hurt by me not wanting to live with him for another six months.

Although we'd only been together for a year and a half up to that point, I compromised. We had been together for almost two years now and I had not seen any violent, abusive red flags or alarms going off around him.

After observing that he was also being responsible with maintaining steady employment and not a crack-head, I figured that it might be okay to take the leap of faith and begin permanently living with him!

After resolving that we wanted to live with each other, we moved out of his one bedroom into our first two bedroom apartment, which was on Hollywood Boulevard and Cherokee.

I loved being able to walk four blocks up the street to the open-air farmers market on Hollywood and Cahuenga Boulevard every Saturday morning, shopping for organic produce and freshly cut flowers. It was also convenient that almost everything that we needed was just a few blocks from where we lived.

When I agreed to us living together, I was by no means expecting it to be some sort of fairy tale, Cinderella happily-ever-after fantasy, because in reality, I know that in almost every relationship after you've moved beyond the lust and infatuation phase, the real work begins.

I will be the first to tell you that our relationship has not been without the everyday challenges of living under one roof together. There have been days that Tevin has gotten on my nerves and I am most certain that there are also days that I've gotten on his nerves. Thankfully, we don't get on each other's nerves as much as we did in the beginning!

However, before arriving at this point after almost three years or so of living together, the one and only time that I ever felt physically threatened by him was when I felt that he was being irresponsible in the manner of which he'd chosen to manage a household bill that he was responsible for maintaining.

I must also admit that I was so angry that he'd felt he could keep the matter hidden from me, which affected both of our well-being. I'd really gotten in his face, calling him some names that I've since learned are inappropriate no matter what.

Setting the scene, Tevin was sitting at the computer in the office when I confronted him and I guess he could not take it that I'd also started threatening to leave the relationship, so he jumped up in a threatening manner making me think that he was about to hit me.

He did not physically put his hands on me, but if he had we would have been done. Period. Like Tina Turner says, "What's love got to do with it?"

You can best believe that there was absolutely no way I was ever going to stay with Tevin no matter how much counseling he promised to seek if he had tried to physically restrain, control or hit me.

Our confrontation also taught me that my response was wrong. However, I was more concerned about the way he'd responded because he had never been that aggressive towards me.

Thankfully we were both mature enough to let things settle down before proceeding to deal with the issue. I'm grateful that I gave him enough time to also calm down and consider what had just happened before we were able to later come together in the living room to calmly discuss the events that lead up to that incident.

I've since realized that Tevin doesn't do well with me yelling at him whenever he makes a mistake, so I'm continuously working on changing the way that I deal with my personal anger management issues.

Tevin has also taught me that forgiveness is a very important factor in maintaining a relationship, because I had been so used to taking things so personally whenever I felt betrayed. As a result of those past relationships, I'd unconsciously and sometimes consciously made it challenging for me to see their point of view and consider that they may have made a regrettable mistake.

Thankfully, I have evolved to not taking everything so personally and learned the power of forgiving the perceived transgressions of others!

During our conversation after the incident in the living room, I expressed my concerns about Tevin's aggressiveness, reminding him about conversations when we first met about my previous abusive relationships.

Although we'd come to a meeting of the minds, I was not totally convinced that Tevin would not let the future pressures of everyday stressful situations cause him to become aggressive or violent towards me during disagreements, which would not be tolerated for one moment in our current relationship.

As a gesture in order to satisfy my concerns, Tevin agreed that he would go to anger management counseling to seek out some tools that would assist him with handling the pressures of life and stressful situations that normally occur in a relationship.

We went to his first counseling session together in order for me to share with the counselor my concerns that lead me to insisting and requiring that he seek counseling if we were to continue our relationship.

Tevin's anger management counselor diagnosed the incident as a mild anger issue, suggesting that he take a six-week course in anger management and coping skills classes. When she diagnosed him with a mild anger management issue during that meeting, I wondered if she'd ever been in an abusive relationship.

I consider myself fortunate and blessed to have learned early that it does not matter if the abuse is just mild, light or tepid, abuse is abuse no matter how it's disguised!

As a means of protection, I've developed a no-tolerance attitude when it comes to allowing anyone to ever mentally or physically abuse me again, especially someone that professes to care for and love me.

So, it really did not matter how mild his anger management issues were, I made it clear to him that I was leaving if I ever felt threatened mentally or physically by him ever again.

Thankfully, Tevin took me seriously and completed his coping skills course and, delightfully, it has now been almost 18 years that we've been together and he has not expressed aggression or displayed that sort of anger towards me since that one and only incident.

In return, I've learned to not cross the line with him by disrespecting his manhood or personal space

A year or so after bringing Savannah home, we felt that she needed a mate, so we answered an ad placed by a couple in the Valley who were selling Shih Tzu puppies.

After scheduling a visitation to see the last puppy from the litter, Savannah immediately bonded with him! We fell in love with the little fur ball that was so playful, yet smart enough to lie underneath the car for shade and then peek out at us in the hot sun!

After inspecting him and becoming satisfied with his current medical records, we decided that we wanted to take him home with us, but the guy's wife was on an out of town movie shoot and she wanted to say goodbye to him before we took possession.

The actress was supposed to be back from her shoot within the next three days, so we agreed to wait until her return before taking him home. We grew discouraged after almost a week of not getting the final word to come pick him up.

Our discouragement turned into joy and excitement when we were finally called to take him home with us! We then named him Baby Bear because he was extremely furry and looked like a little bear cub!

After getting that little booger home, he was such a little tyrant that we joked about taking him back to the couple and leaving him in their gated yard overnight. It was only a joke, because we had both instantly fallen in love with the little terror, so there was absolutely no way that he was going anywhere.

Eventually, with the assistance of Queen Savannah putting him in his place whenever he crossed the line, we successfully trained the little rug rat and he quickly became an irreplaceable member of the family.

Our journey has been fantastic, but it's inevitable that as long as we continue living, we will have peaks and valleys. We have to hold on tightly, riding the waves and knowing that we're better and better every day during those low moments.

One such moment was when I received a phone call from Ma telling me to come home for Grandma's funeral. I knew that Grandma was in poor condition during my previous visits home and at my last visit before her death, I was so overwhelmed as a result of the condition that she was in that I didn't visit with her as I usually did. Writing about that period has been therapeutic to me. So, here we go!

Chapter Twelve

Dear Grandma

Bertie Lee Wingate-McDaniel August 11, 1911, to February 6, 1997

Dear Grandma,

If I had one more day to spend with someone who is not physically here on this earth at this moment, it would be you because I would use that time to apologize for not being strong enough to come into your bedroom during my last visit home before you transitioned from this physical plane.

That afternoon when I arrived at your house, I'd intended to place a big kiss on your cheek while squeezing you tightly and expressing all the love I feel for you as we'd always done before, spending quality time reminiscing about the past while I brushed and greased your hair the way that you liked for me to do!

Then I planned to read some of your favorite Bible verses the way that I'd done back when I was younger, but when I opened your bedroom door and saw you lying there motionless in the bed with those tubes coming out of your body, I became very ill and angered by the condition you were in.

I could just not handle seeing you lying there in such a helpless state, so I couldn't bring myself to come all the way into your bedroom no matter how much I wanted to. I didn't want your condition to be the last image stamped into my memory.

I wanted to remember the way you used to move your shoulders up and down to the music with your lips fixed in such a distinct way, expressing how B.B. King and his guitar Lucille moved you while listening to him on the stereo!

I only wanted to remember the way you were before becoming so ill and unrecognizable from diabetes. I recall you calling me Cat-Eyes when we were little because my eyes were green and according to you, they sometimes reflected in the dark! Additionally, I loved the times whenever the storm knocked the power out and you'd tell us about some of the most unbelievable and amazing stories about events in our family history!

Although most of the times that we lived with you were hard earlier on, I still recall with fondness the year you'd planted the most beautiful garden that was the envy of the entire neighborhood!

You then spent the entire summer sitting guard while watching your stories on television to keep us from raiding the watermelon, cantaloupe and cucumber patches!

I will never forget the sweet corn, tomatoes, and okra that I helped you harvest from the garden to make the most delicious pot of home-made succotash that I've ever tasted, which was the first and only time that I have been able to tolerate the taste and texture of okra!

I also vividly recall the times when I was a teenager and Ma and I were going through our challenges with my orientation. Whenever I ran away from home to your house, you never turned me away or made me feel that you did not love me for who I was. I was your grandchild and it did not matter to you that I was different from your other grandsons.

I suspected during those days that you were aware of all of the pain that I was in being unaware that I was intentionally created different, no matter how many times I was forced to read those Bible verses that condemned homosexuality to hell, I still felt that there was nothing wrong with me. However, the few times back then that I really enjoyed reading the Bible was to you, because I knew that my reading brought you great pleasure!

Grandma, when I left South Carolina to return to California after seeing you that last time, I knew you'd probably not be with us on this earth for very much longer. After you made your transition to finally find peace and rest, when Ma called me home for your funeral, I was comforted knowing that you were no longer suffering.

On the flight to South Carolina to attend your funeral, I felt some anxiety and nervousness about seeing the rest of the family. I'd previously been home to visit after I'd first started transitioning into living full time as a female, and Ma accepted me during those visits. However, I'd never been seen by the other family members who didn't live in Sumter.

I wasn't sure how the other family members would react to the person that I'd become, although it really shouldn't have been a surprise to any of them that I identify as female. On the morning of your funeral, I had a one-on-one, private conversation with Ma as I sponged foundation and powder on her face.

"Ma, I know that my presence might be a distraction to some of the other family members which is not my intention. There also may be some remarks made by some of them about me living and presenting myself as a female," I said. "I just want to reassure you that what they may or may not say or think does not matter to me, because my intentions for being there was to support you in memorializing Grandma."

I'm almost sure that considering the past challenges that Ma and I went through, you would have been very pleased with your daughter, because she replied, "You are very beautiful inside and out, presenting yourself in a very classy manner. I love you just as you are because you are my baby and you will always be my baby."

Ma then turned to me after I gave her a paper towel to blot her lipstick and continued, "If any of the other family members have anything to say about you, they had better keep it to themselves."

Grandma, I did get a few crossed-eyed looks from a couple of the other female family members and I don't know what they were saying about me amongst themselves when I wasn't present, but one thing that I'm happy to say for certain is that no one dared to say anything negative or nasty to me directly because they knew that Ma don't play any games when it comes to her children!

Your daughter, my mother, set the tone by showing the rest of the family that she loves and accepts me for who I am, and that she will not tolerate anyone disrespecting her child in or out of her presence.

Since your funeral, Grandma, all of my cousins, uncles, and aunts have seen me as Tracee and those that matter the most to me have not had anything but positive things to say, telling me how proud they are of the person that I've become!

Also Grandma, your transitioning has inspired the family to come together on more regular occasions other than just funerals, so after your burial, we initiated coordinating annual family reunions to honor you, Granddaddy, Uncle Isaiah, Uncle James, Aunt Connie, Aunt Rebecca, Aunt Dinah, Gail, Judy and all of our other ancestors that have gone before us.

A few years ago on December 25, 2007, a group of our family members visited your grave and as I placed hyacinth and daffodil bulbs into the ground, Tonya kept calling me "him" during the course of the conversation.

Before, it never really bothered me that much that they were being ignorant because

I did not have to be around them all of the time. However, since I am in South Carolina more often now after moving back to the East Coast, whenever family members refer to me with the masculine pronoun these days it is as irritating as fingernails on a chalkboard to me.

It bothers me that even though I present myself as a female and they've all met my husband, they still choose to refer to me as he, him, or his. I think that you'd also be pleased, Grandma, that I've since built up the courage to have conversations with those whom have chosen to be disrespectful to me!

I've individually taken them aside to let them know that I understand that it might be a challenge for them getting used to my transformation and that it's probably easier for them continuing to address me in the manner that they've done since we were growing up.

However, since I legally changed my name on a momentous afternoon after pulling my hair back into a chignon, lightly applying makeup with nude lips and dressing in my sharpest black pinstriped skirt suit with a crisp white blouse accessorized by black and white sling back pumps carrying a black leather case to appear before a Superior Court Judge!

Due to his wisdom, knowledge, and understanding the judge generously and compassionately expressed to me the greatest amount of respect and humanity after summoning me to appear before him in his private chambers along with his administrative clerk and then granting my petition to legally change my name instead of attempting to humiliate me in front of a courtroom full of strangers!

Although I was mentally prepared to professionally deal with the situation if by any chance the judge had tried to embarrass me in that courtroom, his unexpected compassion reaffirmed there are still good people practicing the Golden Rule, "Do unto others as you would have done unto you"!

As for some of our family members, I don't have an issue with them still calling me by my abbreviated birth name because it's unisex.

The problem that I have with them is that it's as if they're living on another planet somewhere, still thinking that transgender people are abnormal, although in my opinion, some of their children and friends are transgender and gender non-conforming.

I know that I haven't all of a sudden been just dropped on this planet from an Alien spaceship and since I don't judge them for their faults or perceived shortcomings, Lord knows, you know as well, that there is plenty to go around in this family, Grandma.

All I want is respect in the same manner that I respect them and to just be addressed as the female energy that I currently present. I'm sure that some of them may have a problem with my request and their moralistic subscriptions may prevent them from paying me the respect that I feel I deserve so, if necessary, I do not have a problem with refusing to respond to anything that blatantly disrespects or makes attempts to discredit who I am, family or not.

I love Ma from the depths of my heart and soul and I never previously envisioned the unimaginable relationship that she and I share at this moment in our lives! I wish that you were able to witness her evolution from the person that she was back then, which inspires and fuels my desire to be all that I was created through her to become!

Also, Grandma, I wish that you were able to meet Tevin, the man who is my husband and spiritual life-partner! We have been together almost 18 years now and he was there with open arms to comfort, support and love me through your passing when I returned to Los Angeles after your funeral.

I know that you would have loved him because he is a really good guy that loves and accepts me unconditionally! I am comforted knowing that you are another guardian angel watching over me and I hope that you're pleased with who I am!

I think about you all of the time, Grandma, and if I had one more day with you, I'd read your Bible to you, grease your hair and tell you how much I love and miss you!

Love Always,

Tony

Chapter Thirteen

World Famous Queen Mary Audition, February 11, 1998, 10:31 P.M. Another great

adventure!

Since the abrupt closing of La Cage Aux Follies, Beverly Hills, the landmark

institution for celebrity impersonators and performance artists, I returned to booking at that

the clubs that had once been my strong foundation.

In addition to snagging continued bookings at Plaza, Catch One, Robbie's in

Pomona, Rage, Love Lounge, VIP, and Peanuts, regular weekend tours at the Palm Springs

Riviera Resort (carving out a substantial salary), I also maintained a part-time sales and

marketing day job. That's what I'm talking about!

After several years of performing on the road from club to club all over California,

I started longing for a more consistent home base to hone my craft.

Frankly speaking, I was also sick and tired of practically packing and transporting

almost a closet full of costumes from club to club, because I'd started incorporating props

and everything else that was mobile enough to create a memorable performance.

Since it had become physically exhausting lugging around so many costumes and

props for one engagement, I started visualizing working regularly in a local venue that

would be financially prosperous enough to take care of my financial obligations without

having to continue being on the road as much as I had been.

After putting my desires out into the universe during meditation and prayer, an

opportunity was presented to audition for the cast at one of only a couple of authentic

showrooms left in California after "LaCage Aux Follies" became defunct.

The club was promoted on its Website as a special events, lesbian, gay, bar and

fetish venue with clientele from all backgrounds and statuses located over the mountain in

North Hollywood at 12449 Ventura Boulevard in Studio City.

Tevin was at work and I was alone in the apartment on a day off unpacking my

show bag from an appearance at Rage the weekend before, when I answered the phone and

heard Patrik excited voice.

"Tracee, are you sitting down?"

I knew immediately by his tone that it was something fabulous! So I replied, "What is it, Shooting Star?" And then I took a deep breath, anticipating what the surprise was.

Historically, Patrik always kept me waiting by chattering about all of the insignificant details leading up to the good news, so I had to interject, "Okay, Patrik, what happened on your lunch break today?"

Finally getting to the juicy part he giddily said, "I got you an audition at Queen Mary in Studio City this coming weekend. What do you think about that!?"

My only reply was, "Patrik, are you serious? Are they aware that my main character is Diana Ross, and is Candace not still their Diana Ross impersonator?"

He replied, "Yes, I am serious. I met with the owner Robert during lunch and he is aware that your main money maker is Miss Ross, and dig this, according to Robert, Candace is having sex-change surgery and plans to permanently leave the show because she feels that she will be a real woman after surgery and real women don't perform at gay clubs anymore."

I could only respond to Patrik, being knowledgeable that Candace had probably become burned out after working at Queen Mary for more than 15 or 16 years consistently. "Patrik, she may be tired or she may also desire to become a former showgirl who has had gender reassignment surgery, therefore making the decision to cut all ties from her past."

Patrik questioned, "I wonder what she's planning to do for a job now?"

My initial concerned response, "I hope that she doesn't become an ex-showgirl whom usually regret their decisions like those that I've personally known who have either committed suicide or ended up starring in transsexual porn and XXX rated Websites, however, there are those who seem happy, God bless Candace, I hope that she will be one of the happy ones and I wish her all the best with her surgery, now what time is my audition?"

He gleefully replied, "The show starts at 9:30p.m. Can you pick me up on your way there?"

"Sure, honey, I'll leave a little earlier and pick you up on the way. Thank you so much, Patrik, for arranging this for me. I'm so excited!"

"Oh wait, that's not all, honey!"He replied.

At that point in time, I could not imagine what could have topped auditioning for the Queen Mary, so I asked, before inhaling another breath, "What is it, Patrik?"

"Bob is letting us barrow a red fringed gown from his Vintage Collection for your audition costume. Now what do you think about that surprise?!"

I was in utter disbelief, so I replied, excitedly, "Wow, are you kidding me, Patrik!?"

"No, I am not kidding. You can come to Elizabeth Courtney Costumes tomorrow for a fitting if you want to!"

I replied, reaching for my appointment calendar, "Of course I'll come for a fitting tomorrow. What time do you want me there?"

"How about 2p.m. after lunch and, honey, you are going to be standing on the very same podium that Miss Ross, Cher and Tina Turner, and so many other icons stand whenever they come in for their costume fittings!"

He continued after a quick breath, "You can wear the "Super Nova" from Portland that Bob taught me how to make for the audition, so that you can make a grand entrance with there being no way at all that Robert won't hire you on the spot for the cast!"

I replied, making sure to get in all of the important details before they slipped my mind. "Wow, all right, Shooting Star, you better work it right on out, this is fantastic news and we can decide at the fitting tomorrow when we're going downtown to Michael Levine's Fabrics for materials in order to touch-up Miss "Super Nova" in addition to shopping for shoes and accessories. I cannot wait to call Tevin and tell him about the great news. Oh my gosh, thank you, thank you, thank you so much for everything, Patrik!"

Responding to my excitement, Patrik replied, "You are so welcome, honey, you deserve this. Say hello to Tevin for me. I got to get back to helping Conrad with an art project. He's been commissioned to sculpt an angel showpiece. I will see you tomorrow!"

When I finished writing in the fitting time into my calendar and then hanging up the telephone after talking to Tevin, I said a prayer: "Thank you mother, father, God, universe for these many blessings being bestowed upon me."

That following afternoon, I arrived early at Elizabeth Courtney for fitting, 30 minutes before my scheduled time. Minutes later, it was as if I'd started another out-of-body experience , standing on the same fitting room podium that my entertainment idols Diana Ross, Cher, Tina Turner and many other superstar legends had previously and recently stood for their costume fittings.

It was as if a part of me was floating above, watching the activities below as I tried on an original vintage Bob Mackie gown! After coming back down to earth after the Elizabeth Courtney Costumes fitting, the night of my audition on February 11, 1998, became another simply amazing evening!

I not only felt great, I was also looking like a million bucks performing "I'm Coming Out/Ain't No Mountain High Enough" and then later "I Will Survive/Take Me Higher" Diana Ross medleys to a sold-out showroom filled with people traveling from all across the world just to see a Queen Mary showcase!

I felt like a queen during my well-received, high-energy performances. Afterwards in the dressing room, I'd never felt as confident about an audition before as I was experiencing that night due to my amazing costumes and the overwhelming positive response that I received from the audience!

Patrik was just beside himself in the dressing room after my numbers, beaming with much- deserved pride and complimenting me on my performance. I was wearing the perfect red fringed Bob Mackie Vintage gown along with a Shooting Star Original floor length duster engulfing me like a brightly beaming super nova!

As Patrik helped me to undress and neatly pack away the outfits so they would not be damaged, the club owner Robert came into the dressing room also excitedly complimenting me on my performance! "Girl, you really knocked that audience out!"

He proceeded without allowing me to respond, "When can you start working for us permanently? "After discussing my salary, I accepted the position on the cast, thusly beginning the evolution from just lip-syncing to actually using my voice and a live microphone to create energy, nuance and excitement during my performances!

I was ecstatic about having a home base to re-create and update some of my old-time favorite numbers from over the years incorporating, "The Men All Pause/Cold Hearted Snake" by Klymaxx and Paula Abdul that I started off on the top of the stage seductively dangling from a chain hanging from the ceiling!

My choreography was designed to seduce the audience as I descended down from the top stage steps wearing a black leather choker, fuchsia sequined-pasties and an all-black Jane of the jungle, shredded sheer top and bottom!

The initial intention was to catch the audience by surprise after concluding the routine by ripping off my sheer top, allowing my pasties to reflect the stage and spotlights!

I'd also updated and turned "Mercedes Boy" by Pebbles into a sexy burlesque-inspired number, concluding with my back turned to the audience teasing them while removing my bra to the beat of the music!

I additionally included "I Don't Want To Lose Your Love," the version by B Angie B, and there were always my ever crowd pleasing routines to re-mixed and updated Sade, Jody Watley and "Tyrone" by another most inspiring current performer, Erykah Badu!

Inspiration and being such a fan lead me to have become adventurous enough to create my Tina Turner illusion, which was a challenge for me at first to really capture her rough-edged rock and roll persona! I don't care how rough she appears on the stage, because Tina Turner also possesses an alluring sexy edge that I connected with during my performances.

One of my other favorite productions was when Robert commissioned Shooting Star to design Egyptian-inspired costumes for me along with two male dancers! Robert also hired an artist to sculpt a huge Egyptian cobra's head rivaling anything that you may have seen at any theme park after sharing the vision with him during cast rehearsal my desire to portray Queen Nefertiti!

The prop was specifically designed to allow me to elegantly pose with burning incense while being glided across the stage by my scantily-clad muscular attendants, Angel, Abraham or Rico, performing a "Swept Away/Eaten Alive" Diana Ross medley.

The Queen Mary fans were a very excitable group of people from various walks of life whose sole purpose for going to the club was to have a great time! During one of my earlier Ross performances, shortly after joining the cast, a very enthusiastic and, might I add, intoxicated fan almost pulled my wig off when she'd stumbled to hug and tip me.

I was mortified that she was able to shift my hair during a performance and after that experience on stage in front a showroom filled slightly beyond capacity with an energetic audience, I knew that just using bobby pins was not the answer.

The following Saturday morning after that horrific experience, I walked up to my then favorite wig store on Hollywood Boulevard and purchased some hair clips and then sewed them into all of my wigs to rectify that previous horror. As a result of hair-clipping all of my stage wigs, I never had to worry about my hair ever being shifted during a performance ever again. Additionally and almost as importantly, I'd also developed a keen eye to spot and readjust my interactions with those that may have tied on a few too many cocktails over the course of the evening!

Just a few short months after joining the Queen Mary cast, I started receiving increased local and national booking opportunities for exclusive appearances one after another! This included a memorable weekend after the show when Robert came into the dressing room to inform me that a guest named Sally, who'd previously attended the show, was interested in speaking with me about booking my services!

According to Robert, Sally requested a quote for a two-hour Diana Ross exclusive appearance at her upcoming birthday Halloween Masquerade Ball, which was to be held at Hotel Nikko Beverly Hills on October 31, 1998!

Also according to Robert, Sally and her husband were scheduled to attend the show together the upcoming weekend to talk with me about my fee and availability. That Friday night after the show the following weekend, Patrik and I met with Sally and her husband in the dressing room.

First, Sally informed me that the group of people in attendance with her the previous weekend really enjoyed my performances and that she and her husband wanted to discuss my booking fee to perform at her 50th birthday celebration that their family and friends from all over the country would be attending.

After negotiating what she wanted, my fee and the deposit requirements, we arranged to meet on the upcoming Tuesday at Jamba Juice three doors up from the club to sign the engagement contract.

I feel that this would be the most appropriate point to provide a little background on Robert. I had been forewarned by a reliable source that it was extremely unusual for him to allow a guest to speak directly with the entertainers about outside bookings.

Robert had issues with being cut out as the middle man, so he'd usually insist on booking off site engagements through the club in an effort to receiving a huge cut of the money. But, according to my reliable source, Sally insisted upon negotiating with me directly.

The entire event, starting with my personal dressing suite was both elegant and exciting. It was rare occasion that Tevin was off on the night of the Halloween show! It was great that Tevin was able to escort me earlier that afternoon, supporting my acclimation to the venue showroom, stage and then organizing my dressing suite.

Later that evening, Conrad and Patrik arrived with the "Super Nova" that he'd taken home from Queen Mary to repair for the show. As usual, he worked his magic and added the boas together from our previous "DreamGirl" Oregon production, creating a beautiful golden-feathered duster that we christened "Big Bird"!

After inspecting and reorganizing my costumes with Patrik, Tevin and I retired to take a quick nap in our private lounge while Patrik and Conrad went to an early dinner. Later that evening at the event, I managed to charm some of the most conservative elderly African-American men in the audience.

During my "Lady Sings the Blues" segment, one of the other younger gentlemen spontaneously re-enacted an impromptu scene from the movie, where Billie Dee Williams tipped Billie Holiday a twenty dollar bill during her performance.

It was an unexpectedly magical evening as a whole!

Almost immediately after the Halloween Masquerade Ball exclusive engagement, I was later once again informed by my reliable source about other exclusive engagement opportunities that were not being presented to me, because Robert was not receiving a large enough commission.

Robert also had a well-deserved reputation of taking advantage of his cast members, usually making almost ten times my salary whenever he received special requests for me to perform. Immediately after learning of Robert's self-serving business tactics, I didn't make it easy for him to continue using me to make money without it also benefitting me.

I felt it important to set parameters during a private discussion with him in his office about our working arrangements when it came to him booking outside events for me.

It was only fair and about business for me to insist on the ability to negotiate my fees for those bookings that came through him, because I felt that the payment arrangement that he and I previously negotiated in the beginning of my employment was based on working four nights at the club.

As far as I was concerned, those previously negotiated fees associated with performing in the club did not have anything to do with outside engagements. I later also insisted on and received a cost-of-living raise after my first year on the cast.

My salary raise request was another monumental accomplishment, considering that there were other cast members who had worked for Robert on the cast for 15 years or more without receiving a raise in their salaries.

I wasn't mad at Robert for running his business, but as far as I was concerned I had a business to run also. It wasn't personal and the ground rules we established benefitted us both. I'm also happy that Robert seemed to understand where I was coming from.

As time passed, my weekends usually consisted of picking Patrik up, giving him a ride to the show before he got his own stylish sports car. Whenever he rode with me, Patrik usually surprised me by saying things like, "Honey, I was telling Bob about our challenge with finding some really nice faux gardenias for your Billie Holiday medley and he gifted you a special surprise!"

After taking the white box from him, opening it and removing the tissue paper, there was a silver beaded sequined three-petal gardenia headpiece sparkling and reflecting the streetlights in the car!

I was not going anywhere until I had gotten a closer look at another unexpected gift from Mr. Mackie, and as I removed the head-piece from the box to get a closer look, Patrik proceeded with the story behind the gift. "Bob said he'd made these for a photo shoot for the model Iman many years ago and since he knew that we were having problems finding nice gardenias that were the right size for the stage, he pulled them from the vintage accessories storage and asked me to give these to you!"

All I could do after receiving such a beautiful and priceless gift from Mr. Mackie was reply, "These gardenias are perfect for my "Lady Sings The Blues" medley. Thank you, Patrik, and will you please thank Bob for me!?

On another occasion when I picked Patrik up, he presented me with two sets of sequined materials that Bob purchased for me while he was shopping for costume material for Miss Ross' upcoming concert tour!

Patrik proceeded to explain that Bob used his designer's discount to purchase two really expensive, amazing AB sequined materials for my next costumes and all I had to do was just pay his cost for purchasing them.

When he pulled the material from the bag, the reflection against streetlights lit up the inside of the car like a disco ball and I was utterly dumbfounded at how beautiful the materials were! All I could say on that occasion in disbelief was, "Patrik, are you serious? Bob picked this material out special for me?"

"Yes, honey, you have a fan!"

He continued before I could respond, "Using the fuchsia material, I'm thinking that I will sketch a dolman-sleeved, ostrich feather-lined, sexy '20s-style gown that will be reminiscent of the one we previously borrowed from Bob for your Billie Holiday number at Love Lounge. You can wear it for your new "Missing You/He Lives In You" medley!"

After I had gazed at the materials for several more minutes and then started the car, Patrik continued speaking. "I'll also get Alexis Delago to work her magic on putting it together, because she owes me a favor, so I'll also make sure that she give you a great discount!"

I liked the sound of getting a discount for an original design, as Patrik continued speaking. "For the blue material, I can design a gown with a similar plunging neckline and back-out like the blue dress Miss Ross wore in Bob's book 'Dressing for Glamour' "!

I finally was able to get a word, in replying, "I know exactly what gown you're referencing, due to previously purchasing Bob's book at one of the bookstores on Hollywood Boulevard when Tevin and I were shopping for rare books."

Patrik continued, as if he didn't hear a word I'd said.

"We also need to make you a form mannequin that's your measurements for Alexis to get the draping just right when she makes the muslin before cutting the material. I will show you the full effect of everything at the club."

Due to me just wanting to listen to whatever new CD that I might have recently purchased, Patrik used to sometimes really get on my nerves always requesting for me to play my Randy Crawford greatest hits CD during our drive from West Hollywood up Laurel Canyon, towards Studio City.

There were also times that I was just tired of hearing Randy Crawford every weekend, but that night after receiving the vibrant designer material, I did not care what we were listening to. All that was on my mind was paying Bob for the materials as soon as possible and getting to the club so that I could fully see everything in full effect.

I'm not sure why Patrik never made himself a copy of Randy Crawford's music collection. Anyway, Patrik and I usually took my new music and costumes that we were putting into the show on trial runs during the Sunday evening shows before featuring them on the marathon Friday and Saturday night madness!

Sundays were usually less hectic as compared to the crazy and off-the-wall Friday and Saturday night long distance run. The show line-up required you to really focus and sometimes rush to change makeup to create a totally different character.

In addition, we were to be dressed and ready in costume for the next number, hoping to avoid Robert coming into the dressing room if there was a hold up in the show. And let us not forget the chaos and drama being multiplied during the continuous interruptions to take numerous requested souvenir photos with the guests!

Finally, after almost snake-crawling in the traffic up and over the Canyon, arriving at Queen Mary that early evening, there was only Monica, P. Levy and Rene in the dressing room when Patrik and I entered.

We greeted everybody in the room and then excitedly retreated to my dressing area. The period of getting to know the other cast members had long past by then with me already figuring out those cast members who were cool and down to earth as compared to the pretentious ones.

As far as the ones that were untrustworthy or shady, I fed them with a long-handled spoon and kept a vigilant eye on them at all times. Those usual suspects were like P. Levy, who regularly got on everybody's nerves always bragging, making himself out to be more than what he really was.

Rounding out the two attention-grabbing, jealous people was also the pageant girl named Rene, who saw everybody as competition. Rene entered the room just as Patrik and I were still drooling over the materials at my dressing station, and the fake, as usual, P. Levy sitting at the station directly left of me complimented us.

Then I recall hearing crazy Monica yelling across the room being her usual comedic self, "Great materials, Destiny! You can just hang that blue one right here so I can get started on my new gown during intermission!"

We all laughed and went on with the task of preparing for the Saturday trip into "Alice In Wonderland"! But Miss Rene could not contain her jealousy any longer, so as the night progressed and after she'd become drunk enough to have built up her nerve, she played her domestic role right as I prepared to go on stage!

Usually, the performer that goes on lineup next stands at the bottom of the steps waiting their turn to go on after the person before them finishes, so I was standing there patiently waiting, wearing my silver-sequined David Hawkins gown and the Shooting Star "Super Nova," ready to have some fun!

My opening number that night was the "I Will Survive/Take Me Higher" medley and I stood there watching Rene in the mirror stumbling from the opposite side of the dressing room to where I was standing.

Patrik was also standing with me, inspecting the "Super Nova" for possible touch-ups while I checked to be sure that the microphone was hot before going on stage. I was ready for Rene when she intentionally stepped on my costume trying to rip the chiffon "Super Nova" with her spiked heels!

I knew that Rene was already drunk, so I just pushed her off my costume, saying, "Rene, I know you see me standing here waiting to go on stage. You need to back your drunken ass up off me!"

Rene replied, stumbling backwards and then towards me again, "Destiny, move out of my way. You think you so special cause you wearing Bob Mackie costumes!"

When she swung at me and missed, I dropped the microphone that I was holding and the "Super Nova" to the floor, and grabbed her hands to move them away from my face.

Then I forcefully backed her up, pinning her against the dressing room bathroom door, replying, "Rene, I know that your ass is drunk right now, but the words are 'excuse me' if someone is in your way!"

I continued to restrain her, but I knew that she was also sick so I had no intention of hitting her. I just wanted her to know that I was not playing around, warning, "Rene, this is not a pageant. We are cast members here to make some money, not competing with each other for a crown, and if you were not such an alcoholic lush getting drunk all of the time before the show even starts, you would make some tips also!"

I was tempted to hit her after I released her and she tried swinging on me again and missing. But my journey consisted of learning to not use violence as the first means to resolve conflicts unless it was unavoidable in order to protect myself from being physically harmed.

Since she was no threat to me in her drunken state, I chose not to whip her ass all over the dressing room that night. For a brief moment I thought that I'd have to at least take her down after backing away when she acted like she wasn't finished acting crazy.

Rene should have thanked our mutual friend Victoria for saving her ass because she jumped between us to ask Rene what her problem was.

After Rene realized that I was serious about whooping that ass if she'd continued being stupid that night, she turned away from me and stumbled back to her station, covering her face with both hands and sobbingly crying out, "I'm sorry, Destiny! It's just that I am dealing with some serious issues right now!"

I replied to her before going on stage, after taking several deep calming breaths, "Girl, I don't invade your personal space, so don't invade mine. Everybody in this dressing room has issues and problems that we're dealing with, but if you ever get in my face like that again drunk or not, it will not be pretty the next time!"

I picked up the "Super Nova," with Patrik helping me to place her back into position and then he handed me the microphone that he'd picked up off the floor during the scuffle.

Once I'd gotten into position at the top of the stage for my introduction, I took a few more deep breaths and it became as if the incident never occurred, because I did not miss a beat. I was determined to not let Rene ruin my night!

I really turned on the energy when the music started after my introduction, and the audience erupted in cheers and applause as the scrim slowly opened to reveal me posed, engulfed in an invigorating "Super Nova"!

After the long show that night, Robert summoned me to his office to request my side of the story about what had occurred in the dressing room. I was nervous knocking on his office door because I never liked having to be questioned by him about being involved in anything that wasn't complimentary.

After closing the office door behind me, Robert pulled a cigarette from the pack on his desk and lit it with a gold-engraved lighter before asking in a calm voice, "What is going on in the dressing room between you and Rene, Destiny?"

After I explained to him what had occurred between Rene and I, which was later corroborated by everybody that was in the dressing room at the time, I told him, "Robert, I don't bother anybody, nor do I disrespect other people or their property in this show. I work hard to afford my costumes, so I had to back Rene off me letting her know that I was not someone she could just walk all over and be disrespectful to just because she was drunk and envious."

Robert proceeded to confide in me. "You know, Destiny, when you first joined my show I was a little concerned about you being so nice and unassuming and I also questioned if you would be able to handle the crazy personalities in the show."

He continued, before I could respond. "Thankfully, you have proven me wrong and I really admire the way that you carry yourself and, due to being in this business for many years, I find you to be one of the classiest ladies and talented performers that I have had in my show in many years, girl!"

Robert took another puff of his cigarette, continuing, "I'm really happy that I don't have to worry about you handling yourself in that dressing room, because you are a tough girl and a shrewd business woman."

I had not expected Robert to tell me that he had been concerned about me being able to handle myself on the cast. If he only knew what I'd had to deal with being the new girl on the scene back in Atlanta and later at Plaza, being the only African-American on a cast full of deceitful Latina queens and showgirls. Whew!

All I could say in response to his concerns was, "Robert, you don't have to worry about me, because I've had to deal with a whole lot worse than this over the years that I have been performing. I'll be okay here and thank you for the compliment, your support and understanding!"

I thought to myself, as I left Robert's office, that I was there to make money, not get into the petty drama that was always present in every cast dressing room. I think that after the incident with Rene, I sort of showed that just because I was a nice person who treated people the way I wanted to be treated, that it was a mistake for anyone to take my kindness for weakness, because I'm not the least afraid to stand up for myself when being threatened or disrespected.

Although I really enjoyed performing, my main goal for working in those bars and clubs has always been a means of survival to pay my bills. I had a low tolerance level for all of the other unnecessary drama and people that were a possible threat to accomplishing that goal, so I continued the practice of feeding those drama queens, who seemed to always needed chaos and dysfunction in order to exist, with long-handled spoons.

It's also common in club environments to always have those people present who are intrusive on your personal space and refuse to take no for an answer. There are also those who do everything possible to interfere and make everyone else around them as miserable as they are, which brings me to the second physical altercation that I was involved in at Queen Mary a year or so later.

The incident occurred after I'd received a personal booking to appear at an exclusive New Year's Eve private event at the Masonic Temple in Studio City in 1999. Patrik and I would have to leave immediately after my last number at Queen Mary to go perform "I'm Coming Out/Ain't No Mountain High Enough" and "I Will Survive/Take Me Higher" medleys at another exciting and financially prosperous engagement.

Thank goodness Tevin rearranged his work schedule in order to be my escort, which also made it possible for us to bring in the New Year together in the dressing room before leaving Queen Mary for the private event!

However, the night after I'd booked the New Year show, a cocktail server named Allen came into the dressing room as we were preparing for the second show and started sarcastically suggesting to me, "Miss Destiny, I know you're getting paid a lot of money for your New Years' Eve show, so there's no reason why you can't buy some jewelry from me, right?"

As far as my personal business was concerned, I'd consciously made every effort to keep my outside bookings on the down low, however, there were those unavoidable connections made through the club which always seemed to spark interest from others.

Whenever someone directly inquired about the details of such engagements, I usually downplayed the little information that I chose to share with them.

Up to that point, Allen and I have never had any major issues with each other, but for some unknown reason he had been extremely annoying the entire evening. Instead of being where he was supposed to be, out on the floor serving cocktails, he was in the dressing room being messy.

I just wanted him to back off a little bit, considering it had been a fast-paced show, requiring us to be mentally and physically prepared for three long shows so I responded, "Allen, it 's really none of your business how much money I'm getting paid for my show."

I turned from the mirror and then faced Allen before continuing, "And furthermore, it's my choice if I choose to buy anything from you or not and right now. I choose not to spend my money on your preschool, art project jewelry."

The rest of the cast chuckled when I said aloud what we all had expressed privately about him trying to hawk jewelry that looked like a 3--year-old could have designed much better. I thought that the conversation was over when he angrily walked out of the dressing room.

I also thought that I had made myself clear that I was not going to just give him my hard- earned money, because I could get better quality costume jewelry at the costume jewelry place on Hollywood Boulevard for half the price of the junk that he was trying to sell.

After Allen left the dressing room, the whole cast questioned why he'd chosen to be messy right in the middle of the weekend whirlwind, knowing very well that we were expected by Robert to pose for photos in addition to being ready for the productions and our solo numbers.

When I performed, I usually had set choreography for each number but I would also do things to feel more connected with the audience! I really enjoy leaving the stage to mingle and connect with an audience on a deeper level, especially during all Diana Ross character performances, where connecting with the audience is a requirement!

Well, as the evening progressed, I was having a great time with the highly enthusiastic audience, unaware that Allen was plotting. He sought his revenge on me by starting to block my set path during the Miss Ross medley routine.

I was sure that Allen was trying to be funny when he kept abruptly stepping in front of me and trying to step on my train in an attempt at tripping me up during my performance.

He stepped in front of me again, and I reached down, picked up my gown train and then, discretely, forcefully pushed him out of my way without skipping a note during my number! Unbeknownst to the audience, I managed to successfully put Allen in check as they erupted in applause!

After my number concluded, as far as I was concerned I had proven to Allen that I was not intimidated by him one bit. I also felt that it was all over after I was immediately ushered outside by Robert to pose for individual fan photo requests!

After the guest photos ended, I rushed to the dressing room to get ready for my Sade makeup and costume change! Within five seconds, Allen slammed the dressing room door as he dramatically entered through the curtain carrying a serving tray! Since my dressing station was at the exit, he approached me at my dressing station, wildly waving his hands in the air and screeching like a crazed nut."Destiny, what's your damn problem, bitch?"

I calmly replied, "Allen, I'm rushing to get changed for my next number, If you like, we can discuss this after the show, but now back the hell off me."

As I turned to continue powdering my face toning down the makeup, he then took the serving tray he was carrying and pressed it up against me in a threatening manner, yelling, "I don't give a damn what you are doing, we are going to discuss this right now! You think that you are so special, but you're not, Destiny!"

I got to my feet and pushed him away, causing him to stumble into the hanging costumes and then I picked up my station chair raising it high over my head warning, "I am not going to tell you again to back the fuck off me Allen. I will take this chair and break your freaking neck if you don't get the hell out of my face!"

Allen screamed, covered his face with the tray and went running out of the dressing room threatening, "I'm going to tell Robert, you hit me with your chair, Destiny!"

I yelled after him, "Go right ahead, the next time you get in my face with another tray , you'll be pulling it out of your ass!"

I then sat back down at my station and took in a few deep calming breaths to compose and center myself in order to finish the show.

After I explained to the other cast members what happened in the showroom with Allen trying to trip me during my number, those that knew me could not believe that he'd threatened me with a serving tray right in the middle of the show! A few minutes later, Robert rushed into the dressing room asking, "Destiny, did you hit Allen with your chair?"

"No, Robert that is not what happened. The truth is Allen followed me into the dressing room after I finished taking fan pictures, getting in my face and threatening me with a tray, and insisting that I talk to him after I told him that we can discuss whatever he wanted to talk about after the show. When he insisted that I argue with him at that very moment and continued threatening me with his serving tray, I raised my chair up to back him off after I repeatedly told him to back up, but I did not hit him with the chair."

After everybody confirmed that Allen followed me into the dressing room and threatened me with his serving tray after I told him that we could discuss his issues at the end of the night, Robert turned back to me, shaking his head and saying "Girl, I don't know what I am going to do with you?"

He then turned facing the exit and announced to the entire cast before walking out of the dressing room with a cola in one hand, a cigarette in the other and his Polaroid camera dangling from his neck, "We've got a hundred guest pictures outside, if you are dressed meet me out front!"

The following weekend, another cast member decided to push their limits to test if they were able to express domination and their perceived superiority over me right after a very exclusive appearance at an Advertising Industry Gala in the Merv Griffin Beverly Hilton Hotel International Ballroom!

I returned to work at Queen Mary that Friday evening still floating on a cloud after being introduced two afternoons previously by Jim Belusci and then performing my "I'm Coming Out/Aint No Mountain High Enough" Diana Ross medley to a receptive, energetic Beverly Hills elite crowd!

P. Levy, who was the self-appointed stage manager always trying to intrude in everybody's business, started getting on our nerves when he once again began bragging the whole night about some movie he'd acted in over 20 years ago.

I knew that he was trying to be competitive with everyone else. Since he was no longer doing crystal meth, cocaine and alcohol, he'd resorted to dealing with his sketched-out nerves by annoyingly, continuously running his mouth at almost a thousand miles per hour, getting on our nerves.

P. Levy also decided to flex his muscles and get an attitude with me after I'd started to wear my Walkman to tune him out whenever he'd started repeatedly telling the same old story about his over 20--something-years of drug addiction, which contributed to him being arrested in between shows by an undercover cop outside of Queen Mary.

The arrests were widely covered on the local news. Two Queen Mary cast members were taken into custody by an undercover cop for soliciting and snorting cocaine in the club parking lot, which required Robert to post bail for P. Levy and another cast member, whom shall remain nameless because I like her.

P. Levy was also upset that night because he did not get the reaction from the crowd the night before during one of our annual offsite cast bookings at The Sportsman's Lodge for talk radio hosts Mark and Brian.

So, he built up the nerve to try and intimidate me when he leaned over as we prepared for the second show saying, "Destiny, the dressing room is really crowded on Saturday nights, so in order to keep Robert from being upset about non-cast members being in here, you need to tell Patrik that he is no longer allowed in the dressing room during the show."

What? Of course, I was taken aback by the crap that was coming out of his mouth, because each cast member were allowed at least one dressing room assistant during the show, so I calmly replied, "P., you are not the boss of me and since Robert has never informed me that he had any problems with Patrik assisting me, your ego-tripping objections mean nothing to me."

P. Levy then started to get loud, yelling, "Destiny, I am the stage manager back here and you will obey my rules!"

I turned to face him, trying to remain calm and looking directly into his eyes, replying, "P., you must be drinking and snorting cocaine or crystal meth again. I tell you what, you can play stupid and jump over here if you want to."

I turned and pointed at Monica's dressing station, continuing, "You must have forgotten about that dent in the file cabinet over there that was made by your head after Monica slammed you into it when you got into her face about being her stage manager. I will clean this entire dressing room up with your ass if you play crazy up in here tonight. P. Levy.

After realizing that I was serious about him staying out of my business, he backed off and he never approached me like that ever again. As I think back throughout my life, I've had numerous experiences with jealous and envious queens assuming that I'm weak just because I am a genuinely nice person.

I guess you can say the majority of said people were shocked upon immediately being stopped in their tracks after they'd foolishly assumed that they could walk all over me just to see how far I would let them go.

I never wanted to get physical with anyone. I just had to make it clear that I would have gone there if pushed and backed into a corner. My mother and grandmother always taught us to treat others the way that you want to be treated, but if threatened, do not ever hesitate for one moment to protect yourself.

As I've matured over the years, I have made a conscious effort to handle those types of situations differently than I used to do back in the day when fighting was the only way that I knew to defend myself from physical harm.

However, in the line of work that I've been in for so many years and since there was usually no one to have my back earlier on when I was out there flying solo, I was sometimes left with no other choice but to do what I had to do when physically threatened.

It seems that the older I've become, the less tolerance I have for the unnecessary drama and shadiness associated being an entertainer in such environments. This has greatly contributed to my diminishing desire to continue being a performance artist.

Even though there were the usual acidic queens in the show, there were also those cool and down to-earth people on the cast that were not drama kings and queens whom I immediately connected with! Included in those cool people I liked working with were Angel, Monica, Catrice, Abraham, Rico, the other Alan, Fontazia and another cocktail server and Diana Ross fan named Chris Hnatsin.

Although we were aware of Chris' impending mortality, I was distraught after we were informed one Friday night by Robert that Chris had died after a long battle with AIDS.

After receiving the unexpected bad news, the cast stopped fighting amongst each other that whole weekend and I somberly dedicated Chris' favorite Diana Ross medleys to him: "Missing You/He Lives in You," and "I'm Coming Out/Ain't No Mountain High Enough," "I Will Survive/Take Me Higher."

Over the next several months, the Queen Mary show continued selling-out, with me also receiving one of the best compliments of my career when Moms Tyson shared that her daughter overheard a conversation about me when she was flying into Los Angeles to visit her from Philadelphia.

According to Moms, during her daughter's flight she became privy to a conversation on the plane between two other women who were flying from France. They were expressing their excitement about going to Queen Mary on that weekend to see Destiny perform!

Moms' daughter then informed the ladies from Paris that her family was also attending the show that weekend as my special guests! Since it has always been a strong desire of mine to be entertaining creating memorable experiences on stage for those people coming to see me perform, that acknowledgement from random people on an overseas flight re-affirmed to me that I was on the right path to living the professional life that I'd always dreamed that I deserved to experience!

Remembering the compliment from strangers on a plane also causes me to recall the time that I was first inspired to become a performance artist—way before I even knew that there was even a name or title for what I witnessed many years ago in Myrtle Beach, South Carolina!

The memorable opportunity for me to shake my tail-feather as a solo performance artist arrived after I managed to book my very first paid show at a gay club that my friends and I often frequented in Florence, South Carolina when we were teenagers.

The out-of-town booking occurred on a fun night that we were all dancing after the show with me deciding that I wanted to perform on the stage like the girls that were in the show earlier that night! I did not have any idea of what I was getting myself into after approaching the club manager and inquiring about what was required to perform in his show.

All I knew was that I was thinking that I could have some fun performing and entertaining the audience like I was entertained by those other performers! I was naively unaware of how much work and effort would be required to put a routine together, because it was not just about dancing around and lip-syncing your favorite songs.

On the ride back to Myrtle Beach later that morning with Vivian driving, I had already chosen my songs before we'd left the club, one of which was "I Feel Good All Over" by Stephanie Mills, "Other Side of The Rainbow" by Melba Moore and maybe something by Natalie Cole!

I'd purchased the hair from the wig store on the boardwalk and my costumes were purchased from my favorite department store, JC Penney, the evening wear collection! I used spray adhesive to cover one of my pumps one in glittery gold and the other in sizzling red!

Vivian was my roommate back then on the beach and I usually worked on costumes and choreography whenever I was alone in the apartment, continuously practicing each song daily, thinking that I was going to turn the show out with my song selections and costumes!

The night of the show, Vivian drove us to Florence and there was also an acquaintance that I'd recently met at Offshore Drilling Company in Myrtle Beach named Gina La'Tate who was also booked on the same show. During my numbers, I went out there performing those slow love songs, compared to Gina performing the high-energy Tina Turner number "Proud Mary," tearing the house down with her performances!

Although my costumes and wigs were right on target, it never occurred to me that I might have needed a mentor to teach me the proper techniques for creating an entertaining performance when I first started out.

However, I quickly learned right then and there after that deflating experience, resolving that in order to be entertaining enough to move the audience, I would have to really bring it with high energy, more popular numbers after learning my audience!

I was so disappointed with the performance that night I did not go to the management afterwards to collect my salary for what was to be a first time paid booking. I was not at all happy about my performance selections, yet determined to strive for excellence and high energy around future performances from that moment forward!

Over the years since that humiliating performance and since I didn't have a drag-mother during those days, I also learned by trial and error what works for me and what doesn't work on stage! I am therefore thankful that all of my hard work has been acknowledged and appreciated by others who may have experienced my alter-ego Destiny (Your Mistress of Illusions) on stage!

Also, I've been rewarded beyond measure for all of the determination and hard work that I have put forth to being exciting, engaging and memorably entertaining on stage which remains my priority.

They paid off I guess, those many hours that I spent alone in my childhood living room practicing and creating routines to everything Madonna, including but not limited to "Lucky Star," "Borderline," "Let Me Show You The Way To Go" and everything else by Michael Jackson, The Jacksons, Cyndi Lauper, Prince, Vanity Six, Jesse Johnsons' Revue, Andre Cymone and many other favorite artists!

Whenever I wasn't creating shows in the living room during my early teen years at home alone, I usually placed the stereo speakers in the garage window, turned the volume on high and created choreography up and down our driveway in my roller skates.

I recall during those early days performing and imagining that our gated yard was filled to the capacity with applauding fans! They all came to see me roller-skate choreographed precise turns and spins to anything Shannon, "I'm Coming Out", "Upside Down" by Diana Ross, all of Melba Moore, including "Loves Coming At Cha," and many other popular songs!

Although I would often get into trouble with my mother for blowing out her stereo speakers, I believe that those earlier rehearsals really prepared me for my future in entertainment! T.U.M.F.G.U.!

Chapter Fourteen

Destiny Fulfilled and a Time for Change!

Almost three years after meeting Tevin, we were both really burned out and in need of a much-deserved vacation from work. In addition to working on a top-secret post for the aerospace industry when we became a couple, Tevin usually worked at least two jobs ever since we started living together!

I continued working part-time sales jobs in the corporate field by day in addition to managing the nonstop club and exclusive stage appearances by night.

Our first official vacation together occurred on November 10, 1999, after Tevin booked airline tickets to Phoenix, Arizona, with the intention of introducing me to his family for the very first time.

That single unsolicited gesture he made for me to meet his family reconfirmed that he was really serious about us being together for the long haul! And he had listened to me in the beginning when we first started dating when I informed him about what I would and would not tolerate in a relationship with him.

Tevin also confirmed without question the level of commitment that he was willing to make regarding our future together! However, I also remained vigilant and in an uncompromising frame of mind about what I would and would not accept from him for our relationship to continue growing together.

Also, admittedly, my vigilance resulting from the negative experiences that I had in previous relationships, including those life threatening nightmares also resulted in there being many times that I may have been unnecessarily harder on Tevin than what was required to get my message across. I'm Sorry "Pumpkinhead"!

However, those past relationships taught me that just because I was born transsexual, I did not have to continue settling for the first guy showing interest in me to fulfill whatever fantasies they may or may not possess about being in a relationship with a transsexual woman.

Additionally, those past experiences taught me to be more aware of those guys being covertly insincere about their personal agendas for being with me. I just knew that I deserved to be with someone who would cherish and value me for who I am and what I have to offer!

So, Tevin's gesture to meet his family also reconfirmed his character and frame of mind as far as our union was concerned. Before landing in Phoenix, I was very nervous, wondering how his family would respond to me and hoping that they would not be able to "Read" me upon sight.

It was a cool desert early evening when Tevin and I left the hotel in the rental car headed to his parents' house and during the drive I felt an instant connection with the rustic landscapes.

I was especially drawn to the almost 30-foot-tall saguaro cacti growing in certain areas on the mountainsides, meditatively reaching toward the sky with their almost 50-foot-long arms!

They were in bloom with creamy white flowers and golden clustered centers at the end of their outstretched limbs, while serving as nesting roosts to flocks of the most colorful parakeets fluttering from cactus to cactus, building nests in crevices of the saguaros!

Later that breezy evening, when we arrived at his parents' house and I was introduced to his family, my nervousness thankfully became less as intense as they were on the flight. At first, Tevin's mother was a little cold towards me when we sat next to each in the back seat of the car on the ride to the casino.

However, as the evening progressed I noticed she seemed to have slightly warmed up just a little bit. I would have taken her coldness personally if not for Tevin warning me that his mother has always been cold towards all of her sons' girlfriends and wives upon initially meeting them.

During the course of the visit back at their house, his father serenaded us with one of the songs that he'd previously sung during his singing career when he was much younger in the military with his smooth vocals very reminiscent of Nat King Cole!

Since our visit was during the beginning of the fall season, the weather was really nice and comfortable, contributing to me also instantly falling in love with the sultry dessert evenings later back in our hotel room.

After meeting his parents, sister and brothers, who are some of the most influential people in Tevin's life, allowing me to understand his motivations for being who he is, I also better understood the reasons that he worked so hard!

Meeting his family also contributed to me really understanding how blessed I am to have such a great guy whose desires and intentions are to unconditionally love, protect and provide for me on all levels!

I was pleased that during our visit with his family we were not confronted about my gender identity, nor was I later made aware by Tevin of any further conversations concerning my gender that may have taken place after we left Phoenix!

On the flight back to Los Angeles, we both fantasized aloud about Phoenix being our first choice to live if we were to ever decide to leave Los Angeles!

Also, on our flight back to Los Angeles, I discovered the true power of verbally putting out into the universe your hopes and future dreams! My power revealed itself after suggesting to Tevin that if we were to relocate to Arizona, I would not feel comfortable making such a life-changing decision to move to another state with him just as his girlfriend.

Without skipping a beat, Tevin suggested that if we got married, then I would be his wife and I wouldn't have to worry about just being called his girlfriend by anyone!

Considering that when we spent our first night together it could have possibly been a one night stand, my suggestion to him was just a thought that I had no idea would come to fruition in the manner that it came to be.

I'd never in a million years expected for one moment that a vacation to meet his family would also result in a marriage proposal thousands of feet in air on a flight from Arizona!

The next day in our living room when I was cleaning our bird cages and sweeping up their discarded feathers, Tevin formally presented me with a beautiful princess-cut, two carat diamond and gold engagement ring, officially proposing that we get married!

In my opinion, my ring was the most beautiful ring ever, due to me never expecting that at the age of 32 years young I would seriously be asked for my hand in marriage for the very first time by the guy of my dreams!

Of course, I said yes again, however, since I did not want to be the only one displaying that I was committed and officially off the market, I insisted on also buying

Tevin a ring, so that we both wore engagement rings!

After getting that minor manner of business resolved, we then, upon much discussion and weighing of the pros and cons, decided that it would be so much easier, stress-free and adventurous if we'd eloped to Las Vegas to get married!

Our Vegas elopement reflected the previous adventurousness on the kinetic night that brought us back together after previously being introduced to each other and then meeting again for the second time at Peanuts almost five years later!

I recall it being a magical night. I'd randomly walked into the club not looking for anything but a change of pace from my mundane life. The thought of finding a boyfriend there was the last thing on my mind and as unexpected blessings come out of nowhere, I found my one and only future husband! Yes, you heard me right I did conclusively say one and only husband!

Although I was floating on air due to becoming engaged after returning from a vacation of a lifetime, I immediately got going back to work at Queen Mary that following weekend, still seemingly extremely chore-ridden and monotonous as before our vacation.

My focus was on making wedding plans all while struggling to not become once again worn down by the monotony of my job in the show. However, I continued pushing myself to experience some great times here and there working on developing my craft!

I recall almost in detail the night that the cast and I were all in the dressing room painting for what was expected to be a busy and crazy Saturday night show, which were usually sold-out from beginning to end!

Usually on the weekends Queen Mary was expected to have continuous lines snaking around the corner into the parking lot, with enthusiastic people vying to for the best seats in the showroom closest to the stage.

On those sold-out marathon nights, we were all required to each perform at least four solo numbers, in addition to the cast productions for each show, which included one of my favorite productions when I played the RuPaul character singing live in our "Love Shack" production that I've posted on Youtube.

The Queen Mary audiences really appreciated our artistic creations that were presented to entertain them and they in turn showed their appreciation by generously opening their wallets and awarding us for our efforts.

I looked forward to and really enjoyed the few and far between drama-free nights in the dressing room when we were all getting along and no one was competing with each other.

We all seemed to have been having a great time during intermission before the second show, laughing about one such hilarious occasion occurring the night before while standing outside in front of the club waiting for the assistant manager Christina to start posing the guests for their requested photos with the cast.

As we stood there in full costume and hair, chatting and acting crazy, waiting for the next guest to be posed with us, some of the crazier cast members were waving and yelling catcalls back at the cars honking their horns as they passed us in front of the club.

Well, all of a sudden it seemed that we were immersed in one of those surrealistic "Girls Gone Wild" scenes when we all noticed this very attractive, shirtless and physically fit guy jogging towards us almost in slow motion, with sweat glistening on his toned chest reflecting in the bright moonlight.

Those of us that were in relationships managed to play it cool as the beefy jogger passed, but Miss Catrice, with her crazy self, dramatically reached down, swept the train of her gown off the sidewalk with her fingertips almost exposing her G-string, and then started jogging behind the jogger in a pair of five-inch stilettos!

You talk about a hilarious sight, watching her running up the street in a beaded gown trying to catch up with the sexy blond guy getting his exercise on, which made us all fall out hysterically laughing!

Anyway, on that night everyone were in a joyous mood until Christina came into the dressing room later that evening to tell us that she'd just received word that Robert had suffered a massive heart attack after the show the night before.

Earlier that evening we were all wondering why Robert wasn't at the club as he usually was to open up. I was stunned after we gotten the news of his heart attack when Monica and P. Levy then told us that this was Robert's second heart attack, and he was previously advised by his doctors after the first one to not continue managing their family owned business.

According to the long-timers in the cast, his mother had established Queen Mary over 38 years or so before. She entrusted Robert with running the business after she became unable to manage the club.

Her intention was to provide a venue so that transgender, gay, lesbian, bisexual, questioning, queer, non gender-conforming and heterosexual people would together all have a place to come to be who they were in a safe and affirming environment.

The loyalty and appreciation for what Robert's family did for the community was such that every now and then, original cast members from over the time span of Queen Mary being in existence would often return to the stage as special guest performers in the show during the holiday and other special occasion shows.

On the night that we were informed of Robert's heart attack, we all dedicated our performances to him and when he finally returned to the club, he informed us that he was going to finally follow his doctors' advice and not return in his previous managerial capacity.

Unfortunately, Robert's son, Robby Jr., was the only other family member physically able to assume responsibility for managing the family business. It was ironic that he assumed managing and running the club daily operations, because he had been fired and barred from the club by his father one month or so before Robert's heart attack for falling off the wagon sneaking around drinking on the job again.

In addition to Robby Jr's alleged drug and alcohol challenges, he was also known to sleep around with some of the cast members even though he was a married man with a newborn.

Often between my sets, I'd sit in the back of the club by the bar watching the other performers. He first approached me in a sexual manner while I was minding my own business watching Angel perform his dramatic geisha production to "What About That" by Janet Jackson.

I was interrupted by Robby Jr. really grossing me out when he began informing me out of the blue that he had a Latina queen, so now he wanted to add me in the mix, becoming his Nubian queen if Tevin and I were to ever break up.

The chances of me and Robby Jr. being anything other than platonic acquaintances was never going to happen in this lifetime or any other even if I wasn't with Tevin. Too many demons!

The weekends that Robert wasn't supervising the club, chaos ensued, including some of the other performers obviously trying to perform intoxicated on stage. Additionally, making things worse during our performances we regularly had to walk over to the DJ control booth and awaken the DJ from her heroin-induced snooze.

It was embarrassing to have your music continuously skipping during your performance and also often performing in the dark, because the spotlight operator had fallen asleep in the middle of the show.

However, I liked the rare occasions when Robert was well enough to manage the club, because he did not play or compromise at all when it came to making sure that all aspects of the show was professional and ensuring that the guests were happy and entertained.

Working at Queen Mary brought immeasurable success professionally and monetarily. I remember my pride and excitement earlier on when I'd gone one sunny afternoon to the car lot managed by my cast member Abrahams' boyfriend and paid cash for my very first of several Chrysler LeBarons to follow!

I confess that you couldn't tell me I wasn't cool cruising around town in my burgundy and black top convertible to rehearsals, usually wearing one of the silk Bob Mackie scarves that Shooting Star illustrated for a limited release and gifted to me throughout the years.

I'd also usually just thrown on an oversized hat and shades and, with the top down, groove to my favorite songs in the six disc changer running errands, going to the gym and work!

I was also privileged during my employment at Queen Mary to have met some fabulous legends like the beautiful Lisa Raye McCoy, Rip Torn, Tracy Bingham, the first African-American "Baywatch" beauty life guard, some of "Living Single" cast members and many other celebrities whom regularly attended the show!

One celebrity in particular, who will not remain nameless was Tim Allen, whom to my surprise turned out to have been one of the most obnoxious rudest celebrities that I have ever performed for.

At first he was fine, but after more than a few drinks he started talking loudly, trying to be the center of attention during the entire show. If he had to be the loudest person in the show-room being annoying the whole night, you would think that he would have at least tipped the entertainers that he'd interrupted during their performances.

Although I obtained much success working at Queen Mary, as time passed I became extremely burned out on continuously working nonstop every weekend. In addition, I was compelled to perform the same regularly requested songs because audiences insisted upon seeing their favorites.

I feel it important to note that totaling my performance schedule included also working some days during the week for almost 20-something years after that period!

My very first time seriously considering retiring from the show circuit occurred during a time that the current Queen Mary management also caused me to become very concerned about the future of the show.

As a result of my observations, I also felt it necessary to start planning for a different future because I wasn't interested in going to another show, nor was I ready to go back on the performance circuit at that point.

I wasn't sure what career I wanted to venture into at the time, although I was confident that I wanted to transition from the entertainment scene, so I decided to enroll in a local community center data processing certification program!

My intention was to take the short-term computer data entry program first to get back in the swing of school and then later transfer to a two-year community college.

Since it had been so long in time that I'd attended classes, the certification program also allowed me to get back in the groove after time off from previously taking an Introduction to Psychology course for a semester at West Los Angeles Community College over nine years or so prior to that point in time.

Fourteen weeks later, years before she died, Mother Chinue and Tevin attended our Computer Data Processing Certification graduation ceremony on a breezy sunny afternoon encircled by birds of paradise and underneath the shaded aromatic magnolia trees in the courtyard of the church associated with the school.

Almost four weeks later after receiving my Computer Data Processing Certification, I then enrolled into an Introduction to Sociology and Beginners Art classes at Los Angeles Community College. I am so happy that I had the foresight to explore other career options, because I'd started to really dread going into work at Queen Mary!

It didn't help that Robert was no longer there effectively managing the club and in addition to the state of the economy that year, Robert's absence also negatively affected the quality of the show, thusly contributing to a decrease in club patronage. Except for the baroness on old consistent Saturday nights, we often performed to an almost empty showroom.

If you've never been a performance artist you may find difficulty understanding how exhausting it is to maintain the required energy level in order to present an entertaining performance each time.

I consciously committed to giving 150 percent whether there was one person or 100 people in the audience taking the time and coming out to see our show!

As the days progressed into weekend nights, I remained committed to remaining professional in dealing with my challenges with my night job. School was a welcomed distraction from the chaotic nights and uncertainty of the club's future.

I really enjoyed being on the campus attending classes and on one particular day that I was reviewing homework in the Student Center during a break in between classes, a guy from my past unexpectedly approached me!

The flame from my past was named Vernon and we met several years earlier at Circus Circus disco club on Santa Monica Boulevard after Ebony's brother Scott talked me into going out with him to dance.

I recall seeing Vernon intensely watching me from the second level before he approached me on my way to freshen-up after a marathon, old-school mega-mix dance with Scott.

After informing Vernon that Scott was my cousin, Vernon and I started passionately dating for a brief while.

When I looked up from my sociology book that day in the Student Center and saw Vernon standing there in front of me looking as cute as I remembered, I was happy that I was also looking cute myself!

Vernon displayed an air of confidence and excitement upon sitting down in the chair beside me and then inquiring, "Hello, Tracee, how are you doing?"

"I am doing very well, Vernon!" I replied as I placed the pen and papers in the book and then inserted them inside my book-bag continuing, "How are you?"

"I'm good, especially after running into you!" He leaned in closer to me and continued, "You look great. How long have you been attending classes here?"

I smiled in response to Vernon's compliment and then replied, "Thanks Vernon, so do you." I then made every effort to change the subject about our looks, continuing, "I've just recently enrolled. How about you, when did you start?"

He replied, almost apologetically, "Well, I had to move back to Michigan for a while and I've just recently returned and enrolled myself."

I sarcastically replied, "Is that why you just disappeared?"

Vernon replied, "Well, that's sort of a long story I would love to tell you about over coffee or something after your last class!" He then placed his hand over mine, continuing, "How many more classes do you have left, Tracee?"

I removed my hand from beneath his and replied, "Vernon, I am actually engaged to be married very soon now!" I then proudly displayed the engagement ring on my left hand as I continued, "So, I won't be able to accept your coffee invitation."

"Wow!" Then he briefly paused before continuing, "I knew that you were special when we first met, so I guess my loss is your new man's gain, huh?"

My joyous response to Vernon's statement was smiling and shaking my head up and down in agreement that it was his loss!

Vernon shrugged his shoulder and inquired, "Are you happy with him, Tracee?"

In response to his question I continued smiling and glancing at my engagement ring, ecstatically replying, "I am immensely happy with my fiancé, Vernon!"

Since Vernon didn't respond, I sat back in my seat getting comfortable before almost relishing in reminding him of a previous discussion we'd had! "Do you recall the conversation that you and I had about my desire to find someone whom was secure enough in his manhood to unconditionally love and accept me the way I deserved to be loved?"

He replied, shaking his head in agreement with my recollection. "I remember that conversation vividly, Tracee, and I regret that I was not brave enough to have been that person during that time. I wish that we could turn back the clock and go back to that night so I could do things differently!"

"Well Vernon, my fiancé is that guy and since we cannot go back in time, nor would I want to go back because he is such a special person and I really love him!" I glanced at my watch and observed that I'd be late for my next class if I did not leave immediately, so I gathered up my purse and book-bag as I stood to leave, concluding, "It's really good seeing you again, Vernon, but I'm going to be late for my next class if I don't leave now!"

Vernon stood along with me, asking, "Can I walk you to the door, Tracee?"

Not seeing any harm in him walking me to the Student Center exit, I replied, "Sure you can walk me to the door, Vernon." He quickly gathered his books from the end table, following me outside of the Student Center, and when I turned to him, he started gazing longingly into my eyes, asking, "Are you sure that I can't convince you to let me be your bachelorette last fling before getting married, Tracee?"

I was admittedly flattered by Vernon's persistence, replying, "I am positive, Vernon, that I can't go there with you!" We briefly embraced each other before bidding our goodbyes then turning in opposite directions to never see each other again.

As time ticked onward, there came a time three years or so after meeting and becoming engaged that it seemed that Tevin and I simultaneously became more tired of the continuous high cost of living in California.

Additionally, we'd also factored in the decreased quality of life due to population increases, which were compounded by the most horrifying earthquakes separately and together that shook the apartment building to the point of us feeling it necessary to gather up our babies and driving away from the continuously shaking foundation!

We probably should not have done that, but we were afraid the entire building was going to collapse. Also, we were both ready for a change of scenery due to the frustrations dealing with the challenges and ridiculous expenses that were associated with even renting a nice house with a yard for our four-legged babies.

The inevitable night that caused us to have a serious intentional discussion about leaving Los Angeles was an unforgettable time after a long hard week at the studio, which contributed to Tevin coming home in a rather sour mood. He'd already endured spending many restless nights having nightmares of being stalked by an actor that he'd previously had to personally escort off the studio lot. Bless his heart!

During dinner that evening, I knew he was serious when he referred me back to our previous conversation on the flight back from Phoenix about once we decided to permanently leave California, Arizona would be our next destination to live.

Since I was engaged to be married, I was also down for the adventure, although my entertainment career as perceived by others seemed to be glamorous and full of excitement over the years that I'd been performing.

Our serious conversation also occurred during the time when I was just simply exhausted from the mental and physical rituals in preparation for being in the club atmosphere for the entire weekend plus days in between and regular evenings during the week.

I was really looking forward to taking a little break from the stage for a while, even though during that time I'd felt that I was at the top of my game, successfully being featured in several historical feature films and music videos that did not exploit me!

Also a contributing factor to my desire to make a complete job change from the entertainment industry was my disinterest in the majority of the acting opportunities spoiling the pot by always subscribing to those negative "Jerry Springer Show" stereotypical characters, which also misrepresented and marginalized transgender people to our detriment.

In addition to being a featured cast member at Queen Mary, which by the way, in my opinion, was one of the last authentic showrooms in California, I concluded that there probably was not going to be a long future for a transsexual performance artist in Hollywood other than the clownish, over-the-top roles that my current agent was sending me to audition for during that time.

Including, but not limited to, the degrading meeting that I'd taken with a production company from Tokyo that was recruiting transsexual performers to work in a lounge patronized by extremely wealthy and distinguished Japanese.

When I'd initially received the call from the agent about the audition, I wasn't expecting to speak directly with their client to schedule the interview. In addition, I found it interesting that the Japanese production company was advertising audition announcements for performers and celebrity impersonators, but during the phone conversation confirming meeting dates and time, they'd suggested that they were looking for "hostesses."

I suspected that something in the milk wasn't clean, so I asked Patrik to attend the meeting with me, and before our appointment with the representatives we'd both just assumed that "hostesses" was a term used by the Japanese to describe performance artists.

When we arrived at the office, there was also immediately something strange about the whole temporary set-up that drew my attention, so I got to the point requesting a clear definition of what "hostesses" were in Japan.

At first the overseas Japanese recruiter was evasive with his response after offering us beverages which were never received. We continued questioning him about what the job entailed.

After several seconds of attempting to disarm us with small talk, he finally proceeded to explain that "hostesses" in Japan were girls hired to mingle and cater to the needs of the elite clientele.

Since I'd immediately observed that not at one time did he ever mention anything about performing on stage, I then shutdown and just listened as he went on to disclose that as a condition of accepting the job, they would take possession of our passports until the contracts ended.

I purposefully verbally unengaged myself from the rest of the meeting, letting Patrik lead the conversation, because I did not want to tell that recruiter I wasn't interested in turning my life over to him and becoming a prostitute in his club on this planet or any other.

However, I remained professional and courteous during the remainder of the interview and after leaving the office, we both agreed that the whole arrangement was a big scam.

The following day when one of the production company representatives called and offered me the Japan contract, I happily declined! After the initial meeting and conversation with them, I never for one second considered ever accepting their offer to sell my soul no matter how much money they were promising.

Unfortunately, a few other girls that I'd personally known became victims to the scam and ended up regretting their decisions to turn their passports over to those pimps after they'd ended up trapped and turned out sex slaves in Japan.

Another typecast and degrading audition that I was sent on was the one in particular that came about in an attempt to compete with Judge Maybelline, Judge Joe Brown, Judge Judy and Judge Mathis in their early days.

I'd received an offer to appear on a new court show, pretending to have borrowed money from a guy and refusing to pay him back just because he was not interested in being in an intimate relationship with a transsexual.

The producers and writers had concocted a script with the intention to have me look like an uneducated ghetto transsexual fool. I don't think so! Another insult offer was when I was asked to appear on "The Drew Carey Show" without being compensated.

Since I didn't want to become one of those bitter and resentful queens, resorting to using alcohol and mind-blowing drugs as a coping mechanism in response to a limiting and in some cases usually humiliating entertainment industry, I chose to bow out gracefully having recently reached a plateau in my entertainment career!

I now believe that my desire back then to take a hiatus from performing may have also been unconsciously as a result of our impending marriage. Our wedding date was set in stone for April 25, 2000, with an agreement to later have a reception for our local friends and family after returning from our honeymoon.

During various conversations as time progressed on, Tevin and I concluded that I should resign from my sales management position at a Hair Club for Men distributor. My resignation was due to the owner of the company demanding that I quit my night job and totally commit to his company, which, by the way, was later raided by federal agents and shut down several weeks after my resignation from the company.

His insistence upon meddling in my personal life outside of work caused me great suspicion about his motives. I was so happy that I had the awareness to always cash my checks at his bank and not deposit them into my checking account like my former friend Nikki had!

After they'd all bounced, leaving her bank account overdrawn and her holding the bag for repayment, I bet Nikki regretted not listening to me after I'd warned her several times to not continue depositing those checks into her account.

That was that, the only thing left to finish was school! Once my school semester ended, we concluded planning our next trip to Phoenix to secure an apartment before our big move!

First, we had to get the wedding ceremony completed and the time leading up to our nuptials was a very exciting time for us after choosing our wedding package! Then Tevin took care of our flight reservations and he also reserved a honeymoon suite in the Pyramid at the Luxor Las Vegas Hotel!

Shooting Star illustrated and accompanied me to purchase the pattern and materials for my '20s-inspired "Lady Sings the Blues" elegant white satin gown! She was accessorized with a seven-foot matching satin wrap and elbow-length white satin gloves in addition to sparkling Swarovski earrings and matching bracelet!

My something blue was a beautiful diamond necklace gifted by Mother Chinue! I then commissioned a friend and cast member at Queen Mary who owned Cuddie Fashions to create my wedding gown!

Three days before we were scheduled to depart for Las Vegas, I went to Cuddie's apartment to pick up my wedding gown after shopping for white satin pumps from a shoe store in the downtown garment district earlier that afternoon.

When I arrived at Cuddie's apartment and parked, I immediately noticed fresh blood all over the walkway as I walked from my car toward the stairs leading to her apartment. When she invited me into her apartment, it looked like a hurricane had just blown through her usually immaculately kept place!

The furniture was turned over and the pictures that used to be on the wall were shattered and scattered all over the living room. All I could ask after seeing all of the destruction was, "Girl, what happened in here?"

Cuddie replied, placing her hand on my shoulder inviting me to sit on the couch next to her, "Destiny, I have really fucked up this time, girl."

Curious as to what she could have possibly done to have caused so much chaos, I asked, "What did you do, Cuddie?"

"Well Girl, you know how I love them right-out-of-prison, hard-as-hell thug boys, right?"

Since I'd never previously seen Cuddie smoke before, I was surprised when she took a cigarette from the ash tray and lit it! I knew that whatever she had done, it was pretty serious.

After taking several puffs of the cigarette, she continued. "I met this fine-ass, muscle- bound motherfucker at the bus stop last week who just got out of jail and I brought him home with me, girl."

"What?" I was shocked that she'd moved another guy in so soon after her recent break-up from the guy that she'd moved from San Diego with! "What about Mich? Has he moved out already?" I asked, in utter shock!

"No, girl, that's where I fucked up at by moving John in here before Mich finished moving out!" She replied, physically exhausted.

"Cuddie, what the hell are you thinking moving another man into the same space that your former man still resides?"

"I don't know what the hell I was doing, girl, because before the fight Mich told me that he'd felt disrespected when I moved another guy in while his toothbrush and other personal shit were still exposed."

She took one last puff from the cigarette and then smashed it in the ashtray until the fire was completely extinguished, continuing, "John just would not stay his ass in the room while Mich and I were discussing how disrespected he felt and John kept coming out and injecting himself into the conversation!"

"Girl, I know Mich was not having that!"

"No, he was not. They started fighting like they were in a caged death match, girl!"

After her reply, she then motioned for me to follow her into her bedroom to show me the damage in there. After seeing the complete devastation, I asked, "Cuddie, is everybody okay?"

"Destiny, they fought from the living room to the bedroom and there was nothing that I could do to stop them!"

She continued speaking and pointing across the room, "Mich fell through the window cutting his wrist to the bone and severing a main artery on the shattered windowpane."

Carefully stepping over the debris scattered all over the floor as I walked over and saw all of the blood inside on the floor and outside the apartment on the ground below. I inquired, "Cuddie, is Mich okay?"

Cuddie replied to my question apologetically and remorsefully. "I feel so guilty and responsible that he's going to be unable to work for a while, Destiny."

I was in disbelief. "Girl, this is serious."

After walking back into the living room and then sitting back on the couch, she continued. "Destiny, girl, I just can't believe that they were like two mad bulls destroying everything!"

She then excitedly pointed to my gown in the clear plastic garment bag hanging on the opened closet door as she continued, "All I could do was grab your gown, girl, and run up the hall to my neighbor's and asked her to hold on to it for me so they wouldn't destroy it, too!"

All I could say was, "Wow, Cuddie!"

Cuddie continued as I sat there almost speechless that my gown survived what was by all appearances seemed to have been a violently destructive incident. "Destiny, after all the hard work and time I spent on your gown, I was not going to let them get a drop of blood on it!"

She pulled the gown and wrap from the garment bag and then handed them to me, continuing, "Go into the bathroom and try it on, honey!"

Ironically, I noticed that the bathroom was the only room that was spared from Earthquakes Mich and John when I entered it to try my gown on. After putting on the gown and then excitedly exiting the bathroom, exclaiming, Cuddie, this is absolutely beautiful!"

Expressing extreme and well-deserved pride in her work, Cuddie responded. "Honey, let me zip you up. Girl, I was not going to let my sister get married in anything but your original design!"

Appreciative that I didn't have to scramble at the last minute to find another gown for my wedding, I inquired. "Are you sure you're okay, honey?"

She replied, "I will eventually be okay. Right now I'm just more concerned about Mich because he won't return my phone calls to let me know if he is okay after being released from the emergency room."

I offered, without judgment, "Well, honey, just give him some time and hopefully after things settle down, he will call you."

She concluded, "I doubt it Destiny, but it's all good!" She then hung her head in shame and continued, "At least I've learned a valuable lesson, which is to leave those jailhouse thug boys the fuck alone."

"Honey, we've all been there with crazy-ass, violent men and hopefully we learn the lesson before it's too late. Are you sure you're okay, Cuddie?"

"I'm okay, Destiny. I've got to clean this apartment and then go talk with the management about the incident."

After removing the envelope containing her commission plus a generous tip from my purse, I replied, aware that a few more unexpected coins would be beneficial to her in that stressful, uncertain period, "Well, here is the rest of your commission fee and a little something extra to help you out, honey!"

After tightly embracing Cuddie, I informed her, "We'll be gone for the weekend for our Vegas honeymoon and we will be back the following Tuesday. Just call me if you need anything, honey!"

"Thank you, Destiny, I might need some help moving when you get back, but you go and enjoy your honeymoon and I will talk to you when you return!"

I concluded, looking at my wristwatch, "I wish I could stay and help you clean up, sister, but I have got to go to the Beverly Center to pick up some lingerie and something sexy to wear out on our wedding night!"

We embraced one final time before I left the apartment with my wedding gown intact, leaving to finish running my errands! As I walked away, stepping over blood splatters, I knew that Cuddie was not going to leave those just-released jailbird thugs alone, because she was addicted to those hot roughnecks.

After successfully completing my errands that afternoon, everything was in order to our specifications when our wedding date arrived. Our flight was on time for departure and arrival in Vegas on a clear, sunny, beautiful unforgettable morning on our life-transforming journey!

After we'd safely landed at the Vegas airport and obtained our rental car, the drive to the hotel was unlike any other trip that we'd ever previously taken other than the engagement proposal on the plane!

After checking into our honeymoon suite in the Luxor Pyramid, we later ate dinner in a realistic Egyptian-themed restaurant. Afterwards we retired to our suite to begin preparing for our nuptials the following evening. I'd strategically hidden my gown behind hanging garment bags filled with clothes after removing her earlier to hang so she would not be wrinkled on our big evening.

The following evening of our ceremony, I still didn't want Tevin to see my gown until I walked down the aisle, so I wore a two-piece denim fitted outfit and carried my gown secured in her garment bag.

My hair, of course, was pulled back into a chignon to accent the sequined three-petaled gardenia hairpiece pinned on the right side which had been gifted to me by Bob Mackie and Shooting Star.

Tevin was as handsome as ever in his black tuxedo and white crisp shirt on our walk downstairs to an awaiting white, stretch limousine and driver to chauffeur us on a pit stop to formalize our union. Then we proceeded to a quaint wedding chapel that was reserved for our vows.

When we arrived at the wedding chapel, we were greeted by the minister conducting our ceremony and his daughter. Upon handing our marriage certificate to the minister, reality set in; I wasn't dreaming, it was really happening that I was both spiritually and mentally committing myself to the man that I would be spending the rest of my life with.

At first, I'd planned to have a bouquet designed in California, but resolved that fresh flowers might not have traveled very well on the plane so, instead, I chose to rent a cute bouquet from the chapel.

After selecting my flowers and confirming our special ceremony requests with the minister, I then excused myself to the changing room to slip into my wedding gown!

The minister's daughter served as our witness and after the wedding march started playing, it was another extremely surreal moment as I walked up the aisle toward my future! My dream turned into reality sooner than expected!

Those moments in our lives were a prime example that dreams really come true. Waiting for me at the altar would be the man I intended to commit my life to, for better or worse! OMG!

I was really nervous as we stood before the minister reciting our wedding vows and I could tell that Tevin was also nervous! Although nervous, he managed to place another beautiful non-traditional two-karat diamond cluster ring on my finger that fit perfectly with my engagement ring.

After the minister pronounced us spiritual life partners as we initially requested, the nervousness disappeared from both of us as we kissed to seal our union! Time seemed to flash back during that tender moment to when we met for the second time after so many years of initially being introduced to each other.

I strongly believe that it was destiny and fate that brought us back to each other and I am so grateful that I found a really secure man who introduced me to his family without any hesitation or concern for what they would think of me!

I was also grateful to have met a mature and intelligent person who was bold enough to choose someone like me as his wife because he loves, respects and accepts me completely just as I am, which is a rare, true blessing from God!

On the ride back to the Luxor in the limousine, all I could do was hold up our marriage certificate, repeating over and over the line from "The Color Purple": "I's married now, Miss Ceelie, I's married now!"

When we arrived back at our honeymoon suite, we changed clothes for a very romantic dinner in one of the Luxor five-star restaurants to toast our wedding. Afterwards, we danced the night away at Studio 54 Las Vegas.

Later that destined evening we consummated our spiritual union. The following day was filled with sightseeing and souvenir shopping for the first time as husband and wife!

After returning from our elopement, I was refreshed and energized that following weekend and ready to get back to work! I was also scheduled to perform an exclusive engagement after that Friday night show and due to the unexpected congested traffic and closed off streets as a result of all the other various concerts and high profiled events going on in town, it took us a whole lot longer to maneuver through traffic.

Fortunately, Tevin took off from work to drive me to work and also escort us to the Burbank private party!

Patrik rode with us to both events that night and I was still wrestling back and forth with what would have been the right time to inform him that we were leaving Los Angeles to move to Arizona.

Opportunity presented itself during the almost two hours it took us in the slow moving traffic to drive up the canyon from West Hollywood to the Valley. After we'd finished discussing the music and reconfirming that I had separately packed my costumes for the special event show in one of the two canvas garment bags that Conrad Wolf created for my previous Halloween Masquerade Ball show!

As we waited motionless in the traffic I knew that I shouldn't delay the inevitable any longer so I just interjected, letting the cat out of the bag, "Patrik I have something to tell you that will take you by surprise, which is we are moving to Phoenix in October!"

Up to that point, Patrik was the only person that was informed of our plans to move and it was obvious by his response that me leaving the show at the height of my success concerned him. "Destiny, are you serious about leaving the show now that you are at the plateau of your career both creatively and professionally?"

Patrik was understandably surprised and slightly disappointed by our out-of-the-blue revelation to him, but our minds were already made up so I explained our decision. "Patrik, I know that this comes as a shock to you. However, the bottom line is that we're both really burned out and ready to leave Los Angeles!"

He replied, questioningly, "I understand that you are ready for a change, but what are we going to do about your future bookings, Destiny?"

I replied, "Well, Shooting Star, I've been performing nonstop for a while now and I am just ready to try my hand at being a housewife for the first time in my life. And besides, we're just a six-hour drive or a really short flight away, so if we receive any special engagement requests I'll return then!"

By the time that we'd finally arrived at Queen Mary, Patrik was more understanding and hesitantly supportive of our decision to leave California, but I knew that he still had reservations about our non-negotiable Arizona re-location decision.

Later that evening, the private show was well received and in the dressing room packing up my costumes Patrik couldn't help but to make one last ditch effort to make me reconsider our decision to leave Los Angeles. "Destiny, your audiences love you, are you sure you are ready to give all of this up?"

I replied, without hesitation, "Patrik, I am absolutely positive that I'm ready to give this up just for just a little while until inspiration hits me to return. I can then go back to the stage refreshed and excited about performing again. It's just that right now I am ready for a change!"

Later that morning in the car after dropping Patrik off at his apartment, Tevin and I both agreed that no matter how convincing Patrik seemed about supporting our decisions to leave California, he really was not happy about me leaving the show so soon, but our minds were made up.

The following month our reception party was a very special and exciting, yet bittersweet May 10, 2000, afternoon due to me wishing for my mother's presence! However, since Ma has never flown on a plane, I did not expect for her to be present for our celebration.

I decided on sending all of my other family members who were not present copies of our wedding photos. Our extended family members and close friends, Mother Chinue, Moms Tyson, her family members and those that we loved were all present!

Since I didn't want any fake people spreading their negative energy around to attend our reception, I only invited those cast members and friends that I was really close with to share in our celebratory occasion.

Our first dance was to "Spend My Life with You" by Tamia and Eric Benet! The food was delicious and after the bridal money dance we celebrated, having a festive time until later that evening!

One of our most memorable reception gifts were given by our friend Harrison, which were a pair of tickets and a backstage tour of the sold-out "Lion King" original cast stage production at Pantage's Theater, in which Harrison was featured!

We knew that Mother Chinue would love to experience such a memorable event, so we secretly purchased an additional ticket and invited her to attend with us! After the extravaganza, in attendance producer and actress Kim Whitley was hilarious as usual during our back-stage tour!

Shortly after settling into our married life, we planned to complete the move to Phoenix by the end of October 2000. With almost six months before our fantastic journey, Tevin secured his job transfer, picked up extra shifts at work and mapped out the travel schedule for our voyage to the desert.

Several months later, we drove back to Phoenix for the second time together to secure an apartment. Happily after three visits to other sites we then found and placed a deposit on a really quaint luxury apartment complex off Nineteenth Avenue and Thunderbird Road.

After we'd successfully completed our apartment search to our satisfaction, we then visited with Tevin's family. We also decided to take a weekend road trip to Sedona,

Arizona, for my first time, which is often referred to by most as "Red Rock Country."

Just imagine there being me, Tevin, his brother and his wife and their infant son departing together in our rental car on my first adventure, visiting one of the global spiritual power-points in the northern Verde Valley region of the United States!

Our amazing Sedona weekend excursion occurred on a clear and sunny drive which contained unforgettable experiences during impromptu detours to explore the running streams and take photos at Oak Creek Canyon off the main highway.

Tevin and I snuggled closely in the crisp, fall romantic air, watching the trout swim with the flow of the stream and posed for pictures taken by his brother. It was the most awe-inspiring magical feeling when the red rock formations of Bell Rock and Cathedral Rock came into view extending more than a mile high each.

Digressing slightly, Tevin and I later went back to hike and further explore Bell Rock on a trip that only the two of us took several months after we'd gotten settled in Phoenix. Back to our first trip together with his brother and sister in-law, I immediately connected to the vibrant energy flowing within the vortex as we lit candles, prayed and meditated on the future that we'd desired inside the Chapel of The Cross!

The chapel is an architectural wonder built into the red-rock mountainside off Chapel Road, which had the most transformative view of the dessert. We later purchased candles that were the rustic scent of the candles burning inside the sanctuary before leaving to further explore Sedona.

As we walked the trails, I became more conscious of the invigorating energy flow throughout my entire being! I was grateful for all of my blessings to be reconnecting to nature in such a placid manner1

During our exploration, I also became more in-tuned and aware that my creator created me in her image using the same magnificent atoms, minerals and molecules she'd used to form the energized Red Rock formations, our planets, stars, moons and universe!

When the time arrived for us to leave Sedona, I didn't want to leave, but I knew that we had to get back on the road traveling onto Flagstaff, where we had another adventure visiting the Lowell Observatory and stopping at roadside stands shopping for the most indigenous native jewelry.

Tevin and I selected two beautiful necklaces for both of our mothers before moving on to also shop for other souvenirs and memorabilia at some of the varied eclectic downtown Flagstaff boutiques.

Later that bone-chilling, crisp evening, after eating dinner in the diner next door to our hotel, we purchased tickets to a late show at the movie theater to watch Denzel Washington and Angelina Jolie in their new thriller "The Bone Collector."

Other than his brother making unsolicited annoying commentary throughout the entire movie, the cathedral seating was very romantic, and the baby slept comfortably through the entire show with us having fun splurging on popcorn and diet soda!

Afterwards, we bundled up for the short drive back to the hotel in the cold evening air and after arriving at our rooms, we bid good nights before retiring to our individual rooms where Tevin built a fire in the fireplace, which allowed us to continue our romantic candlelit evening together in Flagstaff.

We all got up early the follow morning to pack the car and eat breakfast at the diner before our drive back to Phoenix. It was clear to me on our drive back to Phoenix that I had experienced a spiritual awakening during our Sedona and Flagstaff trip that I will never forget!

Also, the fact that Tevin's brother volunteered to drive the entire road trip back and forth, meant that we were able to relax and absorb the energy from the warm sun posing on the hugest sun-dial I've ever seen at one of the rest stops! It was unstated that Tevin and I both were happy about our decisions to relocate to Arizona as the afternoon transitioned into a sultry moonlit evening during our drive back to Phoenix.

We were both well rested for our early drive back to California the following morning after checking out of our hotel, we were also very excited about accomplishing the mission to have successfully placed a deposit down on a really nice apartment nestled right next to Thunderbird Mountain.

Immediately upon returning back to Los Angeles, I wanted to personally inform Robert of our intention of relocating to Phoenix, because I did not want to just leave without talking with him about my resigning from the show.

Neither did I want to write a letter informing him about my pending resignation, due to him not being at the club more regularly. When he'd unexpectedly came in one Sunday evening to just observe how things were going in his absence, I took advantage of that rare opportunity to speak with him about my plans.

Once the show concluded, I was really nervous approaching his office to knock on the door before requesting to speak with him. I stood there for a few seconds gathering up the courage to knock on his office door and after knocking, I inhaled and slowly exhaled when he opened the door and invited me into his office.

I nervously sat down in the chair next to his desk, breaking the ice by enquiring about his health. "How are you feeling, Robert?"

He puffed the cigarette, sipped his Coke Cola , then replied."Well, Destiny, I'm not supposed to even be here or smoking this damn cigarette, but here I am."

I hesitantly responded, not able to stall any further. "Robert, I know that you have a lot going on right now with your health and I don't want to pile extra stuff on your plate to deal with."

I took another deep breath before slowly exhaling and continuing, "I really wanted to personally inform you that Tevin and I are moving to Phoenix, Arizona, in October this year, which means that I am going to be resigning from the show two weeks prior to our scheduled departure date."

Robert took another long puff from his cigarette, inhaled, holding in the smoke, before exhaling then replying, "Destiny, I suspected that after you got married it wouldn't be long before Tevin took you away from the show."

He took another quick puff from his cigarette and continued before I could respond. "You are a very important member of our team here, Destiny so if it's the money, give me a chance to counter their offer if you're going to another show."

In response to both of his incorrect assumptions as to why I was resigning from the show, I replied, "No Robert, whether you believe it or not, it's not the money, nor am I going to another show."

Robert replied, "Then what is it really, Destiny?"

Feeling relieved and more relaxed now that everything was finally out in the open, I proceeded revealing more information about my future plans. "Robert, I'm not going to be working in a show at all in Phoenix, because I need a little break from performing for just a little while. That's it."

Robert leaned back into his plush chair, crossing his legs and replying, "This man is really serious about retiring you from the stage, isn't he, girl?"

Smiling at yet another assumption that Tevin was pressuring me to retire from performing, I replied. "No, it's really not that at all Robert. Our move and my resignation are mutually agreed upon because I've been performing consistently for many years now nonstop. I am within sound mind and willingly making the decision to explore other opportunities outside the entertainment industry!"

He replied, seemingly convinced, "Well, Destiny, girl, I have no doubt that you will be happy no matter what you decide to do and I really appreciate you coming and personally informing me of your decision to resign from the show."

Robert took another puff before putting the cigarette out in the ash tray on his desk continuing. "Destiny, I have known from the beginning that you were a very classy lady and if you ever need a job, this will always be your home to come back to whenever you should need to return."

I was relieved that he wasn't angry as I replied. "Thank you so much, Robert, for your understanding and support these last two years. It means a whole lot to me!"

Sitting back in the chair and reflecting on my initial audition for Robert, I continued, "When you hired me for the show, Robert, you gave me an opportunity to continue being creative in a consistent environment and have a great time doing what I have loved doing ever since I used to make up routines in my living room growing up back home in South Carolina!"

Robert sipped his soda and continued intently listening to my childhood reflections as I continued reminiscing about my past. "I am extremely grateful for the opportunity to continue my childhood dreams and fantasies coming true on stage in Queen Mary showroom!"

He replied, Destiny, you've given an old man the great pleasure of working with such a talented entertainer!"

"Wow, thank you so much for the compliment, Robert!"

I was beaming that Robert thought so highly about me and my talents. As we both stood and embraced each other before ending our conversation with Robert concluding as I reached to open the office door, "Make sure you don't forget about us Destiny!"

Turning to face him before I responded, "This is not the last time that we will see each other because we'll be back for many visits. Good night, Robert!"

"Good night, Destiny!"

Several weeks before my last performances at Queen Mary the cast members were all getting along laughing and acting crazy as we prepared for the laid back Sunday night show!

Monica and Catrice were already tipsy from sharing a bottle of firewater that they'd tried to conceal from the rest of us in her dresser drawer, to no avail! I decided that the rare peaceful moment of togetherness would be a good time to also inform them that I was resigning from the show and moving to Phoenix with Tevin!

After my revelation to the other cast members, Monica questioned unconvinced, "Destiny, are you sure you are doing the right thing by leaving the show, because you know that all of the others that have left usually ended up right back here?"

I replied with confidence. "Well Monica, I cannot say exactly what the future holds for me, but I do know that the only time I will be returning back here anytime soon is to watch you perform for us one of my favorite Candi Staton songs you do -- "Young Hearts Run Free"-- during one of our visits back from Phoenix!"

Everybody laughed and Monica shook her head as she took a sip from the cocktail glass, adjusting her wig, determined on getting the last word in concluding as if she was Nostradamus. "They always come back home at one point or another, I'm just saying."

A few months or so later after getting settled in Phoenix, we did return to California for regular weekend road trips, visiting the club, extended family and friends after we'd got settled in Arizona, not for me to rejoin the cast as Monica suggested, but to check out the show from the audience as I'd predicted!

After officially resigning from the show, I am happy to report that I've never possessed any desire to return to Queen Mary as a result of regretting my choices to temporarily resign from the stage.

Time seemed to fly after also informing Ma of our pending move and then making everyone else of significance aware of our relocation to Arizona! On the days and nights that we were not working, we started packing our two-bedroom apartment furniture and the personal items that were going with us into what seemed to have been several dozens of huge boxes and miles of plastic and bubble wrapping.

When I reconfirmed my two-week resignation notice with the assistant manager who was running the club in Robert's absence, I wanted to keep it as low-keyed as possible and not have a great big farewell show or formal announcement about my leaving.

It took me several weeks to pack and transport all of my costumes from the club to the apartment to prepare them for travel and finally, on the last night at the club, I celebrated my going away with cake in the dressing room with just the other cast members and our mutual friend Victoria Ramirez whom always hung out in the dressing room with us!

I maintained a sense of contentment with my decision during my farewell celebration with the cast and then later I excitedly double-checked to be certain that I had not missed any costumes before making my final exit out the back door!

Once on Ventura Boulevard after exiting the private parking lot behind the club, I started my last drive home from North Hollywood with the convertible roof down, the car stereo turned up playing smooth jazz and the wind on my face!

Upon turning to drive over Laurel Canyon from Studio City and the world famous Queen Mary one final time and seeing the lights reflecting behind in my rearview mirror, I didn't possess any reservations about changing our lives for something better.

Two weeks after my resignation when the day finally arrived for our move to Arizona, I was very excited and anticipatory of the many adventures that living in the desert would present to us.

We started out before dawn on our departure date, loading the U-Haul with our possessions. Unfortunately we'd decided to save money by loading the truck ourselves, which turned out not to be a good idea at all.

At first, everything was moving along smoothly and on schedule until both elevators broke down leaving us livid, because the management had previously been promising us and the other tenants that they were going to replace the constantly out of order elevators ever since we first moved into the building.

As you can imagine, the broken down elevators did not make us happy at all to have to carry the remainder of the boxes down to the truck from the fourth floor using the stairs, which threw us way off schedule.

We'd hoped to be on the road at least by midnight, but we did not finish packing the truck until after 6 a.m., placing us many hours behind schedule.

Many hours later, after finally finishing loading the truck and securing our car onto the trailer that was attached to the back of the U-Haul, we loaded Savannah and Bear into their kennel, placing them on the seat in the cab between us.

The sun had already started breaking through the clouds as we pulled onto the freeway headed towards our new destination and taking turns driving the six hours to Phoenix. We stopped at rest stops along the way for snack breaks and to walk the babies.

During my turn at the wheel, in addition to thanking God that we'd finally escaped Hollywood in one piece, I also reflected on the many adventures that I'd experienced living in Los Angeles over the last decade. Thanking God that I'd managed to survive and avoid the many dangerous pitfalls along the way.

I was also grateful that I did not fall prey to the drug dealer trying to coax me into becoming his drug dealing prostitute, in addition to the other drug dealer that I'd previously met and immediately discontinued seeing after he'd disclosed his occupation.

On my way home from my day job during that time, my brief encounter with the second drug dealer caused him to resort to stalking and following me home after work one evening immediately after I'd rejected him.

He'd boldly entered the gated garage behind me uninvited and then refused to leave when I asked him to do so. Fortunately, I was being escorted home by a gentleman friend and when he got out of his truck and approached me asking if everything was alright, the drug dealer finally left.

I felt somewhat emancipated on the freeway with my favorite mixture of oldies and pop radio stations on, singing along while remaining alert between also thanking God that I wasn't lured into the pornography industry. The fast money bait was set and cast by a big time transsexual porn producer who sent one of his well-known featured girls to approach me in the dressing room after a show at Queen Mary.

Upon approach, she informed me that her producer was interested in meeting me. Knowing very well that she was a porn star, I asked her what her producer could possibly want to speak to me about.

The transsexual porn star actually proceeded to try and recruit me into starring in her producer's next big porn production as she'd called it. Since she was a nice naïve girl who was always at the club, I didn't go in on her really hard when I declined the invitation to meet her producer.

I was also happy about not being persuaded to appear in any of those other degrading movie roles that I'd been offered by mainstream Hollywood!

Additionally, driving merrily along before our next scheduled rest stop and gas fill-up, I was also grateful that I didn't allow myself to be used and just tossed to the side by insecure and immature men, and most importantly, I was not tempted and seduced into indulging in the alcohol and hardcore drug scenes that were so prevalently running rampant, expected and readily available throughout the entertainment industry! Many blessings, I am thankful!

After Tevin took the wheel for the final stretch of our voyage to Phoenix, I was also very satisfied and thankful for the many successes in the entertainment industry and my personal life more importantly. If I say so myself, I believe that I've made some really wise choices over the years living in California and I harbor no regrets about doing it my way!

We were way off our original schedule when we'd finally arrived at our new home in Arizona and rushed to arrive before the leasing office closed for the day, but we made it safely later that evening!

Thankfully, our leasing agent was cool and she'd waited until we arrived before closing the office. I patiently waited in the truck after walking the babies to potty-potty while Tevin paid the balance of the move-in fees.

After he returned to the truck from obtaining our apartment keys, we exhaustedly carried the babies upstairs first to water and feed them. Then we unpacked the bedding, making a palette on the bedroom floor and after eating take-out, we toasted our new home and fell asleep exhausted from the long drive from Los Angeles!

The following afternoon, I seemed to have blossomed into my stay-at-home, domestic diva, home-maker mode! I was also extremely happy that I did not have to plan out a show, which entailed choosing music, costumes and hair for the entire weekend!

I started by hanging heavy curtains in our bedroom blocking out the beaming morning sun from shining through the blinds. While Tevin unpacked the bed, I organized the kitchen and other personal items for our immediate needs.

After Tevin finished assembling the bed, we went on a drive to familiarize ourselves with the neighborhood, then shopping at the local market for cleaning supplies and enough staples to last for a few days until we were able to do more extensive shopping on a later date.

Tevin didn't have very long before he was scheduled to start work, so he unpacked as many boxes from the truck as possible so that I would be able to start organizing our new home while he was at work during the day.

It was the end of October when we completed our move to Phoenix to live, so the weather was really nice and comfortable. I had a lot of fun during the day listening to the stereo while unpacking boxes and placing our things while Tevin worked. I anticipated the evenings when he arrived home, usually building a fire in the fire place!

Often after dinner, we then shared many romantic evenings thereafter lounging on blankets in front of the fireplace or in bed with the blinds and curtains drawn gazing at the beautiful view of the desert skyline blanketed with what seemed to have been millions of twinkling stars and planets.

I love stargazing due to the planets and stars bringing to mind the many guardian angels that are guarding, guiding and watching over us.

I worked diligently from sun up until sun down unpacking and organizing the apartment just in time for our first New Year's Eve party in Arizona!

Tevin and I had a great time hosting and bringing in the New Year with his two brothers and their wives while our godson peacefully slept in our bed.

Since the apartment complex was right at the base of Thunderbird Mountain, Tevin and I loved regularly hiking up the mountainside to stargaze and watch the bright sparkling Perseids Meteor Shower, which rivaled any manmade fireworks display! I later learned that the meteor shower is associated with the Swift Tuttle Comet, which takes 130 years to complete its orbit.

I've always loved the county and state fairs as a child, so I was very excited about getting the opportunity to see Boy George and the original members of Culture Club at the Arizona State Fair a few weeks after our arrival.

Although we occasionally visited the casinos with Tevin's family, feeding our money to those machines really wasn't our thing because we much preferred hiking, mining for quartz stones, fishing, and the theater.

Another of our favorite pastimes was attending live concerts, seeing Erykah Badu, The Mary Jane Girls, The Stylistics and other old-school favorite entertainers in concert at the Celebrity Theater.

We spent our first Phoenix Thanksgiving and Christmas and other major holidays at his parents' house, and in the beginning we often faced questioning from his parents about when we were going to have some babies.

I've never felt that it was my place to tell his family that I am biologically unable to have children. Furthermore, if we had made up a lie, we would have had to continue lying about the condition that prevented me from giving birth.

Lying about my infertility to anyone was never an option, telling one lie after another covering up my gender identity. Personally, it really isn't worth the extra energy required to keep your stories straight.

However, I have chosen to defer to Tevin whenever the "When are you two having babies" questions arose. It's a little more tolerable to avoid because his family knew that Tevin was previously married and expressed no interest in having children.

If I could, I would love to have a mini Tevin or mini me, but I cannot physically give birth to a child, so our four-legged babies and my gardens remain sufficient for now.

I've often questioned Tevin about how he would feel if my transsexual gender identity was to ever become confirmed to his family. His response has always been and remains, "I'm not really concerned about what my family or others may think or respond to you being who you are, because I love you and will continue to do so no matter what."

After completely getting settled into our new life, I thought that I wanted to become a lawyer during that time, so the following year, I enrolled in a few introduction to paralegal law classes, continuing my education and occupying my time while Tevin worked two jobs.

On our days off, we continued exploring the desert, finding interesting fishing holes and eclectic places to go for leisure time after work and school other than the smoky gaming casinos.

Once after resisting for a whole year, we decided to go check out the only gay club in town called Winks. We usually drove back to Los Angeles for weekends to visit Peanuts or Queen Mary to see the shows and visit with extended family members, but this particular weekend, we did not feel like driving all the way back to Los Angeles.

So, we got all dressed in our finest duds one Friday evening and ventured out to see what Winks had to offer after passing it by many times before. After parking the car in the club lot, we were excited about seeing a local show as we walked up to the entrance.

But when we entered the smoke-filled, one-room club, we were barely able to see through the almost blinding thick cigarette haze, so we kept walking from the front door immediately exiting out the side door to never return.

It was my birthday and I was wearing my new faux leopard print, knee-length coat that Tevin had just gifted to me, so I was not about to sit in that smoky club stinking up my new birthday gift!

Neither one of us was able to tolerate the unventilated room, so we went to one of the five-star restaurants at the mall for dinner and mutually agreed that if we wanted to see that sort of entertainment, we plan on driving back to California for weekend club fixes.

As time passed, it seemed like old man winter abruptly ended with no in between before the sizzling hot summer arrived with a bang! Spring was nowhere to be found and I was not expecting or prepared for the immediate onset of an extremely dry, suffocating heat so soon following the winter season conclusion.

Fortunately, my classes were evening courses, after the blistering sunset, and I also went to the gym in addition to running our errands very early, avoiding being active in that extreme heat.

Fate would have it that I was home alone on June 4, 2001, at 4:45 that afternoon while Tevin was at work when I helped to deliver our third baby Sheba after Savannah went into labor, delivering her spitting image!

I was so nervous when she went into labor two days after we'd taken her and Bear on a short road trip with us to Gold Canyon, Arizona. I hadn't been in that sort of situation since the time Ma and Perry went to North Carolina while I was still in school with them getting into an accident checking on our aunt.

I must have been in the fifth or sixth grade on that cold winter day when Ma received the distressed call from our aunt. All I remember is that they were gone upon my arrival home that afternoon when our dog went into labor underneath the carport with me assisting her with delivering the babies, scared and nervous.

I managed to keep things in order until Ma and Perry returned, but I was at home alone for several days with a dog that had just delivered more than eight healthy puppies. In an effort to shield them from the cold and rain I was smart enough to move them into the storage unit, placing them all safely on top of a blanket.

Ever since I'd left home to strike out on my own adventures of self-discovery, I only had myself to depend on. Running back home to live with Ma whenever times were challenging was not an option for me, because I needed to continue facing the tough times in order to learn from those experiences so that I did not have to continue repeating them.

I'm also grateful that I was moving forward and persevering at that point in my life after we finished our move to Arizona and I loved being the stay-at-home wife delivering puppies.

I adapted very well to the household routine of cooking, cleaning, and caring for my husband! Most importantly, I did not miss for one moment having to apply the heavy makeup to appear on stage every weekend.

Due to anticipating our regular road trips to Sedona, Los Angeles and exploring the vast Arizonian desert, I even seemed to have endured the unbearable continuous extremely nauseating heat during those hot days when it felt as if we were struck by an atomic heat bomb!

I was also able to rise above the disgusting racial overtones that were present during the time Tevin and I were dining at a popular family dining restaurant after a movie.

The venom was disbursed not long after Tevin and I were seated by the reception hostess, who then informed us that our server would be right with us and left us alone to allow time to make our menu selections.

We'd just finished commenting that we were the only ones in a nice and comfortable area of the restaurant due to it being early in the week. Six minutes or so after placing our dinner selection orders with our server and once again being left alone, this unassuming elderly Caucasian couple were eventually seated a couple of tables across from us.

The lady immediately started speaking aloud, "Why are they at our table anyway?"

Although I heard her comment and assumed she was referring to us since we were the only other people in that area of the restaurant, I continued enjoying being on date night with my Pumpkinhead!

I concluded that nothing was going to ruin our time until the little old gray-haired lady stated, "They used to be in the fields, now they're sitting at our reserved table."

Tevin and I were both immediately stopped in our tracks by what the little old gray-haired lady had just stated; we'd heard every speckle of poison spewing from her lips.

I responded by calmly rising from my seat and walking over to their table. I looked in her eyes and affirmatively stated, "Ma'am you are absolutely correct about our ancestors once being enslaved in fields. However, what you fail to realize or accept is that those days are long gone and will absolutely never return again."

The little old gray-haired lady and her husband remained speechless and shocked that I'd directly confronted her sense of privileged bigotry. I continued, "Furthermore, if you have a problem with your dining accommodations I'd suggest that you speak with a manager because we were seated at that table by the same hostess who sat you and your husband, which is where we will remain until we are done with our dinner in addition to not letting racists like you spoil our appetite"

As I turned to walk away back to our table she responded with her husband remaining mute, "We're not racist, we're Christian god-fearing people with black friends."

After I settled back at our table with the window view overlooking a plush courtyard filled with vibrant multi-colored flowers landscaping, Tevin and I tuned the lady completely out as we'd enjoyed our dinner!

You'd think that being confronted by an elderly racist couple just as we were continuing our celebration of Tevin's rare night off from both jobs would have made us think twice about our decision to move to Arizona.

Nope. The racist little old gray-haired Caucasian lady wasn't powerful enough to send us running for the hills screaming, "Get us out of there!" However, out of all those experiences the final straw for me that broke the camels' back was climbing into our bed one night and almost getting scared to death and stung by a scorpion underneath the sheets!

Although I was used to seeing the scorpions outside and occasionally inside the apartment in the living room, to find one in our bed was unacceptable. Tevin got rid of the scorpion and expressed concern about the negative effects that living in Arizona during the summer was having on me.

Another contributing factor to our second thoughts about permanently remaining in the desert was the fact that Tevin never really liked living in Phoenix when his parents initially moved them there during his teen years. He'd only agreed to move back to Arizona so that I could get to get to know his family.

Although I was happy to have accomplished the goal of knowing my in-laws, I really didn't like living in the desert during the summer months as much as I thought that I would.

After much discussion and consideration, we decided that once my school semester ended, we'd relocate to the East Coast for the very first time together!

Synergistically, Tevin and I were on the same page, both agreeing that since Atlanta was somewhat of a metropolitan city vibe in addition to being within driving distance from my mother in South Carolina, Georgia was our final destination!

Although I love my family, moving back to my home town in South Carolina was not even an option up for consideration. I am not quite ready to live there right now. Who knows what the future may hold, though?

Also, Tevin had revealed to me that right before we became reacquainted with each other in 1996, he was really considering moving to the East Coast. He'd become really disgusted and discouraged with not being able to meet any quality and real people in California other than his cousin.

Retrospectively, the fact that I'd previously lived in Georgia for two years before making my escape to California being understandably a concern for Tevin, we addressed and discussed in-depth my past situations that contributed to me leaving Atlanta.

I reassured Tevin that those previous relationships would not have any bearing on our decision to move there because, as far as I was concerned, those other guys were done and over with years ago in the past, which is where they shall remain.

However, in preparation for the likelihood that I would run into a former love interest from my past, we mutually agreed that I'd immediately inform Tevin, which was the case when I did have an unexpected encounter with a former boyfriend -- Hilton -- at a certification course I was attending downtown after we'd completed moving to Georgia.

When the encounter inevitably happened that I was confronted by an ex-boyfriend, I was confident that I wouldn't have any problems with him, because there were no feelings or desire on my part to even entertain the thought of resuming what we had in the past.

Also, on that occasion, Hilton questioned me on my way back from a break. " So, why did you not let me know when you moved back to Georgia, Tracee?"

I immediately nipped his inquiry in the bud informing him, "First of all Hilton, I didn't know that I had to inform you of my whereabouts and, secondly, I am happily married to my husband for over 11 years now, so what you and I had in the past will remain in the past."

I was disgusted by his approach and not wanting to ride in the same elevator with him, I took the stairs back up to the training. I reflected with each step on leaving him all those years ago because he was a lying, cheating abuser.

By all appearances, he had not changed or matured a bit, trying to Mack on me with his supposedly current girlfriend right upstairs attending the same training as me.

I've happily moved forward with my life since Hilton, remaining focused on my current commitment to Tevin, because I don't possess any unresolved feelings, regrets or desires to rekindle anything with any of those guys from my past ever again.

I was certain that those old boats have sailed into the sunset. After Tevin was comfortable that we'd developed a firm contingency plan in place for dealing with any unforeseen circumstances, we started making plans for our next great adventure together!

The simple fact that we are not afraid to go out into the world and see what possibilities and opportunities may exist beyond the familiar and safe environments we'd spent our childhood in is very attractive to me!

In addition to informing his parents of our decision to move to Georgia, I called Ma also, informing her that we were making plans to move to Atlanta and requested to live with her until we get settled. Without a moment's hesitation, Ma told me that we could stay with her for as long as we needed to!

Tevin once again arranged for another job transfer, worked double shifts at both jobs and we then submitted notice to the apartment leasing agent that we would not be renewing our lease for the following year.

After our big decision to leave Arizona, I knew that we were only going to take the most cherished material possessions that we'd collected over the years, both individually and collectively before and during our time together.

Resulting from our California move to Arizona I had gotten a sobering idea of how much stuff we'd accumulated over the years, so it wasn't too much of a challenge downsizing in preparation for our cross country excursion.

My first stereo in California that I'd purchased when I joined the Plaza cast was gifted to a really cute little girl who I met with her mother at a complex Easter egg hunt that I'd helped to coordinate. I later found it interesting that there was a huge Confederate flag prominently hanging in their living room covering the wall behind their couch on the day that I dropped the stereo off to the little girl.

The little girl was very ecstatic about the stereo, which was all that really mattered to me! I also then gifted my plants to Tevin's mother and we'd given our Chrysler LeBaron convertible to his parents because we were only able to travel with one car.

Also, in order to avoid the usual stresses and pressures of relocating to another residence, we gave ourselves almost seven months this time for Tevin to process his job transfer and pack the apartment.

My avid researcher and geographical genius also mapped out to the letter every freeway, highway, state and city that we would pass through, stop to rest or spend the night in on our first cross-country trip together!

After several months of packing and planning, the day finally arrived when it was time to repeat the process of relocating to a different state, except this one was very different. Once again, we packed our possessions onto the U-Haul truck, but this time everything was loaded and ready to go the day before in addition to securing the van onto the trailer attached to the U-Haul the day before our scheduled departure.

Early that following morning we completed the walk-through inspection with the leasing agent to secure the return of our full deposit. Then we placed Savannah, Bear, and Sheba in their kennel between us in the cab and were ready to begin our Exodus from Phoenix, Arizona!

I'd anticipated the many adventures that we'd encounter on our fantastic journey to new beginnings and it was an adventure, believe me! We spent the night in Albuquerque, New Mexico, with the awareness that Texas, being such expansive state, would most likely be a challenge to drive through.

We remained on schedule, leaving Albuquerque before dawn the next morning, which was a typical beginning until when we were leaving a gas station after gassing up the U-Haul in a desolate area where the service station driveway entrances were not paved and just all around jacked up, which in turn contributed to us getting stuck as we were leaving.

Several precious hours was spent trying to free the truck and simultaneously arguing with our road service on the cell phone, because they claimed that they weren't able to find our location.

Finally, after our frustration level reached its boiling point, a really nice trucker used his rig to push us off the hump and therefore sending us on our merry way. We were both beyond thankful for the kindness of another stranger, because if we had waited and only relied on the roadside service to get there, we would probably have been stuck there waiting until midnight!

After that fiasco was over, we drove for several hours before pulling into a camping and RV site later that evening to rest. I had forgotten about my previous experience with Texas mosquitoes, so when we stepped out of the truck to use the restroom and walk the babies, I was immediately attacked by what seemed to be an army of militarized mosquitoes poised to strike when they smelled our warm fresh blood. It felt like someone had started blowing needles from a blow gun that created instant red bumps rising and throbbing all over my sleeveless arms.

Thankfully, we had rubbing alcohol, insect repellant and anti-itch cream in the truck. To add to the misadventures along the way, after sunrise, it seemed that we were baked potatoes just placed into an on high pre-heated oven as the sun rose directly in front of us.

The sun instantly started beaming at full force directly into the truck cab to the point that there was no longer any cool air coming from the air conditioning unit, which was turned up to the highest speed, by the way.

The cab of the truck became extremely hot and miserable, leaving us no choice but to resort to taping newspaper pages onto the passenger side windshield and windows to attempt to block out the baking heat waves from the almost blinding sun.

Then after a few miles baking from the heat, all of a sudden and out of nowhere as we listened to the radio station upon finally finding one that didn't put us to sleep, programming was interrupted for an emergency severe weather advisory!

To our dismay, we were driving just a couple miles heading east of the fast moving tornado that was closely roaring from the west behind us! Tevin floored the gas pedal, driving as fast as the truck would go in order to escape from getting caught up in the severe weather!

Just imagine us driving at top speed in a huge, oversized U-Haul filled to capacity through suddenly down-pouring strong rain associated with high-wind gusts, which were strong enough to have blown the U-Haul on its side with our van on the trailer. It was frightening!

After several more miles driving at top speed, we finally escaped the tornado's fury and after what seemed like an eternity driving a straight stretch of unpredictable pavement, we finally made it safely out of Texas still intact! Hallelujah, thank you, Jesus!

The ride eventually became much less stressful after one of our last rest stops at the Tuskegee National Forest in Alabama before by-passing Atlanta on the final leg of our journey to my mothers' house in South Carolina.

As we got closer to my hometown, continuing east on Interstate 20, I remained excitedly anxious about moving back to the East Coast after so many years of living out west. I also started fondly reminiscing about my experiences growing up in the South and how far I had come in life.

I felt blessed to have had what I consider to be a successful Hollywood career, met and married the man of my dreams whom I'd prayed to God for all of those many years ago while growing up in South Carolina.

I was also filled with extreme gratitude for all of my many blessings, grateful for all of the many prayers that my mother and those that prayed for me! The anxiety that I'd felt about going back home subsided once we arrived at my mother's and parked on the side of the house underneath the pine trees!

When I introduced Tevin to Ma, I knew immediately by her reaction that she liked and accepted him as my spouse and into our family! This was so unlike the previous time when I thought that I was grown in the late '80s after returning home from Job Corps.

I remember those earlier times being the first and only time, until Tevin, that I'd invited a love interest to visit me. He was on weekend leave from Job Corps and, at first, I thought about hiding him in my bedroom for the weekend. That made no sense, considering how astute my mother was. She would have inevitably found out what was really going on.

I recall being scared to death introducing Fred to my mother as my friend who just came into town to visit with me for the weekend when she arrived home from work that unforgettable afternoon.

After introducing Fred to Ma I didn't have any knowledge of what I was going to do after she responded questioning me about the depth of our relationship, with me lying telling her that nothing was going on with us.

The investigator continued to cross-examine me as she grabbed my chin, turning my head from side to side and stating, "Do you think I'm stupid. Tony?" She indicated that she saw the fresh passion marks on my neck.

Since I was caught red-handed in a big fat lie about my relationship with Fred I remained silent as Ma concluded, in no uncertain terms informing me, "You can stay, but he has got to go."

When Ma went into her bedroom and closed the door, I knew what that meant, so I called my friend Asia to pick me and Fred up to drive us to stay with our mutual friends Charlene and Carroll until it was time for Fred to return to North Carolina.

After that confrontation and being busted, I never introduced Ma to any of the other guys that I called my little underage self dating when I was a teenager. I've never gotten up the nerve or courage to try that again until recently in adulthood.

Tevin is very important to me and at that time I probably unconsciously wanted my mothers' approval. It's kind of ironic that I introduced Tevin to Ma as my husband because I've just recently become comfortable with referring to him as such.

I'd previously resisted referring to Tevin as my husband as a result of usually hearing every other girls referencing guys that they barely know anything about as their "husband" when they don't even come close to meeting the standards of what being a husband really represents.

It's without a single doubt to me that Tevin exceeds all of those standards to be called my husband, spouse, significant other and spiritual life-partner!

During visits reconnecting with other family members after settling in following our cross-country escapade, it seemed to me in many ways almost as if I'd never really left. Due to my regular visits home for reunions and other family events over the years since I'd lived in California, it was almost as if nothing had changed.

One exception was the waterfall and fountain on Main Street in downtown, but otherwise Sumter really has not changed very much. But in all actuality things were quite different now, because six out of seven of my childhood and high school friends are all dead and gone forever.

The only childhood friend still living as far as I know is the one in New York somewhere allegedly strung out on heroin. I pray that that's not the case.

I also suspected that staying in South Carolina with its limited opportunities and resources instead of going to Georgia and then California would have possibly been an emotional or physical death sentence for me as well.

Whew, I'm so glad I dodged that hollow-point bullet! It saddens me that most of the untimely deaths of my childhood friends and classmates could have possibly been prevented if only they would have taken responsibility for themselves.

I believe that they'd still be alive if only they'd discontinued some of the self-inflicted, life-threatening activities that some of them voluntarily engaged in. Included in the recklessness were drug distribution, domestic abuse and prostitution by some of them.

It was unbelievable to me that a couple of those whom had college degrees and good jobs willingly chose to be self-destructive, risking their precious lives and selling their souls on the streets, jumping in and out of cars just for the thrill of it. Their personal choices were such a senseless waste of education and lives.

For several years after moving to California, I lost contact with most of my childhood friends. According to Asia, due to some of them contracting AIDS and thusly becoming isolated from their friends and support systems by their family members, they weren't allowed to attend the one too many funerals.

Before Tevin and I relocated to the East Coast, I cherished the times that I was fortunate enough to have spent with those that were still living after I started going back home for regular visits from California.

Also, even though I later learned that my best friend Asia was dealing drugs, she never involved me in any of her illegal activities until the afternoon that I was visiting with her and she asked if I would drive her to the store.

I had no problem driving to the store, but when we arrived at Noon's Liquor Store on Lafayette Boulevard, this strange guy came running up to the car before we had a chance to exit and he went directly over to the passenger side where Asia was.

Without saying a word to either of us, he then immediately pulled three humungous rocks from his pocket for her to choose from. I was stunned, speechless and instantly infuriated that she'd involved me in a drug transaction.

Although I was furious that she did not tell me why she'd insisted that I drive, I remained composed, because I was certain that the drug dealer would have most likely had a gun or something for protection. Neither did I want to cause a scene while Asia was inspecting crack cocaine to purchase in broad day light!

After Asia finished selecting the largest of the three huge rocks, I immediately cranked up the car. After pulling out of the parking lot, I let her have it! "You know what Asia, I don't judge you for what you are doing, but do not ever involve me in any of your drug deals again."

She replied, "I'm so sorry, Tracee. I thought you knew what I was going to do!"

I replied, really pissed off as I drove over the Lafayette Boulevard Bridge, "Girl, how was I supposed to know you were going to buy crack cocaine? I thought that you needed to buy wine or beer for Julio."

Asia remained silent as I continued laying into her. "If I had known that we were going on a drug run, I would have declined being involved, but you did not tell me that you were making a drug transaction, did you?"

She knew that she was wrong, stuttering in response, "I understand and promise that it will never happen again, Tracee." Asia remained true to her word keeping the drugs and all other illegal transactions away from me during our visits thereafter whenever I was in town.

A couple years later during a visit from California, Asia and I spent a weekend together in Augusta, Georgia. I was thankful that we'd received an opportunity to hang out and just be crazy to an extent like we'd done back when things were cool!

I did, however, feel that since we were much older during those days Asia should have become a little more mature and wiser, but she was still the wild child, picking up men in the Waffle House after leaving the club.

I was also disappointed that even though she had warrants out for her arrest for using a dead person's social security number, she was also still recklessly running with one guy after another making it do what it did for money.

During one of our heart-to-heart conversations that weekend in Augusta, I made her promise me she was going to follow through with getting an attorney and return to Sumter and face the charges that were pending against her.

Selfishly, I believed that she was serious about getting herself together because I really wanted us to follow through on our plan for her to visit California in the future after she'd gotten her life back on track. After returning to the West Coast upon completion of my Georgia visit, we regularly stayed in touch.

One day after not being able to reach her on the cell phone for several weeks, I called the gay guy who was currently her roommate, whom I'd met during my visit. He then proceeded to nonchalantly inform me that Asia was dead, as if he found some joy in that fact.

I refused to believe what he was saying, so I hung up the phone and immediately called Asia's mother to find out if what I was told was true. It was very difficult for me to digest Asia's mother confirming the devastating news that my best friend for many years was dead.

She further explained that the family wanted to invite me to his funeral, but they didn't have any way of getting in touch with me at the time. I was extremely distraught that my best friend since high school whom I'd shared oh so many secrets and memories with was gone forever. Rest in peace, Fernando Delay. I love you.

Also speaking of childhood friends, I will never forget whom was the last of my friends to have recently died-- Joseph James Jr., aka Miss Josephine and Jay-Lo. I was honored and privileged when his mother, sisters and brothers invited me to speak at his memorial service about the memories that we'd shared growing up together.

After Joseph's minister brother, who was conducting the funeral service called me before the church to speak, it took everything within my power to remain composed. I was briefly silent for a moment after arriving at the podium and then seeing him lying in the coffin.

It was only after a family member passed me a tissue that I was able to begin speaking, quoting Psalms 23. "Yea, though I walk through the valley of the shadow of death, I will fear no evil: for thou art with me:"

Only after wiping away my uncontrollable, rolling tears with the tissue was I able to continue. "Unfortunately, my dear friend, you're no longer here with me. I know that you're chastising our other friends that are eternally with you to get it right and keep it straight, and I also know that you are keeping them in line as usual, but I am going to selfishly miss those times we'd danced all night long at the clubs, in addition to missing our weekends that we shared together when I started performing on the circuit in Columbia, South Carolina, when I first moved back home.

As I stood there reflecting and being appreciative that we'd shared good times before his death, I continued before concluding, "Most of all, Joseph, I will miss being able to reminisce with you on the telephone like we've always done about the crazy things that we all did growing up together in conservative Sumter, South Carolina."

Later that afternoon back at his parents' house, his uncle paid me a compliment that I will always cherish when he approached me with a shocked expression all over his face, saying, "You're so beautiful. I thought that you were a celebrity movie star friend of Joseph's visiting from out of town!"

So, you know that he was talking about me with your sisters whom reminded him of who I was when we were growing up because he'd only known Tony, not the woman that I've become. Rest in peace, my dear friend, I miss and will never forget you!

We stayed with Ma for only a few days or so upon our initial arrival in South Carolina because Tevin was scheduled to report for work that following week.

So, with our babies in tow we drove back to Georgia that following weekend and placed our possessions in storage. We then, as planned, checked into a hotel off Interstate Highway 285 so that we could spend some time together before Tevin started work.

After taking a day off to rest, we began scheduling interviews for prospective apartments and, thankfully after only four interviews, we placed a deposit down on a cute apartment in a gated community with a bridge and pond in Sandy Springs off Roswell Road. Ironically, it was located right across the street from where the Pizza Hut where I'd waitressed at back in the late '80s!

Upon being notified that our lease application was approved, we immediately started moving into our new apartment on Tevin's days off. When he went back to work, I stayed home cooking and organizing our new place!

As time passed and we reflected on the madness that we'd experienced on our cross- country trip in a U-Haul with the van on the back, managing to outrun a tornado, we were really grateful that we came through all of that unscathed!

We're also thankful that we didn't murder each other along the way and remained solidly together through all of that drama! Other than Tevin having a really tough time adjusting to the humidity during his first family reunion in my hometown, (he soon became adjusted to the Southern temperature) we seem to have transitioned quite well! Blessings!

During the process of documenting my memories, I am also very grateful for managing to successfully find the tools which are continuously assisting me with my forward motion in conquering perceived demons or personal issues!

I'm also happy that I was blessed with the ability to have successfully established a productive life and career, taking care of myself in California without ever having to live on the streets!

Additionally, I'm proud that ever since I left my mother's house, I've only returned home for visits and not run back to living with her whenever things got tough. My ability to take care of myself and remain self-sufficient proved those people wrong whom were sitting back, plotting and waiting for me to fail, and come running home to South Carolina broken and defeated.

Several weeks after we were settled into our new environment, the creativity bug started to cause an itching that would only be soothed by me shampooing, styling my wigs, organizing music and costumes for a return to the stage to release some built-up creative energy!

I then re-established relationships with my goddrag-mother Lena Lust and received great booking referrals and contacts on the showgirl circuit. There were no problems booking appearances at clubs in Columbia and Greenville, South Carolina, Macon, Georgia, Backstreet, The Armory and a few solo Diana Ross exclusive engagements at Red Chair and Stage Door that used to be in Tucker, Georgia.

I'd be remiss if I didn't express gratitude for getting the opportunity to introduce Tevin to the Atlanta that I knew back in the late '80s before it started to evolve from the quaint little city in Georgia into the unrecognizable and commercialized metropolis with the giant skyscrapers on Peachtree Street in Midtown and Buckhead.

Once I settled back into the entertainment scene, I was amazed at how prevalent the drugs were on the circuit. The reality of the drug abuse sank in after I accidentally walked into the restroom stalls on several occasions to find some of the other girls two and sometimes three to the same stall, straddling the commodes and snorting Tina and other drugs of choice up their noses before hitting the stage to perform.

My breath was later taken away when I also realized that one of the girls that I had not previously suspected of snorting drugs was also strung out after she asked me before a show one night, "Destiny, do you party?"

After finding her question strange, I quickly learned that the phrase meant something totally different from the way we used it back in the day when things were more innocent.

Now, I'm currently educated that "Do You Party?" means indulging in cocaine, crystal meth, heroine or crack. I don't and haven't ever gotten down like that, nor do I judge those that do; just do not bring it around or invite me to indulge with them.

Also, I might add it has been years since I've been on the dating scene and a lot has changed. I've also been educated during recent conversations with other girls about the difference in the time when I was single that the term "dating" has evolved from just going out for coffee, dinner, dancing or a maybe a movie with someone into now having sex for money and or drugs.

As a result of learning the new and most current lingo, I rarely use the term "dating" in conversations that refer back to my unmarried days. I can't help but to conclude that I am extremely happy reporting that I do not miss those single days one bit, because I'm with someone who knows me inside-out, flaws, personal secrets and all!

Several years after I'd been back on the performance circuit in Atlanta, the whole vibe began to transform from the land of opportunity into what almost seemed like the first wave of a recession. In addition to the economy, the national and local conservative tone in government meant that the city started shutting down the gay clubs and bars at an alarming rate.

The gay clubs were the main sources of income for those showgirls that did not have a day job or something else monetarily sufficient to fall back on in times of financial uncertainty. The transgender, lesbian, gay, bisexual, questioning, queer and inter-sexed community collectively felt that our communities were unfairly targeted when the intolerance sledgehammer was slammed down on the nail's head.

The most unexpected move was the shuttering of the landmark, 24-hour hotspot BackStreet, after a drawn-out, brutal legal battle to renew their alcohol license.

I immediately knew that we were heading in a direction that would have a devastating economic effect on the showgirls, because not only was the local economy negatively impacted, the states that I regularly traveled to for out-of-town bookings were understandably also facing challenges with their economies.

However, in response to the economic drought and as a matter of principle, I purposefully declined those out-of-town booking offers I received that were insulting. I personally view it as an insult and a slap in the face for a club owner to expect a true professional performance artist to travel thousands of miles for a personal appearance for half their rate, and then also expect me to provide my own accommodations.

My one compromise in respect to the economy was agreeing to a reduction in my booking rate by half. Although I understand that flexibility is required during tough economic challenges, I certainly wasn't going to then use my reduced salary to also pay for two, sometimes three, nights of accommodations.

I also learned another valuable lesson many years ago when I first lived and worked in Atlanta that once you started allowing others to diminish your talents by expecting you to work for far less than you are worth, they treat you accordingly.

I also learned earlier on that if I allowed them to treat me in an undignified and disrespectful manner, I would be expected to continue working for nothing and settling for less than my worth. I don't think so!

My entertainment career isn't a game to me, nor am I just playing "dress-up" to show off for others. I feel that since I've put many years of sweat and tears, not to mention monetary investments into costumes and other supplies that are necessary for creating an entertaining and professional image, I at least expect to be fairly compensated for my efforts.

During that period of adjustment to the more conservative tone in Georgia as compared to California and factoring in the entertainment venue closings, I was feeling that I had more to offer my community other than just becoming a source of entertainment for the pleasure of those that did not appreciate or respect my talents.

I've been fortunate enough to have had some wonderful career pleasures and successes in my more than 20-year span as a performance artist and I refused to allow someone else to devalue those memories by becoming the caricature that my current environment seems to expect and prefer so that they're more comfortable with the transgender performers.

Everybody deserves a little bit of respect as the Queen of Soul, Aretha Franklin sings! The way that I see it is that we are all human first and foremost regardless of our gender identities, preferences and professions, so based on that factor, we all deserve to be respected for our choices no matter how abnormal the superior minds perceive those choices to be.

Conclusively, I will not judge you for your decisions so I ask that you not judge me for mine. It's all about mutual respect.com.

I will never deny to anyone the time that I've spent entertaining others on the stage, because those experiences have been very fulfilling professionally and prosperous for me.

However, I refuse to lower my standards just to continue being a full-time professional entertainer in an environment that does not appreciate what I have to offer. I am also filled with gratitude that I'm at a point in my life and career that I can choose or not continue being a full-time entertainer.

I reconciled, going forward, that I'd see those club closings as a perfect opportunity to pivot from the entertainment industry to becoming a more active advocate for my community. Once I dove head first into beginning the transition from stage after researching volunteer opportunities and becoming actively involved part-time, I also started feeling on a much deeper level that I was living a double life, performing on stage at night yet going into the closet during the day functioning in a perceived heterosexual existence with my husband.

It really bothered me to my core that I was living comfortably while shelters were denying my transgender sisters and brothers access to their homeless facilities, solely

based on their gender identity. Since I've always possessed a passion for helping others, I

was not content with not using all of my life experiences to empower and advance my

community in a more affirming manner.

So, I'd committed myself to a self-imposed hiatus from the performance circuit

when the bars started closing at an almost weekly rate in order to give back to my

community.

However, and just to clarify though, I am not opposed to booking HIV/AIDS and

equality fundraisers in addition to booking exclusive engagements if presented with an

offer that I cannot refuse!

Until those opportunities are presented, I enrolled into some college courses,

continuing to expand my mind and I've also become more personally involved in local

community initiatives serving on their volunteer boards of directors and advisory boards.

Chapter Fifteen

Transformation: Making History

I feel it important to begin this chapter with first acknowledging the person whom initially inspired me to become a community Advocate. I consider my Los Angeles former Bishop Carl Bean to be one of the most profoundly inspiring, encouraging and uplifting people that I've been blessed to have known or worked for.

His vision has inspired me to establish an advocacy, consulting, empowerment, prevention and social services referral organization for transgender and gender non-conforming people.

Another pleasure that I miss about California, in addition to the ocean, I also really miss Bishop Bean's sermons due to him always speaking on subjects that supported me through some of my personal challenges, and after the service he'd always made it a point to greet every worshipper with a big hug or solid handshake accompanied by words of encouragement!

I personally believe that being approachable is something that's currently missing from some of the new-age mega-church services that I've most recently attended, where some of the pastors present themselves as elevated rock and pop stars. "Haleluyer" as Tyler Perry's Madea eloquently put it!

I'd never set out to become a poster child for transgender and gender non-conforming people or win awards for my service to community. It's just that there came a point in my life when I figured that I would play to win the hand that I was dealt and, therefore, bring more awareness to our true purpose for intentionally being created in every past and future century.

I feel it very important to note that my decision-making process during those times were also resulting from consciously not allowing others to feel empowered by making endorsement decisions for me.

Additionally, once my decision was reached to become the captain of my own ship and put forth the platform of activism that I was more comfortable with supporting, I also personally and respectfully unsubscribed to other organization leaders' personal activism choices, actions and agendas.

In an effort to give my mission credibility, I resumed moving forward on the spark that was previously ignited in Los Angeles during the time I managed the first of its kind transgender outreach program!

I envisioned an organization that would assist me with accomplishing my personal goals to educate society about the modern day eunuchs while additionally providing advocacy, consulting, social services referrals, HIV/AIDS risk reduction, educational supplies and resources to a largely diverse, underserved and misunderstood community!

Furthermore, it's also my hope that Juxtaposed Center for Transformation, Incorporated, will serve as a vehicle to continue using my voice to speak out against the systemic injustice, discrimination and inequality that transgender-identified individuals face on a daily basis whenever we as a community seek gainful employment, fair housing, quality healthcare services and other basic human resources.

My mission also includes dismantling some of the negative stereotypes that are associated with being a trans person, because I feel I've been blessed with some wisdom, knowledge and understanding from experiences throughout my time on this planet.

Another aspect of my mission that I need to share with others includes the awareness that we are okay just as we were spoken into existence by our Creator as referenced in the books of St. Matthew, Chapter 19 verses 10 to12 and Isaiah, Chapter 56 verses 3 to 5!

Personally being raised Baptist in South Carolina, I find it ironic that I'd never previously read any of those books and verses of empowerment and inclusion from the Holy Bible. I absolutely feel that most religious figures refuse to acknowledge those uplifting verses in their pulpits because revealing the truth is contrary to their desire is to maintain mind control over society.

My life-changing revelation has reinforced to me that we are valuable and are individually required to fully accept that we do not have to continuously justify our existence on our planet.

We don't have to continue enduring abusive people trying to control us mentally and physically by literally beating you down just to prove dominance or way of coping with their own conscious battles and conflicts with being attracted to and quite possibly in love with transgender people!

As far as my becoming a community advocate, Tevin and I have had extensive conversations about the commitment and time that would be required of me to effectively establish Juxtaposed Center for Transformation, Incorporated.

I also believe, most importantly, we've taken into consideration the perceived effects both positive and negative that my commitment to community activism would have on our personal lives. Although our neighbors aren't all up in our business, we were also both aware that another very important aspect of my endeavor would consist of exiting completely out of the closet and becoming comfortable enough to publicly admit without hesitation that I was born a transsexual woman.

I'd never previously considered willingly and publically revealing my gender to others up to that point. Yes, I was a performance artist, but when I wasn't performing on stage, I was just another transsexual person blending in with society, which is the ultimate goal of most pre-operative and post-operative transsexuals!

Although we had those in-depth conversations, I still wanted to be reassured that Tevin was okay with me becoming more of an outspoken public figure when the time came to file the incorporation forms with the Secretary of State.

As usual, Tevin continues to love and support me throughout all of my quests. He purchased a personal computer and business plan software to get me started on the process of becoming incorporated and tax exempt in the State of Georgia.

Before moving forward, I feel it also very important to provide a little more history on how JCT received her name. Around 1994, I devoted precious time and energy helping someone I considered a friend at that time and previous colleague named Fran to establish a community-based, social services organization back in California.

It was during one of the times that I was on hiatus from dating my on-again, off-again former boyfriend, Kedrick, which allowed for spare time that I used to volunteer to projects on my days and evenings off from work.

Fran was in a long-term marriage with a lesbian-identified female when we first met a couple years before we started working on the project together. Fran was also a female to male transsexual, going through the transformation from living as a female to a full-time male.

On the surface they seemed like a committed couple that loved each other. At the time Fran, two others and myself started spending countless hours at their home researching, processing and filing the appropriate paperwork required to become incorporated in the state of California.

Whenever "All I Want to Do Is Have Some Fun" by Sheryl Crow comes on the radio, it takes me back taking me to the times we turned the radio up loudly whenever that song was played while driving around town viewing perspective office space.

We were all excited about finding a really nice and conveniently located headquarters to accomplish our mission providing HIV/AIDS testing and education to the community at large.

Just as things progressed, several months later, Fran unexpectedly revealed to me they were ending their relationship just after his wife was diagnosed with breast cancer.

They'd both eventually started confiding in me their personal concerns and challenges relative to how Fran's gender reassignment was negatively affecting their relationship. Since I was close to them both, I remained as neutral as possible, trying to offer advice that I felt would support them in remaining together and dealing with the devastating cancer bad news and Fran's gender-identity transition.

Unfortunately, right after we'd finished incorporating, I felt the brakes become engaged after all of the work that we'd put into establishing the organization we'd visualized to help our community.

Upon receiving a call from Fran out of the blue, he told me that he was going to announce at our upcoming meeting he was ending his relationship and permanently separating from his wife. During that meeting, Fran made a commitment to us that he would continue with the work we'd started, but I knew that things would be different when, later in the evening Fran started coming on to me.

When he started expressing his infatuation and feelings for me, you could have knocked me over with a feather. I guess he felt the need to prove his masculinity to me right there as he proceeded to remove his shirt, revealing the results of his double-incision, bilateral mastectomy."I know that you like masculine men, Tracee," he said. "You can't even tell that I used to have breasts, can you?"

Believe you me, I was not expecting such a crazy and ridiculous revelation from him that evening while we were alone at their home, so it took me a couple seconds to respond. "Fran, my feelings for you have always been purely platonic in a sisterly, brotherly kind of way and I'm really surprised that you haven't taken into consideration the level of betrayal that your wife would feel if you and I were so stupid and desperate enough as to ever consider getting together with each other so soon after your separation from her."

After an intense conversation about me not being attracted to him in that way and me feeling like a sister to him, I felt it would have been a betrayal to his wife during such a critical period dealing with her cancer diagnosis.

Fran and I mutually agreed not to go there with each other! He then informed me one week later that instead of the agency remaining a non-profit social services organization, he had begun revising the filing process to re-incorporate as a for-profit jazz entertainment and artist management agency.

For a brief moment after that conversation, I felt slightly betrayed and disappointed regarding all of the hard work that we'd all invested into that project. However, I got over it and became more discerning about projects that I'd committed personal time and energy to moving forward.

Bringing us back to the several weeks before starting the filings for incorporation in Georgia, I'd also previously registered for three college classes that were due to start in less than three weeks!

Additionally, I'd attended an Incorporation Workshop, ordered the required forms and inquired with the attorney who facilitated the incorporation workshop about the total cost to file for incorporation and tax exempt status.

The up to $1,500 quote to pay the filing fees, in addition to paying him for his services, was not in the current budget. After I informed him that I could not afford his fees, and that I'd just have to try filing the forms myself, his discouraging response was, "You are going to need somebody experienced in talking to and convincing the Internal Revenue Service into giving you tax exempt status."

Well, I did not have the money to pay someone to file our forms nor was retaining him an option, so I figured nothing beats a failure but a try! Also, I thought that since I possessed what I consider to be pretty good communications skills, I was determined to move forward with the filings on my own and prove him wrong.

At first, I figured that I would wait until the end of the semester to start filing the forms, but during one of my daily meditations, an inner-voice asked, "Why are you procrastinating and putting off filing those forms?"

After completing my meditation and scriptural readings, I immediately went to the phone and called the Secretary of State's office, confirming their fees, and then called the Internal Revenue Service to confirm theirs.

That unforgettable afternoon while on the phone with the Internal Revenue Service representative, I was unexpectedly informed that the fees would be increased almost three times the usual rate in almost three months.

In addition to becoming loaded down with homework and study requirements when school started in three weeks, I was also concerned that the distractions and additional stresses would be a detriment. I was concerned about the negative effects on my grade point average should the IRS require more extensive and complicated information to complete the filing process.

I really did not have a choice but to go forward; I needed to incorporate and submit the forms to the Internal Revenue Service for tax exempt status before the fees were increased that upcoming June.

I figured that I'd just have to provide the Internal Revenue Service with whatever additional information they might require and I would deal with whatever additional stress when and if it occurred, because my tunnel-vision goal was to postdate those forms before the deadline.

It occurred to me during my isolation in our office that we didn't have the very important organization logo, so I called the only person that would be able to interpret my vision. I had fallen in love with the phoenix rising from the ashes and what that transformative symbolism means to me. In addition to falling in love with the Phoenix, Arizona, spring and fall seasons, I wanted our black and white logo to represent inclusiveness of all races and backgrounds! No other person came to mind who could design our presentation other than the one and only Patrik Shooting Star!

I knew that he'd come through for me with flying colors. After receiving the final draft, I immediately submitted it and received a 2005 logo copyright! Once we'd successfully incorporated in the state of Georgia, I figured that I would hire someone with more reasonable fees just to assist me with dealing with the IRS if need be!

So, I asked around for referrals and mistakenly hired this bootleg fake grant-writer who literally tried to invade and take over my personal life during a surreal fatal attraction moment with her in the dressing room after an exclusive sold-out engagement of my "Destiny Is Diana, An Intimate Evening As Miss Ross" one woman show at the Red Chair!

As I was packing away my costumes into their garment bags after the show, she proceeded to inform me that she liked having multiple intimate partners, including other women. I did not have a problem or judge her polyandrous lifestyle, but I was not interested in participating in it.

I was extremely uncomfortable when she kept insisting that I place a kiss on her funky drunk lips as I dressed in street clothes.

Furthermore, I was disgusted that she'd even suggested I engage in a threesome with herself and her boyfriend, whom she'd introduced at our initial interview in reference to her IRS filings experiences and track record.

Earlier that evening in the Red Chair dressing room after my show, I noticed that it didn't take long for the bootlegger to become extremely intoxicated as the night progressed. Then her quick intoxication made sense to me after learning she'd tried to continue ordering drinks on my tab, according to the establishment proprietor, who knew that I didn't drink.

After the Red Chair owner told me that she was pretending to order cocktails for me, it was only due to not wanting to make a scene at my place of employment that I did not let her have it before kicking her out my dressing room.

I decided to wait until the following afternoon to confront her about the inappropriate manner that she'd presented herself at my job the previous night. I called her on the phone the following afternoon and informed her that her services were no longer required.

Although I'd had a winnable civil case against her due to her not delivering contracted services, I informed the bootleg grant writer that she could keep the $250 deposit that I'd given for her assistance with my tax exempt filings.

I also warned her to never contact me again and, of course, she proceeded to insist that I needed her to help me become tax exempt and that I would not be able to complete the process without her.

I just added her to the proving-wrong list and moved on. As a result, in an effort to save others from having to become an unlimited source of income to fake grant-writers such as the one that I had the misfortune to experience, I am offering the following quick checklist that will give you a head start if you're interested in establishing an organization that would be used to educate, empower and benefit your community:

Additionally, I offer this quick incorporation and tax exempt filing 101checklist: Also, I used the legal survival guide that I previously purchased when we lived in Phoenix, Arizona, entitled, "How To Form A Non-Profit Corporation" written by attorney Mark Warda as my personal reference to familiarize myself with the incorporation and tax exemption language and process.

* Attend an incorporation and tax exemption workshop

* Recruit a board of directors

* Create by-laws, mission and value statements

* Individually contact your local Secretary of State's Office to file articles of incorporation and the Internal Revenue Service to confirm fees, order ALL forms, and instructions for incorporating and requesting tax exemption status

After my hair-raising and blood pressure-rising experience with the psychotic perpetrating grant-writer, I was finished with wasting precious time, so while Tevin was at work, I self-isolated in our office, spending anywhere from 16 to 22 hours at a time filling out the Internal Revenue Service forms to beat the deadline.

After wasting so much valuable time with the bootlegger, I remained focused, dedicating myself to the long hours of isolation, processing the required forms because I did not want any other distractions when I started my three days a week school schedule.

I was filled with overwhelming pleasure and relief after finally completing the filings and submissions two weeks before the deadline! To make it even more rewarding, I did not have to go through the drama that I'd previously went through relying on someone else to assist me, because sometimes when you share your dreams with others, they talk a good game about helping you to reach your goals, but in a lot of cases, they mistakenly see you as an ATM and eventually fall by the wayside when it comes time to walking the walk and taking action.

After all of the required forms were certified, postmarked and submitted inside the post office, I expected continuous additional information requests from the Internal Revenue Service.

However, I did not want to worry about IRS requests until they'd arrived, so I mentally prepared myself for the unexpected and moved forward in becoming consumed with school and consciously refocusing my attention on doing well in all classes!

I believe that it was a little over six months to a year that following March when I stopped to check the mail box on my way to class and when I saw the official letter from the Internal Revenue Service amongst the other letters. My heart rate increased slightly.

Before opening the letter, I prayed that I wasn't going to be required to submit an overwhelming amount of extensive additional information to them. After sitting in the car for several minutes, building up my nerve to open and read what was inside of the envelope, I finally gained the courage opening the letter.

Upon reading that Juxtaposed Center For Transformation, Incorporated, was awarded tax exempt status from the Internal Revenue Service, I screamed all the way on the drive to school in disbelief! I then immediately called Tevin after arriving at the student center, informing him of the great news and he excitedly congratulated me on all of the hard work!

It was so much easier for me when all I had to do was make personal appearances and stage performances as my alter-ego Destiny (Your Mistress of Illusions), because I was only representing and responsible for myself, not an entire community that has been traditionally marginalized and ostracized by society.

I did not take the decision lightly to do what I believe that I was born to accomplish, which is to be a vessel used to illuminate our plight because we deserve equality, justice and the pursuit of happiness that's guaranteed to all American citizens by the United States Constitution and Bill of Rights!

I also personally feel that if using my face, voice and experiences in any way helps my community to gain human and civil rights protections just because we are also humanbeings, then so be it!

Tevin and I had discussed that to effectively representing the organization and my community would require me to become more open and honest than usual about my personal life.

As time progressed, I once again felt the need to inquire if he was still okay with me diving head-first into activism. Unflinchingly, he once again reconfirmed his commitment to remaining supportive of my choices to change our lives as long as the advocacy work did not have a negative effect on our marriage!

After JCT became incorporated and tax exempt, I knew that this was when the real work and commitment would begin! My first and most important task was to form an effective board of directors, which was accomplished way in advance before I'd started submitting the forms to the Secretary of State and the Internal Revenue Service.

The advance foot work that I made placed me way ahead, with the board in place and in the writing and adopting of our mission, value and vision statements!

Honestly speaking, it has at times been a challenging, yet rewarding experience learning what is required to maintain a board of directors. I resolved early on to not be so disappointed and take it personally when members resign for whatever reasons.

My experience has been that there will be those who join a board without full knowledge that they are responsible for raising funds and closely working with the executive director to ensure that the organization's mission is accomplished.

Until recently, I've been dealing with those members who joined with their personal agendas without any knowledge of what's really required to be on a board of directors, not excluding those that have systematically tried to come in then immediately attempting to take control of the board. Their intent was to use the organization to serve their own personal purposes and settle ongoing vendettas against other organizations.

But there were also those loyal people who do not possess any personal agendas, because they genuinely believe in the vision that Juxtaposed Center has been designed to achieve. I appreciate all of their hard work, understanding and the continued support they've unselfishly given me personally and to the organization!

Although I did not set out to win awards for service to my community, in 2007 I was honored and privileged to receive a phone call from King Birthday Rally and March organizing committee member Darlene Hudson inviting me to be one of the keynote speakers to represent the T.L.G.B.Q.I. community at the annual celebration.

Now, when I initially accepted the invitation to speak, I had no idea that I would be the very first transgender person ever invited to do so until the morning of the Bayard Rustin/Audre Lorde prayer breakfast.

During the community breakfast that morning, I was informed by one of the other committee members, Kirk Surgon, that I'd be the first transgender person to speak at the event!

Initially, since I'd thought that there were others before me, it would not have been such a shock to those hearing a speech from another trans-identified person, but I was so wrong in my thinking.

King Committee member Kirk's revelation immediately contributed to the increased pressure that I felt. I was going to be the first transsexual woman to speak at the prestigious celebration honoring one of our most cherished and beloved civil rights leaders, whom unselfishly gave his life for the advancement of all people of color and women!

As I stood in the speaker holding-area with Kirk waiting for the march to start, feelings of gratitude flowed throughout my entire body. I was later placed on the front line of the march with civil rights leader Dr. Joseph E. Lowery, Mayor of Atlanta Shirley Franklin and a distinguished African dignitary!

I was so happy that I had my video recorder to document one of the most life-changing moments and experiences I'd experienced up to that point.

Once the parade started, containing thousands of people participating and lining the march route, I gave in to another out-of-body reaction, as I marched through downtown Atlanta and up Auburn Avenue arm-in-arm with people whom have inspired me on the pathway that was first laid by Dr. King, Coretta Scott King, other unsung heroes, she-roes and allies previously chanting together as we were doing, "We Shall Overcome!"

Although I've spent many years entertaining others on stage, some may find it difficult to believe that I'm still somewhat shy and nervous about speaking publically. When we arrived at the rally stage in front of the King Center, which was established by Coretta Scott King to memorialize her husband, it was at first somewhat challenging for me to absorb the massive number of people in attendance during the march and rally that I would be addressing.

As I was ushered to the back staging-area by Kirk, my heart was already racing and my legs starting to feel like the bones were slowly softening with each step. It did not help my anxiety that Tevin had previously expressed the night before his concerns about the possibility of me being physically harmed for speaking out in front of a largely heterosexual crowd about my dreams of transgender equality.

Tevin worries about me and I am so appreciative that he's concerned about my physical well-being! The nervousness caused me to have second thoughts about my speech and I'd briefly considered editing what I was going to say. But, I then thought that an awareness and empowerment speech about transgender people that included curing HIV/AIDS needed to be expressed!

Although my intention wasn't to offend anyone in attendance upon deciding what I'd speak on at the King rally, I did what I felt I had to do in order to remind those in attendance that Dr. King and Mrs. King were inclusive with their message.

Some choose to forget that both Dr. King and Mrs. King were not about intentionally excluding any group of people just based on their gender identity and orientation.

Being honest, it bothers me that others may find my gender identity and orientation offensive, which is another reason I felt that this once-in-a-lifetime opportunity that I had been given to represent my community should be used wisely and appropriately.

As I stood in line waiting my turn to take the stage, I reflected on the fact that Dr. King and Mrs. King also discouraged discrimination against anyone. Although my reservations were not completely eliminated while listening to the others speaking before me, the anxiety was somewhat decreased as I focused on what they'd stood for.

I was the third speaker in line as I stood there waiting to walk up the first step and deliver a message of inclusion, thusly deciding to just speak from the heart regardless of the perceived consequences.

After hearing my named announced as the next speaker, my knees trembled like the Tin Man in the "Wizard of Oz" walking up to the microphone. When I started speaking, the bones in my legs returned to normal, I forgot all about the trembling knees before taking a deep breath and allowing the words that I'd written from the heart to flow freely from my lips into the atmosphere!

I'd hoped that my well thought out words would gain the necessary momentum which was required to create the energy that's necessary for changing the inhuman treatment of my community in regards to gender identity expression, orientation, and HIV/AIDS. In addition it was an opportunity to acknowledge our true history!

Upon releasing my hopes and dreams into the universe, I was so glad that I did not have time to really edit what I was intending on expressing, because I was invited there to bring awareness about the diversity of our community and hopefully engage and encourage others to possibly expand their thinking.

My hope was that my goal would be accomplished if I could contribute to one person in attendance reconsidering their moral beliefs about those that are considered to be less than human, abnormal and strange, which I believe was the case for people of color during the Civil Rights Movement.

It's ironic that transgender, two-spirited people and Hijras who were once highly respected shamans and healers throughout history have now been reduced to positions of disdain and intolerance. My desire is to continue using my life to expose the truth about our birthright so that we may begin to understand our true purpose in society and on this earth.

After my speech, with tears in his eyes Kirk seemed moved by what I'd expressed and my adoring Pumpkinhead was right there waiting for me with open arms! I love the way that he loves me and I love him with all of my heart!

As Tevin and I walked hand in hand to the front stage, watching the other speakers, we were approached by this beautiful elderly African-American lady who hugged and complimented me on my speech. She then proceeded to share with us her experiences when she'd previously marched in the rally many years ago.

As a result of being blessed after hearing her describe personal experiences she'd felt taking part in the Civil Rights Movement before I was born, in addition to my marching on the frontline during the King Birthday Celebration that year, I was energized and more inspired to participate in another march and rally five months later in the June 27, 2007, United States Social Forum "Stonewall"1969 Riots re-enactment on Peachtree and Baker Street, re-creating our idea of the riots that sparked the lesbian and gay rights protections movement.

My purpose for participating in the "Stonewall" re-visit on that early afternoon when the thousands of marchers ascended upon us was also to remind and prove wrong those that claim transgender people have never shown up to participate in civil demonstrations for equality.

In fact and all reality, our transgender and gender non-conforming predecessors, including Marsha P. Johnson, Sylvia Rivera and others, stood up when no one else would to end the discrimination and violence against them, which has also motivated me to show up and make my voice heard whenever I am asked, if appropriate

Almost three months later, I was also very excited to speak and march in a Transgender Employment Rights march and rally at the Georgia State Capitol during Black Pride on September 6, 2008!

One year later, on June 27, 2009, I once again put on my marching shoes and proceeded up Moreland Avenue and delivered a speech at a very necessary transgender rights rally in Little Five Points/Inman Park.

Another justice and equality march and speech that I am particularly fond of is the most recent Worldwide Human Rights march and rally at the Georgia State Capitol on April 21, 2012.

I am thankfully at a point in my life where I cannot just sit on the sidelines and not participate while my community continues to suffer. I remain committed to participating in all forms of public social activism to continue bringing awareness to who I am and my desires for receiving equality and justice for us all.

With that said, I'm keenly aware that the goal of most transgender people is to blend in and not bring any unnecessary attention to themselves. However, I am visible due to my personal need to be reassured that I am treated fairly in my pursuit of gainful employment, quality healthcare, and fair housing.

I'm actively advocating for human and civil rights for my community due to, God forbid, if I'm in a life threatening accident, I don't want anyone to feel empowered with the right to refuse me care just because they morally object to who I am.

Being treated humanely is more important to me than just "passing" stealthily through society undetected! No judgment passed on other individual choices; it's just a personal choice and I don't expect in any way for others to feel the same as I do.

Up until recently I've rebelled against being called an activist, because I don't like feeling that I have to force others to accept me. I prefer to be called an advocate because convincing and showing others that we are all the same in more ways than we differ is more rewarding to me.

I am personally not one for practically beating someone over the head with a club, begging and trying to force them into accepting something that they really do not care for based on their sometimes uninformed personal moral beliefs and biases.

However, with the definition of activism in general being, "intentional action to bring about social, political, economic or environmental change," I happily accept acknowledgement from others whom choose to call me an activist!

Another of my intentional actions is to tell other transgender people, especially the youth, to please, please closely watch those that profess to be your friends who have your back. Do not let your peers influence you into choosing possible mental and physical death over a life that's intended for greatness.

As I've previously mentioned, I didn't start speaking out for the awards and accolades, because I feel that I am doing exactly what I was born to be doing at this precise moment in time.

I will never forget the unsettling experience I had with another transgender person who was associated with another transgender organization that was the original Atlanta Transgender Day of Remembrance Vigil (TDOR) organizer.

The unsettling and unexpected confrontation occurred at the Georgia State Capitol during a vigil. I was minding my own business, video recording the remembrance montage on the opposite side of the courtyard, when I started hearing someone behind me calling another person stupid and ignorant.

It struck me strangely that someone was actually calling someone names at an event that was supposed to somberly remember those transgender people whom have died due to discrimination and hate.

I was unaware that the person was referring to me until I turned around to see who that person was talking to. When I saw that she'd positioned herself directly behind me, and was calling me stupid and ignorant, I stepped over and asked, "Who are you calling stupid and ignorant, Katy?"

Katy ignored me as if I wasn't there and continued referring to me, talking to her girlfriend standing next to her. So, I stood directly in front of them telling her that just because she was in a wheelchair didn't mean that I wouldn't dump her onto the cement ground if she called me stupid or ignorant again.

Her actions took me by surprise, because I was standing at the montage first before she'd decided to park right behind me and then expected me to move upon seeing her with the eyes she'd thought I had in the back of my head.

Now don't get me wrong; if I had been initially aware that she was behind me I would have moved over as a courtesy, but since I was unaware of her presence I was not allowing her to be rude and bigoted just because she was confined to a wheelchair.

Although Katy's blatant bigoted attitude initially infuriated me, I thank God that I remained in control! She should have also thanked god that I've evolved and matured due to embracing my non-violence evolution, or she would have kissed the pavement if she'd continued being disrespectful, in a wheelchair or not.

Although I wasn't going to push her wheelchair into one of the courtyard statues, I felt that regardless of her present physical condition, she wasn't going to get away with her mindlessness and lack of consideration. As I continued confronting her, an associate separated us, because our mutual associate knew that I was not allowing anyone to be outright hateful to me in such a manner for no reason. At, of all events, a transgender vigil for deceased trans people.

Thankfully, I currently know that violence isn't the answer. I'm just saying we should all be a little more thoughtful about how our actions may affect others. People like Katy should also take into consideration that other people might not be as non-violent as I currently am.

During that unfortunate encounter at the vigil, I was unaware until later that I'd unexpectedly captured the entire TDOR vigil incident on videotape. Upon reviewing the tape to recall details, I'm reminded of another experience during which I'd had to confront racists and bigots on the performance circuit during the time I was employed on the Armory cast before she shuttered her doors.

At first when it all started unfolding in the dressing room one night after months of working together, I was startled, surprised and caught off guard because one of the perpetrators spewing hate previously professed to be a friend to me. I didn't expect for someone to be racist who had also previously attended with their boyfriend a barbeque at our home, in addition to me often hanging out at their apartment with them.

Their true colors were exposed during the start of the weekend after a Friday night show when the show director, along with the so-called friend, were both plastered and as usual sketched-out on who-knows-what by the end of the show.

I recall earlier that evening being in a great frame of mind, feeling an immense sense of accomplishment due to successfully incorporating into my repertoire an extended Eartha Kitt mega-mix copy of "Where Is My Man?"

My first number that night was the second of two performances since returning to the entertainment circuit that an audience really lined up, like tipping lines back in the day when people really appreciated the art form!

Later that evening upon completing our cast "Chicago" production and after confirming that my makeup kit was packed into my shoulder show bag and ensuring that all other take-home items were also secured, they'd abruptly started arguing aloud in their adjoining dressing room.

Their craziness and psychotic dependency upon each other wasn't out of the ordinary, and it was also fueled by their drug and alcohol induced co-dependent association. Their dysfunctional interactions were definitely why I'd previously declined their invitation to move into what was considered to be the best dressing room by most in the cast.

There was no way that I was going to willingly move into what I'd considered the "Crazy House" with those two sketched-out queens when the so-called friend suggested the idea hanging out at his apartment one afternoon after previously discussing it with the show director.

What was most unordinary that night, however, was when they both also started calling each other niggers in response to one of many unknown conflicts that must have occurred between them during the course of the night.

Usually, when they'd argue with each other I'd assumed the peacemaker role to make all of our experiences in the show more pleasant and profitable. Not that time, because I was beyond offended that they'd used their addictions as an excuse to disrespect all of the cast members who were people of color.

I knew that they were both too intoxicated and under the influence to really comprehend what they'd done, so I decided to wait until the very next day to tell the person that I was closest to how I'd felt about their actions via telephone.

He apologized with flowers and a card the following weekend, but the damage and the friendship was done as far as I was concerned. In my book, there is no excuse good enough for being purposefully offensive, racist and bigoted to someone whom you claim to respect and care about.

Progressing towards another happier day in time, my pleasures and contentment were multiplied by not having any second thoughts or regrets about leaving the Armory show!

Another beautiful moment happened when Juxtaposed Center for Transformation, Incorporated, later assumed the responsibility of becoming the official organizer of the Transgender Day of Remembrance Vigil after the previous group became defunct. Our first intent upon becoming responsible for the vigil was to make sure that no other person will ever have to endure such venomous racist behavior that I'd received at TDOR!

Transgender Day of Remembrance is an internationally observed annual vigil and memorial held on November 20 and our tradition locally has been to honor and remember our deceased at the state capitol with a names, citations, and candle-lighting as our pledge to never forget them.

A couple years after organizing the vigil, it was not our intention or design during the "Remembering Our Own" TDOR 2009 reception to have two prominent and influential African-American political representatives in attendance at the same time, including our keynote speaker, state Senator Vincent Fort, and then-mayoral candidate Kasim Reed, now Atlanta mayor.

The show of support from these two very distinguished gentlemen, other legislators and hopefuls that were in attendance at an event designed to acknowledge and illuminate a community that is stigmatized, marginalized and discriminated against, gave me hope that we are on the right track to receiving protections from discrimination and hatred.

This was another unimagined personal dream for them to have acknowledged us just by their presence and individual legislative records of inclusiveness of our entire community when it comes to receiving local civil rights and hate crimes protections!

Also, I was deeply moved by their presence on our international day of mourning those that have lost their lives due to murder, hate or even suicide as a result of the many social and psychological challenges we face living in a society that views you as less deserving of basic human rights just because you do not fit the mold that we've been conditioned to conform to.

Although we were not expecting so many politicians to show interest in our vigil and memorial, their attendance also gives me hope that the days of transgender individuals, especially those of color, continuing to be denied access to public homeless shelters in their time of need will no longer be tolerated.

Later that evening, across the street at the Georgia State Capitol during the Candlelight Vigil and Names Citations on the courtyard, I became unusually overwhelmed emotionally each time that I released the pendulum striking the bell as each deceased name was cited by those in attendance.

Yet, another unexpected privilege and personal honor was bestowed upon me. In addition to nailing shingles on a home during my service with Habitat for Humanity, I'd also received an invitation to become a host committee member for then-candidate Kasim Reed during his campaign to become mayor!

Then Tevin and I later attending the inauguration reception of our current mayor at City Hall downtown on January 4, 2009, where I had expected that our mayor might have played the usual politics game when his committee chair invited me to be one of his host committee members.

However, my feelings were changed upon researching his progressive human rights record during the time he was a Georgia state senator before becoming mayor.

Although I don't currently agree with his marriage inequality opinions, I've committed to not actively campaigning against him as others have continuously suggested, because his record also speaks for itself. After attending the mayor's inauguration, our beautiful evening was capped off with Tevin and I later sharing a romantic dinner at Paschal's Restaurant!

I was additionally honored to have been invited by Senator Vincent Fort to become a host committee member and then attend the reception for his 2010 re-election campaign at a restaurant under the stars in Midtown.

I continued to see my hopes and dreams for community come to fruition when our President Barack Obama appointed the first transgender technical advisor, Amanda

Simpson, to the Department of Commerce!

Another dream come true that I believe brings us one step closer to gaining state protections when our President signed into law the landmark Matthew Shepard/James Bird Hate Crimes Protections Bill on January 28, 2009, which included gender identity and orientation as protected categories for federal employees.

Although there still remains a lot of work that's required on a local level, this fully-inclusive federal legislation reassures me that we are heading in the right direction towards receiving full equality for all people, which is reward enough for me knowing that I may have contributed in some small way via my vote and voice.

Speaking of using my voice bringing awareness, I feel it necessary to share some personal observations relative to our interactions with each other, because some people get it twisted with their assumptions that just because we're transsexual and gender non-conforming people, we possess no standards or morals.

From my personal experiences and observations, trans-identified people are expected by most to automatically desire being with them just because they sometimes automatically perceive themselves as what we're attracted to and may require involvement with in order to obtain self-fulfillment.

Please don't flatter yourself Boo Boo, I'm just saying! We ask please don't get insulted and defensive if you should ever be rejected by a transgender, transsexual person, because it's all about chemistry, my darlings.

I also offer a strong message to my transgender sisters and brothers, which is that we don't have to continue just settling for the first person expressing interest in us just because we occasionally fear we're unacceptable to others.

That person may not be the right one for you, because everything that looks good on the outside might sometimes be rotten on the inside. Additionally, with "We Are Resilient" as our message moving forward, we don't have to buy into the notion that since we're transgender and gender non-conforming our options are limited based only on what we've been conditioned by society to believe about ourselves.

I cannot close this personal choices and responsibility dialogue without suggesting to those aggressive transgender and gender non-conforming people whom refuse to accept NO, that I am not interested in you as an answer. Back off dear, they're just not interested in what's being offered and if you persist on being aggressive, you're looking desperate, stupid and may be at risk of being physically hurt.

If you cherish your life and front teeth, please don't forcefully and inconsiderately disrespect the personal space of others just because you're sexually attracted to them. Just a precautious message about assumptions that's all.

Climbing down off my soapbox now and moving forward from the rant, I am happy that my personal service and contributions to an improved society have been acknowledged by peers and colleagues who are also providing educational programming through their non-governmental organizations and associations.

I was also privileged and honored to have received the Unity Fellowship Church Atlanta "Unity in Community," and the Some One Cares, Incorporated, "Advocacy and Leadership" awards in recognition of my service to our entire community.

Although I do not consider myself as being gay, in 2007 I was also awarded with a beautiful silver-engraved "Speakers Award" for representing my community on an annual "State of Black Gay America" panel discussion during Black Gay Pride celebration! I was then thrilled to have been invited back the following year in 2008 and once again in 2010 to engage in the conversation at the summit.

I've recently thought that my year was topped off in 2011 with receiving the prestigious "Fenuxe 50 Most Prominent & Influential" award on November 6, which recognized my commitment to elevating our human race regardless of gender identity, religion or race.

However, the 2012 "Revolutionary Award" recognition that I'd unexpectedly received the following year from Women Healing Women, Incorporated, has meant the most to me, because the acknowledgement came from some of the strong African-American sisters whom I respect for evolving beyond measure with their purposeful actions to make sure that transgender and gender non-conforming people are at the table contributing to the conversations referencing human rights.

As far as identifying as gay, it's unfortunate that I've sometimes had to give in to the labels assigned by the expectations of society, which I personally believe is a marginalizing requirement. However, I am more of a transsexual woman who is loved by her mother, family and a secure man in a hetero-identified relationship.

I emphatically do not identify as gay or a man having sex with a man. I know that my self-description and relationship status may be confusing to most, so I will try to explain it in simple terms. First off, I acknowledge and recognize the beauty in others, regardless of how they identify.

Secondly, I've recently met some very attractive female-to -male transgender people and if I was not a married woman, let's just say that some masculine female-to-male transsexual men have intrigued me. Just keeping it real!

Thirdly, I have never been interested in bumping purses with gay, effeminate, metro-sexual men, biological or other transsexual women in any sexual manner. Additionally, there is no flip- flopping in my relationship with Tevin, nor do we share makeup and clothes, because I am the feminine energy and my husband is the masculine energy in every aspect -- "Three Hundred, Sixty Five Days" of the year as Anita Baker beautifully stated in one of my favorite songs!

Conclusively, I respect and choose not to judge others for their personal self-descriptions of their gender identity, orientation or sexuality, so I hope to be extended the same common courtesy in sharing my story and personal preferences.

Thank you mother, father, god, and universe for progressively moving me forward on my fantastic voyage! In addition to speaking at the King Celebration being a major highlight in my newly established public service career, in 2007 and 2008 I was also afforded the opportunity to work with a national T.L.G.B.Q. gay rights organization. Yes, I did and will continue to take the liberty of putting the T first for a change!

Providing just a little background, I'd previously became one of their former Atlanta Diversity Committee Co-Chairs and as a result, I was excited to travel with them to Washington, D.C., to lobby Congress and our House of Representatives to increase HIV/AIDS funding.

My purpose was also to encourage them to additionally support a fully inclusive Employment Non-discrimination Act (ENDA) that will protect transgender and gender non-conforming people from being discriminated against in the workplace.

During that visit after Lobby Day, I sat in the audience at their national convention listening to my then first choice for the Democratic nominee for president, former First Lady, Senator from New York and previous Secretary of State to the Obama

Administration, Hillary Clinton!

I've always supported Mrs. Clinton and in most ways will probably continue to do so, because I feel that she possess the intelligence to potentially become our first female president! I feel that once the feminine energy has an opportunity to make decisions on the level of the president of the United States of America, things would significantly change to the positive for our world as a whole.

However, in addition to her constantly hitting below the belt during the Democratic debates and the assassination comment, which is unfortunately how the politics game is played, I really was not personally inspired or moved by the passionless campaign stump speech that she delivered that evening at the convention.

However, I was impressed after seeing and feeling the passion, intelligence, drive, composure and enthusiasm that United States Senator Barack Obama possessed and displayed throughout the debates and whole elections process! Presidential candidate Obama inspired me for the very first time in my life to volunteer energy at his Atlanta campaign office, selling banners, yard signs, T-shirts and badges to raise money for his campaign. I had a great time!

Also during my Washington trip, I felt a sense of empowerment during our lobby session with the always supportive and inspiring Congressman John Lewis' office when we'd received his commitment to support a fully inclusive ENDA!

Later I was mesmerized by him, witnessing his impassioned speech about his experiences while organizing demonstrations at segregated lunch counters and ending up with a concussion in addition to being arrested during a March demonstration against the injustice of Jim Crow and segregation in the South.

In addition, I was also moved by an encouraging and uplifting speech from the "Lion of The Senate" Sen. Ted Kennedy, pledging his unwavering commitment to submit, and support a bill to his legislative colleagues that included gender identity and orientation protections language becoming a catalyst for eliminating some of the economic discrimination against our entire community.

Most people are unaware that Sen. Kennedy's over 40-something years in the Senate positively contributed to civil rights, voting rights protections for people of color, women, and the disabled! Your voice will be missed. Rest in peace, Senator Ted Kennedy.

Later that same evening, I also experienced a light-bulb moment during the speech from my home state's representative and House of Representatives Congressional Majority Whip in the 110 Congress James (Jim) Clyburn, then third-ranking Democrat behind Nancy Pelosi and Majority Leader Steny Hoyer.

I'm encouraged, paraphrasing Rep. Clyburn explaining that from his experience, "Great change doesn't happen over-night, incremental steps may sometimes be required to achieve your ultimate goal." Rep. Clyburn went on explaining that the voting rights protections people of color were eventually extended took time and strategic planning.

In my humble opinion, we've become a microwave society, expecting instant results, which may not be as effective over the long haul. Additionally, during the national conference I was also honored to meet one of the influential people whom inspired me during his speech to continue documenting my personal story, the openly gay former pro basketball player turned author John Amaechi!

Although my Lobby Day, convention trips and stay at the infamous Mayflower Hotel were sponsored by members of the Atlanta Steering Committee, I was really angry that the first Employment Non-discrimination Bill was introduced for voting without protections for transgender people.

The result of that insulting bill contributed to no hesitation on the national organization's flip-flop on a promise to not support any legislation that did not include protections for transgender and gender non-conforming people.

Even though I did not necessarily agreed with the incremental steps ideology in that case, I understood their logic behind it. However, I was outraged at what the national gay rights organization had done in response to the non-inclusive legislation.

My intention was to really understand why they'd so blatantly chosen to throw us under the bus after all of the false community pledges promising not to do exactly what they did. It was like a closed fist to the face after all of the support and labor that I'd personally invested.

I do not think that they will really ever comprehend the seriousness and sense of betrayal associated with the message that they'd chosen to send when first refusing to denounce the discriminatory bill.

During one of the national conferences in Washington, I was informed by a very reliable source that their president had misspoken at a previous transgender conference during his speech in Georgia that I'd witnessed when he'd unequivocally committed in front of a ballroom filled with transgender, gender non-conforming people, our allies and supporters that by no means would they support discrimination against our community.

My source proceeded to inform me that the organization's president had no intention of personally apologizing to the community, and that they were going to issue a general statement that should suffice explaining their reasons for betraying us. I was insulted and immediately knew that I would have to make some serious decisions about continuing my membership within the organization.

When they went on to release their official press release confirming that they would not lobby against the disgraceful bill, I was done! In all honesty, I probably would have resigned way before then, but establishing personal close relationships with other members of the diversity and steering committees made it even more challenging for me to do what inevitably needed to be done.

What I eventually got a chance to ask about at a private meeting with their president and other leaders from within the transgender community was, "Why did it take you so long to meet with the community to explain why you did exactly what you'd previously promised us at the conference that you would not do?"

The national president's responses to my questions and those of the others in attendance seemed genuine to me, so I have chosen to personally forgive him, because if I was in his predicament, I would want to be forgiven for my mistakes.

When the moment was right, I eventually resigned from the steering committee on my own terms with my integrity remaining intact! Although I disagreed with the organization's tactics, I refused to lobby against them due to evaluating the bigger picture and concluding that the other work they are doing is very necessary.

My feeling remains. We can agree to disagree without being disagreeable in order to move forward without all of the controlling, antagonistic energy. My hope is to continue being used by my Creator to civilly work with others in promoting hope, equality and justice for our entire community, because it requires all of us united, working collectively in order to achieve the greater rewards!

Before winding down, can we talk about deception and hypocrisy just for one moment? These are my observations of those opinionated, self-righteous, moralistic and family values people that are against human rights protections for everyone regardless of their orientation, including hypocritically high-profile former legislators like Jim McGreevy, Mark Foley and Larry Craig just to name a few.

Just imagine someone that was distinguished, adamant that he is not gay, but frequenting airport bathrooms tapping out Morse Code to attract a stranger of the same sex to engage in public sex with him. My bad … we don't have to imagine the affectation, because it has occurred in Larry Craig's case.

Let us not forget the many others yet to be revealed for who they really are have been declaratively uncompromising about not affording others their constitutional rights just to deflect the spotlight away from their bones stacked in the closet corner.

It's also my humble opinion that those hypocritical liars that are responsible for drafting and enacting legislation that is supposed to be beneficial to all people, who are instead distracted from their duties because they're concealing personal little secrets, should be exposed for who they are or exit the business of being a representative of the people.

My guess is that they probably feel if they were to show any compassion and support for equal protections regardless of gender identity, orientation, race or background, they might be found out to be fraudulent, deceptive hypocrites. They will eventually be revealed to be in the end.

Also, in my personal experience, those individuals that are the most boisterously rude and morally outspokenly are fronting on you in front of their boys, but if you're ever alone with one of them, they're usually the ones revealing their true freaky fetishes and other carefully hidden persuasions that at some point come tumbling into the light of day for all to see!

I've concluded that it's their prerogative to continue denying who they are; just don't be hypocrites about it. That's all I'm just saying!

Thankfully, I've grown enlightened enough to not believe the myths about who I was and I have come to the point in my life where I unconditionally accept and embrace who I am.

I refuse to let anyone convince me into subscribing to the idea that I am inferior to them solely based on my race or gender identity, expression and orientation. I have resolved that I am a modern-day eunuch who is divinely created for purposes that are far beyond my comprehension. I pray for continued knowledge, wisdom, understanding, guidance, and the strength to fulfill my destiny and purpose for living in this modern society

I am additionally grateful that two Story Corps conversations and interviews that I've participated in to share elements of my life story were recently recorded here in Atlanta on February 20, 2010. The reference number is ATL000205 and another interview with the late Lillie Love on April 22, 2010, is reference number ATL000294!

Those interviews have both been selected to be archived in the United States Library of Congress American Folk-life Center so that generations following will hopefully be inspired and encouraged by my testament with the knowledge that transgender and gender non-conforming people who may be like them have resiliently existed against all odds and misfortune throughout recorded history!

In addition to the unexpected sequences of events that lead up to my wedding date with Tevin, I've experienced four other major events in my lifetime. These include the loss of our first-born Savannah, who was stolen shortly after we moved into a new house.

Due to Savannah not being used to the thunder one evening when a freak lightning storm came out of nowhere, she bolted bolt out of an unlatched screened door. I was devastated when I discovered that she was gone and immediately went out in the dangerous lightning to look for her.

I was somewhat comforted after being informed by a neighbor when I was distributing reward flyers for her return that he saw someone pick her up and sped away. Of course, Tevin was hurt beyond measure after I called him at work informing him of what happened.

Although I was torn apart, I was just happy that I didn't find my baby dead in the streets from being hit by a car! Even though Savannah remains irreplaceable, we were somewhat comforted when we later added our baby Solomon to the family.

Next there was the unexpected election of our first person of color president, Barack Obama, Commander In Chief and leader of our nation! I'm happy that I actively volunteered for his campaign in addition to previously and separately volunteering during a non-partisan voter registration drive in Midtown.

Included in the unexpected events occurring before its time, there was also the sudden death of Michael Jackson. The evening of Michael's untimely death announcement, I was sitting on a panel discussion at Charis Bookstore in Little Five Points conversing with a room filled with people about the contributions that transgender and gender non-conforming people made towards the L.G.B.T.Q.I. human rights movement.

Although I was only two years old when the 1969 "Stonewall Riots" occurred, I am happy that the contributions of my predecessors whom contributed to the fight for equality and justice are acknowledged and written in the history books for all to read,

After the panel discussion and question and answer session, we later stood outside chit-chatting with the other panelists and attendees, continuing our conversations. At that time, I had no idea of the horrible news that I would soon receive after getting into our car to leave.

When I turned on the radio, I heard radio hosts somberly discussing Michael Jackson and I then turned off the radio and immediately called Tevin at work asking, "What is going on, why are people talking about Michael Jackson as if something has happened to him?"

He inquired. "Are you driving, Tracee? "Growing impatient that he was evading my question I replied, "Yes, I am getting on the freeway to go home."I asked again more directly, "Tevin, what the hell is going on?"

He hesitated a few ticks before answering my question, he said, "It's true Tracee. Michael Jackson is dead."

All I could say in response was, "Are you serious?" Concerned by my reaction, he suggested, "Tracee, I need you to get off the phone and focus on driving home safely. If you need to pull off the freeway to compose yourself, do so."

I replied in disbelief, "I am okay to drive the rest of the way home. Tevin, I will call you when I get there."I was in utter shock after hanging up the cell phone, but although I was shocked, I was not totally surprised because several weeks previously, I had unfortunately foreseen Michael Jackson's funeral in a dream, right down to the red flowers that adorned his coffin.

I was and will always be inspired by Michael Jackson, starting when I sung his song

"Ben" in the Black History Club talent show up to winning First Place Talent in a Halloween parade when we performed a production of "Thriller" that I choreographed and produced when I was in Job Corps.

Even though I refused to closely follow the trial of the doctor accused of killing Michael, I was happy on November 7, 2011, when he was found negligent and held responsible for Michael's death. I'm happy that he won't be able to negligently practice medicine in the future. Hopefully, you are finally able to rest in peace, dear Michael Jackson. You are missed.

Lastly, I can't even go there about the pain and tears I wept after hearing about Whitney Houston's untimely death. It was completely shattering that she'd be the next to leave.

Moving forward with the highs and lows, there are questions to which I may never receive answers. One thing that I believe for sure is that there are no coincidences.

The people that come into our lives at various times are divinely placed there for a specific purpose or another, with some being there for a short or a long period of time to teach us something about ourselves or for them to learn a lesson about themselves. The purpose may just to be a source of support to help you move forward to the next level in obtaining your goals and dreams!

I strongly continue to believe that I have personal guardian angels all around me, either in the physical or the spiritual forms and I am filled with gratitude that they continue to surround, guide, guard and support me toward fulfilling my purpose!

Another thing that I am also blessed to know for sure is that as a child, before I began to fully comprehend the depth and magnitude of the love and sense of protectiveness that my mother has for me, I was often haunted with the thoughts of being born into the wrong family so I ran away to escape from the confinement, in search of a place to fit into and be unconditionally accepted in order to fully evolve into who I am.

Thankfully, I've come to know without a shadow of a doubt that I was just running away to educate myself about my gender identity and orientation in order to find self-acceptance! Although I was conflicted with my mother growing up, I love her with all of my heart and soul and I thank God that she was conscious and aware of the value in teaching us the importance of family!

I also know that my mother's actions, no matter how right or wrong I'd perceived them to have been during those days, were to protect me from an unforgiving society that would most likely care less about me. I am additionally grateful that she instilled a sense of strength, determination and morality in me by teaching us the importance of being responsible for our actions and knowing right from wrong.

Also, and most importantly I now know that I was born into the family that my Creator chose just for me, because they're exactly what was and are required to set the foundation needed for me wholly becoming who I was created to be.

As for my brother Perry, our relationship has evolved for the better, I love him and he tells me that he loves me. I also believe that his current wife has been a positive effect on the softened and nonjudgmental person he's become.

I am also extremely thankful to have realized that if I am not able to fully accept myself, I cannot expect others to do something that I am not capable of doing. The person that I am today would not be possible if not for unconditional love from my husband and Mother Bear.

Ma never remarried after the untimely death of my father and I now realize the continuous challenges that she faced raising two children without the support of a father figure.

Additionally, during my early adolescence, I thought that I knew everything, but I thank God for my mother's strong will! She's always put our needs before her own and even considering how extreme my punishments were for being transgender, her intentions were to ensure that my brother and I were safe as children, and prepared for what we would have to face in this world during adulthood.

I also now know for sure that Ma loves me and she did the best that she knew how to do at the time, so I have since reconciled those feelings of resentment about how I was treated in my youth. I've also accepted that her intentions were to protect and keep me safe from being abused and hurt by those that had no stake in my mental and physical well-being.

Ma has taken an important step toward reconciliation by acknowledging that she just did not possess the fundamental tools, knowledge, wisdom or understanding to deal with my gender identity challenges, because she just wanted to protect her baby and make my life less complicated and harsh as compared to hers.

I have also resolved that the mental and physical abuse that I endured was the only way that she knew how to deal with her frustrations, confusion, and embarrassment.

By the grace of God, my Mother and I have also conclusively reconciled the feelings associated with the abuse that she contributed to and she has apologized and atoned for those mistakes that she made, especially the misinformed way that she dealt with my gender identity challenges.

The relationship between Ma and I has only gotten stronger and we have become more connected with each other than ever! I am also blessed that over a period of time, she has become one of my most supportive cheerleaders and that she's extremely pleased that I am not hooked on drugs, alcohol, prostitution, in and out of prison or dead like others that I grew up with!

She is also happy that I am in a committed, monogamous relationship with a man that would give his life for me, and that my life is not one of the stereotypically clownish portrayals of transgender people that has been massed-produced and distributed to our society!

It's sort of surreal now when I go home to visit seeing the photos hanging and displayed throughout the house of me as both the person that I was before, and the transsexual woman that I am now, because those pictures show the smiles during my innocent childhood when I was unaware of the paths that I would travel up through the pain, unhappiness and self-hate that I felt during my teen adolescent years.

Oh my, I remember being challenged with extreme acne, trying so hard without success to be the person that my mother wanted and the frowns in some of those pictures revealed the struggles within to understand who I was and why my orientation created such a conflict with the person that I loved the most.

In addition, photos of my alter-ego Destiny (Your Mistress of Illusions) and articles of my community advocacy service are also prominently displayed on the walls throughout our home in South Carolina! The pictures on the walls chronicle my current state of being blessed as an adult to have come full circle to also see photos of my husband Tevin and I with my nieces and nephews that have chosen to address me as Auntie Toni during one of our heart to heart conversations about my gender identity, creating a surrealistic experience.

Speaking of coming full circle, I will always cherish during one of our conversations when my mother told me, "You are a blessing to me from God and you will always be my baby no matter what. I love you just as you are, and I am very proud of who you are and what you are doing with your life!"

I'm filled with overwhelming gratitude that I am able to sit and converse with my mother about our past and future! During the metamorphosis I experienced during the process of writing and researching family history, she has enlightened me further about my youth

Our various conversations explain the independent strong-willed spirit that I believe came from her and my unconditional love for my mother. I was able to select and play her favorite records before I was able to read, which also reaffirms why music and entertainment brings me so much joy!

I am also amazed, that according to Ma, I refused to crawl on hands and knees when I was an infant. I used my back side to scoot around to wherever I wanted to go until I started walking! Ma has also recently recalled with me the time when I was in my Terrible Twos and she picked us up from Miss Bessie' house after a long tiring day at work and after we exited the city bus to walk the rest of the way home, I wanted her to carry me.

Since Ma had her arms filled with packages and she was tired, she would not carry me and I refused to walk on my own. She said that I just refused to go any further with them unless she carried me and as tired as she was, she figured that I would eventually follow them.

After walking just a few yards leaving me standing there pouting, all of a sudden a big Mack truck zoomed pass from behind scaring the day lights out of me, and I took off running to catch up to them as fast as my little bowed-legs would carry me.

Also, I am blessed that she unconditionally loves and accepts my spouse, and whenever he misses family gatherings, she questions the reasons that he is not present and accounted for. It's also surreal when she introduces me as her daughter to her church members during my first visit to her church and those that are not aware of my childhood!

Honestly speaking, it's still somewhat unexpected when I heard her introduce me in church "This is my daughter Tracee" come from her lips or the first of what would become regular occasions when I've been introduced to her co-workers and others.

Those words from her have taken away all of the pain and the sense of lost and confusion that I'd previously felt during childhood and adolescence. I am her daughter. Wow, another blessing! My intention is to continue living with integrity and have conviction about myself so that she continues to be pleased with me.

I've admittedly made some mistakes that I have regretted and I am also grateful that I've learned the lessons that those mistakes and life experiences presented themselves to teach and prepare me for what's to come. I feel that committing myself early on to not doing anything on or off stage that my mother would not be pleased with has served me well!

Additionally, my hope for transgender people is to know that we were created to be all that this world has to offer. You just have to believe it and see it in order to achieve your desires. Our history dictates that transgender and gender non-conforming people were held in high esteem and positions of relevance by Jesus Christ, and Indian, African and Middle Eastern societies.

As far as our relationship is concerned, it has become more noticeable and interesting to me that most people that I'd previously worked with in the entertainment industry here in Georgia are surprised upon meeting Tevin, a heterosexual-identified African-American, masculine man with a JOB.

Some people are also surprised that he happens to be comfortable enough with himself enough to love a transsexual female! It's also funny that some of them have even gone as far to suggest to me during conversations that due to their perception of my sophistication level, they assumed and expected that I would be with anybody but an African-American guy.

Historically, I unapologetically have known men from various cultures, races and backgrounds, and I've never been with someone or not just based upon their skin color due to my heart not seeing color. I am more concerned with their character and maturity level.

It just so happens during another planetary alignment it was ordained that I would meet my once-in-a-lifetime true soul-mate, whom happens to be a man of color in a similar frame of mind upon our re-introduction to each other those many years ago!

The fact that when we were initially introduced to each other when I first arrived on the scene in California and due to my relationship status with a former boyfriend with almost five years in between leads me to honestly believe that we were destined to be together remaining committed to each other for better or worse ever since that divinely planned night on August 19, 1996, at Peanuts on Santa Monica Boulevard in Los Angeles, California!

Tevin has since revealed to me that he had been searching for someone like me for a great portion of his adult life and immediately knew that we were going to be together upon our re-introduction. When he proposed marriage to me on the plane returning from meeting his family his intentions were and still remain for us to be together for the rest of our lives!

Wow! I have never had a man to express such direct strong desires like that to me before, and up to this point that I'm aware, he hasn't cheated. He's definitely not been mentally and physically abusive towards me because he's conscious and aware of my history, feelings and desires pertaining to relationships.

By the grace of our Creator, we've remained committed to each other throughout our past challenges with the expectations of doing the same in order to rise above the inevitable future challenges that may present themselves in the future!

My life, marriage and public career remains a wonderful tango in progress and it goes without mentioning that there will be other obstacles appearing in all areas. But I am confident that we are guided, guarded, directed protected, maintained and sustained from all harm and danger!

I believe that what Tevin and I share will assist us with rising above, conquering and overcoming physically and mentally whatever is not positive and affirming that may come our way!

Furthermore, I am happy that over the years we've effectively learned to compromise with each other, making the wisest decisions affecting both of our lives together, and I can't say enough about him teaching me patience and trust.

As importantly, he's taught me the amazing power of forgiveness! I feel and hope that I've done the same for him in return!

In conclusion, if one younger person receives any inspiration from my journey, then the process of revealing the intimacies of my life has been worth every moment I've spent writing my memoir "Transitions"!

This is not THE END, for there are many more chapters yet to be written!

The following chapter is the entire speech that I was honored to deliver at the King Birthday Celebration march and rally for Martin Luther King Jr. Day on January 15, 2007, five days before my birthday!

Chapter Sixteen

My Dream Speech

The man that we are here to celebrate and honor today once wrote, "I have a dream that one day this nation will rise up and live out the true meaning of its creed. We hold these truths to be self-evident, that all men are created Equal." End quote.

My dream today is that there will be a cure for HIV/AIDS so that we can all live without the constant familiar sense of lost and separation!

I have a dream that one day we will not have to justify or apologize for being born transgender, lesbian, gay, bisexual, or questioning. It is nobody's business what I do in the privacy of my bedroom.

This dream contains the hope that all transgender individuals will begin to really know, and understand, the truth about our true destiny for being created within, and apart of this society.

I also have a dream today that we as a community will unite, and insist that our lawmakers write, and honestly support, human rights protections, including gender identity and orientation language for every human-being within our society!

Now, I know that this dream will not begin to exist without the support of our allies outside of the T, L, G, B, Q and inter-sexed community, so I invite all of you present today for this very necessary tribute and remembrance to be conscious that every member of our largely diverse society should be included in the dream that a man named Dr. Martin Luther King Jr. spoke so eloquently and passionately about the need for justice and equality for all human-beings! Thank you for your attention.

Written by Tracee McDaniel

GLOSSARY OF TERMS

Note: Some of the following communicative terms commonly used by transgender and gender non-conforming people are not usually found in Webster's Dictionary, so they may be unfamiliar to you. Here is a short glossary of terms.

Beating/Painting: Application of makeup.

Big-Ego: Possessing an extremely large penis.

Bumping Purses: Engaging in sex with another female, lesbian, transsexual, gay or otherwise effeminate person.

"Climbing Trees": Smoking marijuana.

Kool-Aid: Personal business.

Miss Alice: Police, Cop, law Enforcement.

Mones: Female hormone therapy.

Mug: Face, personal space.

Passing/Stealth: The ability to blend into society, living undetectably, flying below the radar.

Read: Possessing the ability to tell that someone is transsexual, transgender, gender non-conforming or quite possibly gay, lesbian, bisexual, undetectably queer or inter-sexed.

Our home on the Strip, window where I got caught kissing Roy Lee at Grandma's house. I was pleased with myself posing in cap and gown during Job Corps graduation, and with my Homecoming King Court.

Atlanta, GA Destiny promos, on stage at Crazy Ray'z, Tara Holiday and I at "Marquette" club and Diamond Girl Revue late '80s. Posing with my dog Goldie, Valentine's Day S. Work photo shoot at Lake Lanier, modeling for topless costumes designer during brief Clermount Lounge days late '80s.

In "Plaza" club dressing room before a performance and on stage during various productions early '90s. Posing with choreographer Jaime and Cinco De Mayo production with Melissa Deljano.

In my first apartment with guardian angel and landlord Alva, posing at Malibu Beach and with Patrik Shooting Star early '90s.

Posing with Brown Sugar during my first Portland, Oregon tour and scrapbook dried

flower bouquet from first date with Mr. Debonair early '90s

My cherished and affirming 5 page letter from Ma responding to my grievances letter to

her in early '90s.

"LaCage" Bevely Hills in dressing room with makeup artist Adam early '90s and
performance montage at "Queen Mary" Studio City late '90s

Our April 25, 2000 Las Vegas elopement and bringing in the New Year in between shows
with Pumpkinhead in "Queen Mary" dressing room! I received some unforgettable
wisdom from a beautiful lady after speaking at Dr. M. L. King Jr. birthday march and rally.
Standing on U.S. Capitol steps during Lobby Day 2007.

Made in the USA
Charleston, SC
09 April 2013